DECEPTION AND DETECTION IN EIGHTEENTH-CENTURY BRITAIN

In Memoriam

Paul J. Korshin

Deception and Detection in Eighteenth-Century Britain

JACK LYNCH
Rutgers University, USA

ASHGATE

Published by
Ashgate Publishing Limited
Gower House
Croft Road
Aldershot
Hampshire GU11 3HR
England

Ashgate Publishing Company
Suite 420
101 Cherry Street
Burlington, VT 05401-4405
USA

Ashgate website: http://www.ashgate.com

British Library Cataloguing in Publication Data
Lynch, Jack (John T.)
Deception and detection in eighteenth-century Britain
1. English literature – 18th century – History and criticism 2. Literary forgeries and mystifications – History – 18th century 3. Fraud in popular culture 4. Impostors and imposture – Great Britain – History – 18th century 5. Enlightenment – Great Britain 6. Fraud – Great Britain – History – 18th century 7. Fraud in literature 8. Great Britain – Intellectual life – 18th century
I. Title
364.1'63'0941'09033

Library of Congress Cataloging-in-Publication Data
Lynch, Jack (John T.)
Deception and detection in eighteenth-century Britain / by Jack Lynch.
  p. cm.
Includes bibliographical references and index.
ISBN 978-0-7546-6528-1 (alk. paper)
1. Great Britain—Intellectual life—18th century. 2. English literature—18th century—History and criticism. 3. Literary forgeries and mystifications—History—18th century. 4. Fraud in popular culture. 5. Impostors and imposture—Great Britain—History—18th century. 6. Enlightenment—Great Britain. 7. Fraud—Great Britain—History—18th century. 8. Fraud in literature. I. Title.

DA485.L96 2008
364.16'3094109033—dc22

2007047668

ISBN: 978-0-7546-6528-1

Printed and bound in Great Britain by MPG Books Ltd, Bodmin, Cornwall.

Contents

Preface

The study of hoaxes is a growth industry. In recent years, the critical literature on forgers, frauds, and fakers has become substantial: Anthony Grafton, Susan Stewart, Paul Baines, Howard Gaskill, Nick Groom, and others have published important studies that explore many impositions from many perspectives. Even within the comparatively narrow field of eighteenth-century British forgery, there are studies of single fakers and broad comparative analyses; some relate forgery to fiction, some to law, some to epistemology. It may seem that there is little room for another book in an already crowded field.

Most of that scholarship, though, is concerned with those who would blur the lines between fact and fiction. This book is different. It addresses those who had the more difficult challenge of separating the two—not the fakers, but the critics who argued over their hoaxes, forgeries, and counterfeits. I therefore hope this study answers a need: although there are now several excellent studies of the careers of the forgers themselves, the discussions of the debates they engendered are often disturbingly unsophisticated. These discussions tend to fall into three categories: naive positivism (did he or didn't he?), petulant dismissal (the genius was misunderstood by his narrow-minded contemporaries), and poststructuralist casuistry (who's to say what truth is anyhow?). These approaches neglect what seem to me the most important questions raised by forgery, fakery, and fraud: How were these cases actually debated and discussed by eighteenth-century inquirers, and what do they tell us about eighteenth-century conceptions of the world?

My method, therefore, is to look not directly at the frauds themselves, but at the controversies they spawned and the critics who sought to bring the perpetrators to justice. *Deception and Detection* examines those who questioned, challenged, and debunked these famous fakers. To use the inevitable legal metaphor, whereas most studies have focused on either the crimes or the verdicts, I look at the intervening trials.[1] My concern is the rhetoric of disproof, the modes of argument employed by both sides in the ensuing debates over authenticity: I hope to discover how eighteenth-century readers sifted through evidence and weighed competing claims. The book is therefore about the way cultural resources were mobilized to discover the truth in the midst of controversy, and particularly about the difficulties they faced in making their cases. It might be called an attempt at a "cultural forensics."

---

1   So pervasive is the association of literary fakery with criminal fraud that we sometimes need reminders that the association is strictly metaphorical. In fact, most of the fakers considered in this study broke no law. Of the major cases considered in the book, only one, Elizabeth Canning, resulted in a trial specifically on the question of fraud, and only one other, the Popish Plot, resulted in legal action. Nothing in the common law prohibits claims of having given birth to rabbits, and even though authors' rights were being defined in this very period, no statute protected the public from attributions of new poems to old authors.

My focus is on Britain during the long eighteenth century, from Psalmanazar's Formosan hijinks through William Henry Ireland's Shakespearean impostures of 1794–96. Eighteenth-century Britain is an exceptionally rich period for this sort of study. It is a commonplace that the age abounded in frauds—as Vicesimus Knox wrote at the time, "The present age, it must be owned with regret, is an age of literary deception."[2] It may be more accurate, though, to say that eighteenth-century Britain abounded in *arguments* over frauds. The presence of a half-dozen famous literary forgers is not on its own enough to earn any place of distinction. The medieval Church, for example, was positively overrun with what we would now dismiss as forgeries, and history is littered with impostors, faked documents, and manufactured wonders. What is unusual about the eighteenth century is the copious and detailed debates over these deceptions, with their growing sophistication and skepticism. As late as 1640, an account of "the Hog-Faced Gentlewoman Called Tannakin Skinker" reported soberly that "about the beginning of the Marsick Warre, one *Alcippe*, a woman of especiall note, at the time of her childing, was delivered of an Elephant; and another (whose name is not left unto us of) a Serpent."[3] No one seems to have thought the claims worth disputing. But when, in 1726, Mary Toft claimed to have given birth to rabbits, she prompted dozens of pamphlets by physicians, would-be philosophers and scientists, satirists, and ballad-writers, all trying to sort out the truth of the remarkable story. Toft's case deserves our attention not because of the prodigious birth—history is full of them—but because it prompted so much learned debate (and much more unlearned satire). One of the goals of this book is to account for the increased attention given to deception in eighteenth-century Britain by tracing a number of cultural shifts—in epistemology, in the natural sciences, in law, in psychology, and in rhetoric—that made investigations of these frauds both possible and necessary.

Behind all these questions about fakery is a much bigger one, and it is the reason fakery should interest us at all: *Quid est veritas?* Any study of deception is really a study of authenticity, for misrepresentation always depends on notions, whether explicit or unspoken, of genuine representation. To enquire into eighteenth-century Britons' reactions to hoaxes is therefore to explore their notions of reality itself. What conception of truth did these critics have that allowed, or even required, them to challenge the fictions of their opponents? What, for them, were the hallmarks of authenticity?

In their attempts to expose deceptions, the critics of forgery reveal by implication their ideas of reality—ideas that may sometimes come into conflict with those of their targets. This is why eighteenth-century Britain in particular makes for so many fruitful inquiries into forgery: not because there was an uncommon number of cases, but because the period saw significant changes in conceptions of authenticity. Locke's often-cited foundation of knowledge on sense perception and his redefinition of personal identity as continued consciousness; the first systematic studies of the

---

2   Knox, "On the Prevailing Taste for the Old English Poets," in *Essays*, 1:217. See also Baines, who refers to "the deuterocanon of eighteenth-century forgers: Psalmanazar, Lauder, Bertram, Macpherson, Chatterton, Ireland" (*The House of Forgery*, pp. 2–3).

3   *A Certaine Relation of the Hog-Faced Gentlewoman*, sig. A2ᵛ.

foundations of legal evidence; the development of a new scientific epistemology; the rise of historicist criticism; the genesis of diplomatics and other sciences that let skeptical inquirers test the authenticity of legal documents—all of these provide rich contexts in which to study these clashes over what was real and what was fictitious.

A few words about nomenclature. We all *feel* there is some connection between the many kinds of liars—commercial and legal forgers, counterfeiters, coin-clippers, perjurers, plagiaries, quacks, confidence tricksters, creators and distributors of apocrypha and pseudepigrapha, impostors, inventors of legendary authors, attributors of new works to familiar authors—but it is not easy to describe the relations among these members of what Horace Walpole called "the house of forgery."[4] I have often thought a comprehensive taxonomy of falsehood would be a useful thing, and have occasionally attempted notes toward one. It would start with innocent misstatements; proceed through simple lies, propaganda, plagiarism, counterfeits, and forgery of both banknotes and *objets d'art*; and end, perhaps, with impostors such as Psalmanazar and the Tichborne Claimant, whose very lives were extended falsehoods. A consistent terminology would not be the least advantage to arise from such a system: it would allow us to distinguish among the many dozens of varieties of cheats, liars, and charlatans.

I have never, however, completed this taxonomy. As I devoted more thought to it, it grew exponentially, demanding the services of a good Scholastic philosopher.[5] Where to place pseudepigrapha?—fiction?—verbal irony? What about art students trained to imitate the masters?—dancers at masquerade balls? All are involved in "deception" of a sort. John Vignaux Smyth even considers clothing, designed to conceal the naked body, a kind of fraud.[6] I soon realized that this taxonomy would be a book-length work in its own right, and probably unreadable, with ever-nicer distinctions constantly interfering with any coherent argument. And in the absence of my own system, I cannot depend on readers to understand the words in the same sense that I intend them. This leaves me, I am afraid, with no clear set of terms by which to call the various impositions and deceptions that interest me. I have therefore been forced to resort to broad terms like "forgery," "fakery," and "fraud" for the whole panoply of falsehoods, introducing qualifications and explanations whenever the exact nature of the falsehood seemed important.

I discuss a variety of eighteenth-century cases of deception, focusing especially on the more familiar literary forgeries and hoaxes. I hope to justify this attention paid to literary forgeries on several grounds. The simplest is that my own training in literary studies means I am best qualified to speak about literary matters. I cannot

---

4   Walpole, *A Letter to the Editor of the Miscellanies of Thomas Chatterton*, in Walpole, *Works*, 4:217.

5   The scholarship on fraud is littered with similarly unfinished and unsatisfactory taxonomies: see Ruthven, *Faking Literature*, pp. 34–41, for his own abandoned attempt "to devise ... a critical lexicography of fakedom." Groom tries, more modestly, to distinguish the words *original, copy, counterfeit,* and *forgery* in "Original Copies; Counterfeit Forgeries." Umberto Eco devotes a chapter to sorting out the varieties of deception: see *The Limits of Interpretation*, Chap. 12. Other modern philosophers, both analytical and Continental, have devoted considerable energy to such taxonomies.

6   See Smyth, *The Habit of Lying*, chap. 7.

presume to comment authoritatively on the ways eighteenth-century forgeries differed from the genuine classical sculpture found at Herculaneum, but I know at least a little about the history of the language and the history of English literature. I am also drawn to literary forgeries because eighteenth-century Britons were at their most sophisticated in discussing them. Forged artifacts abounded, but their obscure foreign provenance, the lack of a precise vocabulary with which to discuss them, and the importance of materials science in determining the age of artifacts means there was little memorable discussion of such forgeries in eighteenth-century Britain. There were many schemes to prevent the counterfeiting of money in the eighteenth century, but they attracted the attention only of specialists: layfolk were ill prepared to discuss specific gravities and new intaglio techniques. Literary deception, on the other hand, attracted countless commentators. Henry Fielding, Samuel Johnson, Thomas Warton, Hugh Blair, and Edmond Malone were just a few of the big-name men of letters to serve as combatants in these cases, and men of letters write. But while most of my attention has been directed to the high-profile literary forgeries, I have also examined smaller cases, as well as less literary deceptions that have left a written trail. Despite focusing especially on literary forgeries, therefore, I have ventured comments on many fields of knowledge in which I have no real expertise. As Steven Shapin complained more than a decade ago, "the resources to conduct an inquiry about the grounds of credibility do not presently belong to any one academic discipline."[7] Rhetoric, paleography, psychology, epistemology, law, antiquarianism, linguistics, numismatics, even mathematics and medicine—I can claim mastery of none of them, and even a passing familiarity with only a few. I hope, though, that the wider scope of the study compensates for some of my own failings.

Writing about liars poses a special set of challenges: we can take no one's reliability for granted. Even the few fakers who ostensibly came clean often loaded their confessions with distortions and outright fabrications: George Psalmanazar's posthumous *Memoirs* may contain nearly as many lies as his original fantastic *Description* (despite his declared intention "publickly to disclaim all the lies and forgeries I had formerly published in that monstrous romance"[8]); William Henry Ireland, despite his self-serving *Confessions*, spent his twilight years mass-producing forgeries of his forgeries and reshaping his past to suit his present. Legendary liars, moreover, tend to attract other liars who comment on them, as when in 1837 John Dix published a biography of Chatterton that showed a cavalier disregard for evidence. Many works and letters once confidently attributed to Chatterton are now being questioned as spurious.[9] And many combatants published anonymously or pseudonymously, and plagiarized from one another brazenly.

Devoting years to the study of forgery can therefore make a person suspicious, perhaps unjustifiably so. I have sometimes been inclined to reject as spurious any story not documented by multiple and independent contemporary accounts. The only authority for some of Johnson's comments on Chatterton, for instance, is a

---

7   Shapin, *A Social History of Truth*, p. xv.
8   Psalmanazar, *Memoirs*, p. 66.
9   See, for instance, Groom, "The Case against Chatterton's 'Lines to Walpole' and 'Last Verses.'"

letter by the hostile Anna Seward 15 years after Johnson's death. Is that sufficient evidence to allow us to attribute the sentiments to Johnson? Much of what we know about Chatterton himself comes from nineteenth-century transcriptions of letters now lost. Can we treat them as reliable sources of information? Perhaps not, but to exclude any evidence that I could not authenticate to a moral certainty would leave me with little raw material. As I note in the final chapter, runaway skepticism leads to intellectual paralysis.

I have therefore worked to maintain a healthy skepticism toward my sources, and have tried, whenever possible, to examine the evidence at firsthand rather than accepting anything on authority. I hope I have been sensitive to the rhetorical occasions that produced the statements I use as evidence, according different degrees of credibility to published attacks or panegyrics, private letters, and diaries still in manuscript. I have worked, moreover, to document my sources conscientiously, and to indicate the provenance of doubtful documents. In my notes I have tried to indicate whether a line can be safely attributed to Johnson himself or whether it comes from someone's recollection; whether a story was documented in a forger's lifetime or whether it first appears in a nineteenth-century biography; whether the original manuscripts exist or whether we are forced to rely on transcriptions of dubious reliability. These are good scholarly habits in any situation, but in a book like this, they are indispensable. I cannot promise that I have approached all questionable stories with the right degree of circumspection, but it is not for want of effort.

Since many investigations of forgery turn on the details of orthography, I reprint all texts *literatim* and try to reproduce manuscripts as closely as print will permit. I have allowed spelling errors to stand uncorrected, generally without a *sic*, and have supplied missing punctuation in square brackets only when the original sense is unclear. I have, however, silently corrected typographical errors that are clearly errors of the press, such as turned letters, and I have rendered manuscript underscores as italics. In passages predominantly in italics, italics and roman are reversed. Notes provide short-title citations to books and articles, with full details in the bibliography. Manuscripts and eighteenth-century periodicals are cited fully in the notes. I indicate both author and recipient of all letters cited, in addition to page or folio numbers when available.

Acknowledgments

I have benefited from conversations with a great many friends and colleagues, and am glad to have the opportunity to thank some of them by name: Nicolas Barker, Tom Curley, John Davenport, Anthony Grafton, Jim Green, Nick Groom, John Gunkel, Kristine Haugen, David Hoddeson, Jonathan Lamb, John Logan, Bob Perelman, Fiona Ritchie, John Scanlan, Richard B. Sher, Susan Stewart, Dan Traister, David Venturo, and Bruce Whiteman.

The research on this book would have been impossible without the generous support of a number of organizations. The Raymond K. Denworth Fellowship allowed me to spend several months in the Rosenbach Museum & Library in Philadelphia, where the staff was unfailingly helpful. The Richard H. Popkin Travel Fund Award from the American Society for Eighteenth-Century Studies supported a research trip to Great Britain. At Rutgers University, the David Hosford Scholarship, the Trustees Research Fellowship Program, and two semester-long sabbatical leaves made it possible for me to do much of the reading and writing.

These scholarships, fellowships, and sabbaticals allowed me to work in some of the finest libraries in the world. In addition to the Rosenbach and the Dana and Alexander Libraries of Rutgers University, I did research in Firestone Library of Princeton University, Van Pelt Library of the University of Pennsylvania, Bobst Library of New York University, Butler Library of Columbia University, the John Hay Library of Brown University, the Houghton Library and the Theatre Collection of Harvard University, the Beinecke Library of Yale University, the Free Library of Philadelphia, the New York Public Library, the Boston Public Library, the Library of Congress, the Pierpont Morgan Library, the William Andrews Clark Memorial Library, the Huntington Library, the Folger Shakespeare Library, the Library Company of Philadelphia, the British Library, the Shakespeare Birthplace Trust Records Office, the Bristol Central Library, the University of Edinburgh Library, and the National Library of Scotland. Arthur Freeman and Janet Ing Freeman were exceptionally kind in sharing with me the results of their research. I am also grateful to the curators at the British Museum and the Metropolitan Museum of Art, who took the time to show me items in their collection and to discuss questions of authenticity as they arise in the visual arts.

Two friends who advised me as I began this book are not around to read my thanks now. One is Lana Schwebel, a dear friend of many years, whose wit, energy, and passion for learning helped me through many dull days. Much of this book emerged from long discussions with her, and she generously answered a thousand miscellaneous queries. More important, she gave me reason to think this career was a worthy way to spend a life. Finally, I would like to acknowledge my career-long debt to Paul J. Korshin. I still recall him writing words like *pseudepigrapha* on the board when I was an undergraduate in his classes; he first introduced me to many of the characters whose bizarre stories have fascinated me ever since. His premature death leaves me only the minimal consolation of dedicating it to his memory.

Some of the material in this book originally appeared in "Samuel Johnson's 'Love of Truth' and Literary Fraud," *SEL* 42, no. 3 (2002): 601–18; "Forgery as Performance Art: The Strange Case of George Psalmanazar," *1650–1850: Ideas, Aesthetics, and Inquiries in the Early Modern Era* 11 (2005): 21–35; and "Horry, the Ruffian, and the Whelp: Three Fakers of the 1760s," *The Age of Johnson: A Scholarly Annual* 18 (2007): 225–42. I am grateful for permission to reproduce this material here.

List of Abbreviations

BL	The British Library, London
Bodleian	The Bodleian Library, Oxford
Folger	The Folger Shakespeare Library, Washington, D.C.
Huntington	The Huntington Library, San Marino, Cal.
Hyde Collection	The Donald and Mary Hyde Collection of Doctor Samuel Johnson, Houghton Library, Harvard University
NLS	The National Library of Scotland, Edinburgh
Rosenbach	The Rosenbach Museum & Library, Philadelphia

Introduction

The "fake studies" genre has been around long enough to have developed a number of conventions. The first is to declare an allegiance at the outset with either the universalists or the particularists, the lumpers or the splitters. Chicanery is both universal and perennial, but it assumes different forms in different ages; a critic may therefore choose to emphasize either its timeless or its timely aspects. Anthony Grafton, the most prominent of the universalists, begins his polymathic survey of fakes with some of the oldest surviving fragments from Egypt's Middle Kingdom, and every few years we are treated to new frauds, whether as sinister as Kujau's Hitler diaries or as trivial as the lip-synching antics of Milli Vanilli. "A relatively restricted group of colors," Grafton observes, "makes the forger's palette, now as two millennia ago."[1] Others, however, prefer to talk about forgeries as the products of a specific age, understanding them only against the background of that age. Ian Haywood, for example, notes that "The forgeries of Macpherson and Chatterton were intimately related to eighteenth-century British historiography," and limits his discussion to that period.[2]

Though I appreciate the virtues of both approaches, in this study I cast my lot with the particularists. This is partly because eighteenth-century Britons were convinced that theirs was an exceptional age of deception, and they became increasingly concerned with authenticity over the course of the century. This evidence from the English Short Title Catalogue should not be accepted without qualification, but it shows an unmistakable trend: in the first decade of the eighteenth century, only one English book included the word *authentic* in its title. In the next decade there were 6; in the twenties, 7; in the thirties, 15; in the forties, 77; and so on, increasing each decade, to fully 324 titles asserting their authenticity in the nineties. Words like *genuine* and *real* show similar, albeit less dramatic, rises:

Table 1

	Authentic	Genuine	Real
1700–1709	1	10	27
1710–19	6	31	70
1720–29	7	36	56
1730–39	15	86	31
1740–49	77	187	52

---

1   Grafton, *Forgers and Critics*, p. 49.

2   Haywood, *The Making of History*, p. 15. Haywood has also written a more universalist book: although *Faking It* devotes much of its attention to eighteenth-century cases, it also looks back to the biblical Apocrypha and continues into the late twentieth century.

	Authentic	Genuine	Real
1750–59	90	254	89
1760–69	105	268	111
1770–79	139	390	106
1780–89	233	237	116
1790–99	324	302	214

Part of this increase can be attributed to the overall growth in the number of publications, but the constant increase, with the use of *authentic* rising more than 30,000 percent from the first decade to the last, cannot be entirely explained away: something was in the air. Authors and booksellers sensed that readers in 1749 would be more impressed with *An Authentic Account of the Whole Conduct of the Young Chevalier* than *An Account of the Whole Conduct*, presumably because inauthentic versions of the story might be circulating and consumers needed reassurance.

More important than any apparent rise in the amount of actual forgery, though, is the way people responded to it. The forgers' palettes may have been limited, but I have come to believe that some of the *responses* to deceptions were genuinely new in eighteenth-century Britain. However limited the varieties of forgery, and however little modern fakers differ from their ancient predecessors, the methods of *detecting* and *arguing about* fakes have changed in important ways. The obvious methods for detecting, say, a questionable painting or manuscript today—ultraviolet light, carbon-14 dating, dendrochronology, spectroscopy—did not exist in the eighteenth century; even tools like the *Oxford English Dictionary*, which allow critics to spot potentially anachronistic words in a suspicious document, were unavailable. Eighteenth-century writers had to work only with taste, with their knowledge of the language, and above all with forensic rhetoric, and they had to develop the techniques for conducting these debates largely on their own. I am therefore convinced it is more productive to talk about these eighteenth-century British disputes in a specifically eighteenth-century British context. More to the point, by examining eighteenth-century British debates over authenticity I hope to understand something about eighteenth-century Britain itself.

A second common convention in the genre of forgery studies is to declare an allegiance with the fakers. This can take at least two forms: either denying that they committed any crime, or celebrating them for upsetting the status quo. There is a long critical tradition, for example, of exculpating forgers by suggesting they are not really forgers: James Macpherson's *Fingal*, says one critic, is not a forgery but "a synthetic epic"; Thomas Chatterton, says another, was "not a cunning forger ... but an undisciplined Puckish Romanticist."[3] Many writers seem to take for granted the assumption that all forgers are villains, and therefore unsympathetic. They therefore

---

3   Gaskill, *Ossian Revisited*, p. 6 (the phrase is repeated in "Ossian in Europe," p. 646); Meyerstein, *Life of Thomas Chatterton*, p. 109. Nick Groom asks in the introduction to his collection of essays on Chatterton, "Were they really forgeries?" (*Thomas Chatterton and Romantic Culture*, p. 3).

scramble to save their subjects from ignominy and to prove they do not deserve the name "forger." Other commentators have decided rather to embrace the label of "criminal" and to delight in the outlaw's powerful romantic imaginative appeal. The tradition stretches back at least to the Romantic reception of Chatterton, but it is especially common now, when cultural transgression is hip. K. K. Ruthven goes further in this direction than most in a recent book "about the power of literary forgeries to disturb the societies in which they are produced": frauds, he insists, "destabilise the dualism which represents the fake as a nefarious singularity, whose virtuous adversary is another putative singularity called the genuine."[4] Forgers, embodiments of the folkloric Trickster, are the heroes of his book for their relentless deconstruction of society's binary oppositions.

For both sets of partisans of the fakers, the debunkers are the enemy, and the critics set their sights accordingly. For the exculpatory school, the investigators are literal-minded boobs unable to appreciate the forgers' true genius; for Ruthven and other champions of the fakers, they are mean-spirited and conservative spoilsports. It is no surprise that scholars who have devoted years to Macpherson or Chatterton should come to appreciate, even to identify with, their subjects, and to resent those who brought shame to them. Sometimes the attacks get downright nasty: Howard Gaskill, Macpherson's most distinguished modern champion, accuses Samuel Johnson of "dogmatic close-mindedness and racial bigotry (for that is what it is)."[5] E. H. W. Meyerstein has few kind words for Horace Walpole, and Edmond Malone comes in for a drubbing in the works of some students of William Henry Ireland.

I have no intention of replacing these attacks with hagiography, turning bitter establishment killjoys into selfless champions of truth and justice. They were not always on the side of the angels. The motives and actions of the skeptics were sometimes as complicated as those of the fakers; several even had their own brushes with fraud of one sort or another. Walpole, who played a role in discrediting Chatterton, has sometimes been accused of forging his *Castle of Otranto*; it is now widely accepted that George Steevens, who helped to debunk William Henry Ireland's claims, committed his own fabrications. There is evidence that Thomas Warton's *History of English Poetry*, which contains an important attempt to contextualize the Rowley poems in English literary history, includes a number of outright deceptions.[6] Even Samuel Johnson, one of the century's most tireless enemies of fraud, published his own compositions as if they were parliamentary debates, as one of his antagonists in the Ossianic disputes reminded readers.[7] Still, while the work of the fakers has come to be appreciated for its complexities and its engagement with the cultural

---

4   Ruthven, *Faking Literature*, pp. 2, 66.

5   Gaskill, "The Manuscript Myth," p. 14. See, however, his admission that "he was not entirely the anti-Scottish bigot he is often made out to be" (Gaskill, "'Ossian' Macpherson," p. 130).

6   See Freeman and Freeman, *John Payne Collier*, 1:184–93. On Steevens, see also Paull, *Literary Ethics*, p. 33. John M. Ellis argues that the Brothers Grimm "deliberately, persistently, and completely misrepresented the status of their tales" (*One Fairy Story too Many*, p. viii).

7   See Meek, *A Small Tribute*, p. 5. For more on Johnson's parliamentary debates, see Thomas Kaminski, *The Early Career of Samuel Johnson*, pp. 29–30, 123–43.

currents of eighteenth-century Britain, the work of their critics has usually been treated reductively. I hope to take the critics of the fakers as seriously as others have treated the fakers themselves.

The approach I take in this book deserves some attention, beginning with how I define "deception." Forgery and fakery cannot always be reduced to a simple and self-evident matter of right or wrong: instead they constitute a continuum ranging from perfectly innocuous misrepresentation through the utmost perfidy. But while we may know deception when we see it, it is difficult both to define it and to explain exactly what is wrong with it. "There are, we sometimes tend to think, artistic crimes," writes Stephan Körner, "but they are not as clearly defined or graded as are murder, theft, or treason."[8] In an essay on artistic forgery, Michael Wreen acknowledges "a disturbing truth in Körner's remark: we do tend to think that there are artistic crimes, but we are ill prepared either to define or to say what is wrong with them."[9]

Many twentieth- and twenty-first-century critics have worked to understand the complications inherent in any notion of authenticity, and much of this work is fascinating. Susan Stewart's meditations on authenticity in *Crimes of Writing* are consistently thought-provoking, even exemplary—and yet, as I came to write this book, I found *Crimes of Writing* offered little direct help. The problem is that books like Stewart's, for all they help us to understand what authenticity means today, have little to tell us about what authenticity meant in the eighteenth century. Consider Thomas Chatterton. For some modern critics, his Rowleian poems are not properly forgeries because he never intended to deceive anyone about their origin—they are works of fiction, not of fraud. They combine a pseudonym with an exotic setting, and are therefore no different from, say, Defoe's *Robinson Crusoe* (published as "a just History of Fact" without "any Appearance of Fiction in it"[10]), Swift's *Gulliver*, or Walpole's *Castle of Otranto*.

Is that, however, what eighteenth-century readers thought about Chatterton? My reading in eighteenth-century sources convinces me it was not, and determining how eighteenth-century Britons thought about forgery and authenticity is the central concern of this book. My approach is therefore resolutely empirical, and from this empirical approach to the subject I derive a resolutely empirical definition of forgery: if contemporaries argued over its authenticity, however innocent we think it today, it is grist for my mill; if they did not, however culpable we think it today, it is not. My only concern is whether the cases were actively debated in the eighteenth century. I mention above that Thomas Warton has been accused of fabrication, but (apart from some cavils by Joseph Ritson) serious doubts arose only late in the nineteenth century. He therefore is of little use for my purposes. I do not pretend to settle for all time the question of what is true and what is false, but I do hope to show that eighteenth-century conceptions of authenticity were not always ours, nor were they necessarily more simplistic than those promulgated by recent critics. The result of this empiricist method is that many matters treated as uniform and uncomplicated by modern critics are shown to have been irreducibly plural in the eighteenth century.

---

8   Körner, *Fundamental Questions of Philosophy*, p. 140.
9   Wreen, "Is, Madam? Nay, It Seems!," p. 188.
10 Defoe, *Robinson Crusoe*, p. 1.

I exclude, as far as possible, only two areas of investigation. The first has to do with religious fraud. The libraries of seventeenth- and eighteenth-century Europe were packed with arguments over the authenticity of sacred visions, the reliability of Scripture, and the evidence for Christ's divinity. Humphrey Prideaux published the first edition of his popular *True Nature of Imposture Fully Display'd in the Life of Mahomet* in 1697; a year later John Jeffery published *The Dangerous Imposture of Quakerism*; in 1712 Charles Owen followed them with *The Scene of Delusions Open'd: In an Historical Account of Prophetick Impostures, in the Jewish, Christian, and Pagan World*—titles like these abound. Religious fraud, though, is such a large topic in its own right, and the methods of debating it are so different from investigations into secular deceptions, that it threatened both to take this book in a very different direction and to double its size. I therefore discuss religious questions—Richard Simon's approach to biblical criticism, Hume's critique of miracles—only when they touch directly on the secular cases that are my real concern.

The second and more important exclusion is fiction, the "legitimate" genre in which reality and lies collided most spectacularly in the eighteenth century. This omission demands some justification. Many people throughout history have accused fiction of being indistinguishable from deception, beginning with the lead counsel for the prosecution: Plato leveled the most famous charge against poets, though he was neither the first nor the last to do so.[11] Augustine devoted two works to falsehoods, the early *De mendacio* and the later *Contra mendacium*; the preposition in the latter title leaves no doubt where he stands. *De mendacio* offers a taxonomy of eight kinds of lie, each with several sub-types, in which fiction figures; in the end he argues that all are immoral.[12] Aquinas concurs, as do many Renaissance critics anxious about the truth claims made by fiction. And Plato found allies among the Puritans of the seventeenth century. Though most Puritan charges against literature concern the specific immorality it cultivates—Stephen Gosson's concern about the wickedness of the stage led him to write his "pleasaunt inuective against Poets"[13] in 1587—plenty of critics disparaged fiction itself.

The most lasting reply to these attacks, at least in England, came from a contemporary of Gosson. In *An Apology for Poetry* (1595), Sir Philip Sidney cleverly proceeded by redefining truth, and separating higher truth from what we might call mere actuality. It was a bold step, and Sidney's masterstroke was to answer the charges against the poets with a plea of *nolo contendere*: "To the [charge] that they should be the principal liars, I answer paradoxically, but truly, I think truly, that of all writers under the sun the poet is the least liar.... The poet, he nothing affirms, and therefore never lieth. For, as I take it, to lie is to affirm that to be true which is

---

11   See Plato, *Republic*, 2.377d. Aristotle says Solon was the first to make the argument: see *Metaphysics*, 1.2 (983a), and Pindar's *First Olympian Ode*. "By the time of Plato," writes Geoffrey Shepherd, "the debate was a stock theme" (in Sidney, *Apology for Poetry*, p. 199).

12   The only exception: "Jocose lies ... have never been considered as real lies, since both in the verbal expression and in the attitude of the one joking such lies are accompanied by a very evident lack of intention to deceive" (*De mendacio*, in *Saint Augustine: Treatises on Various Subjects*, p. 54).

13   Gosson, *The Schoole of Abuse*, title page.

false." Fiction's lies are not *real* lies because they do not ask to be taken for true—or, rather, not "true" in any vulgar sense, though they may deliver a higher-order truth in the guise of lower-order falsehood. As Sidney writes elsewhere in the *Apology*, "Though [the poet] recount things not true, yet because he telleth them not for true, he lieth not."[14] Literature is somehow outside of, or exempt from, the laws of truth and fiction that govern other situations. The poet makes some kinds of truth claims, but when he relates events "he telleth them not for true." The class of genres we call imaginative literature somehow invokes a set of quotation marks that serve to insulate its statements from the scrutiny any other claim should expect. Michael Riffaterre says as much when he opens his *Fictional Truth* with the confident assertion, "Fiction is a genre whereas lies are not.... A novel always contains signs whose function is to remind readers that the tale they are being told is imaginary."[15]

The signs are not always noticed. There are probably readers naive enough to believe any story, however preposterous; Swift famously reports on the dimwitted bishop who "hardly believed a word" of *Gulliver's Travels*.[16] Perhaps we can brush him off as (a) stupid, (b) insane, or (c) an invention of Swift's, but not every patsy is so easily dismissed. Consider John Langhorne, taken in by Walpole's *Otranto*. He did not believe in gigantic helmets or sighing portraits, in "Miracles, visions, necromancy, dreams, and other preternatural events."[17] He did, however, take the story's stated provenance as true, believing the title page's declaration that it was by one Onuphrio Muralto, and that caused him to misread the novel. His harsh review of the second edition shows that his credulity was genuine:

> When this book was published as a translation from an old Italian romance, ... we could readily excuse its preposterous phenomena.... But when, as in this edition, the Castle of Otranto is declared to be a modern performance, that indulgence we afforded to the foibles of a supposed antiquity, we can by no means extend to the singularity of a false taste in a cultivated period of learning.[18]

Even Walpole's friend William Mason confessed, "when a friend ... returned it me with some doubts of its originality, I laughed him to scorn.... it proves me your dupe."[19] Some have suggested Chatterton's work was no different. Chatterton himself seems to have thought of Rowley as Onuphrio Muralto *redivivus*; Walpole's dismissal of his Rowleian poems prompted a venomous verse epistle in reply: "Thou mayst call me Cheat—/Say, didst thou ne'er indulge in such Deceit?/Who wrote

---

14   Sidney, *Apology for Poetry*, pp. 52, 53. Sidney was not the first to advance this line of argument: see, for instance, John of Salisbury's attack on eloquence: "sed sub verborum tegmine vera latent" ("but truths lie concealed under the veil of words," *Entheticus maior*, line 186); "Nec ut est in fabulis, quoniam et mendacia poetarum seruiunt ueritati" (*Policraticus*, 3.6.46–7).

15   Riffaterre, *Fictional Truth*, p. 1.

16   Swift to Pope, [27] Nov. 1726, in Swift, *Correspondence*, ed. Williams, 3:189; see also *Correspondence*, ed. Woolley, 3:56. Woolley defends the date traditionally assigned to the letter, 17 Nov. 1726.

17   Walpole, *The Castle of Otranto*, p. 4.

18   *The Monthly Review* 32 (May 1765): 394.

19   Mason to Walpole, 14 April 1765, in Walpole, *Correspondence*, 28:5.

Otranto?"[20] Herbert Croft, in writing about Chatterton in 1780, was sympathetic: "in the preface to the first edition of the *Castle* of *Otranto* ... we are solemnly told that it was found in the 'library of an antient catholic family.'"[21] So were the Rowleian poems forgeries, or merely pseudonymous works of fiction?

This sort of anecdotal evidence of incompetent readers, though sparse, is valuable because it shows that not all contemporary readers picked up on the necessary clues. And the problem was not merely with delusional Quixotes—there is evidence that seemingly sane readers addressed letters to Pamela B., as they still do to Sherlock Holmes at Baker Street and even to Romeo and Juliet in Verona (though these correspondents apparently never reached the end of the play; otherwise they would realize the star-crossed lovers are in no condition to reply). And even Swift's satire—which seems easy to spot as fictional because of its implausibility—is probably clearer to us than to Swift's contemporaries, who were expected to swallow ludicrous representations of exotic lands in travel narratives, filled with anthropophagi and men whose heads do grow beneath their shoulders.[22] The absurdity of flying islands and talking horses may not have been enough to cue some members of Swift's reading public. We have already seen one reader, proud of his powers of deduction, who "hardly believed a word of it," while another, more gullible still, supposedly sought in vain for Lilliput on a map. These readers have missed the generic clues that *Gulliver* is to be read not as one would read a news account—that its truth claims, if any, are of a different nature altogether.

Comparisons between fraud and fiction are tempting, and can often be fruitful. They can also, however, be superficial and even specious. Even if we admit, with Lisa Zunshine, that "there is no 'one-size-fits-all' definition of the truth-value of a given text and no cross-cultural yardstick against which such a value could be measured,"[23] we can still recognize that most readers—an overwhelming majority—did pick up on most of the cues, whatever they were. In 1726, most treated *Travels into Several Remote Nations of the World* by Lemuel Gulliver as a work of fiction and *A History of the Voyages and Travels of Capt. Nathaniel Uring*, published in the same year, as a work of fact. According to my empirical approach, then, however worthwhile it may be to examine the problematic borderline between novels and histories, fiction need not concern us much here.

That does not, however, mean that we can afford to neglect "literary" language and techniques, and in exploring these cases, I try to pay attention to the metaphors

---

20 Chatterton, *Complete Works*, 1:341. This poem was first published by John Dix, Chatterton's biographer and a known forger. Chatterton's editor, Donald Taylor, summarizes the case: "I am not absolutely sure that [the manuscript] is in C[hatterton]'s hand ... The fact that the poem was first printed by Dix arouses one's scepticism, but nothing in the poem ... argues against C's authorship" (*Complete Works*, 2:986). Nick Groom, however, offers both internal and external evidence leading to the conclusion that this is "extremely dubious and should be regarded as [a] forger[y]" ("The Case against Chatterton's 'Lines to Walpole' and 'Last Verses,'" p. 278).

21 Croft, *Love and Madness*, p. 136.

22 Percy G. Adams wrote the classic account of the "pseudo voyages that were designed to make the public believe them real" (Adams, *Travelers and Travel Liars*, p. vii).

23 Zunshine, "Eighteenth-Century Print Culture and the 'Truth' of Fictional Narrative," p. 216.

in which fakery is discussed. Discussions of deception are most often cast in terms of criminal law: the most common analogue is forgery, "the *crimen falsi*," which Sir William Blackstone defines as "the fraudulent making or alteration of a writing to the prejudice of another man's right."[24] Another common metaphor is to liken literary deception to monetary counterfeiting. Both metaphors are imprecise, but remain significant: eighteenth-century British thinking about authenticity was often informed by law, and it is possible that legal theory was informed by thinking about authenticity. I have therefore tried to take metaphorical and analogical language seriously.

Organizing this unruly mass of materials has been challenging. I originally considered taking up one episode of deception in each chapter—a chapter on the Popish Plot, another on Mary Toft, and so on. But some of these stories of deception are short and sweet, others long and complicated; some promised to be difficult to stretch out to chapter length, while others seemed to spill into multiple chapters. The Cock Lane Ghost was a celebrated case, and raises enough important questions to warrant a closer examination than it has yet received, but the controversy was over in a matter of weeks. Not so the debates over Ossian. The popularity of the poems and the belief in their authenticity long outlived Macpherson; the arguments raged from the early 1760s until well into the nineteenth century, and are still being played out, in attenuated form, in modern scholarly studies. After much experimentation, then, I settled on a topical arrangement, with each chapter advancing another argument about how debates were conducted. In deciding not to structure chapters around episodes laid out in chronological order, I have given less attention to developments that took place over the course of the eighteenth century—since there seemed to be no tidy narrative of progress during the period, I saw no point in giving priority to chronology. Another result is a degree of repetition. The richer deceptions come up in multiple chapters, while other cases may be mentioned only in passing once or twice. This seemed to me to be warranted by the nature of my material. The Ossianic disputes, for instance, came up in virtually every discussion of deception, and therefore deserve the repeated notice; William Lauder's effrontery, on the other hand, was striking but, once Douglas demonstrated that his quotations were fabricated, there was little more to say. Readers who hope for straightforward narratives of each episode of deception will be well served by the many other books on the subject.

I have tried to distinguish this study from other works on eighteenth-century forgery in at least three respects. The first, as stated above, is my question: it concerns not the actions of the fakers themselves but the disputes they produced. The second difference is that I have done my best to avoid empty rhetorical questions. Francis Bacon begins his examination of truth by invoking the Gospel of John: "*What is Truth*; said jesting *Pilate*; And would not stay for an Answer. Certainly there be, that delight in Giddinesse; And count it a Bondage, to fix a Beleefe."[25] The study of forgery has attracted many modern jesting Pilates who delight in giddiness, and the rhetorical question is one of their favorite tools. Why is Macpherson's reworking of the Ossianic stories any worse than Percy's reworking of his ballad

---

24 Blackstone, *Commentaries*, 4:245. Baines offers the most extended consideration of the relationships between legal and literary counterfeits in *The House of Forgery*.

25 Bacon, "Of Truth," in *Essayes*, p. 7.

sources? (Implied answer: It's not.) Isn't Chatterton's imagined medieval Bristol just as valid as Walpole's imagined medieval Otranto? (Clear suggestion: It must be.) Why should literary forgery be seen as less ethical than any sort of creative literary representation? (Inevitable conclusion: They're interchangeable.) But these unanswered questions are sometimes disingenuous and always question-begging, assuming a sly wink can take the place of serious explanation. I have done my best not to leave questions hanging in the air.

Most of these rhetorical questions are directed at readers today, and especially at modern notions of how forgeries differ from other kinds of representation. Such questions may be worthwhile, but they are not my concern. Rather than how *we* should think about forgery, I am trying to recover how *eighteenth-century* readers thought about it. That leads to the third area of difference from most previous studies, my method, which I have tried to make resolutely empirical and historical. "Always historicize!" exhorts Fredric Jameson at the beginning of a manifestly ahistorical book.[26] I have not hesitated to introduce modern examples and analogues when they promise to illuminate earlier cases, but I have worked to restrict my conceptions of authenticity and forgery to notions that actually circulated in eighteenth-century Britain.

My disdain for the unanswered rhetorical question and my fondness for the historical approach have consequences that may demand justification. If I seem at times to belabor the obvious, as when I discuss the principle of non-contradiction, it is because I hope to make explicit what is often only implied by the participants in the eighteenth-century debates. Often one party in a dispute will be guilty of a logical fallacy, and only by beginning with the basics can the fallacy be identified. It may also be the case that something obvious in the twenty-first century was less so in the eighteenth—not because we have benefited from some inevitable progression from ignorance to enlightenment, but because even conventional wisdom has a history. The kind of historicist argument now taken for granted by every undergraduate was alien to many early-modern sensibilities and, although we may feel embarrassed to dwell on the impossibility of finding eleventh-century events in third-century documents, such things have not always been obvious to all observers.

I have also tried to focus on the arguments actually advanced by the disputants in these cases, rather than offering my own speculations about their ulterior motives. Through much of the twentieth century and into the twenty-first, a favorite mode of examining disputes over authenticity has been to reduce the various perpetrators and critics to bundles of prejudices. According to a favorite modern scenario, a dogmatic Englishman like Samuel Johnson could not possibly admit the Scots had a literary tradition at once greater and older than England's, elitist male physicians could not bear to defer to uneducated women like Mary Toft or Elizabeth Canning on medical matters, and powerful Londoners like Horace Walpole could not tolerate antiquarian posturing from poor provincials like Thomas Chatterton. Much of this work has been valuable in contextualizing the debates and revealing what is at stake, and I do not deny that prejudices of many sorts—nationalist, sexist, racist—influenced many of these discussions. I worry, though, that this line of argument has sometimes been taken too far: if one were to read only recent criticism, it would seem as if no

---

26 Jameson, *The Political Unconscious*, p. 9.

eighteenth-century opinion was ever offered in good faith, and no piece of evidence was ever evaluated honestly. My reading in these cases has convinced me that, while not everyone was perfectly disinterested, the Will to Truth was not completely lost in the Will to Power. If the true state of things were so simplistic, there would be no way even to approximate the truth: Scots would always support Scots and Englishmen Englishmen; men would support men and women would support women; and so on. The remarkable fact is that the larger eighteenth-century British public arrived at something like the truth in most of these cases, insofar as we can determine it today. English critics of Ossian may have resented Scottish presumption in "discovering" epics, but they were mostly right that Macpherson had doctored his evidence. Elizabeth Canning's prosecutors may have been unreformed misogynists, but they were right that her story presented enough difficulties to warrant questioning her. Besides, this sort of argument takes for granted that the set of concerns and prejudices that matter to us must have been determinative in the eighteenth century. We care about race, class, gender, sexuality, and nationality, but our understandings of these terms sometimes correspond poorly with eighteenth-century concerns. As Clement Hawes has argued, "The mutual antagonism of England and Scotland … is, in fact, ultimately of very limited value as a lens through which to interpret the nuances of 'Ossian.'"[27] I have resolved to look for evidence about, say, Samuel Johnson's attitudes toward Ossian not in what I can discern about his general attitudes toward Scotland, but in what he actually wrote and said about Ossian.

The book's argument is that forgery, fakery, and fraud make explicit the usually unspoken grounds on which Britons made sense of their world—confrontations with inauthenticity, in other words, bring tacitly understood conceptions of reality to the surface. To make this case, I have tried to account for some of the involved and drawn-out disputes over things that strike us as absurd now, but that provoked serious debate in the eighteenth century. Why were these fakes not dismissed out of hand?— why did Mary Toft's imposture require hundreds of pages of learned disquisition?— why did two dozen distinguished literary men line up to avow their belief in William Henry Ireland's crude forgeries?—how could even learned men accept Psalmanazar as a Formosan? The central argument of *Deception and Detection* is that the era's remarkable surge of interest in deception is the result of a series of cultural shifts that took place in the seventeenth and eighteenth centuries, and that these shifts not only rendered the investigation of deception possible, but made it an urgent task. And the reason many of these questions seem obvious to us today is that we live in a world shaped by the eighteenth century's struggles with deception: our laws, our philosophy, our history, and our criticism all emerge from the debates considered here. Revisiting those initial skirmishes that helped to shape our modern worldview may help to make some of those disputes more comprehensible. We need to know about them because fakery takes us to the heart of eighteenth-century notions of the value of evidence, of the mechanisms of perception and memory, of the relationship between art and life, of historicism, and of human motivation—deception, in other words, opens up eighteenth-century culture.

---

27   Hawes, *The British Eighteenth Century and Global Critique*, p. 33.

Chapter 1

Recognizing a Fake
When You See One

What is *Truth*, was an Enquiry many Ages since; and it being that which all Mankind either do, or pretend to search after, it cannot but be worth our while carefully to examine wherein it consists; and so acquaint our selves with the Nature of it, as to observe how the Mind distinguishes it from Falshood.   —John Locke[1]

James Boswell once naively asked Samuel Johnson, "What is poetry?" "Why, Sir," replied Johnson, "it is much easier to say what it is not. We all *know* what light is; but it is not easy to *tell* what it is."[2] We might say the same thing about forgery: we all *know* what forgery is, but it is not easy to *tell* what it is. A large vocabulary of relevant terms seems to promise precision—forgery, fakery, fraud, hoax, counterfeit—but we have no clear ideas attached to most of these words. And here I mean not only which variety of deception is involved—whether something is properly a forgery or a counterfeit, say—but whether something is a deception at all.

Very Little Resemblance

Sometimes it can be a fairly straightforward matter, at least in principle, and these cases are often pleasingly dramatic, with a definitive "gotcha!" that unambiguously reveals the nature of the imposture. Given the appropriate data, we can usually distinguish the authentic from the false. The data, of course, may be hard to come by; but once the questions of fact are settled, the questions of law usually follow inevitably. George Psalmanazar claimed to be a native of Formosa; he had never been east of Germany; his claim was therefore a lie. Unless our twenty-first-century understanding of human reproduction is grossly inadequate, Mary Toft did not give birth to rabbits; her claim is unambiguously false. A forged banknote, however difficult it may be to discover in practice, is in principle straightforward. The claims it makes about its own status leave no room for ambiguity: this piece of paper was issued by this organization on this date and entitles the bearer to this amount of money. If any one of these claims is false, the document is fraudulent and its monetary worth is nil. In most investigations of fakery, therefore, the task is to come up with the evidence, and the conclusion follows naturally. Most of this book is

---

1   Locke, *Essay*, p. 574 (4.5.1).
2   Boswell, *Life*, 3:38.

concerned with attempts to turn up and then to marshal the necessary facts, with the understanding that the verdict will follow quickly on the discovery.

Not every criminal, though, had a dramatic unmasking at the hands of a single Sherlock Holmes, and not every imposition vanished the moment it was touched by Ithuriel's spear. We know what it means for a banknote to be forged, but a forged poem is endlessly complicated. Because poems are aesthetic and historical objects, judgments about their authenticity are far more involved. What does it mean to be a "fake poem" as opposed to a "real poem"? Questions like this mean that some forgeries were never definitively squelched: they simply faded away. A few did not result in a satisfying Q.E.D., and continue to be debated today.

To explore these complexities, I begin with the works of Ossian, the most famous forgeries in British literary history—if forgeries they are. Many modern critics who debate the true nature of the Ossianic poems are more concerned with our own notions of what constitutes authenticity than with the notions shared by James Macpherson's original audiences. Many are ignorant of even the basic claims made by the eighteenth-century factions. Some of Macpherson's modern critics take a malicious glee in pointing out that he had no third-century manuscripts, and that he stitched together separate pieces from oral tradition, as if that definitively disproves the authenticity of the poems—but Macpherson himself admitted as much. One of his defenders, Anna Seward, believed "he had [no] ancient manuscripts," "weaving [songs] together for the Fingal, into something like a regular epic": the poems were still, as far as she was concerned, genuine.[3] Robert Heron went even further: he acknowledged

> That the age of their composition cannot now be ascertained, nor can it be determined whether they are the compositions of Scotland or of Ireland; That they are in many instances mutilated fragments, pruned, or eked out by the Translator; that such of them as exhibit any considerable regularity of complexity of structure owe their form probably to the cares of the Translator; That the Translator has connected their history with a superficial and ill-founded theory of the early part of the history of Scotland; and they have not been given to the Public in a form sufficiently simple.

And yet, despite all these concessions, he added, "with so many problematical circumstances against them, I however esteem them to be unquestionably genuine."[4] Clearly Heron's understanding of "genuine" is very far from that of many of Macpherson's modern critics.

Some modern Ossianic partisans, on the other hand, praise Macpherson for courageously advocating a modern folklorist's conception of oral composition, invoking (in the words of one recent critic) the "diminishing idealism about the 'purity' and 'authenticity' of folk traditions"[5]—but Macpherson himself expressed contempt for these very "folk traditions," using all the conventional eighteenth-

---

3   Seward to Dr. Gregory, 25 March 1792, in Seward, *Letters*, 3:127.

4   Heron, *Observations*, 1:355.

5   Porter, "'Bring Me the Head of James Macpherson,'" p. 398. Porter here argues that "what was meant by 'originals'" in the Ossianic dispute "has come to be less important" in light of our current knowledge of oral literature.

century language about authenticity and corruption that today's folklorists reject as inadequate for oral culture. In this chapter I hope to strip away modern preconceptions about authenticity to try to recover what eighteenth-century readers thought was genuine or bogus in the Ossianic poems.

That *Fingal* and *Temora* are not literal translations of verbatim transcriptions of two epic poems written by a third- or fourth-century Scottish poet named Ossian is now nearly universally accepted.[6] We have long known that, at least in the case of *Fingal*, Macpherson collected scraps of oral tradition from the Highlands, combined with a few pieces from manuscript, and assembled them into a heroic poem. Modern scholars have determined that Macpherson drew on *The Book of the Dean of Lismore* and other manuscripts when he composed *Fingal*.[7] Derick Thomson, the twentieth-century commentator best equipped to describe Macpherson's use of traditional material, concludes that he "collected a considerable quantity of Gaelic Ossianic ballads from oral and manuscript sources, and used characters and stories, related traditions and history, as and when it suited him; sometimes following the gist and sequence of the ballads but more often altering these, always adding ideas and incidents which have no Gaelic counterpart, and imposing on the whole a style which bears very little resemblance to anything in Gaelic literature."[8] (Thomson was unable to find evidence of much oral literature in either the *Fragments* or *Temora*, which seem to be almost entirely of Macpherson's creation.) In assembling his materials, he arranged the traditional fragments and reworked them to suit their new context, adding long passages of his own. The arrangement changed the character of his originals, sometimes drastically: "Macpherson's refining and bowdlerising pen," writes Thomson, "has often changed the atmosphere of the ballads almost beyond recognition .... Some of the imagery and sentiments are new, some of them are beautiful, but they are not Ossianic."[9]

So these are the facts. What to do with them? For some commentators, they constitute proof that Macpherson was stained with the blackest dye of turpitude; for others, they exculpate him and reveal that the poor Scot got a bad rap. How best to characterize the poems remains unsettled after nearly a quarter-millennium of squabbling. One reason is that we lack a good term for this sort of pastiche-writing, probably because there are so few examples. When it does happen, however, it is not necessarily dismissed as unethical. Had Macpherson been candid about his role in assembling the fragments into a larger poem, there may never have been an Ossianic controversy. His method, after all, was little different from that of Zacharius Topelius in assembling the *Kalevala* from oral tradition in 1822. The problem apparently arose from the manner in which he presented this work. I take

---

6   I say "nearly universally accepted" because at least one eccentric work, published as recently as 1996—Allen and Allen, *Fingal's Cave*—treats Macpherson's versions of the Ossianic poems as literal and unadorned translations of third-century epics.

7   See Mackintosh, "James Macpherson and the Book of the Dean of Lismore," and Gaskill, "'Ossian' Macpherson," pp. 126–34.

8   Thomson, "'Ossian' Macpherson and the Gaelic World of the Eighteenth Century," p. 14. Thomas M. Curley offers a more detailed account of Macpherson's use of Gaelic sources in "Samuel Johnson and Truth."

9   Thomson, *The Gaelic Sources of Macpherson's "Ossian,"* p. 84.

up these questions of authenticity, therefore, not with any expectation of settling "the Ossianic question," but rather in the hope of raising some of the questions that appear in many investigations of eighteenth-century fraud. I want to understand what fraud meant in Macpherson's day.

Genuine in Spite of My Teeth

The first lesson to arise from a careful examination of an eighteenth-century dispute over literary deception is that "authenticity" meant different things to different people, and even to the same people at different times. Many arguments about the poems, both pro and con, have been marked by ignorance—whether of the facts of publication, the Gaelic language, or the nature of oral literature—but even those who had most of the facts at hand still showed a tremendous variety of opinions. What is remarkable is the diversity of interpretations that emerged from the same set of undisputed facts—a diversity of opinion that can sometimes be seen in a single person.

Even so knowledgeable an antiquarian as Thomas Percy did not know what to make of the Ossianic poems. He knew about the *Fragments* by July 1761, when he wrote to Evan Evans about the "favourable reception the public has given to an English version of some *Erse* Fragments imported from the Highlands of Scotland." This early letter betrays no suspicion about the poems' authenticity. A month later, though, Rice Williams wrote to him expressing his doubts of Macpherson's honesty about his scholarly abilities: "I am really afraid the world is grossly imposed upon when I consider Mac Pherson's pretension to the knowledge of the Welsh, Cornish, Armoric Erse, Irish and Gallic languages." Williams seems to have captured the skeptical opinion of those in Percy's circle, and Percy was soon a convert to the anti-Ossianic party. In another two months, he wrote to Evans about Macpherson's success in gaining subscribers for a translation of *Fingal*, "Tho' hardly one reader in ten believes the specimens already produced to be genuine."[10] Percy had joined the doubters. Not long after *Fingal* was published, he described his concerns to William Shenstone: "There is too little simplicity of narration: all is thrown into metaphor and sentence: the latter too often affected and stiff: the former too frequently turgid and harsh. An affectation of the Erse Idiom is too generally studied: so as to betray (I think) a consciousness that the piece is not what it is made to pass for."[11] His language here is cautious: he has not yet called the work a forgery or a fraud, but *Fingal* is "not what it is made to pass for."

As the debate continued, though, Percy became less circumspect. In July 1764, for instance, he wrote to Evans, "every penetrating Person I have ever conversed with look[s] upon it, as almost all an imposition, and that of no very artful kind. A little attention will convince any discerning reader of the imposture: and the world

10   Percy to Evans, 21 July 1761; Rice Williams to Percy, 14 Aug. 1761; and Percy to Evans, 15 Oct. 1761, in Percy, *Letters*, 5:2–3, 161, 19.

11   Percy to Shenstone, 22 Feb. 1762, in Percy, *Letters*, 7:141–2.

begins pretty generally to smell out the cheat."[12] In the same letter, he declares that "every page of the Greater Poems contains evident marks of imposition." His verdict is now unqualified: "the Erse Poems ... contain so bold an attempt to impose on Mankind as was ever practised."[13]

A year and a half later, though, that confidence was beginning to waver. A trip to Scotland brought Percy into the company of Hugh Blair and Adam Ferguson, prominent supporters of Ossian, who led him to reconsider his skepticism. A letter he sent to *The Gentleman's Magazine* in 1781 describes the scene:

> On October 8, 1765, I arrived at Edinburgh, where I passed five days with the Rev. Dr. Blair, who ... introduced me to Dr. FERGUSON.... he mentioned some doubts I had entertained concerning the genuineness of Ossian's Poems: and he ... produced a student, a native of the Highlands, who recited several passages, or verses, in Earse (some of which he afterwards sung me) as what he had heard in his own country; and I perfectly remember, that when he interpreted the verses to me, some of them appeared to contain part of the description of Fingal's chariot.[14]

The details of this visit were soon thrown into doubt, and for decades partisans on either side argued over exactly who said what to whom when in whose company.[15] But from this account it seems that the student's ability to recite passages from *Fingal*—or, since Percy knew no Gaelic, passages he was told were from *Fingal*— tipped the balance, and he grudgingly found himself a believer again. "When I was in Scotland," he wrote to Evans in December 1765, "I made great inquiry into the Authenticity of Ossian's Poetry; and could not resist the Evidence that poured in upon me; so that I am forced to believe them, as to the main, genuine in spite of my teeth."[16]

Evans, still convinced the poems were phony, tried to set him straight:

> You say you are at least convinced of the genuineness of Ossian's poems as published by Mackpherson of Perth; I suppose you mean by that that you are satisfied there are extant such pieces in the Erse language as he has translated into English. I grant this may be true. But if you mean that they are really Ossian's productions and of so great antiquity as averred by him, I beg leave to dissent from you, the proofs that he brings of it are to me far from being satisfactory.[17]

This passage warrants particular attention. For Evans, the existence of old ballads or fragments on Ossianic topics does not settle the authenticity of the epic poems;

---

12 Percy to Evans, 23 July 1764, in Percy, *Letters*, 5:96. The manuscript letter has *cheat* deleted and *imposition* written over it, suggesting Percy chose his words with care.

13 Ibid., 5:96, 97–8.

14 *Gentleman's Magazine* 51 (Dec. 1781): 567–8.

15 Some little-known unpublished material on the question is collected in Edinburgh Univ. Library MS La.II.243, including several letters from Blair to the Rev. Dr. Carlyle, 18 April and 22 April [1782], and in a letter from Henry Mackenzie to John Pinkerton, 6 Jan. 1806, in BL Add. MS 29747, fols. 86^{r-v}.

16 Percy to Evans, 24 Dec. 1765, in Percy, *Letters*, 5:117.

17 Evans to Percy, 17 Jan. 1766, in Percy, *Letters*, 5:121.

it does not prove "that they are really Ossian's productions," or that they are "of so great antiquity as averred by him." For Evans, "authenticity" means at least two things: first, that Macpherson's poems were written by the person, Ossian, to whom they are attributed; and second, that this person lived in the distant past, what Blair called the "uncultivated ages," which were "abounding ... with that enthusiasm, that vehemence and fire, which are the soul of poetry."[18]

Evans's letter had little immediate effect on Percy, who had heard Gaelic verses with his own ears. He had been convinced that they were both traditional and the source of at least some passages in *Fingal*. Fair is fair: he was willing publicly to acknowledge his newfound faith in the authenticity of Macpherson's poems, and so when Blair "desired me to mention the recital I had heard, in the next edition of the Reliques of Ancient Poetry," Percy complied. To the second edition of his *Reliques* (1767) he added a note: "those beautiful pieces of ERSE POESY ... were lately given to the world in an English dress by Mr. MAC-PHERSON: Several fragments of which the editor of this book has heard sung in the original language, and translated *vivâ voce*, by a native of the Highlands, who had, at the time, no opportunity of consulting Mr. Macpherson's book."[19] He was now firmly, albeit grudgingly, among the believers.

Percy's story, however, does not end there. "Some years after," he wrote, "a very judicious friend, a native of Scotland also, ... made it credible to me, that there might be some deception in the case, and advised me to suppress the passage in question."[20] What exactly this "judicious friend" told him is uncertain, but it is probably similar to what Evans had told him long ago: hearing short passages in a language he did not understand should not sway him. The compliment added to the second edition of the *Reliques* in 1767 therefore disappeared from the third in 1775. He was careful to add that "I never believed Dr. Blair to have been conscious of any deception." Macpherson, though, was another matter. Until the end of his life, Percy remained convinced that the poems were fraudulent throughout, as when in 1803 he wrote to Robert Anderson, offering to send him "my Testimony that Sir John Elliott his friend assured me that his Ossian and Temora were all his own invention."[21]

It is worth pausing to consider what caused Percy to change his mind several times—what, in other words, he regarded as the essential characteristics of authenticity or deception. At first it seems he was content to accept the popular verdict without much direct consideration of the evidence. He then shifted to a critique on stylistic grounds: that "all is thrown into metaphor" and that the poems were "too frequently turgid and harsh" constituted evidence that they could not be genuine. He was apparently convinced that authentic primitive poetry was less metaphorical, less turgid, less harsh. But the testimony of a Highlander—whose recitation he could not understand, but whose character seemed unlikely to deceive him—led him to reconsider. Finally, a friend led him into another volte-face as he once again rejected them as fraudulent.

---

18   Blair, *A Critical Dissertation*, p. 345.
19   *Gentleman's Magazine* 51 (Dec. 1781): 568; Percy, *Reliques*, 2nd ed., 1:xlv.
20   Ibid.
21   Percy to Robert Anderson, 20 July 1803, in Percy, *Letters*, 9:123.

Manuscript Questions

With all this confusion in a prominent antiquarian well versed in oral literature, is it any wonder that other critics have been equally baffled? It makes sense, then, to spell out as clearly as possible the claims that Macpherson made about the Ossianic poems, and to see how they measure up against the facts that have emerged over the last two-and-a-half centuries. Even this is a big, messy task, and for now I would like to set aside the personal, national, and aesthetic concerns that swirled around discussions of the works' authenticity. Any such separation is artificial, because squabbles between Macpherson and Samuel Johnson, between Scotland and England (and often Ireland), and between genius and hackwork were all part of the debate. Matters are, however, complicated enough already; besides, most recent commentary on the Ossianic poems has been concerned with such questions—the ulterior motives that led Scots to support Scotland and Englishmen to support England, for instance. I would prefer to limit my discussion to the facts about the composition and the translation, and look at the arguments the participants in the debates actually presented, rather than trying to guess at their hidden motives, however influential they may have been.

The question comes down to the claims Macpherson made about the works he attributed to Ossian. What did he mean by the often-repeated word "originals"?—what was the nature of the manuscripts of which he wrote?—what part did oral transmission play?—were the works supposed to be entirely by Ossian, who lived in or near the third century?—what role did Macpherson, both "editor" and "translator," play? Answers to these questions are rarely clear. Sometimes the evidence is lacking; sometimes it is contradictory; sometimes we can only guess at what might have been said in unrecorded conversations and lost correspondence. More irksome still, Macpherson cultivated a studied ambiguity. His modern defenders often insist that Macpherson never made some of the claims commonly attributed to him—but, to be fair, neither did he deny them. Our desire for reliable information on Macpherson's representation of the poems is constantly frustrated.

Information from Macpherson comes in at least four forms, and it is worthwhile to separate them and to pay attention to the different degrees of confidence we can place in each. First are the explicit statements by Macpherson that have survived in writing, whether published or not. The poems themselves, the advertisements and dedications, the *Dissertation concerning the Antiquity of the Poems of Ossian*, Macpherson's correspondence—all are strong evidence of the claims he made for his poems. However misleading or ambiguous they may be about the poems, we can confidently attribute their contents to him, and he must take responsibility for any statements in them.

Next in reliability come written statements by those in Macpherson's circle, especially Blair, which were given Macpherson's imprimatur by appearing in his books. Blair's *Dissertation concerning the Poems of Ossian* and his *Critical Dissertation*, for example, were published with the Ossianic poems, and many of the facts in them seem to have come directly from Macpherson.[22] *The Monthly Review* suggests that another defender of the poems' authenticity, John Clark, also spoke for the silent Macpherson: "Though Mr. Macpherson hath declined to appear in person in a controversy which he himself hath excited, ... yet on his authority Mr. Clark informs us ...."[23] Since there is no reason to believe that Macpherson ever took Blair or Clark into his confidence about whatever deceptions he may have engaged in, he probably either suggested many things in these works or gave his implicit assent by not correcting them. But by not publicly declaring them himself, he kept his distance, preserving what modern bureaucrats have christened "plausible deniability."

Less dependable still are statements made by Macpherson, whether orally or in writing, that do not survive but that have left traces. James Macdonald and others report that Macpherson took credit for the authorship of the epics late in his life, although no firsthand evidence of this has been preserved. His exact words would provide valuable evidence about his claims, but we will likely never recover them. A famous response from Samuel Johnson to Macpherson survives, but the "foolish and impudent letter" that prompted it does not; we can only speculate on what it contained. Johnson armed himself out of fear of a physical assault, but the exact nature of Macpherson's threat will probably never be known.

All of these sorts of evidence are positive; we must also reckon with at least one kind of negative evidence: stories that circulated during Macpherson's lifetime that he never bothered to correct. Even if Macpherson did not encourage misleading inferences to be drawn from the evidence, he certainly often allowed it; even though a simple comment could have clarified a great deal of doubt, he rarely made it.

Even this complicated taxonomy is too simple, and it is not always easy to keep these four categories distinct. Blair wrote the Preface to the *Fragments* but, because it was unsigned and appeared in Macpherson's book, many early readers believed it was Macpherson's (and many critics continue to attribute it to him). Stories such as the discovery of a manuscript of four books of *Fingal*, or of a surgeon who could recite the entire poem, may have originated with Macpherson himself; they may have circulated with his tacit consent; it is just possible that he never heard them. We also have to reckon with different kinds or degrees of assertion within each of the categories. A statement now thought to be false might have been widely believed in

---

22   The exact relationship between Blair and Macpherson in the early days of the Ossianic affair remains obscure, though an unpublished letter of 1787 sheds some light on the matter: "I know no way in which literary persons who are advanced in years can do more Service to the World than on forwarding the efforts of rising genius, or bringing forth unknown merit from obscurity. I was the first person who brought out to the Notice of the World the Poems of Ossian, first by the *Fragments of Antient Poetry* which I published, & afterwards by my Setting on foot the undertaking for collecting & Publishing the Works of Ossian; and I have always considered this as a *meritorious* Action of my Life" (Hugh Blair to Robert Burns, 4 May 1787, in NLS MS.3408, fol. 3ʳ).

23   *Monthly Review* 66 (Jan. 1782): 52.

Macpherson's day; repeating a false commonplace may be less blameworthy than inventing a false story from whole cloth. In attributing the poems to the third-century Ossian, Macpherson was simply repeating what tradition had told him. And there are even various degrees of belief in a falsehood, any of which Macpherson and the members of his circle might have held about the claims they made: passionate conviction, probable judgment, credulous acceptance, wishful thinking, outright mendacity. Macpherson's tentative speculation might receive enthusiastic support from Blair, and the 24-year-old poet may well have been flattered enough to think his speculation had earned the credit of a prominent critic, thereby intensifying his belief in it. It is probably impossible to turn this messy set of categories into a tidy system for considering various kinds or degrees of falsehood, and I am not convinced that any such system would be very useful. I do believe, however, that much of the confusion about whether Macpherson deserves condemnation or exoneration arises from insufficient attention to these problems, from giving all Macpherson's statements equal weight.

Probably the most pressing question in the entire Ossianic affair concerns where Macpherson found his material—whether it was in written or oral form. This "manuscript problem" has been at the center of much subsequent discussion. On this Macpherson himself is frustratingly silent, but he seems to have authorized Blair to speak for him. In the Preface to the *Fragments*, Blair argues that, "By the succession of these Bards, such poems were handed down from race to race; some in manuscript, but more by oral tradition."[24] Note that he refers to short poems, fragments; his phrase "some in manuscript, but more by oral tradition" probably means that different works ("such poems") were transmitted in different forms. There is no logical problem there: there is no reason not to suppose that some of the *Fragments* came from oral tradition, and others from manuscript. Applying this to the epics, though, is more complicated: was *Fingal* supposed to be in manuscript, in oral tradition, or some combination of the two?

If *Fingal* was supposed to be "in manuscript," was it a single complete manuscript or several partial manuscripts? If partial, on what principles were the fragments assembled into a coherent whole? How old were these manuscripts? In what condition were they? By whom were they written? Were there multiple witnesses of any passage and, if so, were there textual variants among them? By 1760 there had been much discussion about textual transmission, both in classical and in vernacular texts. At least Ossian's more educated readers would have wondered about these questions.

Perhaps, on the other hand, *Fingal* came entirely from oral tradition. In that case, it is unlikely that the entire six-book epic could have been recorded from a single performance. Did the bards, however, recognize the pieces they performed as parts of a larger unified work, or as a cycle of related songs? Or was it Macpherson who first realized that the disconnected poems were in fact the remains of a once-unified epic? What led him to suspect this? How were the oral performances recorded? The work of the great twentieth-century folklorists was made possible by portable tape recorders; their eighteenth-century equivalents were without even a reliable system

---

24 Macpherson, *The Poems of Ossian*, p. 5.

of shorthand. Did, then, Macpherson ask a single bard to repeat his songs slowly enough that he could record them? Did he listen to real-time performances on many occasions, perhaps by many performers, until he had learned them by heart and could transcribe them at leisure? Did he consider whether the conditions of transcription would interfere with the performance? Did he later check his transcriptions against new performances? Did he consider whether performances of the same piece differed, either in multiple performances by the same bard, in performances by different bards in one region, or in different regions of the Highlands? Did he consider whether orally transmitted poems supposedly handed down from the third century to the eighteenth would bear any resemblance to their archetypes? Did he conceive of a "pure" text from which departures were "corruptions," or did he entertain the possibility of equally valid improvisations?

The most complex possibility is that the epics were drawn from a combination of manuscript and oral tradition. In this case all the questions above continue to apply, along with a new set. How were the orally transmitted pieces integrated with the manuscript pieces? Did any passages in the oral versions coincide with the same passages in manuscript? If so, were there any variants among them? On what grounds should one reading be preferred over another? If there was no overlap between the spoken and written fragments, how did he know they came from the same work? How did he know the order in which the pieces should be arranged?

Finally, whether the epic came from oral tradition, from manuscript, or from some combination of the two, more questions apply. How did Macpherson know that the pieces he had collected constituted a single work?—that it was complete, or nearly so?—that it was originally by Ossian?—that the version he found early in the 1760s bore any resemblance to the third-century original? If there were gaps in the text, on what principles did he fill them? Did he rely on his personal knowledge of traditional songs heard in his childhood? Did he ever resort to conjectural emendation and, if so, what kinds of knowledge did he use to overrule readings in the text he collected?

To these dozens of questions, Macpherson provided only a few sketchy answers, many of them contradictory or deliberately ambiguous. Subsequent research has turned up the truth behind some of them, but most remain obscure. Unfortunately, this has meant that many critics have felt free to project their favorite answers onto Macpherson, depending on whether they want him to be a hero or a villain. Some imagine him as a naïf for whom the only "genuine" work must have come from a single third-century manuscript, others as a sophisticated harbinger of twentieth-century theories of improvisatory oral composition and transmission. In fact he was somewhere between the two, as were virtually all eighteenth-century commentators.

Few early commentators believed in an intact third-century holograph manuscript; not even William Shaw, Macpherson's most brutal critic on the manuscript problem, expected anyone to produce a complete manuscript in Ossian's hand (how would a blind bard have written it?). What, then, did people mean when they demanded to see "originals"? There seems to have been little consensus even at the time. Macpherson claimed he had left his originals at the shop of Thomas Becket, but James Boswell had no idea what that meant: "What does Becket mean by the *Originals* of Fingal and other poems of Ossian, which he advertises to have lain in his shop?"[25] Macpherson's manuscripts of his English translations would have impressed no one: that they, or someone's fair-copy transcript, were used as printer's copy was evident to everyone. "Original," therefore, would almost certainly have to refer to some Gaelic-language version of the poems; which version, however, was rarely specified. Henry Home, Lord Kames, stated confidently that Macpherson "saw in the Isle of Sky, the first four books of the poem Fingal, written in a fair hand on vellum, and bearing date in the year 1403,"[26] a manuscript which, if it actually existed, would have settled countless debates—but no one else seems to have seen this document, and other commentators have had to hope for something less definitive. Some might be content to see just the text, a printed transcription of the Gaelic text from which Macpherson made his translations. Others wanted to see, or at least to have some information about, the manuscripts. These manuscripts might be Macpherson's own transcriptions of oral performances, or old manuscripts from which he assembled the materials. There is no evidence that Macpherson offered to publish engraved facsimiles of old manuscripts, whether of the third century or the fifteenth, so it is likely that he was offering some kind of printed Gaelic text from which he putatively translated the Ossianic poems.

No one, then, expected a 1,400-year-old manuscript. Neither, however, did any of Macpherson's contemporaries believe in equally legitimate improvised recreations of a story on the principles of Milman Parry and Albert Lord: virtually everyone took a literate culture for granted, and assumed that a single, coherent Ur-text would have been "corrupted" by oral transmission. Attitudes toward oral transmission of literature were complicated in eighteenth-century Britain, and they were undergoing a great deal of flux in the 1760s and '70s.[27] "It is no accident," Nicholas Hudson observes, "that the Ossian controversy occurred at a time when scholars were generally more aware of the difference between speech and writing, and between 'oral' and 'literate' forms of discourse." He argues elsewhere that Blair's comments on Ossian mark "an important reassessment of oral tradition among scholars during the middle decades of the eighteenth century," and helped to "pav[e] the way for our modern appreciation of oral tradition as a legitimate basis for poetical expression and social organization."[28]

---

25   Boswell to Johnson, 27 Jan. 1775, in Boswell, *Letters*, 1:209. Many experts now believe it was *The Book of the Dean of Lismore* that Macpherson left at Becket's shop, but it is impossible to be certain.

26   Kames, *Sketches of the History of Man*, 1:423. Thomas Campbell repeats the story in *A Philosophical Survey of the South of Ireland* (1777), but concludes that "this report proves ill authenticated" (p. 85).

27   The scholia on oral transmission in the eighteenth century are extensive and growing. For accessible overviews of theories of orality from Vico to Wolf, see Hudson's works cited below, Korshin's "Reconfiguring the Past," and Wickman, "The Allure of the Improbable."

28   Hudson, *Writing and European Thought*, p. 103; "Constructing Oral Tradition," pp. 240–241. See also Hudson's *Writing and European Thought*: "By mid-century, many reputable

However much the controversy may have done to prepare the world for oral literature, though—and by the early nineteenth century, theories of oral composition were beginning to become accepted[29]—virtually no one was really ready for them during Macpherson's lifetime. For Henry Mackenzie, multiple versions of the oral texts must be compared, and one proclaimed authentic: "by a careful and well informed collection of which, the most perfect piece may be found. This is the common and legitimate method of obtaining what it is fair to denominate authentic copies of all genuine traditionary poetry, and must necessarily be followed with regard to compositions which had never been fixed by publication."[30] And most people who had considered tradition could not bring themselves to believe that an epic could be transmitted over more than a millennium without being corrupted to the point of incomprehensibility.

Even Macpherson admitted that "The strongest objection to the authenticity of the poems ... is the improbability of their being handed down by tradition through so many centuries."[31] Since he never offered any details on textual variants, and since his society had no coherent theory of oral composition and transmission, most readers assumed that Macpherson wanted the world to believe that the poems had been handed down intact, largely through oral tradition. David Erskine-Baker said in 1762 that he inferred as much from the front matter to the poems, where the author "laid it down as a fundamental point, to avoid as much as possible the blending any base alloy of his own with the sterling poetry of the immortal *Ossian*."[32] Blair made the point explicitly: "tradition, in a country so free of intermixture with foreigners, and among a people so strongly attached to the memory of their ancestors, has preserved many of them [the poems] in a great measure incorrupted to this day."[33] And Ewen Cameron, while acknowledging that "The extreme Length of these Pieces is very surprising," insisted that "such Hold they take of the Memory, that few Circumstances are ever omitted by those who have received them only from oral Tradition. What is still more amazing, the very Language of the Bards is still preserved."[34] In 1779, Donald M'Nicol, fully aware that readers would be skeptical of such an account, explained that "The practice of committing much to memory seems to be very old, and probably was borrowed from the *Druids*, who, as we are

---

scholars were willing to entertain the possibility that the history and literary works of a people could be preserved without books" (p. 102).

29   In 1807, Sir John Sinclair was able to take it for granted that oral transmission had been used to deliver works of literature down through the ages from the most remote antiquity. "As to Homer," he notes, "there is hardly a doubt that writing was either totally unknown, or at least very little practised indeed, when he lived. The Iliad and the Odyssey, are apparently addressed to an audience, as if they were to be recited, and not read" ("A Dissertation on the Authenticity," 1:lxvi–lxvii).

30   Mackenzie, *Report*, p. 19.

31   Macpherson, Preface to the first edition of *Fingal*, in *The Poems of Ossian*, p. 48.

32   Erskine-Baker, *The Muse of Ossian*, p. v.

33   Blair, Preface to *Fragments*, p. 5.

34   Cameron, *The Fingal of Ossian*, pp. 333–4 n.

assured by authors of credit, were obliged to get 20,000 lines by heart, before they were judged fit to exercise their office."[35]

Few others, though, could conceive of the possibility. "What are we to think of a work of this length," asked Richard Hurd, "preserved and handed down to us entire, by *oral tradition*, for 1400 years, without a chasm, or so much as a various reading, I should rather say, *speaking*?"[36] David Hume had the same concern:

> Consider the size of these poems.... they were composed, you say, in the Highlands, above fifteen centuries ago; and have been faithfully transmitted, ever since, by oral tradition, through ages totally ignorant of letters, by the rudest, perhaps, of all the European nations.... Did ever any event happen that approached within a hundred degrees of this mighty wonder, even to the nations the most fortunate in their climate and situation?[37]

Joseph Ritson left a manuscript annotation in his copy of *The Poems of Ossian*: "The history of Fingal, & of the heros his contemporarys, is, doubtless, entirely fiction; & not older, most probablely, than the tenth century.... to maintain that Fingal inhabited, in whatever age, any part of the present Scotland, & that his son Ossian composed poems, of many thousand lines, preserved to this day by highland tradition, & actually here given to the publick, in English dress, is of the essence of falsehood and imposture."[38] And in the 1790s, Malcolm Laing expressed the same worries to Samuel Parr: "It is easy to conceive that twenty thousand verses might be treasured up by a single retentive memory; but the difficulty is to conceive the transmission of such poems as the Iliad or Odyssey, from generation to generation, by tradition alone, without any written copy to which the rhapsodists might resort .... the acquisition of such long poems ... by means of recitation only, is a theory not confirmed by any known facts in the histories of nations."[39]

---

35 M'Nicol, *Remarks*, p. 325. Compare John Pinkerton's assertion that "The Druids of Gaul and Britain afford a noted instance [of oral transmission]. Such firm hold did their traditions take of the memory, that some of them are retained in the minds of their countrymen to this very day" (Pinkerton, *Select Scotish Ballads*, 1:xix).

36 Hurd to William Warburton, 25 Dec. 1761, in Hurd, *Early Letters*, p. 86

37 Hume, "Of the Authenticity of Ossian's Poems," p. 416. Compare Hume's private letter to Blair: "the preservation of such long, and such connected poems by oral tradition alone, during a course of fourteen centuries, is so much out of the ordinary course of human affairs, that it requires the strongest reasons to make us believe it" (Hume to Blair, 19 Sept. 1763, in Hume, *Letters*, 1:399 [letter 215]).

38 Joseph Ritson's autograph notes in his copy of Macpherson, *The Poems of Ossian*, in Yale Osborn pc124, vol. 1, flyleaf.

39 Malcolm Laing to Samuel Parr, 19 Dec. [1796?], in Parr, *Works*, 8:45. Compare Laing's published observations on the subject: "That the poems were preserved by oral tradition, in an obsolete diction, or, in other words, a dialect already disused by the people, is alone sufficient to confute their authenticity. The mutability of language is counteracted only by letters and the art of printing; which, reacting as a model on conversation, preserve and perpetuate an uniform and refined dialect, through the whole nation, from age to age. An unwritten language diverges in each province into a different dialect, and in every age assumes a new form" (Laing, *The History of Scotland*, 2:388).

Samuel Johnson, like Hurd, Hume, and Laing, was convinced that no significant body of poetry could survive oral transmission: "Whence could it be had? It is too long to be remembered, and the language formerly had nothing written."[40] We, coming after Parry and Lord, know better, and Macpherson's modern defenders seem to revel in pointing out where Johnson's critique missed the mark. But it is wrong to blame Johnson—first because he was at least willing to consider the possibility of some oral transmission, and second because Macpherson himself insisted on the existence of manuscripts. When Macpherson alluded to "the erroneous orthography of the bards,"[41] he clearly suggested that he had old written records of some sort, since oral tradition has no orthography to speak of. As Johnson wrote to Boswell, "If [Macpherson] had not talked unskilfully of *manuscripts*, he might have fought with oral tradition much longer."[42] He always admitted that Macpherson worked at least partly from traditional materials; his charge was that scraps of oral tradition were fraudulently represented as a coherent poem: "This is just what I always maintained. He has found names, and stories, and phrases, nay passages in old songs, and with them has blended his own compositions, and so made what he gives to the world as the translation of an ancient poem."[43]

A Poem in Six Books

Although the mysterious manuscripts kept the controversy brewing for decades, not everyone considered their origin the most important factor in discussing the authenticity of the poems. For many, a more important consideration was *genre*: some of Macpherson's critics were most concerned about the claims was he making about the type of poems he discovered. Even if we grant that Macpherson worked largely with genuine traditional materials, does it follow that the end results—"An Epic Poem in Six Books" and "An Epic Poem in Eight Books"—were also genuine?

---

40   Johnson, Yale *Works*, 9:118. Ernst Mossner says bluntly that Johnson was "indisputably right" (Mossner, *The Forgotten Hume*, p. 94). Howard Gaskill, on the other hand, Macpherson's most astute and vocal modern advocate, writes of "the questionable premises from which Samuel Johnson and his followers launched their attack on Macpherson," and argues that "Johnson got it wrong ... his obsession with manuscripts has served to muddy the debate ever since" (*Ossian Revisited*, pp. 2, 6). Gaskill hopes to disqualify the witness for prejudice: "What was to be done in the face of [Johnson's] dogmatic close-mindedness and racial bigotry (for that is what it is)?" ("The Manuscript Myth," p. 14). For a fairer assessment of Johnson's real mistakes, see Curley, "Johnson's Last Word on Ossian," p. 379.

41   Macpherson, "A Specimen of the Original of Temora," in *The Poems of Ossian*, p. 330.

42   Johnson to Boswell, 25 Feb. 1775, in Johnson, *Letters*, 2:181. Macpherson himself refers to both manuscripts and oral tradition in the preface to the *Fragments*. His insistence that "a copy of the originals lay, for many months, in the bookseller's hands, for the inspection of the curious," together with his reference to "the erroneous orthography of the bards," leaves little doubt that he hoped to leave the impression of at least some written originals. See Macpherson, *The Poems of Ossian*, pp. 5, 330.

43   Boswell, *Life*, 5:242.

Or does a change in genre from a collection of ballads to a unified heroic poem change their status from authentic to forged?

The epic genre was advertised from the very beginning of the Ossianic episode: as early as the *Fragments*, Blair wrote, "Though the poems now published appear as detached pieces in this collection, there is ground to believe that most of them were originally episodes of a greater work which related to the wars of Fingal." In particular, he identified "The three last poems in the collection" as "fragments which the translator obtained of this Epic poem."[44] Johnson once again was prominent here. He never questioned the presence of much authentic folk material in the poems, but "always maintained" that Macpherson "has found names, and stories, and phrases, nay passages in old songs, and with them has blended his own compositions, and so made what he gives to the world as the translation of an ancient poem." But it was the "blending" into a unified whole that bothered him. Boswell observed that "it was wrong to publish it as a poem in six books," prompting Johnson to reply, "Yes, Sir; and to ascribe it to a time too when the Highlanders knew nothing of *books*, and nothing of *six*."[45] Richard Hurd had the same complaint: "what are we to think of a long epic poem, disposed, in form, into six books, with a *beginning*, *middle*, and *end*, and enlivened, in the classic taste, with episodes."[46]

Johnson seems content with "fragments"—though no enthusiast for folk poetry, he supported his friend Thomas Percy in his collection of anonymous ballads. But he balked when Macpherson claimed that the poems constituted a unified whole, and he was particularly bothered by testimonies of people who claimed to remember hearing these epics long ago. Johnson was convinced that their memories were playing tricks: not merely with the fact of hearing old stories, nor even with the plots, but also with the genre. He recognized and was suspicious of a natural habit to turn fragments into a coherent whole. Boswell reports Johnson's boast: "He would undertake … to write an epick poem on the story of *Robin Hood*, and half England, to whom the names and places he should mention in it are familiar, would believe and declare they had heard it from their earliest years."[47]

Johnson was not alone in rooting his objections in the genre of the poems. As early as 1762, a contributor to the *Monthly Review* admitted that "it is with reluctance we should enter into a strict examination of the work before us, as an epic poem; in which light, however, we conceive ourselves, in some measure, obliged to consider it, as many of its admirers have allowed it consummate merit *as such*."[48] The same complaints were echoed decades later. James Macdonald grew up in the Highlands, where he might be expected to know something about Gaelic oral tradition—and yet his letters from the 1790s show that he was no clearer than the Sassenachs on the authenticity of the poems. In 1796, he wrote to Johann Gottfried von Herder, acknowledging at the outset that he was a believer in Ossian. He went on, however, to offer a significant qualification of what that means:

---

44 Blair, Preface to *Fragments*, pp. 5–6.
45 Boswell, *Life*, 5:242.
46 Hurd to William Warburton, 25 Dec. 1761, in Hurd, *Early Letters*, pp. 385–6.
47 Boswell, *Life*, 5:389.
48 *Monthly Review* 26 (Jan. 1762): 44.

I *by no means* believe that [Ossian] is the author of all that goes under his name, nor do I think that he ever once took it into his head to write an epic poem, or any regular continued narration of any specific historical facts. He sang detached military expeditions, or battles, or events of importance which had no particular connection with each other.... I have no doubt but Mr. Macpherson has formed the connections of his great pieces of Fingal and Temora from traditions; indeed I had myself a pretty good idea of the poem of Fingal before I ever saw his work, by means of the traditions and descriptions which I had been accustomed to hear. To say the truth, I wish Mr. Macpherson had *not* given them in that form for it is not the natural dress of Ossian.[49]

A year later he wrote to K. A. Böttiger, answering some questions raised by Klopstock, and clarifying his opinion of the poems' relation to the oral tradition:

With regard to the pieces which pass current among the Highlanders of Scotland as having been composed by Ossian, they are numberless; for every poem that pleases them, and the occasion of whose composition they do not know, passes for one of Ossian's.... Hence I am convinced that one tenth part of what is ascribed to Ossian [by Macpherson] has not been composed by him, but by other poets who succeeded and imitated him.[50]

It was the genre, the epic form, that bothered Macdonald, as it bothered Johnson before him: "among all the pieces I have heard recited or have learned myself in my infancy I never heard any that had the smallest analogy with an epic poem."[51]

For others, though, the same evidence leads to a very different evaluation. The generally enthusiastic *Critical Review* notes that Macpherson "succeeded so well in this expedition, that by the assistance of several gentlemen in the Highlands, he was enabled to complete the Epic poem of Fingal,"[52] suggesting that this reviewer had no trouble with Macpherson's "completion"; the same journal soon pronounced *Fingal* "a perfect Epic poem."[53] Writing in 1792, Anna Seward is persuaded that Macpherson combined orally transmitted songs "into something like a regular epic," but that his achievement was that of a plodding editor, not of a perfidious forger on the one hand or a literary genius on the other:

Not that I believe he had ancient manuscripts, any more than I believe his imagination responsible for the original, the solemn, the sublime mythology....

---

49   Alexander Gillies, *A Hebridean in Goethe's Weimar*, p. 61.

50   Gillies, *A Hebridean in Goethe's Weimar*, p. 64.

51   Ibid. Compare Bailey Saunders's comments on the implications of the genre in which Macpherson presented the Ossianic poems: "when he collected a large number of these waifs and strays of Highland poetry, and under the notion that he was dealing with fragments of a regular epic assigned to them all a like antiquity, and gave them a unity which perhaps they did not possess; when he rendered them in an orderly form, and in a free and polished paraphrase, and presented the six books of *Fingal* and the eight of *Temora* as translations of epic poems composed by Ossian in the third century, and handed down from mouth to mouth for fifty generations, suspicion ripened into an open attack on the translator's honesty" (Saunders, *The Life and Letters of James Macpherson*, pp. 9–10).

52   *Critical Review* 12 (Dec. 1761): 406.

53   *Critical Review* 13 (Jan. 1762): 53.

Catching a portion of their fire, he connected them, doubtless, with much of his own, weaving them together for the Fingal, into something like a regular epic. Probably the episodes are entirely Erse. Internal evidence lies here, with all its weight, for the originality of the Erse poetry, as it is totally against it in the Rowleyan.

I impute the fustian passages, of which it must be allowed there are several, to Macpherson; and it is almost all I can allow him as to the images and ideas.[54]

The Poetry of the Heart

Others seem to have been less troubled by Macpherson's generic claims than by the name that appeared on his title pages: Ossian, son of Fingal. Much critical attention was being shifted from the work to the author in the late eighteenth century, as works increasingly came to be seen as expressions of the unique personality of the author. We can see this process in action in the account given by Thomas F. Hill, one of the first investigators to travel through the Highlands in 1780 looking for traces of the oral tradition that had produced the Ossianic poems. Unlike Shaw, he seems to have approached his task with an open mind, and Richard Sher rightly calls him "one of the few eighteenth-century figures in the entire Ossianic controversy to whom the word 'impartial' may fairly be applied."[55] In 1782–83 he published a series of articles in *The Gentleman's Magazine* describing his findings. Noting that he heard a number of ballads on Ossianic subjects, he reports that "these songs contain portions of the very poems published ... under the name of Ossian. We may therefore justly conclude, that those poems are not wholly the forgery of their editors, but compiled at least from original songs." He is careful to note that Macpherson was not reproducing the traditional songs verbatim: "The foregoing songs ... are by no means uniformly consistent with the poems, in which the parallel passages are found, but frequently relate to different events, and even contain different circumstances."[56] This leaves him in a state of doubt, unable to determine "What portion ... of the Ossian of Macpherson ... is original." But on what had become the fundamental question— whether the poems could be ascribed to a historical Ossian—he is clear: "The Ossian of Macpherson ... is a mutilated compilation from Highland songs, ascribed indeed to that bard, yet very little likely to be his composition."[57]

Macpherson's first Ossianic publication, the *Fragments of Ancient Poetry*, made no claims about authorship; the fragments came from anonymous "bards." With the publication of the longer works, though, the terms of the dispute change: they now sport the name of a single author. Much of Hugh Blair's *Critical Dissertation on the Poems of Ossian* is devoted to describing the expansive soul of the author, whose identity serves to provide a kind of unity and authenticity to the epics that the *Fragments* never claimed. The *Critical Review* makes the same point in 1763: "One consistent face of manners is every where presented: one spirit of poetry reigns: the

---

54 Seward to Dr. Gregory, 25 March 1792, in Seward, *Letters*, 3:127.
55 Sher, "Percy, Shaw and the Ferguson 'Cheat,'" p. 220.
56 *Gentleman's Magazine* 53 (Aug. 1783): 662.
57 Ibid., 663.

masterly hand of Ossian appears throughout: the same rapid and animated stile; the same strong colouring of imagination; and the same glowing sensibility of heart."[58]

If Blair and the *Critical* could use a unified author as an opportunity to praise the poems, though, others could use it to blame them. The later eighteenth century placed a new premium on authorial personality, as a predominantly rhetorical conception of art gave way to an expressive one and authenticity became nearly synonymous with sincerity. As the evidence mounted that Macpherson's claims for a single author were bogus, many of the ardent defenders of the poems rejected them as inferior. The fact is that Ossian's *Fingal* was far better than Macpherson's *Fingal*, even though they were literatim the same; Ossian was a true poet of sublime conception and expansive soul, Macpherson merely a pedestrian editor and translator. When it turned out the true poet was not even a true human being, and that the textual fragments were unified not by a sentimental primitive but by a surly and petulant Scottish propagandist, the game was at an end.

The History of the Times

For others still, the problem was neither genre nor author but historical context. Blair was also largely responsible for this, as he was one of the most prominent historicist critics of his day. Historicism is one of the most important currents in eighteenth-century British criticism, too often neglected by modern scholars who have focused on the references to timeless truths, universals, and generalities.[59] Historicist criticism is grounded in three related convictions: that each historical period has its own character, distinct from that of every other period; that works of art and literature are products of the age in which they were created; and that understanding works of art and literature requires an understanding of that age. Despite the familiar critical bromides about "universality," the major critics of the eighteenth century were more attuned to historical particularity than any earlier age, and indeed than many subsequent ages.

It is only natural that Blair should appear in this role, because his passions were often more historical than aesthetic: much of the poems' appeal for him lay in the information they offered about third-century Scotland. As soon as the first Ossianic work appeared, he speculated that "it might serve to throw considerable light upon the Scottish and Irish antiquities."[60] And when the second epic was published, Blair praised it specifically for offering a window on ancient Scottish culture. "What renders Temora infinitely more valuable than Fingal," he writes, "is the light it throws on the history of the times." This is for Blair the best reason for reading the poems: we should care about them because "the most natural pictures of ancient manners are exhibited in the ancient poems of nations."[61]

Blair was not the only believer to defend the authenticity of the poems on historicist grounds. The *Critical Review* insisted that "the compositions of Ossian are not less

---

58   *Critical Review* 15 (Feb. 1763): 125.
59   I have made this point in *The Age of Elizabeth in the Age of Johnson*, chap. 2.
60   Blair, Preface to *Fragments*, p. 6.
61   Blair, "A Dissertation," p. 215; *Critical Dissertation*, p. 345.

valuable for the light they throw on the antient state of Scotland and Ireland, than they are for their poetical merit."[62] John Smith follows Blair in *Galic Antiquities*, sometimes repeating his arguments verbatim, insisting "the train of ideas are every where so much out of the common line of modern composition, that nothing but the real circumstances which they describe could possibly have suggested them."[63] And the antiquary William Stukeley makes a similar argument about how "much may be collected" from the Ossianic poems "to inlarge our most antient Brittish history,"[64] and he was delighted to allow his bizarre antiquarian theories to back up the poems' authenticity. When he saw that *Fingal* was consistent with his notions that the ancient Britons were descended from Phoenicians, he wrote an open letter to Macpherson: "your history has confirm'd my mature thoughts about them."[65] Stukeley's work of seven years "in considering Abury & Stonehenge" taught him about the ancient Britons, especially their funerary customs. He excavated some "of the innumerable burrows, & *tumuli*, … & found such remains, as are mention'd in *Fingal*." The result of his investigation—*mirabile dictu*—was that "I found all the notions I have conceiv'd in my mind … very much confirmed & illustrated by *Fingal*."[66]

Once again, though, there were just as many historicist adversaries as there were historicist defenders. Edward Davies, seduced at first by Blair's claims for the Ossianic poems, was finally forced to reject them for the same reason that Blair valued them: "His sketches, as far as they can be verified by history, exhibit the *Gothic*, rather than the Celtic style." But the "sketches" are not even consistently Gothic: "the manners and sentiments which present themselves in the poems of Ossian, were not fully appropriate, either to the Celts or the Goths. The painting is far above nature, and can by no means be considered as verified, in the age and country in which Ossian is supposed to have lived."[67]

Where does all this leave us? What have we learned from this exercise of piling complications on complications? The short answer is that different eighteenth-century readers had different criteria for what constitutes deception, and we ignore them at our peril. These criteria show us what contemporary readers found most valuable about authentic poetry—here is where forgery teaches us its most valuable lessons. For some, what might have been authentic when applied to fragments turned to forgery when applied to epic poems; for others, the lack of a single authorial hand was enough to constitute fraud; for others still, the problem was violating good eighteenth-century historicist principles. If I may shift my language from the legal to the spiritual, Macpherson was variously charged with sins against the epic, sins against the author, and sins against history. All of these sins will be the subject of later chapters of this book.

So what, in the end, was James Macpherson's real crime? I am being only half facetious when I say it was making a book like this one necessary. I am not usually

62 *Critical Review* 12 (Dec. 1761): 406.

63 John Smith, *Galic Antiquities*, p. 88.

64 Stukeley, notes on Ossian, Bodleian MS Eng.misc.e.383, fol. 16^r.

65 Stukeley, *A Letter from Dr. Stukeley*, p. 7.

66 Stukeley, notes on Ossian, Bodleian MS Eng.misc.e.383, fols. 4^r–5^r.

67 Davies, *The Claims of Ossian*, pp. 24, 35.

interested in assigning blame, but it is safe to say that Macpherson was culpable for remaining silent when a few words would have settled decades of fierce disputes, added considerably to our knowledge of the Highlands, and begun the serious investigation of oral folk literature decades before it was in fact taken up. By publishing a single sentence in a newspaper in 1762—"Mr. Macpherson wishes to inform the public that he drew on both a number of manuscripts, some dating back to the fifteenth century, as well as ballads collected from oral tradition in reconstructing the lost epic of *Fingal*"—he could have ended the debates well before the most rancorous ones began. Henry Mackenzie made the point in a letter of 1806: "I had no doubt of his having used freedoms when collecting & translating such *mutilated* ancient Poetry I think it is fair enough, (perhaps unavoidable) to use; but I said to him what I think You among others of his friends w^d have said, that a frank Avowal of such Additions or Alterations would have been favourable, not injurious, to his Character both as a Man & an Author. He thinks, however, he has kept to his resolution of an obstinate, & I think an ill-judged Silence."[68] Much of that reticence can be traced to his pride, which alienated many of his one-time supporters: David Hume, originally a supporter, found his patience tried by "so strange and heteroclite a mortal, than whom I have scarce ever known a man more perverse and unamiable."[69]

I do not pretend to have settled the Ossianic question; in fact, my thesis is that *we* cannot settle it, at least not by imposing our own answers on the messy realities of the dispute. What I hope I have shown is that the only way to understand what eighteenth-century Britons made of forgery is to listen carefully to them. I am drawn to this empirical approach to forgery because I am convinced that imposing our own notions about forgery on eighteenth-century writers inevitably reduces the richness and complexity of their arguments. I am convinced, too, that the most valuable lessons we can learn from eighteenth-century forgery, fakery, and fraud lie in the way real people wrestled with real questions, which will be the subject of subsequent chapters.

---

68   Henry Mackenzie to John Pinkerton, 6 Jan. 1806, in BL Add. MS 29747, fols. 85^v–86^r.
69   Hume to Blair, 1763, in Hume, *Letters*, 1:403 (number 217).

Chapter 2

Conviction on the First View

"Mr. James Macpherson," wrote Samuel Johnson brusquely, in a letter second in venom only to his famous reply to Lord Chesterfield in 1755, "I received your foolish and impudent note. Whatever insult is offered me I will do my best to repel, and what I cannot do for myself the law will do for me. I will not desist from detecting what I think a cheat, from any fear of the menaces of a Ruffian."[1]

The motivation behind this letter—the nature of the "foolish and impudent note," now lost, that prompted it—has been the subject of much speculation. Macpherson, it seems, threatened Johnson with bodily harm, or at least Johnson perceived such a threat, prompting him to carry "an oak-plant of a tremendous size" to ward off attacks. However chimerical the threat, the stick was real enough. "Its height," writes Hawkins, "was upwards of six feet, and from about an inch in diameter at the lower end, increased to near three: this he kept in his bed-chamber, so near the chair in which he constantly sat, as to be within reach."[2] The image of the 63-year-old Johnson wielding a staff against Scottish thugs in London's dark alleys is in equal measure farcical and pathetic.

Fortunately for both the health and the dignity of all involved, Johnson was never obliged to raise his stick in anger. Other kinds of sparring, though, are much more

---

1   Johnson to Macpherson, 20 Jan. 1775, in Johnson, *Letters*, 2:168–9.

2   Hawkins, *Life*, in *Works*, 1:491. In "Dr Johnson and the Ruffian," Fiona Stafford questions Hawkins's account, but neither Hawkins nor Boswell doubted the story, and William Duncan avowed in 1806 that he was personally "the bearer ... of a letter of challenge [Macpherson] wrote to the late Dr. Samuel Johnson" (Sinclair, "A Dissertation on the Authenticity," 1:ccxx n). Giuseppe Baretti also recounts the story: "Macpherson was of opinion, that Johnson had given him the lie, and desired him by letter, that he would unsay what he had said.... Macpherson took fire at his answer, and has vowed in his reply, that, if he ever meets with him, he will do him a mischief.... Johnson replied again, that he shall not give himself the trouble of avoiding him on purpose, and that he will defend himself as well as he shall be able, if any ruffian should ever attack him" (Baretti, *Easy Phraseology*, pp. 257–8). William Shaw reprints Johnson's famous letter, adding, "A meeting ... was so certainly expected between these two literary heroes, that for some time after Johnson never went abroad without a stout cudgel, and his antagonist it is also alledged, was furnished with a similar weapon" (Shaw, *Memoirs*, pp. 147–8). An unpublished note from Sir William Forbes, however, is also illuminating: "Mr Mc tells the Dr, that after his having obstinately shut his eyes against every Species of Conviction with regard to the Authenticity of the Poems, he thinks himself at liberty to load the Dr with the most opprobrious epithets; since the Dr's age & infirmities debar Mr Mc from demanding the satisfaction of a Gentleman" (Sir William Forbes to John Forbes, 15 Feb. 1775, in NLS MS.3112, fol. 26v). See also Curley, "Samuel Johnson and Truth," pp. 154–63.

common in eighteenth-century disputes over authenticity, and they are sometimes little more dignified than fisticuffs. Although ridicule may not seem worthy of serious discussion, our implicit hierarchy of means of proof or disproof runs from rational debates through arguments *ad hominem* all the way down to brute violence; all of these have had their place in actual disputes over authenticity, and all deserve attention.

Truth May Bear All Lights

Eighteenth-century Britain produced at least one important defense of a disreputable means of argument. Anthony Ashley Cooper, the 3rd Earl of Shaftesbury, contends that while falsehood may escape many tests, truth will withstand every sort of inspection:

> We may be charged perhaps with wilful ignorance and blind idolatry for having taken opinions upon trust…. They may perhaps be monsters, and not divinities or sacred truths, which are kept thus choicely in some dark corner of our minds. The spectres may impose on us, while we refuse to turn them every way and view their shapes and complexions in every light. For that which can be shown only in a certain light is questionable. Truth, it is supposed, may bear *all* lights.[3]

Since truth can stand up to any kind of scrutiny, it is the obligation of those who would know the truth to try every test of it, including one of the least respectable—ridicule. Shaftesbury, whose "Sensus Communis" is subtitled "An Essay on the Freedom of Wit and Humour," is unusual for speaking "in commendation of raillery." Ridicule, Shaftesbury suggests, may be especially useful in exposing fraud, for "Gravity," he says, "is of the very essence of imposture." He therefore recommends using ridicule to discover the weakness of fakers' cases. "The main point," he advises, "is to know always true gravity from the false, and this can only be by carrying the rule constantly with us and freely applying it not only to the things about us but to ourselves…. Now what rule or measure is there in the world … to find which are truly serious and which ridiculous? And how can this be done unless by applying the ridicule to see whether it will bear?"[4]

Perhaps this defense of raillery encouraged some satirists to enter the fray in public disputes over authenticity. More likely it served only as an after-the-fact justification of what they planned to do anyway. Whatever the case, satirical attacks on apparent instances of fraud abound, and sometimes they were on target. Boswell records Johnson's sharp-tongued dismissal of the Ossianic poems: "Dr. Blair, relying on the internal evidence of their antiquity, asked Dr. Johnson whether he thought any man of a modern age could have written such poems? Johnson replied, 'Yes, Sir, many men, many women, and many children.'"[5] Then again, Johnson himself did not escape satirical treatment for his involvement in a famous deception. In *The Ghost*

---

3   Shaftesbury, *Characteristics*, pp. 29–30.
4   Ibid., pp. 29, 8.
5   Boswell, *Life*, 1:396.

(1762), Charles Churchill remembers Johnson's role in the episode of "*Lauder*'s spight/O'er MILTON," and takes aim at the too-credulous "Pomposo": "Whilst HE, *our Letter'd* POLYPHEME,/Who had *Confed'rate* forces join'd,/Like a base Coward, skulk'd behind."[6] We must admit that attacks like these, however impressive as *belles lettres*, are rarely good forensic science. The most famous satirical dispute over authenticity was Jonathan Swift's *Battle of the Books*, particularly the attack on Bentley's methods of dating the *Epistles* of Phalaris—a thrilling performance of satirical excoriation. But even Swift's most devoted admirers today have to admit that Bentley was right where Swift was wrong, and that the *Epistles* were late forgeries.

Not all the derision aimed at deception had anything like Swift's wit and literary merit. Would-be satirists were not above the lowest sort of ridicule, and the more ridiculous the imposture, the greater the potential for mischievous fun. Women in particular were favorite targets, since the ancient tradition of misogynist satire was easily adapted to new uses. Elizabeth Canning, for instance, claimed to have been abducted and locked in an attic for four weeks in 1753; when interrogated, she admitted that she had not had a bowel movement the entire time. Scatological humor is difficult for some ballad-writers to resist: as one explained,

> So she staid there a Month with a very good Grace,
> But at length she grew weary and tir'd of the Place;
> Then out of the Window she flew like a Bird,
> And left not behind her so much as a T—d.
> *Derry down, &c.*[7]

Mary Toft, supposed mother of rabbits, had to withstand even more bitter attacks in 1726–27. Many commentators drew attention to the fact that the supposedly fetal animals she delivered were discovered to have feces in their intestines: as Thomas Brathwaite puts it, "the Lungs of all *Fœtus* Animals that have not breathed sink in Water; … A plain Proof that these Lungs belong'd not to a *Fœtus* that died before Birth, but to one that had breath'd…. 'Tis a little strange that these Rabbets should have Pellets of Dung if they had never fed."[8] The satirists, though, were less interested in chains of reasoning than in the cheap shot:

> Is this a Rabbit or a Cat—in troth
> Tis hard to say it looks so like 'em both
> But hold—this dung will soon decide ye Matter,
> By this I judge it cannot be the latter,
> And by its weight—I can as Safely Swear
> Tho it has Shit—It never breath'd in Air.[9]

A fourpenny pamphlet called *À Propos Mr. St. André's Case* attacks the physician in the Toft case with a catalogue of scurrilous comments about venereal disease, vomiting, diarrhea, and hemorrhoids.

---

6   Churchill, *The Ghost*, 2.230–232, in *Poetical Works*.
7   *The Devil Outdone*, p. 5.
8   Brathwaite, *Remarks on a Short Narrative*, pp. 14, 17–18.
9   "The Doctors in Labour."

More popular than scatological jokes about Toft, though, were sexual ones. Many likened her genitals to a rabbit warren, which conveniently rhymed with "barren." "There are some that would account for this wonderful Production," wrote one satirist, "by saying, The Woman had a criminal Conversation with a Buck-Rabbit."[10] Bawdy puns were common. Few of Toft's satirical prosecutors could resist punning on *hare* and *hair* or *coney* and *cunny*—as Alexander Pope and William Pulteney put it,

> On Tiptoe then the Squire he stood,
>   (But first He gave Her Money)
> Then reach'd as high as e'er He cou'd,
>   And cry'd, I feel a Cony[11]

—and some took advantage of the fact that, early in the eighteenth century, one word for a rabbit's tracks was *prick*.

The nastiest of the anti-Toft satires is *Much Ado about Nothing; or, A Plain Refutation of All That Has Been Written or Said Concerning the Rabbit-Woman of Godalming*, signed by "Merry Tuft." The supposed editor claims to have learned the story from Toft "by touching *her in the Tenderest part*, viz. her Conscience." By pretending "to print this Confession … in her own Stile and Spelling" he not only ridicules her illiteracy but makes a number of obscene allusions hinting at her promiscuity. Tuft's "Affucktation" for her neighbor, whose "Rawbit" was far superior to her husband's, made her receptive to his flattery: "I wos a Wuman as had *grate natturul parts*, and a *large Capassiti*, and kapible of beng kunserned in depe *Kuntrivansis*." The whole story about giving birth to rabbits, she explains, was just a misunderstanding: she simply "wanted to mak a *Kunny-Warren* of my *Parsly-Bed*." The narrative ends with "thare barbirus Experiment wich tha intended, of sending *a chimni-sweper's boy up my fallopin Tubb*."[12]

Offe Mannes Fyrste Bykrous Volunde

The birth of rabbits was a natural source of mean-spirited mirth, but even more sober and scholarly debates could be conducted in satirical terms. The authenticity of the Rowley poems, as we shall see, depended on arcane details of orthography, prosody, and accidence, such as only a small part of the public could hope to judge. When the disputes were played out in public, though, those who attacked Chatterton's works often resorted to low humor. William Mason's *Archaeological Epistle* (1782), for example, tries to reduce the whole Rowley matter to an elaborate Shandean joke. There he sarcastically develops a new "archæological" method of writing, paying ironic homage to "my Archetype, the immortal Rowley." He proposes "a complete Anglo-Gothico-Saxonico-Chattertonic dictionary for the use of tiros," with "the modern words before the Archæological ones," as an aid to future forgers. The most

---

10   *A Philosophical Enquiry into the Wonderful Coney-Warren*, p. 2.

11   Alexander Pope and William Pulteney, "The Discovery; or, The Squire Turn'd Ferret: An Excellent New Ballad," lines 57–60, in Pope, *Poems*, 6:261.

12   *Much Ado about Nothing*, pp. 7, 9, 12–13, 18, 20–21.

visible sign of forgery in Chatterton was his bizarre spelling; even those who had never read real Middle English could recognize the oddity of Rowley's orthography. Mason therefore has a suitably ironic comment: "As to orthography, there is only one rule, and that the most simple that can be imagined ... and this is, to put as many letters as you can possibly crowd into a word, and then rest assured, that the word will look truly Archæological." Meter too becomes easier for would-be forgers in Mason's method:

> But the last and best thing I shall mention is that great and unspeakable emolument, which the Anglo-Saxon prefix *y* brings to a necessitated versifier: as *yprauncing* for *prauncing*, *ymenging* for *menging*, &c. &c. By having this always at his beck, that poet, who cannot write a smooth line in any given number of syllables, deserves, in my opinion, never to write a line at all.

Finally, he offers examples of the results of his new method, beginning with an "archæological" translation of Milton:

> Offe mannes fyrste bykrous volunde wolle I singe,
>   And offe the fruict of yatte caltysnyd tre
> Whose lethal taste into thys worlde dydde brynge
>   Both morthe and tene to all posteritie.

Then on to Shakespeare: "To blynne or not to blynne the denwere is ...." He finishes with a *Jabberwocky*-style "Epistelle to Doctoure Mylles" in parodic Rowleian verse, decked out with the appropriate notes (where we are informed, for instance, that "The *lordynge* toade" is "Standing on his hind legs, rather heavy, sluggish").[13] No readers, whether the professional antiquarians or the marginally literate, stood to learn much from this pamphlet, but even amateurs would come away having been confirmed in their initial impression that the unusual spelling of the Rowley poems was evidence that they were frauds.

Similar jests were rehearsed in the wake of William Henry Ireland's similar imposture. His faux-obsolete spelling was a favorite target, as a short notice in *The Telegraph* reveals: in a letter dated "Jannuarrie 27, 1658," Shakespeare invites "Missteerree BEENJAAMMIINNEE JOOHNNSSONN" to lunch, "too eatte sommee muttonne choppes andd somme poottaattoooeesse."[14] Even Ireland's most prominent and vehement critic, Edmond Malone, was not above ridiculing the would-be old-fashioned orthography. "I may perhaps be expected to say a word on the far-famed tragedy of KYNGE VORTIGERNE," he advised, "and all the KKYNGES and all the QQUEENES which have been announced from the same quarter."[15]

Malone's sense of humor, sometimes waspish, sometimes mischievous, occasionally gets the better of him. After suggesting that a single sample of Elizabeth's true handwriting would be enough to prove Ireland's letter spurious, he resolves nonetheless to go through his four usual method of disproof:

---

13   Mason, *An Archaeological Epistle*, pp. 6, 5, 8, 10, 11 n.
14   *The Telegraph*, 14 Jan. 1796, in BL Add. MS 30349, fol. 36ᵛ.
15   Malone, *An Inquiry*, p. 314.

A certain Potentate of Spain happened to pass through a town in his dominions.... The deputy-bailiff ... began an harangue, ... lamenting in the first place his own insufficiency ... his principal being unable to attend. For his absence, he added, he should presume to state several substantial reasons, the first of which was, that he was *dead*.... By following the example of this provincial orator, and producing at once a genuine specimen of her Majesty's hand-writing, I might certainly save myself some trouble.... Though I am perfectly aware that the [complete] disquisition is supererogatory, it may tend to produce a more full and complete conviction in the minds of many of my readers.[16]

Malone's disquisition is indeed supererogatory: the attempt at a witticism goes on too long, and falls with a thud. Passages like this in his attack on Chatterton prompted Walpole's complaint that Malone "unluckily has attempted humour which is not an antiquary's weapon."[17] Malone is more successful when his touch is lighter. In turning his attention to Shakespeare's supposed letter to Anne Hathaway, he borrows a favorite technique of the mock-epic poets: "But now I ought in due form to invoke Venus, and her son, and all the Loves and Graces, to listen to my tale; for lo! I am next to present you with a letter from the Stratford youth to the lady whom he afterwards married."[18]

Sometimes Malone resorts to the crudest ridicule, intending only to make Ireland look preposterous. Shakespeare's supposed "Confession of Faith" includes the lines, "O cherishe usse like the sweete Chickenne thatte under the coverte offe herre spreadynge Wings Receyves herre lyttle Broode," prompting Malone's sarcastic query, "whence the absurd introduction of a *chicken*?"[19] As Malone's most distinguished modern biographer observes, "A number of people thought he had been too harsh, and something of a backlash did occur that pilloried him for heaping arrogant and lofty scorn on an adolescent."[20] At other times, though, the satire was more strategic in its function. Malone worked to associate the Irelands' narratives with the worst sorts of fiction, which served not only to link them to *bad* literature but, more important, to bad *modern* literature—reminding readers that the Shakespeare papers were a product not of the age of Elizabeth, but of the age of Radcliffe. The Deed of Gift, for instance, is "the first deed that I have ever perused, (though I have examined not a few,) in which the story, with all its circumstances, was regularly told. It is, however, we must acknowledge a very pretty story, and almost as interesting as some of our modern novels."[21] Sometimes the stories do not rise even to the level of modern novels, but are no better than adolescent attempts at them: of the "Tributary Lines to Ireland," Malone asks, "Is this the composition of Shakspeare, or of a young lady of fifteen, after reading the first novel that has fallen into her hands?" And the versification of the manuscript of *Lear* was not even up to

---

16 Ibid., pp. 30–31.

17 Walpole to Mason, 7 Feb. 1782, in Walpole, *Correspondence*, 29:176.

18 Malone, *An Inquiry*, pp. 142–3.

19 Ibid., p. 201.

20 Martin, *Edmond Malone*, p. 195.

21 Malone, *An Inquiry*, p. 213. Compare Thomas Warton's contempt for Chatterton's attempts at antique diction: "Who does not perceive in some of these instances the cant exclamations of modern tragedy?" (Warton, *Enquiry*, p. 27).

the standards of young ladies of fifteen: "the verses which have been supplied are not better than any school-boy who had ever composed a line of poetry could write."[22]

Searching Their Old Trunks

Chatterton and Ireland had more than their eccentric antique spelling in common: both claimed to have discovered their manuscripts in an old chest. Chatterton's chest, found in the muniment room of St. Mary Redcliffe, was the subject of any number of japes; Thomas Warton noted that "of literary contention there is no end. The Bristol-chest has become the box of Pandora to the critical world."[23] From that casket flew many critical evils. As Mason sarcastically predicted,

> should all the old chests in all the parish churches in the kingdom, after a pregnancy of four centuries, choose to bring forth a tuneful progeny of pastorals, tragedies, epic poems, and what not, it cannot be imagined, that the said chests will ever pretend, that they were impregnated in the same wonderful manner, and by the same occult personage, with that of St. Mary Redclift. I must, therefore, if her pretty bantlings be proved supposititious, or illegitimate, necessarily rise up the first Archæological Poet in Great Britain.[24]

And when Ireland had the bad judgment to locate his own discoveries in a suspiciously Chattertonian chest, found in the house of his fabulously generous benefactor, his critics could hardly resist pointing out the coincidence. *The Herald* facetiously suggested that London was bristling with literary treasure-chests: "As *Shakespearean* manuscripts have lately been found in such abundance, many old Ladies are now at work in searching their *old trunks*, in hopes of finding a few Comedies from the pens of *Congreve* or *Vanbrugh*."[25] Ireland is pictured as a simpleton in John Nixon's engraving, *The Oaken Chest or the Gold Mines of Ireland a Farce*, who sits on the floor reading a children's book while his father roots through a chest turning up documents labeled "The Virgin Queen," "Deed of gift to Ireland," "Verses to Anna Hatherrewaye," Holinshed's *Chronicles*, and a mouse.[26]

The attempt to liken Ireland's chest of literary masterpieces to Chatterton's—and thereby to liken Ireland's questionable new documents to Chatterton's discredited old ones—is just one variety of a technique employed by many of those who would discredit supposed fakers. "All of the house of forgery," wrote Horace Walpole, "are relations," and a favorite ploy of self-appointed champions of truth was to draw out the family resemblances. We therefore see many detectors of forgery trying to liken a doubtful new case to a known old one. Walpole himself was a master of this technique, as when he called George Psalmanazar "the prototype of Chatterton," likening the

---

22 Malone, *An Inquiry*, pp. 239, 309.

23 Warton, *An Enquiry*, p. 6.

24 Mason, *An Archaeological Epistle*, pp. 3–4.

25 *The Herald*, 12 Jan. 1796, in BL Add. MS 30349, fol. 33ʳ.

26 The attribution to John Nixon appears in G. Hilder Libbis's manuscript annotation in Huntington MS 287173, p. 37. See also Bate, "Shakespearean Allusion."

modern poet with the faux Formosan.[27] An anonymous enemy recognized Walpole's technique of conflating Chatterton with other forgers, and in this ironic praise for the technique he shows a clear understanding of how the technique works:

> I much approve of the repetition of Psalmanazar's name, and indeed of as many impostors as we can well crowd together, they cannot be rung too often into the ears of the public. This manner of proceeding will have an excellent effect: for let a man but once suspect that there is a design on foot of imposing on his understanding, and he will not believe his reason and his senses, although they tell him to the contrary.[28]

Malone was an opponent of both the Rowleians in 1782 and of Ireland in 1796, and clearly had the former case in mind when he set out to prosecute the latter. Early in his examination of the Ireland matter, he makes a sly anonymous reference to himself as "the author of one of the earliest pamphlets" on the Chatterton imposture, which "proved, with irresistible force, that the authors of those [genuine] specimens, and of the pretended ancient reliques, could not have lived within the same period."[29] Other comparisons between the cases pop up from time to time. "After the detection of Chatterton, and the demolition of the chest with six keys," he writes, "I did not expect to have heard again, for some time at least, of such a repository for ancient Manuscripts." In providing this little history, he reminds us of some of the least plausible facts of the Chatterton case. This implausibility is then turned on Ireland: "from a similar receptacle, however, the *unknown* gentleman is hardy enough to draw all his *speciosa miracula*."[30] The sarcasm is palpable, and serves to liken the new subject to the known forger. Two chests, two mysterious provenances: Malone invites us to draw the conclusion that their stories are similar in other details as well.

Similar strategies underlie many similar conflations of fakers. When Thomas Birch criticizes Charlotte Lennox's "Freedoms" in quoting Shakespeare's sources, he adds, "Mr. Garrick has fix'd a Name upon her, which she highly resents, that of Mrs. Lauder"[31]—the meaning is clearly that Lennox is engaging in the same falsification of quotations as William Lauder, notorious for the false plagiarism accusations he had leveled at Milton. And George Colman goes much further in this direction, attacking the Reverend Mr. Moor for his involvement in the Cock Lane Ghost imposture by likening him to every fake he can think of:

> We hear that the Rev. Mr. M. is preparing a new work for the use of families, especially children, to be published in weekly numbers, called The Ghost's Catechism. We have been favoured with a transcript of the Creed, which is as follows:

---

27   Walpole, *A Letter to the Editor of the Miscellanies of Thomas Chatterton*, in Walpole, *Works*, 4:217, 211.

28   *The Genuine Copy of a Letter*, pp. 11–12.

29   Malone, *An Inquiry*, pp. 31–2.

30   Ibid., p. 289.

31   Thomas Birch to Philip Yorke, 23 June 1753, in BL Add. MS 35398, fol. 121. I am grateful to Fiona Ritchie for bringing this to my attention.

Mr. M——'s BELIEF.

"I Believe, in signs, omens, tokens, dreams, visions, spirits, ghosts, spectres, and apparitions.

"And in Mary Tofts, who conceived and was brought to bed of a couple of rabbits.

"And in Elizabeth Canning, who lived a whole month without performing any of the usual offices of nature, on six crusts of dry bread and half a jug of water.

"And in A[rchibal]d B[owe]r who made his escape from the Inq[uisition]n at M[a]c[e]r[a]ta.

"And in all the miracles of the Holy Roman Catholic Church.

"I believe in fairies; I believe in witches; I believe in hobgoblins; I believe in the shrieking woman; I believe in the death-watch; I believe in the death-howl; I believe in raw-head-and-bloody-bones; I believe in all stories, tales, legends, &c. &c. &c. &c. &c. &c. &c. &c. &c. &c. &c. &c. &c. &c. &c. &c. &c. &c. &c. &c. &c. &c. &c. &c. &c. &c. &c. &c. &c. &c. &c."[32]

The goal is to encourage the metaphorical jury to associate new witnesses with known perjurers. To associate Ireland with Chatterton, Chatterton with Psalmanazar, Charlotte Lennox with William Lauder, or the Cock Lane impostors with Mary Toft was an attempt to exclude their testimony as unreliable.

My Noble Friend's Name

No one wanted to be seen as unreliable. Authority is often the key to success, and in these debates the combatants are always sizing one another up, hoping to improve their standing in the eyes of onlookers. Displays of honors, the more conspicuous the better, might serve the purpose. A boast about being "Fellow of the Royal Society" or "Member of the Royal College of Physicians" could do much to impress an audience, predisposing them to look favorably on one's abilities and trustworthiness. It is likely that these ostentatious displays of credentials and initials sometimes meant no more to some readers than so much Erse, but a string of impressive-looking abbreviations could do much to establish the expertise of the bearer.

Title pages were a favorite place to make claims to authority. On the title page of his investigation of the Rowley poems, Thomas Warton is "FELLOW OF TRINITY COLLEGE OXFORD, AND F.S.A." William Shaw's *Enquiry* into the Ossian affair is "By W. SHAW, A.M. F.S.A., Author of the GALIC DICTIONARY and GRAMMAR," showing in just a few words his education, his publications, and the honors conferred on him. Manningham's observations on Mary Toft are "By Sir *RICHARD MANNINGHAM*, Kt. Fellow of the *Royal Society*, and of the *College of Physicians, London*"[33]— indicating at once his social rank, his proficiency in pure and applied science, and his acceptance by his peers.

When credentials were not so easily displayed in a series of degrees and initials, authors sometimes had to resort to more explicit boasting. The antiquary William Stukeley says of the Ossianic poems, "I can't call it vanity in me, if I think no

32 Colman, *Prose on Several Occasions*, 2:4–5.
33 Warton, *An Enquiry*; Shaw, *An Enquiry*; Manningham, *An Exact Diary*.

one can be a better judge of their authenticity."[34] Shaw, likewise, claims "to know and understand the [Erse] language as well as many man living; having bestowed more labour and expense upon it than all that went before me." He can say—like Stukeley, "without vanity"—that "I understand Galic as well as any man living; for I wrote a Grammar and Dictionary of it." In explaining the pains he took in collecting his information, he borrows the language of romance: "Many mountains I traversed, many vallies I explored, and into many humble cottages I crept on all four, to interrogate the inhabitants. I wandered from island to island, wet, fatigued, and uncomfortable. No labour I thought too much, no expense too great."[35]

Malone opens his treatise on Ireland with a personal narrative to establish his Shakespearean credentials. After mentioning "the publication of my edition of this great poet's work" six years before, he attacks the spelling *ande* by insisting that "From the time of Henry the Fourth, I have perused, I will not say several hundred, but some thousand deeds and other MSS., and I never once found the copulative *and* spelt as it is here, with a final *e*."[36] The attempts to establish his authority are especially clear here. In a single sentence, he reveals both the breadth and the depth of his antiquarian research, the attentiveness of his reading, the accuracy of his memory, and his grammatical expertise, not least by referring to *and* as a "copulative," a term of art likely to be unfamiliar to many of his readers.

What makes for an acceptable credential is not always clear. Membership in a prestigious professional organization or learned society is helpful, as is a distinguished professional title—"Physician to His Majesty"—or a title of nobility or decoration. Beyond that, though, the rules are less clear, and various sorts of posturing may be called for. Signs of classical learning are often useful. Edward Burnaby Greene's attack on Malone's work on Chatterton is decked out with all the flamboyant learning he can muster: numberless Latin and Greek tags appear throughout his pamphlet, all unattributed; even the page references show off their learning: "Id. et. pag. eadem." His vitriol often turns into sarcasm: "Heigh Presto in the next paragraph!" "Soft and soothing *Bathos!*" He is particularly fond of sarcastic exclamation-laden Latin tags: "Obscurum per Obscurius!" and "vix crederem, etiam si jurasset!"[37] Thomas James Mathias litters his *Essay on the Evidence ... Relating to the Poems Attributed to Thomas Rowley* (1783) with offhand Latin and Greek quotations, likewise without attribution. (Similar exhibitions of arcane learning may have led Swift to include the epigraph from Irenaeus on the title page of his *Tale of a Tub*—"Basima eacabasa eanaa irraurista, diarba da caeotaba fobor camelanthi"—and certainly prompted the author of *Gisbal*, a satire on the Ossianic affair from 1762, to emblazon his title page with the meaningless "*¶ (b)* = ‡*, &, ‖:‖† (p) = ,, xy. Vet. Inscript. ap.* GRONOV."[38]) Other critics make claims to inside knowledge, hinting that this makes them better judges than other, more benighted, participants. Shaw, for instance, has firsthand information

34 *Gentleman's Magazine* 36 (March 1766): 119.

35 Shaw, *An Enquiry*, pp. 70–71, 84, 108.

36 Malone, *An Inquiry*, pp. 3, 33.

37 Greene, *Strictures upon a Pamphlet*, pp. 46 n, 32, 45, 34, 43.

38 Swift, *A Tale of a Tub*, p. 1; *Gisbal*, title page.

that debunks a public story: "In this manner a collection hath been made up and published at Edinburgh, three years ago, by an ingenious *translator*, Mr. Clarke, entitled *The Caledonian Bards*.... Mr. Clarke, when I charged him with it, confessed that it was entirely made up."[39] Shaw never explains why Clark's admitted imposture should cast doubt on Macpherson's story, but the implication is clear.

A work's authority may be increased not only by the author's credentials, but by those of his associates—his sources of knowledge, the lord to whom he has dedicated his book, and so on. Samuel Ireland sought to improve the credit of the Shakespearean papers by trotting out a catalogue of distinguished names, whose authority would answer all the nagging questions about authenticity:

We whose names are hereunto subscribed have in the presence and by the favor of Mr Ireland inspected the foregoing papers, and are Convinced of their authenticity. Feby 25th 1795.

Samuel Parr	James Boswell
John Tweddell	Lauderdale
Thomas Burgess	Revd James Scott
John Byng	Kinnaird
James Bindley	John Pinkerton
Herbert Croft	Th Hunt
Somerset	H. Pye
Is: Heard, Garter King of Arms	Rev^{d}Nathl Thornbury
F. Webb	Jon^n Hewlett
R. Valpy	Translator
	of old Records—
	Common Pleas office
	Temple
	Matt Wyatt.[40]

On the other side, his rival Malone knew how to play the game of invoking prominent names. His attack on the Shakespeare papers is framed as "A Letter to the Earl of Charlemont"; on the first page of text comes a footnote on Charlemont's name:

As my noble friend's name appears in the List of Subscribers prefixed to the MISCELLANEOUS PAPERS, &c. here examined, I am authorized by him to say, that he subscribed to that work at the request of a gentleman who furnished him with a splendid PROSPECTUS of it, which he carried from hence to Ireland; and that if Lord Charlemont had known as much of it as he now does, he would not have given either his name or his money to the publication.[41]

When building oneself up does not suffice, there is always the option of tearing others down by attacking their character. Many eighteenth-century Britons found this principle so obvious that they felt no need to justify it—"The necessity of an honest character," writes an anonymous commentator on Aristotle, "is so plain, that

---

39 Shaw, *An Enquiry*, pp. 59–60.

40 BL Add. MS 30346, fol. 82^v. Ireland reproduces the list in *Mr. Ireland's Vindication of His Conduct*, pp. 21–2.

41 Malone, *An Inquiry*, p. 1 n.

to offer any arguments in defence of it, were a folly"[42]—but it is worth expanding the enthymeme left implicit in such charges. The implied logic: you are a cad; cads generally have little regard for the truth; one who generally has little regard for truth is probably lying in this particular case. This tactic turns the investigation from the nature of the doubtful texts to the character of their discoverers or defenders; it therefore depends on a strong association of works of art, whether genuine or fake, with the personalities who produced them. This association was by no means new in the long eighteenth century, but it seems then to have been stronger than ever before, and grew during the course of the century.

Sometimes it is enough simply to mention a group to which a disputant belongs to discredit him. During the Popish Plot, the Protestant accusers often made at least half their case simply by identifying their enemies as Roman Catholics. In an "Epistle Dedicatory to All Protestants," for example, Miles Prance disparages the defendants' religion: he is telling his story so "That both the present Age, and Posterity may take right measures of *Popery*, as a thing so *destructive* to Government and Humane Society in general, and so directly opposite to all the *Ennobling*, Holy, Humble, Meek and Peaceable Designs of *True Christianity*, That the *Better Roman-Catholick* any person is, the *worse man* he becomes."[43] William Ireland, a defendant in the Popish Plot trials (and unrelated to the Shakespeare forger of a century later), faced the same prejudice even from the Lord Chief Justice: when he offered evidence of an alibi, the testimony was dismissed because it came from Catholics:

> *Ireland.* My Lord, I will prove, That I was not in Town in *August* all the Month, by twenty Witnesses: I'le bring those that saw me in *Stafford-shire*, and spoke with me all *August*....
>
> *L. C. J.* If [the witness] did see you, he must see you in such Company as you keep, they were Priests and *Jesuits*, and of your own Religion; and we know very well what Answers we are likely to be put off with by men of your own Persuasion at this time of day.
>
> *Ireland.* My Lord if no body's Oath can be taken that is of another Persuasion than the Church of England, it is hard.[44]

It was hard indeed: Ireland was sent to the gallows.

Not many years later, George Psalmanazar used similar religious bigotry to defend himself. Almost the only people who had seen real Formosans were Jesuit missionaries, and some of them lined up to challenge his story. It was enough for Psalmanazar merely to remind his auditors that they were, in fact, Jesuits, and that

---

42   Aristotle, *Hobbes's Translation of Aristotle's Art of Rhetorick*, p. vii. Aristotle gives much of a chapter in the *Rhetoric* to the necessity of demonstrating the superiority of your character to that of your opponent (1.15.18–19). Compare Cicero, *De Oratore*, 2.42.178.

43   Prance, *A True Narrative and Discovery*, sig. A1[r].

44   *The Tryals of William Ireland, Thomas Pickering, and John Grove*, pp. 44–5. Bitter attacks on character could be found on both sides: many accused Titus Oates of sodomy (see, for instance, Elliot, *A Modest Vindication of Titus Oates*, p. 33). An anonymous critic wrote that, when Oates was a child, "he was so Famous for Lying amongst his Companions, that several did presage his future Villanies," and that at "the University of *Cambridge* ... he was equally remarkable for his Dulness" (*The Life of Titus Oats*, p. 2).

their word should never be accepted when it contradicted an Anglican. In a defense published after the first accusations of deception had been leveled, he wrote, "now we may expect it will be inquired *how P——r came to be at all suspected*, since all the Objections against him are so very easily answer'd? And truly we find this the harder Question to resolve, unless we may be allowed to say *His first Enemies were the Jesuits*."[45] Even in his *Description*, he warned his readers "how great a prejudice the Jesuits have done to Christianity, and what a Reproach and Disgrace they have brought upon the Christian Name, by imposing their Popish Errors upon the People as necessary Articles of Faith, and by contriving that barbarous and bloody Massacre which they intended against all the poor Pagans."[46]

Perverse and Unamiable

An episode in which character loomed especially large was the dispute over Elizabeth Canning's supposed abduction. This was an exceptionally difficult case, because the testimony on both sides seemed so plausible—and yet many of the witnesses on at least one side must have been lying. Malvin R. Zirker points to "the extraordinary fact that at the trial forty-one witnesses for Squires were in nearly direct contradiction with twenty-seven witnesses for Canning."[47] As a reviewer for the *Gentleman's Magazine* put it on examining the two most important publications in the controversy, "the writers do not seem to agree about any single fact."[48] The battle raged and divided London society for more than a year, with the partisans for Canning and those for the gypsy falling into two clear camps: "The Appellations *Whig* and *Tory*, *Court* and *Country*," writes one commentator a full year into the affair, "have entirely subsided, and seem with us all to be merged into *Canningite* and *Egyptian*."[49]

The Canningites were uniformly eager to insist on Canning's unblemished character. One supporter, Daniel Cox, observed that "The character of Elizabeth Canning is well supported by several tradesmen of probity and integrity in the neighbourhood of Aldermanbury."[50] Another anonymous supporter reminded readers that Canning had "her Education in the Charity School belonging to the Parish where they lived, and, from her Infancy, behaved in such a Manner, as to acquire the Applause and Esteem of all who knew her." And if Canning's character looked good in its own right, it looked far better by comparison with those of her supposed captors, "Mother Wells," a bawd, and Mary Squires, a gypsy. "Is there not as much Reason for believing," asked one commentator, "that the *Widow* of an *executed Felon*, one who had long *kept* a notorious *Brothel*, and a *Vagabond* of the *worst Sort*, a *Gypsy*, ... were capable of committing this, or any other Crime, whereby they might interest themselves, as that a Girl *possessed, from her Infancy,*

---

45 Psalmanazar, *An Enquiry into the Objections*, p. 49.
46 Psalmanazar, *An Historical and Geographical Description*, 1st ed., pp. 322–3.
47 Fielding, *A Clear State of the Case*, p. xciii.
48 *Gentleman's Magazine* 23 (March 1753): 109.
49 *Canning's Magazine*, p. 2.
50 Cox, *An Appeal to the Public*, p. 10.

of a moral Character, exemplary, as well as blameless, should be willing to forge a false Accusation?"[51] Another makes the same case: "Is there not a considerable difference between the character of E. C. and those of a bawd and a gypsey; a sort of people, whose very professions, generally speaking, entitle them to the gallows? Had the gypsey happened to have been hanged, the consequence would have been, that there had been in the nation one vagabond less."[52]

Others, though, hinted that Canning's character was not quite so exemplary as it had been made out to be. An anonymous ballad describes the actions of the supposed kidnappers:

> They sought not a Maiden-head, for if they had
> They went to the wrong Shop to find it, Egad.
> *Derry down, &c.*[53]

Besides, as an anonymous supporter of Squires points out, although "*Wells* ... is notorious for keeping a bad House, and entertaining Company of very loose Morals," it does not follow that she was guilty of kidnaping Canning: "Shall a Man be condemn'd to the Gallows for Petty Larceny, because he has the Character of a Pick-pocket or Highwayman?" he asks. "No, 'tis not his Character, but real Facts that condemn him, and for such Facts only as he shall be proved guilty of."[54]

This argument, however, had little success, and character continued to trump "real Facts" in many eighteenth-century disputes over authenticity. And no one's character came under more serious attacks than James Macpherson. His enemies never forgot that Macpherson was not the most sympathetic man, and even his friends found him hard to take: David Hume, once a supporter, later admitted he never knew "a man more perverse and unamiable."[55] William Shaw dwells at length on Macpherson's perversity: "Strange to tell!" he marvels, "when the public might have looked for a deposit of the manuscript, ... Mr. Macpherson's irascibility flamed forth, and he only had recourse to the single argument that always remains for the defence of imposture, the *argumentum ad hominem*, or *baculinum*." Macpherson, then, is both ungentlemanly and brutal; worse still, his threats of violence do nothing to advance his cause, for "the incompetency of the *argumentum baculinum* to prove a literary truth was manifest."[56] So widespread were the complaints over Macpherson's character that the Committee of the Highland Society, investigating the Ossianic poems in 1805, worked hard "to conduct its inquiries, and to frame its report, in a manner as *impersonal* as possible"—but even they felt obliged to "produc[e] some documents relative to the character and disposition ... of Mr James Macpherson."[57]

The forgers were not the only ones to be attacked, and Macpherson was not the only participant in the Ossianic disputes whose personal character was impugned.

---

51 *Genuine and Impartial Memoirs of Elizabeth Canning*, pp. 3, 11.
52 *A Collection of Several Papers Relating to Elizabeth Canning*, p. 11.
53 *The Devil Outdone*, p. 4.
54 *The Truth of the Case*, pp. 2, 8.
55 Hume to Blair, 6 Oct. 1763, in Hume, *Letters*, 1:403 (no. 217).
56 Shaw, *An Enquiry*, pp. 20–21, 25.
57 Mackenzie, *Report*, p. 15.

Sometimes Macpherson's critics came under fire as much as Macpherson himself. Shaw complains that "My adversaries, instead of proving the genuineness of Fingal, have contented themselves with insulting me."[58] But the attacks on Shaw were as nothing beside those on Samuel Johnson. For his enemies, Johnson's "favourite and leading prejudice" against the Scots was supposed to explain everything; in this version of the tale, the close-minded and snobbish John Bull was disqualified from testifying.[59] Sometimes the vituperation was scathing: Donald M'Nicol argued in 1779 that "The Doctor hated Scotland; that was the *master-passion*, and it scorned all restraints. He seems to have set out with a design to give a distorted representation of every thing he saw on the north side of the Tweed."[60] And not all of the invective has survived: R. Carruthers observed in 1843 that "The acrimonious controversy with Johnson irritated [Macpherson] extremely; and there are many coarse epigrams, lampoons, and parodies, among his unpublished papers, in which the great moralist is treated very unceremoniously."[61]

Anna Seward, whose relation with Johnson was always complicated, wrote to Walter Scott:

> Apropos of Ossian, ... Dr Johnson's scornful assertions on the subject, have no weight with me; believing, as I have ever done, that his impatient jealousy of a new classic, of such high antiquity, emerging from the mists of time, and in the land of his detestation, was the motive of his journey to Scotland; that he went thither for the express purpose of giving weight and credence to his verdict in a cause which he had prejudged, long before he pretended to examine the evidence.[62]

Similar attacks, often in similar language, emerged when Johnson later considered the Chatterton case. Seward herself—apparently unaware of Johnson's minimal role in selecting poets for the edition to which he wrote the prefaces—writes, "Yet would not Johnson allow Chatterton a place in those volumes [the *Lives*] in which Pomfret and Yalden are admitted. So invincible were his grudging and surly prejudices— enduring long-deceased genius but ill—and contemporary genius not at all."[63]

No dispute over authenticity did more damage to Johnson's character, though, than that over William Lauder's Milton. Johnson, like many others, was duped by Lauder's claim that Milton was a plagiary; worse, he was persuaded to contribute a preface to Lauder's book, which later provided his enemies with plentiful

---

58 Shaw, *An Enquiry*, p. 51.

59 Mackenzie, *Report*, p. 35. James Boswell wrote to Johnson in 1775, worried by these attacks, and able to reply only with a general reference to Johnson's good character: "You may believe it gives me pain to hear your conduct [toward Macpherson] represented as unfavourable, while I can only deny what is said, on the ground that your character refutes it" (Boswell to Johnson, 2 Feb. 1775, in Boswell, *Letters*, 1:209).

60 M'Nicol, *Remarks*, p. 5.

61 Carruthers, *Highland Note-Book*, pp. 308–9.

62 Seward to Scott, 20 June 1806, in Seward, *Letters*, 6:277.

63 Seward to Park, 30 Jan. 1800, in Seward, *Letters*, 5:273.

embarrassing ammunition.[64] When he discovered that Lauder had cooked the books, he composed a sincere confession: Johnson, writes Hester Thrale Piozzi,

> convinced Lauder, that it would be more for his interest to make a full confession of his guilt, than to stand forth the convicted champion of a lye; and for this purpose he drew up, in the strongest terms, a recantation.... That piece will remain a lasting memorial of the abhorrence with which Johnson beheld a violation of truth.... As a critic and a scholar, Johnson was willing to receive what numbers at the time believed to be true information: when he found that the whole was a forgery, he renounced all connection with the author.[65]

With Lauder's confession, Johnson says, "the shade which began to gather on the splendour of Milton totally dispersed." Johnson overcame his own political aversion to the "acrimonious and surly republican,"[66] but Lauder never learned his lesson, and later unsuccessfully reasserted his charges. When Johnson later became the prosecutor of fraud rather than its unwitting perpetrator, his critics delighted in bringing up the Lauder affair. Johnson's friends rushed to his defense; Shaw found him "too sincere a friend to truth" to let Macpherson's charges go unanswered, and Piozzi declared that his "ruling passion may be said to be the love of truth."[67] It is no surprise that, with the archetypal Englishman going up against the Scottish literary establishment, the debate often took on a nationalistic character. Shaw reminds us how closely the two are intertwined in his italics-laden self-righteous protestation: "*Truth* has always been *dearer* to *me* than my country; nor shall I ever support an ideal national humour founded on an imposture."[68]

Common Sense, and the Observation of All Mankind

At other times the idea was not to focus on the characters of the participants, but to eliminate them entirely from the discussion—to eliminate everything but the works themselves. The eighteenth century helped to create, or at least to codify, an important critical myth: that works of genius are proofs of themselves, irrespective of their authors, irrespective of the circumstances of their creation. *Res ipsa loquitur.* Even today, we hear the argument that some documents are powerful enough to be self-authenticating. In 1998, Daniel Ganzfried accused Benjamin Wilkomirski of falsifying his Shoah memoir, *Fragments.* As Wilkomirski's supporters rallied to his defense, even those who questioned his facts argued that his text carried with it indisputable marks of its authenticity. For Guta Benezra, "his voice is so true, so comparable to her own innermost voice of horror and sorrow that it is beyond

---

64   See Blackburne, *Remarks on Johnson's Life of Milton*, pp. 4–22. The most thorough overview of the Lauder affair appears in the four articles by Michael J. Marcuse cited in the bibliography.

65   Piozzi, *Anecdotes*, pp. 397–8.

66   Johnson, 1825 *Works*, 5:273; *The Life of Milton*, in *The Lives of the Most Eminent English Poets*, 1:276.

67   Shaw, *An Enquiry*, p. 2; Piozzi, *Anecdotes*, p. 398.

68   Shaw, *An Enquiry*, p. 21.

doubt."[69] Similar conviction can be found in many eighteenth-century cases. Vicesimus Knox describes this dynamic in his essay on Rowley's poems:

> There are many truths which we firmly believe, though we are unable to refute every argument which the extreme subtilty of refined learning may advance to invalidate them. When I read the researches of those learned antiquaries who have endeavoured to prove, that the poems attributed to Rowley were really written by him, I observe many ingenious remarks in confirmation of their opinion.... But I no sooner turn to the poems, than the labours of the antiquaries appear only a waste of time and ingenuity, and I am involuntarily forced to join in placing that laurel ... on the brow of Chatterton.[70]

The faker who gained the most from the enthusiasm he generated in his readers was Macpherson, whose Ossianic poems were often defended as authentic only because they were appealing. Enthusiasm for the poems could be intense. Many modern readers of *Fingal* and *Temora* are at a loss to discover what so appealed to early audiences; they are more likely to discover what Johnson found, "a mere unconnected rhapsody, a tiresome repetition of the same images."[71] And yet countless readers were positively enthralled by the supposed Scottish antiquities. William Duff's valuation is somewhat more forceful than most, but not different in kind: "In a period of about six thousand years," he writes, "that is from the creation of the world to this day, there have arisen only three complete *original Geniuses* in the art of *Poetry*, whose compositions have descended to our times; and these are Homer, Ossian, and Shakespeare."[72] Goethe's Werther famously declares "Ossian hat in meinem Herzen den Homer verdrängt"—in the first English translation, "Ossian has taken the place of Homer in my heart and imagination."[73] And for many, this excellence was itself evidence that the poems were authentic—not merely that they were fine in their kind, but that they were of the kind that Macpherson represented, and that their provenance was genuinely ancient. As the *Critical Review* put it, "It is impossible for a reader of taste, acquainted with the manners of the present Highlanders, to refuse his assent to the authenticity of these poems, or to believe them the production of any other country."[74]

Anna Seward, one of Ossian's most passionate admirers, makes much of the link between beauty and truth, truth and beauty. She scolds a friend for not being sufficiently alive to the sublimity of *Fingal* and *Temora*: "And so you fancy you do not like Ossian. You, who are so alive to the sweet, the majestic, and the terrible graces in actual prospect, to be insensible when they are finely presented by the old Bard to your internal sight!!!" This sublimity is what convinces her that the Bard is indeed old, for "The scenic painting in Ossian's works gives them their high and exquisite value. They represent, in every variety possible, amidst an uncultivated,

---

69   Maechler, *The Wilkomirski Affair*, p. 143.

70   Knox, "On the Poems Attributed to Rowley," in *Essays*, 2:247.

71   Boswell, *Life*, 2:126.

72   Duff, *Critical Observations*, pp. 2–3.

73   Goethe, *Die Leiden des jungen Werthers*, pp. 170–171; translated as *The Sorrows of Werter: A German Story*, 2:68.

74   *Critical Review* 15 (March 1763): 200.

and naturally barren country, its wild and solemn features."[75] Years later she wrote to another friend that "I must acknowledge that no poetry is more dear to me;—that I think Macpherson's must be a consummate translation, since it glows with the strength, spirit, and grace of original composition"[76]—in other words, "strength, spirit, and grace" are guarantors of "original composition," and the excellence of the poems is proof that they are what Macpherson insisted they are. Seward likewise complained about John Sargent's poem *The Mine*, which, in its second edition (1788), included "an inscription against the originality of Ossian. It is impolitic," Seward insisted, "as well as disgraceful to his sensibility, which ought to furnish internal evidence of originality, powerful enough to do away all the testimony which Macpherson's disingenuous pretences have thrown into the opposite scale."[77]

If documents could authenticate themselves, however, they could just as easily proclaim their falsehood. Thomas Warton made that case about Chatterton when he wrote that "the cast of thought, the complexion of the sentiments, and the structure of the composition, evidently prove these pieces not antient."[78] And one of Malone's favorite rhetorical techniques in his attacks on the Ireland Shakespeare papers is to insist that the documents betray *themselves*: the reflexive pronoun shows up many times. Consider the time when Samuel Ireland and his supporters insisted that the papers must be genuine because no one could pull off such an elaborate fraud: "it was impossible amidst such various sources of detection, for the art of imitation to have hazarded so much without betraying itself."[79] Malone saw an opening: "I entirely agree with these gentlemen: the fabrication of these manuscripts … *has* accordingly betrayed itself in almost every line." Notice that he gives the documents agency by the active verb *betrayed*; passive verbs applied to the investigators divorce their inquiry from volition. On the publication of the Shakespearean papers, Malone says, "we are naturally led to ask one or two questions": led, presumably, by the forgeries. He also insists that "The absurd manner in which almost every word is over-laden with both consonants and vowels will at once strike every reader." It is the forgeries that disprove their own authenticity; Malone and Ireland are merely spectators to the self-destruction of the *Miscellaneous Papers*. Critics can be struck, but they can do no striking. In fact the papers are granted agency to such a degree that they are suicidal. One of Ireland's most daring (and foolhardy) deceptions was to write a letter from Shakespeare to a long-lost ancestor, William Henry Ireland—ostensibly at a time when two forenames were almost unheard of. As Malone notes, "no other three words in the language could have been selected more unpropitious to the cause of imposture than the names—William Henry Ireland.—The deed in which they are found is so perfectly a *felo de se*, that were there no other denotations of fraud in the other instruments and papers, (as they are spangled all over with them,) the whole would [be exposed]." As Malone writes elsewhere in the same book, "The

---

75 Seward to Miss Weston, 23 Dec. 1786, in Seward, *Letters*, 1:240–241.
76 Seward to Miss Wingfield, 29 Oct. 1796, in Seward, *Letters*, 4:265.
77 Seward to T. S. Whalley, 10 April 1789, in Seward, *Letters*, 2:259.
78 Warton, *The History of English Poetry*, 2:156.
79 Ireland, *Miscellaneous Papers*, p. vi.

proofs of fraud are so numerous," he writes, "that they produce conviction on the first view."[80]

This is, of course, manifestly untrue; many readers, even some who had reason to think themselves knowledgeable in such matters, had found the papers plausible even on multiple readings. Malone therefore spends more than 400 pages and roughly a hundred thousand words making sure the audience's impressions are the ones they should have had "on the first view." The very existence of his book is proof that his curt dismissal was unsuccessful. Many of those words are devoted to his catalogue of things he need not bring to readers' attention: "I have not collated nor ever shall collate a single line of [the manuscript of *Lear*] .... Life is not long enough to be wasted in the examination of such trash, when almost a single glance is sufficient to shew that it is a plain and palpable forgery."[81] But life was long enough for Malone to examine a great deal of such trash, often with so much malicious glee that he prompted many readers to agree with John Byng, who called the *Inquiry* a "weak, futile captious illiberal Performance, written by the Pen of an inferior Special Pleader."[82]

All of these attempts we have seen to answer *quid est veritas* with a simple punch line, a flip conflation of fakers, or a pompous assertion of critical authority have something in common: they suggest that a deception should be visible at a glance. When cases of authenticity start to get complicated, the quickest way out is an appeal to good old common sense. As William Davy, the prosecutor in Elizabeth Canning's case, put it,

> These are not all, nor the fiftieth part of the objections to which this unexampled tale is liable. It would be mispending time to enumerate them—they are obvious to every understanding.
>
> Does there need much evidence to contradict this? Does not common sense, and the observation of all mankind upon the course of nature refute it in every instance?[83]

"Common sense, and the observation of all mankind"—implicit in all these dismissals is the idea that the judgment of a questionable story requires not weeks or months of careful scrutiny, but simply a few moments and a sound judgment. The truth is perceptible all at once, and our ability to discern it comes not from minute inspection of details but from a general impression of a *Gestalt*. "'Tis not a *Lip*, or *Eye*, we Beauty call," wrote Pope, "But the joint Force and full *Result* of *all*"[84]—the same focus on "joint Force" often took the place of the careful examination of evidence.

This has to be understood in context, for eighteenth-century Britain was in the middle of a long-running battle between two schools of critical interpretation, which might be called the appreciative and the analytical, or perhaps the aesthetic and the antiquarian. It will not do to separate critics into two clearly delineated camps; lines are difficult to draw, and the two sides are always intermingling with one another. As

---

80   Malone, *An Inquiry*, pp. 7, 34, 227, 171.

81   Ibid., p. 305.

82   John Byng to Samuel Ireland, 1 April 1796, in BL Add. MS 30348, fol. 178[r].

83   *The Trial of Elizabeth Canning*, p. 9.

84   Pope, *An Essay on Criticism*, lines 245–6, in *Poems*.

we have seen, even the detail-obsessed Malone often resorts to aesthetic judgments. In his attack on Chatterton's poems he offers "a fixed principle": "The authenticity or spuriousness of the poems attributed to Rowley cannot be decided by any person who has not a *taste* for English poetry, and a moderate, at least, if not a critical, knowledge of the compositions of most of our poets from the time of Chaucer to that of Pope."[85] A supposedly Shakespearean simile in the Ireland papers comes in for criticism as "faulty" for "being little more than a comparison of a thing with itself"— a genius of Shakespeare's stature, we are to understand, would not be guilty of an artistic solecism. In Elizabeth's genuine letters, says Malone, "every reader must be struck by the quaintness of the expression, (the quaintness of the age,) tinctured with good sense, for which we look in vain in the pretended Letter to Shakspeare."[86] So even scholars could turn to "good sense" when it suited them. With that caveat, however, we might imagine a spectrum running from pure appreciation to pure technical analysis. On such a spectrum, we could range Addison, Swift, and Pope closer to the more appreciative end, and Bentley, Theobald, and Malone closer to the more technical end.

Ocular Demonstration

This chapter has focused on the attempts to settle questions of authenticity with reference to taste rather than to careful scholarship—a talent that many were eager to claim for themselves, but few were willing to grant to others. The great critics were supposed to have been born with this faculty. Samuel Johnson noted this ability in the learned Joost Lips, who detected a forgery by Sigonius, "a Native of *Modena* eminently skilled in History and *Roman* Antiquities. He was so great a Master of the Stile of *Cicero*, that he wrote a Treatise *de Consolatione*, and published it as a Piece of *Cicero*'s Works newly discovered; many were in Reality deceived by the Counterfeit which was performed with great Dexterity, but *Lipsius*, having read only ten Lines, threw it away, crying, *Vah! non est Ciceronis.*"[87] And as Paul Korshin points out, Johnson's own "reading and learning were so wide that, rather like the great classical scholar Lipsius, he could often spot a non-canonical work or a forged passage by inspirational judgment."[88] Johnson himself, though, thought little of this sort of subjective appreciation when it ventured into the province of scholarship. Boswell uses these categories to celebrate Johnson in the *Life*. In 1776, the two men traveled to Bristol, where they investigated the Rowleian controversy. Boswell gives us this report of Johnson at work:

> I was entertained with seeing him enquire upon the spot, into the authenticity of "*Rowley's* Poetry," as I had seen him enquire upon the spot into the authenticity of "*Ossian's* Poetry." George Catcot ... with a triumphant air of lively simplicity called out, "I'll make Dr. Johnson a convert." Dr. Johnson, at his desire, read aloud some of Chatterton's fabricated

---

85   Malone, *Cursory Observations*, p. 2.
86   Malone, *An Inquiry*, pp. 101 n, 115.
87   Johnson and Osborne, *Catalogus*, 3:150.
88   Korshin, "Evidence," p. 145.

verses, while Catcot stood at the back of his chair, … now and then looking into Dr. Johnson's face, wondering that he was not yet convinced.

In Boswell's scene Johnson plays the sober and rational judge; "Honest Catcot," unthinkingly believing his fondness for the poems constituted evidence of their antiquity, is the comic foil. Boswell clearly relishes the ingenuous Catcott, with his "bouncing confident credulity," and his suggestion that Johnson and Boswell "*view with [their] own eyes* the ancient chest in which the manuscripts were found."[89]

Catcott's "*ocular demonstration*," with its conflation of the aesthetic and the historical, is hardly less convincing than Hugh Blair's rapturous defense of the Ossianic poems on the basis of their sublimity: "The compositions of Ossian are so strongly marked with characters of antiquity," he insists, "that although there were no external proof to support that antiquity, hardly any reader of judgment and taste, could hesitate in referring them to a very remote æra."[90] In the face of self-evidently heartfelt poetry, say Catcott and Blair, qualms about provenance are supposed to melt away.

But not for Johnson, who was notable for refusing to allow impressions to overrule judgment. He was always skeptical about "taste," and it is surprising how rarely he uses the word: although the phrase "good taste" was widespread during his lifetime, Johnson never once uses it in his writings.[91] The only relevant *Dictionary* definition is "Intellectual relish or discernment," which leaves no room for the sort of impressionistic faculty Blair and Catcott have in mind. Johnson was unimpressed by uninformed enthusiasm. The Rowley manuscripts "were executed very artificially," he admitted, "but from a careful inspection of them … we were quite satisfied of the imposture, which, indeed, has been clearly demonstrated from internal evidence, by several able criticks."[92] Whereas Blair and Catcott expect the truth to be evident even to the eyes of the amateur, Johnson is diffident about his abilities as an antiquary, and relies on both meticulous observation and the verdict of more authoritative critics. Though far more knowledgeable about fifteenth-century poetry than most, he knew he was no better than a dilettante beside Tyrwhitt, Percy, Malone, and Warton, and deferred to their judgment. He did the same in the Ossianic controversy: when he challenged Macpherson to make his manuscripts available, he suggested that he should "deposite the manuscript in one of the colleges at Aberdeen, where there are people who can judge."[93] Johnson reveals his high opinion of antiquarian scholars as well as his awareness that his own comparative ignorance leaves him liable innocently to mistake falsehood for truth. In the quest for authenticity, Blair's "judgement and taste" are poor guides, likely to lead searchers astray.

The danger was that relying on taste pushed the discussion into the realm of the purely subjective. Eighteenth-century commentators did not want to believe taste

---

89 Boswell, *Life*, 3:50–51.

90 Blair, *A Critical Dissertation*, p. 353.

91 "Good taste" does appear in a translation of his, "A Dissertation upon the Greek Comedy, Translated from Brumoy," in Johnson, 1825 *Works*, 5:396. Boswell also attributes the phrase to him in conversation in *Life*, 2:191.

92 Boswell, *Life*, 3:50.

93 Ibid., 5:95.

was subjective, and Hume's essay "Of the Standard of Taste" is only the most famous of countless attempts to ground that faculty on objective principles. But when one party declares that something is obviously true, no explanation needed, and another replies that it is equally obviously false, no explanation needed, both parties should quickly see the need for further explanation. Vicesimus Knox is all too aware that taste can easily lead the investigator astray. "Few studies," he writes, "are so much exposed to the delusion of forgery as those of antiquaries." The problem comes from the antiquarian who "has sometimes made his palate the criterion of a genuine rust"—the faculty is likely to fail, and "by the temporary indisposition of the organs of taste, he has often been known to admit into his invaluable collection pieces of less value, and of less antiquity, than the lowest coin of the current specie."[94]

It would be unfair to declare a winner in the battles between the advocates of taste and the advocates of scholarship but, at least in the cases considered in this book, the dry-as-dust scholars have the better record. Those who resorted to catalogues of verb forms and paper chemistry were occasionally deceived, whether in favor of a questionable document or against a genuine one, but taste proved an even more unreliable guide. The classic instance is the dispute over the *Epistles* of Phalaris, in which the avatar of literary taste, Sir William Temple, was soundly thrashed by the pedantic but meticulous Richard Bentley. To go beyond the limitations of taste and authority, we have to give up the expectation that the truth will be evident on first glance, and instead devote time and effort to sorting through evidence. That will be the subject of the next several chapters.

---

94   Knox, "Objections to the Study of Antiquities," in *Essays*, 1:320.

Chapter 3

The Utmost Evidence

All the varieties of detection considered in the previous chapter have one thing in common: all demand of the reader a rapid summary judgment whether a story is true or false. Most would-be detectors, though, lack the ability to survey the whole case in a glance. Samuel Johnson acknowledges that a few "gigantick and stupendous intelligences … are said to grasp a system by intuition, and bound forward from one series of conclusions to another, without regular steps through intermediate propositions." Most people, though, have to "make their advances in knowledge by short flights between each of which the mind may lie at rest."[1] Perhaps a genius like Isaac Newton—at least the Newton of myth—could see an entire system at once, could grasp intuitively all the facts that determined the shape of the universe. Lesser mortals had to be content with shedding light on only a small part of the whole. They could hope to answer large questions only by beginning with small pieces of evidence.

The Doctrine of Presumptions

Understanding early modern notions of evidence requires a kind of imaginative leap, since many ideas we now take for granted were only beginning to come into being in the seventeenth and eighteenth centuries. New conceptions of historical and scientific evidence emerged from a substantial reconsideration of the nature of fact itself, as chronicled by Steven Shapin in *A Social History of Truth*. The most obvious forum in which theories of evidence were being developed, though, is the law, and while few of the cases of deception discussed in this book resulted in actual legal proceedings, notions derived from the law did much to shape the debates over authenticity.

Footprints left by a tall man with a slight limp; ashes from the suspect's preferred brand of cigarettes found at the murder scene; a dog's failure to bark—since the nineteenth century, clues like these have been at the heart of the crime fiction genre. Legal writing from before the eighteenth century, though, suggests that what are now clichés would have been nearly incomprehensible to many early modern readers: seventeenth-century audiences would not have known what to make of Edgar Allan Poe, Wilkie Collins, or Agatha Christie. Detective fiction as we know it was a nineteenth-century invention, but it would not have been possible without the epistemological shifts that took place in eighteenth-century British theories of evidence. It was the period in which circumstantial evidence came into its own, and

---

1   Johnson, *Rambler* 108, in Yale *Works*, 4:212–13.

without it the debates over Ossian, Rowley, and William Henry Ireland would have been impossible.

The Continental legal tradition had little room for circumstantial evidence: conviction in a criminal case usually depended on "positive" evidence, usually in the form of a confession or the testimony of witnesses who had seen the crime with their own eyes. We can trace the tradition of requiring a fixed number of witnesses (usually two) who could provide positive evidence back to Scripture: "At the mouth of two witnesses, or three witnesses, shall he that is worthy of death be put to death; but at the mouth of one witness he shall not be put to death."[2] Positive evidence was almost always needed in Continental criminal trials, for it alone could produce the degree of confidence the eighteenth century called "demonstration"—in Johnson's definition, "The highest degree of deducible or argumental evidence; the strongest degree of proof." This need is in keeping with earlier conceptions of legal fact, and it is based on a conception of evidence that allows no room for doubt: legal evidence was about producing certainty, not swaying opinion. As Ian Hacking puts it in his study of the history of probability theory, "For the medieval, evidence short of deduction was not really evidence at all."[3] Medieval trials by ordeal and trials by combat were supposed to reveal God's own summary judgment, and these early trials left no room for a judge or jury to suggest that God's verdict might not be true. And as the ordeals receded in favor of more formal legal proceedings, new standards of evidence were adapted from the old canon and civil law, but the expectation of certainty remained. Under the new regime, the testimony of some specified number of witnesses was both necessary and sufficient to convict a defendant. These systems could be very sophisticated, with one eyewitness being the numerical equivalent of two hearsay witnesses and so on. Still, all witnesses were expected to have some sort of direct experience of the supposed crime, and a case that depended entirely on circumstantial evidence was almost certain not to proceed.[4]

Early English law followed Continental practice, usually demanding positive evidence in the form of either confessions or eyewitnesses. The two-witness rule was not always followed; as Sir William Blackstone explains, "One witness (if credible) is *sufficient* evidence to a jury of any single fact; though undoubtedly," he admitted, "the concurrence of two or more corroborates the proof." After all, "our law considers that there are many transactions to which only one person is

---

2   Deut. 17:6. See Franklin, *The Science of Conjecture*, p. 4 and n. 12.

3   Hacking, *The Emergence of Probability*, p. 22.

4   This is not to say that the principles of imperfect circumstantial evidence were entirely unknown on the Continent. Although their legal system had no formal provision for dealing with evidence that was not positive, circumstances could sometimes compel belief. In cases where authorities had strong circumstantial evidence but recognized that it could not be used to secure a conviction in court, they often resorted to judicial torture, extorting a confession and thereby rendering the circumstantial evidence unnecessary. And exceptions were made for crimes like rape, which, by their very nature, precluded the possibility of witnesses. The *crimen exceptum*, "known to both the common and the civil law, was composed of secret crimes unlikely to produce the usual kinds of evidence or witnesses. The *Carolina*, for example, treats clandestine murder, infanticide, secret poisoning, and sorcery separately from other crimes" (Shapiro, *"Beyond Reasonable Doubt" and "Probable Cause,"* p. 165).

privy; and therefore does not *always* depend upon the testimony of two, as the civil law universally requires."[5] Still, for a long time English law allowed only positive evidence to be admitted into legal proceedings, and circumstantial evidence was excluded from consideration.

Some early modern English thinkers, though, did begin to think about how to deal with evidence that seemed to warrant conviction—both in the sense of "firm belief" and of "successful criminal prosecution"—but that still fell short of strict demonstration. The favorite example of evidence that was less than certain but still compelling was a murder committed behind closed doors, with a man seen running out of the room holding a bloody sword. Sir Edward Coke, writing in 1628, follows Henry de Bracton in offering a familiar example: the would-be jurist was to imagine "if one be runne thorow the bodie with a sword in a house, whereof he instantly dieth, and a man is seene to come out of that house with a bloody sword, and no other man was at the time in the house." This Coke called "*violenta praesumptio*," an overwhelming belief that still falls short of demonstration, which for him "is many times *plena probatio*."[6]

As the seventeenth century turned into the eighteenth, British legal thinkers gave increasing attention to the kinds and degrees of presumption that might produce a conviction: not a man seen running from the house with a bloody sword, perhaps, but a trail of blood leading from the crime scene to a man's house, or a man with a grudge against the victim seen to ask where he might buy a sword. Such arguments, even though they were unable to produce perfect certainty, were generally considered good enough to secure even a criminal conviction—the old standard of "demonstration" gave way to a new standard in which evidence "beyond a reasonable doubt" sufficed.[7] Many Britons, after all, complained about the inadequacies of the Continental dependence on positive evidence, lamenting both the false convictions and the false acquittals it could produce. And so they began to formulate, for the first time, a coherent system for dealing with circumstantial rather than positive evidence.

Blackstone therefore breaks from the older practice when he argues that, "next to *positive* proof, *circumstantial* evidence or the doctrine of *presumptions* must take place: for when the fact itself cannot be demonstratively evinced, that which comes nearest to the proof of the fact is the proof of such circumstances which either

---

5   Blackstone, *Commentaries*, 3:370.

6   Coke, *The First Part of the Institutes*, sig. B2ᵛ (lib. 1, cap. 1, sect. 1). The example was widely repeated in eighteenth-century legal writings: see, for instance, Burn, *The Justice of the Peace*, p. 200.

7   See Shapiro, who documents the rise of the "beyond reasonable doubt" standard in detail: "The similarity between the casuistical and the legal conception can also be seen in the formulations of Robert South, another Anglican cleric. South, like Taylor, insisted that the mathematical certainty of demonstration was not necessary in order to be assured of the rightness of one's conscience. It was sufficient 'if he know it upon the grounds of a convincing probability, as shall exclude all rational ground of doubting it.' The language of rational or reasonable doubt was thus part of the language of the right and sure conscience in England before it entered the legal sphere" (*"Beyond Reasonable Doubt" and "Probable Cause,"* pp. 16–17).

necessarily, or *usually*, attend such facts; and these are called presumptions, which are only to be relied upon till the contrary be actually proved."[8] In this he is typical of the new age of legal thinking, when Britain was learning to treat these kinds of evidence with a greater degree of sophistication. Hacking describes the state of understanding before the modern period: "Concepts of testimony and authority," he writes, "were not lacking: they were all too omnipresent as the basis for the old medieval kind of probability that was an attribute of opinion. Testimony is support by witnesses, and authority is conferred by ancient learning. *People* provide the evidence of testimony and authority. What was lacking, was the evidence provided by *things*."[9] In the eighteenth century, the evidence provided by things was being taken ever more seriously. Many critics and legal theorists started to consider it the equivalent of positive evidence; in 1785, William Paley even went so far as to argue that it was inherently superior, challenging the "popular maxim ... 'that circumstantial evidence falls short of positive proof.' This assertion, in the unqualified sense in which it is applied, is not true. A concurrence of well-authenticated circumstances composes a stronger ground of assurance, than positive testimony, unconfirmed by circumstances, usually affords. Circumstances cannot lie." The advantages to circumstantial evidence, after all, are many. "The danger of being deceived," for instance, "is less; the actual instances of deception are fewer in the one case than the other. What is called positive proof in criminal matters, as where a man swears to the person of the prisoner, and that he actually saw him commit the crime with which he is charged, may be founded in the mistake or perjury of a single witness." But circumstantial evidence cannot easily be faked or even mistaken; it "requires such a number of false witnesses as seldom meet together; an union also of skill and wickedness, which is still more rare." Moreover, "this species of proof lies much more open to discussion, and is more likely, if false, to be contradicted, or to betray itself by some unforeseen inconsistency, than that direct proof, which ... is incapable, by its very simplicity, of being confronted with opposite probabilities."[10]

An Imperfect Kind of Information

For all its advantages, though, circumstantial evidence raises some serious problems. The degree of belief that results from circumstantial evidence, for example, may be stronger than mere opinion, but it always stops shy of demonstrative certainty, and for many, that meant it was not true knowledge. Douglas Lane Patey summarizes the status quo ante: "In the central Western tradition from late antiquity to the Augustans, the ideal of knowledge—*scientia*, 'science' in its pre-nineteenth-century sense—was demonstrative knowledge.... By definition, *scientia* excluded all nondeductive, nondemonstrative proofs—all probability—locating these in the subordinate fields of dialectic and rhetoric."[11] But this was changing in the age that saw the birth of systematic philosophies of empiricism. Mathematics and logic were

---

8   Blackstone, *Commentaries*, 3:371.
9   Hacking, *The Emergence of Probability*, p. 32.
10   Paley, *The Principles of Moral and Political Philosophy*, pp. 551–2.
11   Patey, *Probability and Literary Form*, p. 9.

supposed to allow for demonstration but, in the words of one important eighteenth-century theorist of evidence, "most of the Business of civil Life subsists on the Actions of Men that are transient Things, and therefore oftentimes are not capable of strict Demonstration ... and therefore the Rights of Men must be determin'd by Probability."[12] This was frustrating, but most Britons realized that no higher degree of certitude was possible. As Bishop Joseph Butler explained in 1736:

> Probable Evidence, in its very nature, affords but an imperfect kind of Information; and is to be considered as relative only to Beings of limited Capacities. For nothing which is the possible object of Knowledge, whether past, present, or future, can be probable to an infinite Intelligence; since it cannot but be discerned absolutely as it is in itself, certainly true, or certainly false: but to us, Probability is the very Guide of Life.[13]

The problem of degrees of certitude was much discussed in eighteenth-century Britain, and not only in law. Locke devotes considerable space to the question in *An Essay concerning Human Understanding*, cataloguing the "degrees ... from the very neighbourhood of Certainty and Demonstration, quite down to Improbability and Unlikeliness, even to the Confines of Impossibility; and also degrees of *Assent* from full *Assurance* and Confidence, quite down to *Conjecture*, *Doubt*, and *Distrust*."[14] Less familiar thinkers were doing similar things. Joseph Butler writes that "Probable Evidence is essentially distinguished from demonstrative by this, that it admits of Degrees; and of all Variety of them, from the highest moral Certainty, to the very lowest Presumption," and Anthony Collins distinguishes three varieties of knowledge, and organizes them in order of decreasing reliability:

> When the agreement or disagreement is visible at first sight, or by the help of an intermediate Idea, which has a necessary Connexion with the Ideas join'd, our Assent is then call'd *Science*. When the agreement or disagreement by the intervention of intermediate Ideas that internally discover the agreement or disagreement, is but probable, our Assent is then call'd *Opinion*: and when we perceive by Testimony, our Assent is then call'd *Faith*.[15]

After spelling out the various kinds of evidence and the degrees of knowledge associated with them, John Wilkins reminds his readers in 1675, "When a thing is capable of good proof in any kind, Men ought to rest satisfy'd in the best evidence for it, which that kind of things will bear, and beyond which better could not be expected, supposing it were true."[16] Where early modern inquirers saw no middle ground between "demonstration," which was beyond dispute, and mere "opinion," which was only subjective, seventeenth-century theorists began considering a wide range of kinds of evidence, each of which produced a degree of credibility somewhere between opinion and fact. History, epistemology, medicine, natural history—all

---

12 Gilbert, *The Law of Evidence*, p. 3.

13 Butler, *The Analogy of Religion*, p. iii.

14 Locke, *Essay*, p. 655 (4.15.2).

15 Butler, *The Analogy of Religion*, p. i; Collins, *Essay concerning the Use of Reason*, p. 5.

16 Wilkins, *Of the Principles and Duties of Natural Religion*, p. 25. For a catalogue of similar comments, see Shapin, *A Social History of Truth*, pp. 207–10.

came to depend on these new intermediate degrees of credibility. Steven Shapin puts it well when he argues that

> the whole of the factual testimony with which early modern practitioners were concerned—including the stopping of the sun, the multiplication of loaves and fishes, and the existence of "men whose heads do grow beneath their shoulders"—fell somewhere short of absolute plausibility. Such things might be so, and both Christian apologists and early modern natural philosophers devoted much energy to arguing that there were adequate grounds for assenting to highly implausible claims.[17]

The Weight of Improbability

By the early nineteenth century, such notions had been elaborated and codified into systems, and soon a new language was being introduced into discussions of degrees of belief—the language of mathematics. This resort to mathematics is consistent with the many new applications of numbers to things that had previously resisted precise quantification, beginning with the "arithmetization" or "algebraicization" of classical geometry by Descartes and Fermat,[18] continuing through the mathematical descriptions of planetary movement by Galileo and Newton and the increasingly precise quantification of probabilities in the later seventeenth century,[19] achieving its most obvious expression in the "political arithmetic" of the later eighteenth century, eventually culminating in the statistical descriptions of every imaginable population in the nineteenth. The age was fascinated with the prospect of assigning numbers to everything that could bear it, and it is characteristic of this fascination that Benjamin Franklin could write in 1772 of a "Moral or Prudential Algebra" and Capel Lofft could call for a "moral algebra" in 1779.[20] Numbers were everywhere.

Thus, in 1825 Jeremy Bentham makes a point similar to those made by Butler, Collins, and Wilkins a century earlier: "Nobody can be ignorant," he writes, "that belief is susceptible of different degrees of strength, or intensity. In one case we say, *I am inclined to believe*; in another, *I believe*; in another, *I know*; but these expressions are far from marking all the intermediate shades, from simple probability, up to moral certainty." All of this is conventional enough. Bentham was, however, unhappy with the imprecision of this vocabulary, and therefore invited his readers to "Imagine a scale divided into ten degrees. It has a positive side, inscribed with the degrees of positive belief (that is, affirmative of the fact in question); and a negative side, inscribed with the degrees of negative belief (that is, denying the same fact); at the

---

17 Shapin, *A Social History of Truth*, p. 236.

18 For an overview, see Mahoney, "Die Anfänge der algebraischen Denkweise."

19 See Hald, *A History of Probability and Statistics*; and Franklin, *The Science of Conjecture*; and Hacking, *The Emergence of Probability*. Hald argues that "Before the Renaissance, probability was nonmathematical. It was not until the beginning of the 16th century that Italian mathematicians began to discuss the odds of various outcomes of games of chance" (p. 29).

20 Franklin to Joseph Priestley, 19 Sept. 1772, in Franklin, *Papers*, 19:300; Lofft, *Elements of Universal Law*, p. 6.

bottom of the scale is 0, denoting the absence of all belief either for or against the fact in question."[21]

This use of the language of mathematics to describe degrees of certainty was possible only in the wake of seventeenth- and eighteenth-century thinking about mathematical probability. People must have had some intuitive sense of probabilities for a very long time; the popularity of dice games since antiquity suggests that people have long been willing to stake money on their understanding of chance. As Abraham de Moivre warned in 1718, though, "some of the Problems about Chance having a great appearance of Simplicity, the Mind is easily drawn into a belief, that their Solution may be attained by the meer Strength of natural good Sence," but this is rarely the case.[22] Hacking states the shortcomings of ancient understandings of statistics more dramatically: "Someone with only modest knowledge of probability mathematics could have won himself the whole of Gaul in a week."[23]

The seventeenth century not only saw increased sophistication in the calculation of mathematical probabilities; it also began to develop some of the connections between "aleatory" or "stochastic" probability on the one hand and "epistemic" probability on the other. As Hacking argues, "Epistemic probability did not emerge as a significant concept for logic until people thought of measuring it."[24] Aleatory or stochastic probability is a statement of the likely number of times a repeatable event will occur in a given number of trials—a fair coin tossed a large number of times will tend to produce roughly equal numbers of heads and tails; a playing card selected at random from a standard deck will be the knave of hearts roughly one time in 52. Epistemic probability, on the other hand, does not depend on repetition, but on the degree of plausibility we are willing to assign to a unique event. Most modern audiences would agree that the probability that the Seven Years' War took place is so high as to approach certainty; that the Trojan War took place is somewhat less likely, but still probable enough to justify at least tentative belief; and that the Battle of the Cranes and the Pygmies took place is so slim as to approach certainty that it is untrue.

It is not at all obvious that the one kind of probability can be converted into the other, that the language of aleatory probability can express degrees of certitude. If I say there is a 50 percent chance a tossed coin will show heads—an aleatory probability—it means that, as I repeat the coin toss a large number of times, the ratio of heads to tails will approach 50:50. But in events that cannot be repeated, the meaning of probability is more mysterious. If we ask about the likelihood that Caesar crossed the Rubicon, we cannot look at large numbers of worlds, in some of which Caesar did and in some of which he did not. In this case we are trying to

---

21 Bentham, *A Treatise on Judicial Evidence*, pp. 40, 41–42. Patey finds a precursor: "One of the earliest systems of mathematical probability in England was a quantification of Locke's canons of testimony. In 1699 John Craig published his *Theologiae Christianae Principia Mathematica*," in which he "argues that Christ will return to the earth in the year 3153, when the probability of the Biblical account of his first appearance will have dropped nearly to zero" (Patey, *Probability and Literary Form*, p. 24).

22 Moivre, *The Doctrine of Chances*, p. iii.

23 Hacking, *The Emergence of Probability*, p. 3.

24 Ibid., p. 73.

assign a number not to the real-world frequency of an event, but rather to our degree of confidence in a fact which either did or did not happen. The actual "chance" that Caesar crossed the Rubicon is either zero or 100 percent, but we have learned to assign numbers not to the event but to our degree of certainty. What we mean by "probable" here is less mathematical than psychological: we are willing to grant the same degree of belief to this fact that we would to an aleatory outcome assigned the same degree of probability. And as the understanding of aleatory probability increased over time, Britons' ability to discuss degrees of knowledge short of demonstration also improved. As Paul J. Korshin observes, "The laws of probability helped justify the collection of large quantities of statistical evidence, for it had now become possible to interpret such materials. The concept of probability allows us to establish a scale or certainty or likelihood, so that the collecting of additional evidence clearly was likely to heighten one's chances of attaining certainty."[25]

This new understanding of probability was central to the developing "scientific" epistemology that informed seventeenth- and eighteenth-century natural investigations. The fields we now group together as natural sciences were all dependent on the collection of large bodies of evidence, and only these new notions of statistics and probability allowed for the necessary induction from individual observations to general principles. This induction is the process that made science as we know it possible, as demonstrative proof became less important than probabilistic judgment. Britain's Royal Society abandoned the Cartesian fantasy of explaining all phenomena with a few rational principles, and instead focused on the many small pieces of evidence they could reasonably hope to collect. Virtually all the fellows believed that their small pieces would eventually add up to a coherent big picture, but most British natural philosophers recognized that they would have to be content with making small contributions.

As natural philosophers began accumulating large collections of experimental and observational data, the new mathematical advances would allow them to discern patterns. Hacking suggests that these "low sciences"—alchemy, geology, astrology, and medicine—were instrumental in shaping a probabilistic approach to knowledge, because

> By default these could deal only in *opinio*. They could achieve no demonstrations and had to resort to some other mode of proof. The high sciences, such as optics, astronomy, and mechanics, still lusted after demonstration and could, in many cases, seem to achieve it. They could scorn *opinio* and any new mode of argument. New modes of argument arose, perforce, among the students of opinion.[26]

And these conceptions of probability went beyond the laboratory, infusing even common life with the language of observation, measurement, and calculation. Even when the mathematical language was entirely metaphorical, it still allowed people to speak as if belief could be measured and, more important, compared. When Johnson recounts Richard Savage's murder trial, for example, he uses mathematical language to indicate degrees of likelihood short of certainty. He notes of the witnesses that

---

25   Korshin, "Evidence," p. 137.
26   Hacking, *The Emergence of Probability*, p. 35.

"There was some difference in their depositions," and while he acknowledges that the discrepancy "was very far from amounting to inconsistency," he insists "that it was not easy to discover the truth with relation to particular circumstances, and that therefore some deductions were to be made from the credibility of the testimonies."[27] The "deductions ... from the credibility" treat a question of epistemic probability, whether or not Savage had killed a man, as if it were a question of aleatory probability—as if it were possible to reckon the number of universes in which Richard Savage did and did not kill a man. The reason for this fanciful metaphor is that it allows us to compare two uncertain events with one another—rather than dismissing either or both as mere "opinion," we can accept that one uncertain event can yet be more likely than another.

The comparison of probabilities is sometimes described in terms of arithmetic, but the more common metaphor is weighing, with opposed cases figured as weights in the scales of a balance. Henry Fielding, for example, writes of the Elizabeth Canning affair, "In all Cases, indeed, the Weight of Evidence ought to be strictly conformable to the Weight of Improbability; and when it is so, the wiser a Man is the sooner and easier he will believe."[28] Although the metaphor was nearly universal in the eighteenth century, it was comparatively recent—before the middle of the seventeenth century, evidence was rarely "weighed." The earliest example of English evidence-weighing I have been able to find is from 1587, when George Gifford complained that "Many Iurers neuer weigh the force of the euidence which is brought, but as if they had their oth for coniectures or likelihoodes." The same metaphor appears in a sermon of 19 November 1627 by John Donne, who describes a man who "should heare a *Christian* pleade for his Bible, and a *Turke* for his Alcoran, and should weigh the evidence of both."[29]

Presumptions Not Proofs

All of this language of "weighing" probabilities, comparing the plausibility of one uncertain event with that of another, eventually made its way into the courtroom, as eighteenth-century common law practice responded to the new developments in philosophy and the natural sciences. This is the period in which systematic theories of legal evidence came into their own. Many commentators have noted the lack of sophistication in the theoretical foundations underlying theories of evidence before the nineteenth century. A few philosophers took up the question of how best to interpret legal evidence beginning in the nineteenth century, but before that, as Korshin points out, information about the theory of evidence "is casual, unsystematic, even anecdotal."[30] William Twining likewise finds the study of evidence shackled by "a rather naïve, commonsense empiricism, which failed to confront a variety of sceptical challenges to orthodox assumptions," and complains that it has generally

---

27 Johnson, *The Life of Savage*, in *The Lives of the Most Eminent English Poets*, 3:134.

28 Fielding, *A Clear State of the Case*, p. 291.

29 Gifford, *A Discourse of the Subtill Practises of Deuilles*, p. 57; Donne, *Fifty Sermons*, p. 325.

30 Korshin, "Evidence," p. 133.

"proceeded in almost complete isolation from developments in relevant branches of philosophy."[31]

In eighteenth-century Britain, though, philosophy and law began to be intertwined. This is clear even from the first page of the most influential evidentiary treatise of the period, *The Law of Evidence*. "It has been observed by a very learned Man," the author explains, "that there are several Degrees from perfect Certainty and Demonstration, quite down to Improbability and Unlikeliness, even to the Confines of Impossibility."[32] The "very learned Man" is John Locke, whose *Essay concerning Human Understanding* recognizes that "most of the Propositions we think, reason, discourse, nay act upon, are such, as we cannot have undoubted Knowledge of their Truth."[33] And the author of the book is Sir Geoffrey Gilbert (1674–1726), the most important eighteenth-century British theorist of evidence. His influence was not only widespread but lasting: in 1801 Thomas Peake said *The Law of Evidence* "must form the basis of every subsequent work on the subject."[34]

In most legal theory in the eighteenth century—and, for that matter, today—to discuss evidence meant to discuss the rules for the admissibility of evidence. Such procedural matters are of limited interest in a more general study of deception, since courtroom rules do not apply in the wider world. This has not always stopped disputants from trying to invoke admissibility rules outside the court. Edmond Malone, for example, tries to eliminate some of the evidence adduced by Samuel Ireland: "In the Prerogative Court," he lectures, "if any Will or testamentary writing is exhibited at a time when, or from a quarter where, it might not reasonably be expected, the party producing it is always asked, in the first place, in what cabinet or coffer belonging to the deceased, or where else, it was found." In the absence of this sort of justification, he insists, "the claimant is not allowed to advance a single step.[35] Such attempts to exclude evidence from public discussion, though, were hardly ever successful, and legal notions of admissibility are of little help outside the courtroom.

What to do with that evidence once it has been admitted, though, is both a more vexed and a more interesting question, and here Gilbert is one of our first reliable guides. Like other treatises on evidence, most of Gilbert's book—first published in a posthumous Dublin edition in 1754, and then in seven more editions before century's end—is concerned with admissibility, offering a taxonomy of the varieties of evidence that might be admitted in a trial, along with the rules appropriate to each: written and unwritten, public and private, and so on. All of this is familiar stuff in legal history. But with one of his principles, the "best evidence rule," Gilbert began

---

31 Twining, *Rethinking Evidence*, p. 2.

32 Gilbert, *The Law of Evidence*, p. 1.

33 Locke, *Essay*, p. 655 (4.15.2). Gilbert's own *Abstract of Mr. Locke's Essay on Human Understanding* appeared in 1752. Shapiro argues for an extensive network of connections between legal and philosophical thought: see *"Beyond Reasonable Doubt" and "Probable Cause,"* pp. 25–6.

34 Peake, *A Compendium of the Law of Evidence*, p. iv.

35 Malone, *An Inquiry*, p. 15.

the serious consideration of evidence—not only what evidence is admissible, but how it should be analyzed once it has been introduced into the proceedings.

This is how Gilbert formulates his best evidence rule: "The first ... and most signal Rule, in Relation to Evidence, is this, That a Man must have the utmost Evidence, the Nature of the Fact is capable of."[36] In one sense, this is nothing new: it is an old legal maxim that had long been applied to the admissibility of evidence. Hearsay evidence, for example, is of no use if there is an eyewitness; an eyewitness's recollection is of no use if there is a document; and so on. Gilbert, however, expanded the scope and applicability of the notion, and went beyond the traditional concern with whose testimony might be allowed in court—he thought instead about which *pieces* of evidence might legitimately be expected. His contribution to legal thinking was to encourage the world to consider critically how evidence might be applied and weighed *after* it has been admitted into the courtroom.

Information of this sort is useful, because discussions of the proper use of evidence are surprisingly few. Even today judges routinely instruct jurors on what evidence they are allowed to consider, but rarely give any guidance on how they should interpret it. "The jury," as Barbara J. Shapiro observes, "is a black box. We cannot know what goes on inside it, and, indeed, it is often viewed as somewhat unseemly to inquire. Moreover, at least in criminal cases, what comes out of it is a general verdict of guilt or innocence, and it is altogether forbidden to inquire into the pieces and processes that went into that verdict."[37] It is a curious state of affairs. The jurors' skill in sorting through and evaluating evidence is the very heart of the Anglo-American court system, and yet very little is known about how the system works.

Gilbert's advice on how to evaluate conflicting claims is therefore valuable because it explicitly allows for degrees of belief short of the complete certainty supposedly provided by eyewitness testimony. Gilbert's demand for "the utmost Evidence, the Nature of the Fact is capable of" is important for what it presupposes: that less-than-demonstrative evidence may still be sufficient to produce conviction. Gilbert brings Lockean concerns about our usual inability to "have undoubted Knowledge" to legal proceedings, and the result is a new degree of sophistication in jurisprudence.

"When the Fact itself cannot be proved," Gilbert advises, "that which comes nearest to the Proof of the Fact is, the Proof of the Circumstances that necessarily and usually attend such Facts, and these are called Presumptions not Proofs." He therefore advises jurists to consider how to balance these presumptions against one another: "Now what is to be done in all Trials of Right, is to range all Matters in the Scale of Probability, so as to lay most Weight where the *Cause* ought to preponderate, and thereby to make the most exact Discernment that can be, in Relation to Right." And this notion of probability is not stochastic or aleatory, but the fundamentally psychological category of epistemic probability, which arises, he says, "from the Agreement of any Thing with a Man's own Thoughts and Observations from the

---

36 Gilbert, *The Law of Evidence*, p. 4.

37 Shapiro, *"Beyond Reasonable Doubt" and "Probable Cause,"* pp. xi–xii.

Testimony of others who have seen and heard it."[38] *Plausibility* might seem to be the more apposite word, but *probability* is more valuable because it allows us to measure different degrees of plausibility against one another, as if with mathematical precision. The concept of epistemic probability was entering the courtroom at just the moment that legal theorists were acknowledging the acceptability of evidence that was compelling but that did not aspire to demonstrative certainty.

Gilbert was not the only eighteenth-century legal theorist to bring contemporary notions of epistemology and probability to the study of the law. James Wilson, an early Associate Justice on the U.S. Supreme Court, composed a series of lectures on law in the 1790s that anticipated some of the most important advances in evidentiary thinking of the nineteenth century. Like Gilbert, he recognized the relationship between law and philosophy, drawing on (and often challenging) Locke and Beccaria; he also recognized and expounded on the connection between the principles of legal fact-finding and the need to discern the truth in the real world. "Evidence," he explains,

> is not confined, in its operation and importance, to the courts of justice. Its influence on the human mind, human manners, and human business is great and universal. In perception, in consciousness, in remembrance, belief always forms one ingredient. But belief is governed by evidence.... So large a share has belief in our reasonings, in our resolutions, and in our conduct, that it may well be considered the mainspring, which produces and regulates the movements of human life.

Although he recognizes that "The love of system, and of that unnatural kind of uniformity to which system is so much attached, has done immense mischief in the theory of evidence," he offers an elaborate list of "fourteen distinct sources" of evidence, ranging from "the external senses" and "the internal senses," through "human testimony in matters of fact" and "human authority in matters of opinion," to "reason" and "calculations concerning chances."[39] It is the most thorough consideration of the subject attempted to that date, and might have put the study of evidence on a firm footing in the 1790s. The lectures were not published until 1896, however, and their influence was therefore severely limited.

The most thorough and influential analyses of the nature and use of evidence to be published before the twentieth century, therefore, are two works by Jeremy Bentham: *A Treatise of Judicial Evidence* (1825) and *The Rationale of Judicial Evidence* (1827). Although the dates lie outside the period at the center of this book, Bentham, for all his originality, is not *sui generis*; while he effectively begins a new tradition in the theoretical study of evidence, he also summarizes much of the thinking on the subject to date. It may therefore sometimes be allowable to introduce some of Bentham's ideas when they seem to capture ideas that were circulating, perhaps in inchoate form, in the eighteenth century. As Korshin notes, "A legal theory of evidence ... does not exist in a vacuum. Rather, it represents a distillation of a climate of ideas that covers all aspects of a society's culture. Accordingly, we

---

38   Gilbert, *The Law of Evidence*, pp. 160, 2, 147.
39   Wilson, *Works*, 1:479, 481, 486–8.

will find that new evidentiary principles in the law reflect and are reflected by the state of knowledge in other areas."[40]

Like Wilson, Bentham expatiates on the connection between legal evidence and evidence in everyday life: "questions of evidence," he writes, "have a much wider application than we are usually aware of. They occur in circumstances of life, where one would least suspect that he was following a logical, and, so to speak, a judicial process; the management of domestic affairs depends entirely on evidence; our most frivolous amusements imply the most subtle applications of its rules." He offers an elaborate Aristotelian taxonomy of the varieties of evidence, far more extensive than anything Gilbert or Wilson had attempted. He begins somewhat conventionally, distinguishing what had been called "positive" from "circumstantial" evidence, but in doing so he introduces new terms: "As to its source, proof is drawn either from *persons* or *things*: *personal evidence*, and *real evidence*. Personal evidence is that furnished by a human being, and is generally called testimony. Real evidence is that deduced from the state of things." Real evidence, he explains, "is a branch of circumstantial evidence."[41]

Bentham is clear about the relationship of theories of evidence to theories of cognition, and especially to notions of plausibility. He acknowledges that "this state of mind, this interior of man, can be known only through material facts, through external acts. Thus all psychological evidence depends at last on physical evidence." He then goes on to offer a definition of what he calls "psychological or moral improbability," which "means, that certain actions, ascribed to an individual, do not correspond with his intentions as learned from other acts, with his habits, with his dispositions, such as they are displayed in the ordinary course of his life. The different kinds of improbability of this nature might be designated by the word *inconsistency*."[42]

He has also taken his predecessors' arithmetic habits to new extremes, treating the various factors that "probabilize" and "disprobabilize" a fact as quantifiable and comparable—sometimes even developing an elaborate moral calculus by which one can balance factors pro and con to arrive, as if by algebra, at a reliable answer:

> Supposing one evidentiary fact, and only one infirmative supposition applying to it: then, to estimate ... the quantity of probative force remaining to the evidentiary fact,—deduct from the ratio expressive of practical certainty, the ratio expressive of the probability of the fact the existence of which is by the infirmative supposition supposed: the remainder will be the neat probative force.
>
> To one and the same evidentiary fact, suppose a number of different infirmative suppositions applicable; and, of each of the several supposed facts, suppose the probability the same; the sum of their infirmative forces will be as their number.[43]

Most relevant for our purposes in this book, he applies this system to forgery, which "takes in a vast field, affording abundant occupation for the sagacity of judges

40 Korshin, "Evidence," p. 141.
41 Bentham, *A Treatise on Judicial Evidence*, pp. 8, 12, 40.
42 Bentham, *A Treatise on Judicial Evidence*, p. 19.
43 Bentham, *Rationale*, 3:221–2.

and lawyers."[44] He notes that "there is not perhaps a single article that has not, at one time or other, been taken for the subject of that sort of deceptitious operation which, applied to other objects, has received the name of *forgery*; yet it is among the modifications of *permanent* real evidence that we are to look for that modification of forgery which is most in use, most readily apprehended, and most apt to present itself under that name."[45] In Bentham we see the culmination of all the eighteenth-century theorizing on the nature and uses of circumstantial evidence.

The Best Reason to Doubt

Bentham's work is the result of a series of changes in thinking—in epistemology, in theology, in natural history, and in law—that also made possible the disputes in this book. Not all the combatants in the authenticity wars had direct access to these fields of knowledge, but at least some were well read in legal theory. Consider Edmond Malone, a practicing lawyer who knew Gilbert's works. He even quotes the jurist in his attack on the Ireland Shakespeare papers: "It is an established rule," he writes, "that the best evidence the nature of the case will admit of, shall always be required."[46] He was therefore able to bring an uncommonly sophisticated understanding of the law to discussions of deception. Most of those who engaged in arguments over literary frauds and other hoaxes had no formal legal training, but the rudiments of the new theories of circumstantial evidence and the means of comparing epistemic probabilities were not confined to law, to science, and to mathematics: they had entered the wider culture. Without this transition, the tremendous amount of debate over deception in eighteenth-century Britain would not have been possible. Few fakers have ever been caught red-handed by eyewitnesses. Those who engaged in disputes over authenticity therefore knew that they would have to depend not on positive but on circumstantial evidence. They had to know how to marshal facts.

But "facts," insisted William Shaw, "are stubborn things: there is no contending with them but by facts." Many of those who argued over authenticity in the eighteenth century made the same point. "This relation of facts which I have given," Shaw boasted to Macpherson and his partisans, "may be contradicted, but can never be overborne."[47] John Douglas, in another case, likewise asked "that no farther credit may be given to the facts which I shall relate, than as they shall be authenticated by proofs too stubborn to be invalidated by all the sophistry which can be displayed by low cunning when it hath credulity and ignorance to work upon."[48] "I was always open to the Conviction of facts," professed George Chalmers of the Ireland forgeries, "believing that general Reasonings must give way to special Facts."[49] "Truth is secure

---

44   Bentham, *A Treatise on Judicial Evidence*, p. 140.

45   Bentham, *Rationale*, 3:52.

46   Malone, *An Inquiry*, p. 17. Malone quotes Gilbert, p. 5, and Blackstone, 3:368. Margreta de Grazia discusses the way Malone's experience in handling legal documents allowed him to shore up his Shakespeare text in *Shakespeare Verbatim*, esp. pp. 98–104.

47   Shaw, *An Enquiry*, p. 172.

48   John Douglas, *Six Letters*, p. 27.

49   Chalmers to Mackenzie, 14 April 1796, in Rosenbach EL3 f.I65i MS4 vol. 5.

in its own, native Simplicity," writes an anonymous attacker of Elizabeth Canning, "and seeks no other Assistance but plain Facts."[50] Facts are indeed stubborn—but they are often stubborn in more than one way. They refuse to speak for themselves, and therefore demand to be interpreted. And only after people began to think about circumstantial evidence was it possible to put these facts to their best use.

That Gilbert's best evidence rule was rarely, perhaps never, invoked in disputes over authenticity before the middle of the eighteenth century suggests that what may strike us as commonsensical was in fact a genuine discovery, for after Gilbert's work appeared, arguments about circumstantial evidence begin to show up in many surprising places. And this newly discovered principle proved particularly damaging to Macpherson, whose perverse refusal to provide evidence even to those kindly disposed toward him served only to ruin his reputation: by declining to show the world his "originals," whatever their nature, he earned a place in literary history as the most perfidious of forgers.

Samuel Johnson's dismissal of the Ossianic poems in the *Journey to the Western Islands* is well known: "The editor, or author, never could shew the original," he complained. "To revenge reasonable incredulity, by refusing evidence, is a degree of insolence, with which the world is not yet acquainted." Thus his insistence that "It would be easy to shew it if he had it."[51] As he said to Boswell, "Let Mr. Macpherson deposite the manuscript in one of the colleges at Aberdeen.... If he does not take this obvious and easy method, he gives the best reason to doubt."[52] This is an elegant application of Gilbert's best evidence rule, and seems to anticipate Jeremy Bentham's formulation from decades after Johnson's death of the "obvious practical rule, viz. not to receive real evidence in the form of reported real evidence, when, without preponderant inconvenience, it can be had in the form of immediate real evidence."[53] It may seem that Johnson is simply resorting to common sense—if Macpherson had reliable evidence, he would show it—and yet Johnson's comments closely echo the language of contemporary legal treatises, and suggest he was applying cutting-edge legal theory in his debates with the surly Scot. In this way, he gives an instance of how theories of evidence, derived from courtroom practice, had entered the larger culture. As he said about Erse manuscripts, "We have seen none; and we have no reason to believe that there are not men with three heads, but that we have seen none."[54]

---

50 *Truth Triumphant*, p. 6.

51 Johnson, Yale *Works*, 9:118.

52 Boswell, *Life*, 5:95. See also Shaw's *Reply to Mr. Clark*, pp. 54–5, for which Johnson was partly responsible, and Johnson's letter to Boswell of 7 February 1775: "Where are the manuscripts? They can be shown if they exist, but they were never shown. *De non existentibus et non apparentibus*, says our law, *eadem est ratio*. No man has a claim to credit upon his own word, when better evidence, if he had it, may be easily produced" (*Letters*, 2:177). Compare Malone's argument about the supposed full-length portrait of Shakespeare, which the Irelands refused to produce: "Till however that day shall arrive, we may safely regulate our judgments by the old law maxim—*de non apparentibus et de non existentibus eadem est ratio*" (*An Inquiry*, p. 317).

53 Bentham, *Rationale*, 3:34.

54 *Boswell: The Ominous Years*, p. 89.

Johnson's friend William Shaw agreed: "Mr. Macpherson often promised me a sight of [the manuscripts] .... And yet, although he appointed, at least at six different times, a day for showing them to me, and I as often waited upon him, there was always some apology made:—the manuscripts were at his house in the country; or mislaid; or the key lost; or I should see them some other time." He elaborates, offering an analogy to make Macpherson's offense clearer to his audience:

> If a man says he has a gold watch in his pocket, and I deny it; if he has it, is there any thing easier than convincing me by shewing it? But to persist in affirming that he has it, and publishing dissertations to prove it; to rail and abuse all who will not believe him, is an insult on the party, and a "degree of stubborn audacity the world has hitherto been unacquainted with." It is the last subterfuge of guilt.[55]

It is worth noting that this application of the best evidence rule is not really about how to handle evidence, but how to handle its lack. "The absence of evidence," a familiar maxim warns, "is not evidence of absence"—but Gilbert's best evidence rule did, to some degree, authorize the presumption that the one implied the other. Gilbert himself makes the point, for immediately after he states the best evidence rule, he goes on to add the corollary that "less evidence doth create but Opinion and Surmise."[56] As Shaw lectured his Ossianic opponents, "An enquirer after truth, always expects evidence before he gives his assent to a proposition; and ... will never believe as true, upon conjectural and probable evidence, that which facts alone must prove."[57]

Thus, one of the recurring arguments in the charges made against Macpherson was that his refusal to produce evidence for the Ossianic poems' authenticity was itself evidence of their inauthenticity. One is to accept "the utmost Evidence, the Nature of the Fact is capable of," the argument goes, but if a fact can be demonstrated simply through the production of, say, a manuscript, and that manuscript is not forthcoming, one is justified in believing that "the utmost Evidence" has not been produced. Shaw was therefore blunt: "When the proposition to be proved is a fact, and not mere speculation, or matter of opinion, facts alone, not internal evidence, which always give latitude to conjecture and uncertainty on both sides, can be a reasonable proof; and nothing less can procure the assent of the dispassionate and unbiased mind."[58] His long catalogue of Highlanders who should have been able to produce old Erse poetry, but did not, served him as evidence that the poems were not authentic.

Malcolm Laing was also convinced that withholding evidence was itself evidence of guilt. In the Highlands Commission Report of 1805, he speaks of a commonplace book in which Macpherson had written some unpublished poetry. He disingenuously offers Macpherson's supporters the opportunity to prove their case: "Having arraigned Macpherson at the bar of the public, as one of the first literary impostors in modern times, I have imposed an opposite obligation on his friends to vindicate and rescue his memory, if they can, from the imputation of forgery; after which no reason can be

---

55   Shaw, *An Enquiry*, pp. 84–5, 160–161.

56   Gilbert, *The Law of Evidence*, p. 4.

57   Shaw, *An Enquiry*, p. 81.

58   Ibid., pp. 99–100.

assigned for withholding the book, but that it would serve for his conviction."[59] These ostensibly missing papers, whether Macpherson's notebooks or the manuscripts from which he assembled the Ossianic poems, are the issue in many of the Ossianic quarrels, since for many people it seemed that papers were "the utmost Evidence" that could be expected in a literary "trial." The Highlands Commission asked Macpherson's executor "if he had left behind him any of those MSS. particularly those ancient books which the Committee understood he possessed .... after a strict search, no such books could be found, and ... the manuscripts left by Mr Macpherson were not ancient."[60] Macpherson and his supporters often promised to publish the "originals," though nothing that deserved that name was published until "A Specimen of the Original of Temora" appeared, with the second epic, in 1763 (Gaelic versions of the other poems were still unpublished at the time of Macpherson's death in 1796). The defenders of Ossian often pointed to Macpherson's seeming willingness to publish these originals as strong evidence of their authenticity. As early as September 1760, they felt the need to assure readers of *The Gentleman's Magazine*: "As the original *Erse* is intended to be printed, with some future edition of them, it will irrefragably prove their authenticity, which might otherwise be reasonably doubted."[61] Of course "the original *Erse*" did not appear, and the reasonable doubts were still not settled by the time *Fingal* was published. Selections from the epic were printed in *The Gentleman's Magazine* in January 1762—by coincidence in the very issue that first reported on another famous hoax, the Cock Lane Ghost—bearing the note, "It might reasonably be expected, that to put the authenticity of these poems out of question, they should have been printed in the original language with a translation."[62] Readers are meant to infer that the investigator's inability to discover appropriate evidence means such evidence does not exist.

However, the best evidence rule and its corollaries were not limited to the case of Ossian. In his discussion of the Canning affair, Allan Ramsay explicitly reminds his readers of the need for the proper kinds of circumstantial evidence. Under the traditional rules, he says, even an innocent defendant must be prosecuted if two witnesses agree in their story, no matter how improbable their testimony may be. "To prevent this absurd method of proceeding, and the cruel consequences attending it," he says, "it is incumbent on the learned, who know the rules of probability, to divulge all those rules to the public, and especially to explain more fully, and enforce the principle with which I set out in the beginning of this letter, *that no evidence is to be received in proof of any fact, unless its weight is strictly conformable to the improbability of the fact it means to prove.*"[63] And the author of the *Genuine and Impartial Memoirs of Elizabeth Canning* identifies one of the sources of his probabilistic reasoning in one of Gilbert's most important sources: "These are, as near as I can remember, Mr. *Locke*'s Grounds of Probability. Let us examine how far this Tale coincides with them.—Is it agreeable to common Observation that Two

---

59 Mackenzie, *Report*, p. 87.

60 Mackenzie, *Report*, p. 79.

61 *Gentleman's Magazine* 30 (Sept. 1760): 407.

62 *Gentleman's Magazine* 32 (Jan. 1762): 9.

63 Ramsay, *A Letter to the Right Honourable the Earl of* ——, p. 56.

Footpads should be at the Trouble of half-stripping, in *Moorfields*, a Person whom they intended to make their Companion for ten Miles, when the same Robbery might have been committed with more Ease and Security to themselves at the End of their Journey?" And he clearly has something like Gilbert's principle in mind when he takes up the case of the missing girl: "when the Truth of any Matter is ascertained by all the Evidence it is capable of, and we have greater Reason to believe that it is, than that it is not; this alone ought to serve for Conviction." The author's "Conviction" here means "belief," but he was well aware it also meant criminal prosecution. The author here is exercising a surprising irony, however; this passage is disingenuous. The *Genuine and Impartial Memoirs* are presented as a series of letters, written as the Canning affair unfolded, and he presents his belief in Canning's story at the beginning, only to see it erode as more evidence comes out—in other words, the truth of the matter was *not* yet ascertained by all the evidence it was capable of. And the language of epistemic probability shows up in the same work, where the author demands, "what is commonly understood by the Probability of any Relation, but that its constituent Parts and Circumstances shall be consistent with one another, and not incongruous to general Observation, Knowledge, and Experience."[64]

All of the discussions of evidence in this chapter have addressed only the need for the best possible circumstantial evidence, along with the ways in which new conceptions of circumstantial evidence combined with the language of aleatory mathematical probability to make it possible to balance likelihoods. Nowhere, however, has this chapter addressed what should be done with this evidence once it is collected—what, in other words, might lead one to accept or reject a conclusion based on the evidence. But the practical definition of probability offered in the *Genuine and Impartial Memoirs* suggests most important criterion for addressing the value of evidence: its consistency. And the author usefully distinguishes the two kinds of consistency which, while often applied together, can be productively considered separately. The first, internal consistency—the notion "that its constituent Parts and Circumstances shall be consistent with one another"—is the subject of the next chapter. The latter, external consistency—the notion that it is "not incongruous to general Observation, Knowledge, and Experience"—will be the subject of Chapter 5.

---

64 *Genuine and Impartial Memoirs of Elizabeth Canning*, pp. 49, 35, 48.

Chapter 4

Truth Is Uniform

Francis Webb, one of the most prominent defenders of the Ireland Shakespeare papers, put it well, albeit in a losing cause: "When ten thousand rays, all darting from one great Circle, point directly to the same Centre; they illuminate the mighty Round with the steady beams of Truth.—Truth is uniform, simple, One—Error, multiform, perplext, infinite."[1] Reality, he insisted, is always consistent with itself, and inconsistency is a sure sign of error. Even as he was inadvertently lending support to one of the most audacious literary impostures of the century, he was spelling out one of the most reliable means of spotting fakery.

Falsum in Uno

Among the most common eighteenth-century criteria of authenticity was consistency —a fine principle, at least in theory. To base a case on consistency is to draw implicitly on the principle of non-contradiction, formulated by Aristotle and a cornerstone of subsequent Western philosophical thought. This principle holds that no statement can be both true and false: as it is often expressed in formal logic, for any proposition P, $\neg (P \wedge \neg P)$.[2] An important corollary is that no true statement can contradict any other true statement, since contraries cannot both be true. Aristotle's works, especially the *Metaphysics*, were little read in eighteenth-century Britain, but the Aristotelian principle was widely known at second hand. Samuel Clarke presents it clearly in a sermon: "every Doctrine of Truth," he writes, "is consistent both with *itself*, and with every *other* Truth; and stands clear of Objections, equally on *All* sides."[3] William Adams makes the same case: "Truth," he said in 1770, "is always uniform, and every truth consistent with every other. In other words, whatever contradicts a known truth must be false."[4] Eighteenth-century critics knew this principle well, and the criterion of consistency lies at the heart of many discussions of authenticity.

Consistency can take two forms, internal and external. An account is internally consistent when it never contradicts itself; it is externally consistent when it does not contradict our knowledge of the larger world that produced it. In most investigations of fraud, tests of both internal and external consistency are used in tandem, but it is possible, and sometimes necessary, to treat the two separately. Sometimes internal

---

1   Webb to Samuel Ireland, 30 June 1795, in BL Add. MS 30346, fol. 100[r].

2   For a recent and thorough discussion of the philosophical background, as well as a consideration of the limits of the principle, see Priest, Beall, and Armour-Garb, *The Law of Non-Contradiction*.

3   Clarke, *Sermons*, 2:228.

4   Adams, *A Test of True and False Doctrines*, p. 14.

inconsistencies can be so striking that further tests are considered unnecessary. Richard Simon was able to identify many inconsistencies in the text of the Hebrew Bible without reference to history, archeology, or any other field: because Moses could not be both alive and dead at the same time, he could not have been the author of the passages in the Pentateuch that narrate his own death. There is no need to turn to historical or archeological evidence when the internal evidence is so compelling. Thomas Warton thought he had attained a similar degree of certainty in investigating the Rowleian poems: "The internal proofs," he writes, "had always appeared to me so convincing against the probability of the existence of that pretended antient poet, as to supersede the expediency of collecting facts, and of attending to any external arguments."[5] In other cases it is not desirable but necessary to rely entirely on internal evidence, as when reliable external evidence is wanting. The surest way to test the authenticity of Psalmanazar's ethnographic claims in his *Description of Formosa*, for example, would simply be to travel to Formosa: one could see whether Formosans wore the clothes, spoke the language, and engaged in the rituals described in that book. In 1704, though, a visit to Formosa was anything but simple; even finding a witness who had visited the country—at least one whose claims were as plausible as Psalmanazar's—was all but impossible.

Tests for internal consistency proceed on the assumption that every true narrative is consistent with itself, and that any unexplained inconsistency disqualifies it from being genuine. Steven Shapin refers to Locke's advice—one should assess testimony according to "the Consistency of the Parts, and Circumstances of the Relation"—and goes on to explain the implications:

> Here the maxim might be formulated: "Inspect for contradiction or inconsistency the internal and external relations of testimony, and, if you find any such problems, take these as an indication that the testimony may be untrue."… [Montaigne offered this] pragmatic counsel against lying: the truth was one, lies were many, and he who lied might reliably be found out through discrepancies in his utterances. A man might say that he had seen a mermaid near Newfoundland and on another occasion say that he had seen it near Iceland.[6]

Most avid detectors in eighteenth-century Britain knew how to use these tests, latching on to inconsistencies in their rivals' accounts and insisting that they disproved the authenticity of the whole. It was a well-known legal principle that someone convicted of lying before was likely to lie again; Geoffrey Gilbert therefore excluded certain classes of people from testifying: "there are several Crimes that so blemish, that the Party is ever afterwards unfit to be a Witness, as Treason, or Felony, and every *Crimen falsi*, as Perjury, Forgery, and the like."[7] The same logic was widely applied, even extended, in contemporary discussions of authenticity.

This means that there was a kind of economy of detection: one falsehood was considered to be enough to disprove the lot. This principle had been embedded in a

---

5   Warton, *An Enquiry*, p. 4.

6   Shapin, *A Social History of Truth*, p. 215. The passage from Locke comes from *An Essay concerning Human Understanding*, p. 656 (4.15.4).

7   Gilbert, *The Law of Evidence*, p. 142.

civil law maxim, and was later picked up in common law: "*Falsum in uno, falsum in omnibus*"; an account that can be shown to be false in any detail can be assumed to be false as a whole.[8] The implication for those who sought to discredit a story, whether criminal prosecutors or detectors of literary deceit, is obvious: finding any falsehood in an account is enough to discredit the whole. A questioned account must be able to withstand any sort of examination, and pass every reasonable test. No number of truths or consistencies adduced by the supporters of a document can ever definitively prove it genuine, but a single inconsistency can disqualify it. As Otto Kurz puts it, "Each detected forgery is apt to betray a whole group. Fakes hunt in packs."[9]

In strict logic, *falsum in uno* does not prove *falsum in omnibus*. There is no reason a habitual perjurer may not tell the truth on occasion: as Jeremy Bentham points out, "Supposing the general habit of mendacity ... ever so clearly established; the judge should not regard the inference from such general mendacity to mendacity in the individual case in question ... as being by any means conclusive."[10] The same principle applies to fakes: even if we discover one of Macpherson's poems or Ireland's letters has a modern origin, it does not follow necessarily that all of them must be modern. Still, it produces a strong presumption against the forger: a single false document causes us to become far more critical of the authenticity of the others bundled with it. Occam's Razor comes into play here: we are being asked to believe that, in discovering a corpus of genuine texts, the discoverer produced some imitations and introduced them among the genuine ones; in telling her story of her abduction, Canning was honest about most of the details but did falsify a few. Few are willing to entertain such a probability, and we usually allow a single falsehood, if it cannot be attributed to innocent misunderstanding, to discredit an entire narrative.

And so we see many investigators of fraud asserting that a single inconsistency is enough to disqualify an entire narrative. Edmond Malone makes this sort of argument, in his characteristically acerbic manner, when he notes two inconsistent dates in the Shakespearean documents published by the Irelands. He points to "The indorsement on the deed now before us—'20th Maye 9th: Iam^s.'" But "the deed itself has already informed us that it was made on the 'twentieth day of Maye in the *eyghth* yeare' of King James." He never bothers to investigate whether the eighth or ninth year of James's reign is the more plausible date for the deed—in other words, he cannot be bothered to search for external evidence. The internal evidence is on its own enough to render the document invalid: "When two such *great authorities* differ," he asks disingenuously, "to which of them are we to give credit? I conceive, in the

---

8   The maxim also commonly appears with the masculine *falsus* for the neuter *falsum*. The more literary often preferred a Virgilian tag to the same effect: "accipe nunc Danaum insidias et crimine ab uno/disce omnes"—"Now listen to the deceptions of the Danaans, and from one crime learn about all of them" (Virgil, *Aeneid*, 2.65–6, in *Opera*). Malone applies "the old adage—*crimine ab uno disce omnes*" against Ireland (*An Inquiry*, p. 259).

9   Kurz, *Fakes*, p. 17.

10   Bentham, *Rationale*, 3:205–6.

present instance it will be safest to believe *neither*."[11] Edward Davies too spotted some curious shifts in diction in the preface to the Ossianic poems—"He styles himself, indifferently, the *author*, the *writer*, and the *translator*"[12]—and regarded them as evidence that Macpherson had no consistent account of his relationship to the poems he published. Davies went on to spot hundreds of variants between the 1778 and 1807 editions of the supposed Gaelic "originals," suggesting the editor-*cum*-author-*cum*-translator was tinkering with his material: he found such changes "not the work of the *file*, but of the *forge*."[13]

Giving Verisimilitude to His Fictions

Davies was able to make such discoveries because he looked carefully at the texts—he immersed himself in details in order to spot inconsistencies. All but the most incompetent fakers will create a story that is superficially consistent, but the investigators of fraud often proceed on the assumption that any sufficiently rich collection of details is likely to reveal inconsistencies. Some detectors were convinced that the lack of details was itself evidence of deceit. Samuel Johnson knew that reality is seldom neat, and that a certain amount of messiness lends credibility to an account—one that seems too tidy is less likely to be believed. "Round numbers," for instance, "are seldom exact." On another occasion he went further still: "Round numbers, said he, are always false."[14] Investigators of fraud often kept principles like this in mind. In his *Remarks on the History of Scotland* (1773), for example, David Dalrymple advises would-be detectors that a lack of circumstantial details may be a sign of fraud: he should be suspicious "When the writer limits himself

---

11   Malone, *An Inquiry*, pp. 264–5. Ireland himself admitted as much, though he would never give credit to his arch-enemy Malone. Before he began on the Shakespearean papers, he forged a dedicatory letter to Queen Elizabeth and showed it to a bookbinder who supplied him with the ink he used throughout the impostures. When his ink ran out he had to return to the same bookbinder, thus risking all: "I scarcely need remark," he wrote in 1805, "that the circumstance of the dedicatory letter to queen Elizabeth, with the having twice procured the same liquid preparation, would in themselves have been quite sufficient to overturn the whole Shaksperian mass, and display to the world the naked truth" (*Confessions*, p. 41).

12   Davies, *The Claims of Ossian*, pp. 11–12. William Shaw noticed the same thing: "Mr. Macpherson, ready to snatch those laurels that might best adorn his brow, sometimes insinuated he was the author" (Shaw, *An Enquiry*, p. 10). Thomas Warton catches Chatterton in the same mistake: "The attentive reader will also discern, that our poet sometimes forgets his assumed character, and does not always act his part with consistency" (*The History of English Poetry*, 2:155).

13   Davies, *The Claims of Ossian*, pp. 302–3, 313.

14   Johnson, Yale *Works*, 9:126; Hill, ed., *Johnsonian Miscellanies*, 2:2. The principle may well have played out in at least one real-life situation. It is said that in 1856, when the British India Survey of Mt. Everest was undertaken by Andrew Waugh for the Royal Geographic Society, his team arrived at a measurement of exactly 29,000 feet. Fearing that people would interpret it as a rough estimate, Waugh falsified the result, reporting it as 29,002 feet: close enough to the real answer, but seemingly much more precise, and therefore more plausible. It was more circumstantial, and therefore less likely to be faked.

to general topics, although his subject, and the passions and situation of the person whom he represents, naturally lead into a detail of circumstances."[15] Authentic narratives, Johnson and Dalrymple argued, are filled with details, and the more details the liar provides, the more chances the detector has to catch him out. "If a lie is made circumstantial," Allan Ramsay explains, "with the names and descriptions of persons, places, dates, and other furniture, it will be plausible and gain immediate credit; but then every one of those circumstances, which at first gave it authority, may administer means of tracing, and discovering its falshood."[16]

The knowledge that helped the detectors to spot fakes, though, also helped the fakers to elude detection, for if a lack of detail was evidence of deception, then the presence of circumstantial details, even false ones, could give the illusion of authenticity. So familiar was this principle that it became the subject of satirical fun. In Richard Brinsley Sheridan's *School for Scandal*, for example, Crabtree and his nephew, Sir Benjamin Backbite, trade accounts of a duel that never happened. In Sir Benjamin's version it was a fight with swords; in Crabtree's version, it was a gunfight in which "the Ball struck against a little Bronze Pliny that stood over the chimney piece—grazed out of the window at a right angle—and wounded the Postman, who was just coming to the Door with a double letter from Northamptonshire." Sir Benjamin, clearly bested, grudgingly admits, "My Unkle's account is more circumstantial I must confess."[17] The more concrete and specific the details, the less likely they seem to have been invented.

Real-life liars learned Crabtree's lesson: the "more circumstantial" the account, the more verisimilar. They therefore began manufacturing endless details that supposedly could not be invented. Consider the case of John Carleton, who in 1663 published his sad narrative about being duped by a "Grand Impostor, Late a Pretended Germane-Lady." This confidence trickster claimed to be a "Person of honour lately come out of *Germany*," whose tales of her sad past were enough to win sympathy from all who met her. Carleton admits to some suspicions when he began courting her: "indeed I wondered she could speak English so well, and I would ask her how she came to learn it, she answered, that her *Governess being an English Lady, she would speak English to her.*" This ability to provide quick answers to all his questions put his mind at ease: "Thus would she answer all objections as readily as you could ask her." The circumstantiality of her answers was enough to outweigh all the suspicions prompted by the gaps in her story: "in answering one, she would traverse over so much, and such a seeming real story, that she would satisfie me in very many points, that my private suspitions thought to propose to her; by which freeness of hers to declare her self, she ... procured of me a greater beleife to what she said."[18] She was an impostor, but her quick invention took her far.

Another impostor used the same tricks 40 years later: "when any question has been started on a sudden," admits George Psalmanazar, "about matters I was ever so unprepared for, I seldom found myself at a loss for a quick answer, which, if

15   Dalrymple, *Remarks on the History of Scotland*, p. 209.
16   Ramsay, *A Letter to the Right Honourable the Earl of*——, pp. 11–12.
17   Sheridan, *The School for Scandal*, in *Dramatic Works*, 1:429 (act 5, scene 2).
18   Carleton, *The Ultimum Vale of John Carleton*, title page, pp. 2, 6, 10.

satisfactory, I stored up in my retentive memory."[19] He too managed to conquer most doubts in his audience with his thick description of a culture, and especially its language, which William W. Appleton memorably describes as "a Formosan jabberwocky."[20] Nonsensical the language may have been, but the circumstantial richness of its details managed to convince a great many people. Susan Stewart notes some of the effects which allowed Psalmanazar to convince much of the world:

> The con man's rule, "give 'em what they want," became for Psalmanazar a way of structuring an imaginary social whole.... Two aspects of this ethnography immediately present themselves as paramount. First, there is the reproduction of a system of differences—that is, an immediately apprehensible and hence comparable system of categories of the social: manners, gestures, means of transport, architecture, costumes, ritual, and so on. Such categories then internalize the situation of difference.... And second, there is an internal consistency whose cumulative effect will be that of a rational necessity.... Psalmanazar's brilliant move was to forge an entire social world.... If this was the dream of Enlightenment reason, it was also the dream of Enlightenment authorship: to usher in whatever is necessary to make the world, as a textual whole, cohere.[21]

K. K. Ruthven discusses the way these "authenticity-effects" can be produced by circumstantial evidence:

> "inconsequential" episodes that would be edited out of a text by any self-consciously literary author who had internalised that functionalist and ultimately Aristotelian economy of writing which promotes the importance of carefully concatenated episodes in the cumulative development of a plot. Another authenticatory device is ... vivid but "irrelevant" details—"authentication by density," as Taylor calls this technique apropos Chatterton—which are frowned upon in a functionalist aesthetic committed to eliminating superfluities.... In October 1726 Mary Toft did not claim merely to have given birth to a rabbit ... instead, she gave birth to *seventeen* rabbits.[22]

This passage, though, is only partly about Chatterton and Toft: Ruthven's real concern is with the "authenticity-effects" of Daniel Defoe, who learned the same lesson that the forgers did—a dense collection of circumstantial details lends an air of truth to any narrative. Alexander Welsh makes a similar point, linking the authenticating function of rich details to the passion for detail evident in so many eighteenth-century novels: "Paradoxically, the thesis that circumstantial evidence could not be falsified was of the most lasting use to inveterate falsifiers.... Novelists

---

19　Psalmanazar, *Memoirs*, p. 138.

20　Appleton, *A Cycle of Cathay*, p. 130.

21　Stewart, *Crimes of Writing*, pp. 41–2, 55. James Beattie noted in 1786 that Psalmanazar's imagined language did much to make his story plausible: he "was in no danger of detection; his island being little known, and at a great distance. He contrived a probable tale; and, to make it the more probable, he did what he knew nobody would suspect him of having done, because no one man had ever done so before,—he invented a new language" (Beattie, *Evidences of the Christian Religion*, 1:133). For the best modern scholarly consideration of Psalmanazar's language, see Thomas A. Reisner, "Graphic Affinities" and "'Tongue with a Tang.'"

22　Ruthven, *Faking Literature*, p. 149.

... demonstrated that a narrative so connected was 'within the reach and compass of human abilities.'"[23] Many works of fiction advertised themselves as true stories, and backed up this claim with a dense collection of details. One of the most famous examples is Crusoe's description of the physical remains of the shipwreck: "as for [my comrades], I never saw them afterwards, or any Sign of them, except three of their Hats, one Cap, and two Shoes that were not Fellows."[24] Ian Watt puts it well: "Defoe would seem to be the first of our writers who visualised the whole of his narrative as though it occurred in an actual physical environment."[25]

Watt was not the first to notice Defoe's minute attention to authenticating detail; it was a commonplace of Defoe criticism from the beginning. In 1892, Leslie Stephen wrote about "De Foe's powers as a liar," noting that "he had the most marvellous power ever known of giving verisimilitude to his fictions; or, in other words, he had the most amazing talent on record for telling lies."[26] A half-century before that, in 1841, Thomas De Quincey pointed out that Defoe's style created a much more intense experience of the physical world than other authors, for "De Foe is the only author known who has so plausibly circumstantiated his false historical records as to make them pass for genuine, even with literary men and critics." This notion of "plausible circumstantiation" is a powerful one. "How," asks De Quincey, "did he accomplish so difficult an end?" His answer shows he understands the power of trivia to lend an air of authenticity:

> Simply by inventing such little circumstantiations of any character or incident as seem, by the apparent inertness of effect, to verify themselves; for, where the reader is told that such a person was the posthumous son of a tanner, that his mother married afterwards a Presbyterian schoolmaster, who gave him a smattering of Latin, but, the schoolmaster dying of the plague, that he was compelled at sixteen to enlist for bread—in all this, as there is nothing at all amusing, we conclude that the author could have no reason to detain us with such particulars but simply because they were true. To invent, when nothing at all is gained by inventing, there seems no imaginable temptation. It never occurs to us that this very construction of the case, this very inference from such neutral details, was precisely the object which De Foe had in view—was the very thing which he counted on, and by which he meant to profit.[27]

Do I Contradict Myself?

Because liars, both innocent and culpable—both novelists and fakers—learned to fabricate details that produced the illusion of verisimilitude, investigators of hoaxes usually had to comb through the evidence in search of contradictions. The method, though, was not always as reliable as it should have been. Strict logic holds that an inconsistency in an account means the account cannot be true: the law of non-contradiction tells us a proposition cannot be both true and false. Inconsistency

---

23 Welsh, *Strong Representations*, p. 41.
24 Defoe, *Robinson Crusoe*, p. 46.
25 Watt, *The Rise of the Novel*, p. 26.
26 Stephen, *Hours in a Library*, 1:3.
27 De Quincey, "Homer and the Homeridae," in *Collected Writings*; 6:84–5.

seems, therefore, a foolproof test for fakery. In practice, though, it is not always conclusive, because it is too easy to misapply the strict logic and to ignore shaky unstated assumptions in critical enthymemes. In his attacks on Macpherson, Edward Davies is often spot-on, but some of his shafts miss their target. When he drifts from verbal to other sorts of internal evidence, his accusations against Ossian become less convincing. Davies complains that Macpherson's "characters ... do not appear to have been immediately drawn from real life," and that "He has not informed our judgments, with the colouring of history, but amused our fancy with that of poetry. It follows that the work cannot be ascribed to Ossian."[28] Such accusations claim to invoke no specialized knowledge of the historical or linguistic context—just good old reliable human nature—but the supposedly internal judgments are actually riddled with implicit assumptions about what an age was capable of. And although they often make for stirring rhetoric, they are liable to embarrassing blunders.

Virtually all internal tests, in fact, can be unreliable, and they can sometimes condemn the innocent. In the early days of the "Homeric problem," a favorite sport was attributing portions of the epics to interlopers on the basis of internal contradictions. Sometimes these inconsistencies were factual: in the *Iliad* Hephaestus is married to one of the Graces; in the *Odyssey* he is married to Aphrodite. Sometimes they derived from concerns about character: the Achilles of *Iliad* book 24 seems far more brutal than the Achilles of book 22. Some episodes—the tenth book of the *Iliad* was the most common example—lacked the sort of plotting that marked the rest of the epics. And sometimes Homer simply did not sound like Homer: "After *Od.* 4.620," writes F. A. Wolf in 1795, "there follow four verses, extraordinarily harsh in the unusualness and ambiguity of their diction and entirely devoid of the Homeric quality."[29] To many, it was evident that the same author could not have produced all these passages—something must have happened to Homer's authentic text. In the nineteenth century, such concerns about corruption thrived, sometimes growing into paranoid fantasies. The analysts rejected passage after passage from the Homeric canon until, by the end of the century, very little of Homer was left intact. Only in the twentieth century did Milman Parry and Albert Lord demonstrate convincingly that such seeming contradictions are inherent in oral composition. The standards of coherence we expect in print or even manuscript do not always apply.

Even in a more conventionally literate culture, it does not always follow that inconsistencies render a text inauthentic. Not all apparent contradictions, for example, are necessarily contradictions. The question "How many children had Lady Macbeth?" has provoked irritated eye-rolling since L. C. Knights twitted A. C. Bradley with it in 1933; critic Michael D. Bristol calls it "a byword for asinine literal-mindedness."[30] The question depends on an apparent contradiction in Shakespeare's play—Lady Macbeth insists "I have given suck" (1.7.54), whereas Macduff, seeming to refer to Macbeth, says "He has no children" (4.3.216)—but many explanations are possible. Perhaps Lady Macbeth had a first husband; perhaps

---

28   Davies, *The Claims of Ossian*, pp. 24, 35.

29   Wolf, *Prolegomena*, pp. 128–9.

30   L. C. Knights, *How Many Children Had Lady Macbeth?*; Bristol, "How Many Children Did She Have?" p. 18.

a child died; perhaps the antecedent to Macduff's "He" is not Macbeth at all. More to the point, such questions may not even be worth asking: perhaps Shakespeare simply forgot a detail. Who, after all, has not contradicted him- or herself? If on page 95 of this book I contradict page 37, it does not follow that the book is not my own; it means only that I wrote too hastily, or that I am not entirely in control of my meaning. When confronted with such inconsistencies, our documents may well give a Whitmanesque reply: "Do I contradict myself?/Very well then I contradict myself,/(I am large, I contain multitudes)." As Horace Walpole wrote to Mason in 1772, "We live in an age of contradictions."[31]

Using apparent internal inconsistencies to spot a fake is risky enough; using apparent internal consistency to verify something as authentic is riskier still. Hannah More of Bristol wrote to George Catcott, "In Miss Hannah More's *humble Opinion*, the Authenticity of Rowley's Poems is so clear from the *Internal Evidence alone*, that it stands in need of no other Proof."[32] And the dispute over the *Epistles of Phalaris* provides a telling example of seemingly internal evidence used improperly to authenticate a spurious document. Sir William Temple offered a now-famous defense of their antiquity and authenticity:

> I know several Learned men (or that usually pass for such, under the name of Criticks) have not esteemed them Genuine.... But I think he must have little skill in Painting that cannot find out this to be an Original; such diversity of passions upon such variety of actions and passages of Life and Government, such Freedom of Thought, such Boldness of Expression, such Bounty to his Friends, such Scorn of his Enemies, such Honour of Learned men, such Esteem of good, such Knowledge of Life, such Contempt of Death, with such Fierceness of Nature and Cruelty of Revenge, could never be represented but by him that possest them.[33]

Temple is clear about his distaste for modern advances in philology: "I know not what to make of it.... he must be a Conjurer that can make these Moderns with their Comments, and Glossaries, and Annotations, more learned than the Authors themselves in their own Languages."[34] There is no need to draw on all the abstruse arcana of *Altertumswissenschaft*; it is enough for a well-read gentleman to sit down with the work open before him, and common sense will show him the way. The danger is that common sense can be downright wrong. Temple, despite his pride in being above the plodding pedantry of fact-obsessed antiquaries, turned out to be entirely misguided in his judgment of Phalaris, as Richard Bentley delighted to point out.

Bentley was a virtuoso in the use of circumstantial detail: his *Dissertation upon the Epistles of Phalaris* (1699) takes 549 pages to answer a much shorter work, and every page is filled with notices of inconsistencies in the supposed *Epistles*. Bentley's adversary had the misfortune to suggest an untenable emendation, reading

---

31 Whitman, *Song of Myself*, lines 1324–6, in *Leaves of Grass*, p. 88; Walpole, *Correspondence*, 29:71.

32 Hannah More to Catcott, 17 March 1777, in BL Add. MS 47865, fol. 29[r].

33 Temple, *The Epistles of Phalaris*, sig. A1[r].

34 Temple, *Miscellanea, The Third Part*, p. 256.

"*Heraclean* or *Herculean* Cups instead of Thericlean."[35] Bentley will not hear of it. "I won't contend with him about the unreasonable Licence he takes in changing a plain Reading against the Authority of three MSS, and the whole set of Editions," he explains—but contend he does, and for dozens of pages on the "Thericlean cups" alone, backed up by citations to Pliny, Theophrastus, Hesychius, Eubulus, Aristophanes, Pamphilus, Athenaeus, Casaubon, Julius Pollux, Plutarch, Clement of Alexandria, and many others. And yet Bentley is not always concerned with pointing out the ways in which the *Epistles* of Phalaris contradict other classical texts; instead he is often content to point out that the *Epistles* are sometimes inconsistent with themselves. "What an inconsistency is there between the LI and LXIX Epistles?" he asks. "In the former he declares his immortal hatred to one *Python*," who poisoned his wife. "But in the LXIX Epist. we have her alive again."[36]

Bentley's tone is often petulant and always ostentatious. Every objection is met with dozens of details; Bentley buries his adversary in an avalanche of responses from which no one could hope to emerge. In criticizing his enemies' handling of details, he shows himself to be a master of detail—thereby defeating one set of circumstantial details with another. To the casual reader it does not even matter whether the details are correct—their sheer volume does much of the rhetorical work. In resorting to this sort of overkill Bentley may have harmed his reputation as a gentleman—he was berated, "Pedantry in the Pen, is what Clownishness is in Conversation; it is *Written Ill-breeding*"[37]—but Bentley left little doubt among learned readers that his argument was superior to Boyle's, Atterbury's, and Temple's.

Even more proficient at using details—and maybe even more petulant and ostentatious—was Bentley's intellectual heir, Edmond Malone. Sir James Prior, Malone's nineteenth-century biographer, notes, "Of the internal evidence he was perhaps the most complete master then living," and it seems a fair estimate. No investigator of forgery was more adept at piling detail on detail. There are hints of this technique in his brief investigation of Chatterton, but he truly shines in *An Inquiry into the Authenticity of Certain Miscellaneous Papers*, his 400-page exposé of Ireland's Shakespeare forgeries. For Malone, too much is never enough. "Nothing," said Prior of the *Inquiry*, "can be more complete than the exposure. Not a point is neglected, not one remains doubtful."[38] Critics found his obvious delight in amassing evidence impolite and ungentlemanly: as John Byng wrote to Samuel Ireland, Malone's "Conduct, all Must Disapprove,—as most Malevolent, mean, and Mischievous."[39] Malone, though, was unapologetic. "I cannot think that I was too copious in accumulating proofs of the forgery," he wrote to Charlemont, "for my business was to make a book that would live; and if I had omitted any proof,

---

35   That is, not the textus receptus of ποτηρίων Θηρικλείων but ποτηρίων θ' Ἡρακλειων: see Bentley, *Dissertation*, p. 113. He was answering *Dr. Bentley's Dissertations on the Epistles of Phalaris*, which bore Boyle's name on the title page but was largely ghostwritten by Francis Atterbury.

36   Bentley, *Dissertation*, p. 482.

37   Boyle, *Dr. Bentley's Dissertations*, p. 93.

38   Prior, *The Life of Edmond Malone*, pp. 222, 224.

39   Byng to Samuel Ireland, 5 April 1796, in BL Add. MS 30348, fol. 179ʳ.

Steevens, or some other kind friend, would have immediately pointed it out, and shewn how very superficial and short-sighted I was."[40]

Thickening detail is one of Malone's favorite means of claiming both authority and verisimilitude. In his attempt to date the construction of the Globe, he pauses to comment on another theatre: "The Rose Theatre," he tells us, "of which the total cost was 103l. 2s. 7d., was built by Mr. Philip Henslowe in 1592, and opened by him in that year, as appears from his theatrical Register now before me." Such information does nothing to fix the date of the Globe. By reckoning amounts to the penny, however, it allows Malone to portray himself as a master of detail, thoroughly versed in the theatrical history of the era, and the possessor of rare works on the history of the stage ("his theatrical Register now before me"). And if one detail is good and two details are better, dozens must be better still. In trying to demonstrate that some of Ireland's spellings were unattested, he resolves "to produce a few specimens of orthography from the time of Chaucer to near the end of the sixteenth century … out of some hundred books of that period, with which I am surrounded" (again portraying himself as a well-equipped scholar).[41] These "few specimens" turn into an anthology of fifteenth- and sixteenth-century literature stretching to 34 pages. And even 34 pages is not enough detail for some of his assaults. Perhaps the most extreme example of Malone's fondness for breaking butterflies on a wheel is his exposure of Ireland's forgery of Elizabeth's letter to Shakespeare. The letter itself runs to just 82 words; Malone's dissection of it runs to 90 pages and one fold-out engraved plate.

A Silly Young Man

The task facing the detectors was a difficult one, for the fakers were often well schooled by fiction. They had learned that a rich selection of circumstantial details gave the illusion of authenticity. As historian G. Kitson Clark observes, "A forgery whose success must depend on the faking of a large number of documents, or a very long document, is less likely to have been perpetrated than one which would only need the faking of a single document or a short one."[42] The Committee of the Highland Society made essentially the same point nearly two centuries earlier when it admitted it "does not recollect any instance of a fabrication in a foreign language, or in a language supposed to be that of an ancient period, where, upon an accurate examination, internal proofs of the forgery have not been discovered in the very language alone in which the forgery was attempted to be conveyed"[43]— an uncommonly prolix way of saying that no one is smart enough to pull off an extended forgery in an unfamiliar language. This led many of the fakers' defenders

---

40 Malone to Charlemont, 29 July 1796, in Charlemont, *Manuscripts and Correspondence*, 2:276.

41 Malone, *An Inquiry*, pp. 86, 34.

42 Kitson Clark, *The Critical Historian*, p. 71. Kitson Clark shrewdly adds that "It would be a great mistake, however, to underestimate the possible industry and enterprise of forgers, some of their efforts having been very massive indeed."

43 Mackenzie, *Report*, p. 137.

to argue that so much internal consistency could not possibly have been the product of deceit—that only Ossian, or Rowley, or Shakespeare could have written the texts in question. The accused forger, in other words, would not have been capable of carrying out the forgery, and his story must therefore be true.

This produces an odd kind of paradox among the defenders of fakes, in which the accused forger (Macpherson, Chatterton, Ireland) is accused of incompetence, and therefore declared unequal to the task of producing the resulting masterpieces—which leaves only the putative original (Ossian, Rowley, Shakespeare) as the true author. Many critics paid Macpherson the backhanded compliment of supposing him incapable of writing *Fingal* and *Temora*. Anna Seward, for instance, refers to "the weakness" of Macpherson's translation of Homer, which for her

> becomes the strength of our internal evidence, that its author was not responsible for the production of some of the noblest poetry which has been since the world began. We also find a powerful support of its claim upon early time, in that exemption from involuntary adoption of recent phraseology, from which no confessedly modern writer is free.... Powerful also, on the side of its ancientry, is the utter absence of every allusion to arts and sciences, or to agriculture. We scarcely conceive the possibility of imposition thus guarding itself at all these points.[44]

And according to her defender, publishing under the name Philologus, Elizabeth Canning "had not Wit enough, was she sufficiently wicked, to invent such a Story, which would require better Heads than yours or mine."[45] Since Macpherson and Canning were not bright enough to create such brilliant narratives unaided, they must be innocent of imposture, and their accounts must be true.

Thomas Chatterton was the eighteenth century's greatest beneficiary of this sort of logic. The *Gentleman's Magazine* informed readers in 1777 that "when Chatterton gave this fragment to his friend, he was utterly (and ever after continued) unacquainted with any language but his mother-tongue."[46] "I never heard it surmised," writes Jacob Bryant, "that Chatterton was in the least acquainted with the French language: much less with the Latin and Greek. Whence then was it possible for him to have made such an exotic collection?"[47] Thomas James Mathias makes the same argument: "Those who contend that the Poems are a forgery, resolve all objections into the strength and power of Chatterton's genius. I think it should be considered, that it is necessary to distinguish what is extraordinary from what is impossible."[48] Samuel Seyer insisted firmly on this point: "Is it possible," he asked, "that a boy upon leaving a Charity school, without having read any books, should immediately take up the Idea of forming such a complicated forgery as the present.—I do not deny but that a Person might acquire the knowledge necessary for this forgery, the question is, whether Chatt: could." His objections fall into several categories:

---

44   Seward to Scott, 20 June 1806, in Seward, *Letters*, 6:278.

45   "Philologus," *The Inspector Inspected*, p. 26.

46   *Gentleman's Magazine* 47 (Sept. 1777): 413.

47   Bryant, *Observations*, 1:27.

48   Mathias, *An Essay on the Evidence*, p. 91.

He must not only have written the poetry & learned the hands, & executed the forgery, but have acquired a perfect knowledge of Saxon & Norman histories & manners, which the writer of these pieces certainly had. He was besides an idle boy, & I much question whether Bristol could furnish the books. He was besides utterly ignorant of Latin; & had only about a year and a half before he produced his MSS.; & under all these disadvantages is it possible for a boy of 15 to produce such a quantity of forgeries, all which abound with allusions to particulars, & yet have escaped actual detection from so many learned men as have examined.[49]

And one "P.T." wrote to *The Lady's Magazine* in 1784, asking, "Was this young person, when a boy, at the Blue-coat school at Bristol, favoured by CELESTIAL INSPIRATION? if he was, there is an end of the business—if he was not, he did not write the Ballad of *Sir John Baudwin*, or indeed, any of the other poems attributed to *Rowley*. Such a prematurity of genius as was necessary for the production of such poems, and under such circumstances as Chatterton lived, NEVER YET HAD AN EXAMPLE."[50]

Another pathetic adolescent was often exculpated because of his supposed inability to write works of genius: William Henry Ireland offers the most extreme example of a defense resting on the supposed incompetence of the suspected forger. Ireland's father never thought much of him; we hear the result of years of hostility in Ireland's forged letter from "H," the ostensible owner of the papers, to his own father: "He [W. H. Ireland] tells me [the fictional H] he is in general look'd upon as a young man that scarce knows how to write a good Letter ... he often told me his blood boils a little when he is stiled a silly young man."[51] The father never gave up his low opinion of the "silly young man," and died convinced his son was innocent—not because of his honesty but because of his lack of talent. Even after Ireland's first public confession in the *Authentic Account*, his father refused to believe him capable of the forgeries. The young man's late letter to his father makes an impassioned plea for recognition: "If the writer of the papers ... shows any spark of Genius and deserves honour *I Sir YOUR Son* am that person."[52] And yet, two days later, Samuel declared his conviction that his son's confession was "Prompted ... by Vanity," because "not any of his Friends have ever discovered the least trait of *Literary Genius* in his Character." He concludes, "I who know his Talent for Romancing so well, can never credit the report."[53] Three weeks later, he wrote again to Talbot: "he has publicly avowed himself author of all the papers, deeds &c., to wch I give no credit not even to a Syllable—it is his Vanity, that has urged him to this."[54] Even after young Ireland wrote a letter to his father in Shakespeare's hand dated "No 24 1796," Samuel "told him I neither did, nor would believe him to be the author of the papers, till he gave specimens of his abilities equal to what I had in my possession."[55] This is especially

49 Seyer, *Mr. Seyer's MSS*, Bristol Central Library MS B4533, facing fol. 119.
50 *The Lady's Magazine* 15 (Feb. 1784): 62.
51 "H" [i.e., W. H. Ireland] to Samuel Ireland, 25 July 1795, in BL Add. MS 30346, fol. 54^v.
52 W. H. Ireland to Samuel Ireland, 14 June 1796, in BL Add. MS 30346, fol. 243^r.
53 Samuel Ireland to Montague Talbot, 16 June 1796, in BL Add. MS 30346, fols. 250^r–v.
54 Samuel Ireland to Montague Talbot, 5 July 1796, in BL Add. MS 30346, fol. 264^v.
55 BL Add. MS 30346, fols. 304^r, 312^r.

revealing, for it shows Samuel's preconceptions about his son's abilities completely overriding the immediate evidence of his senses. The facts did not fit the theory, and the facts must therefore be rejected.

The spectacle of the father's refusing to believe the son's confession—even that his son was capable of writing the confession itself—may be the most pathetic example on record of a plea of innocence based on incompetence. But it was not Samuel Ireland alone who believed his son was incapable of creating the Shakespeare papers, and it was not William Henry Ireland's extraordinary incompetence that tipped off others. For many inquirers, no one—certainly no modern—could have written the Shakespearean documents. For Webb, the Shakespearean papers are "attended with such minutiæ of Circumstances, Subjects, & Characters, which all the Art, Cunning, & even Wisdom, of Man united, could not have possibly devised, or invented."[56] And Henry Mackenzie, in a letter to George Chalmers, confessed that he "cannot believe that any Man … is capable of passing a Forgery of such Magnitude as that of an entire Tragedy on the Critical World."[57] So much internal consistency, the argument went, could not emerge from a fraud.

Shakspeare's, & Shakspeare's *Only*

It was not merely "an entire Tragedy," though, that Ireland claimed to have written: it was an entire tragedy by *Shakespeare*, whose position at the head of the English canon was firmly established by the 1790s. The Bard was being recognized not merely as a great author, but as an author beyond compare. As Webb wrote to Samuel Ireland, "All great & eminent Geniuses have their characteristic peculiarities, & originality of character, which not only *distinguish* them from *all others*, but *make* them *what they are*. These none can rival, none successfully imitate. Of all Men & Poets perhaps Shakspear had the most of these. He was a peculiar Being—a unique—he stood alone. To imitate him, so as to pass the deceit upon the World, were impossible."[58] The belief that Shakespeare was inimitable shows up in many of the defenses of the Shakespeare papers. *Vortigern*, Francis Webb insisted, "must be Shakspeare's, & Shakspeare's *only*. It either comes from his pen, or from Heaven: For two were never cast from his peculiar Mould. This is a proof of such a Nature, that without arrogance, presumption, or figure, We may truly say the authentic Seal of Heaven is stampt thereon."[59] And Samuel Ireland noted of Shakespearean Profession of Faith, "This piece of writing has been generally admired by all persons who have seen yᵉ Mss but particularly by yᵉ Revᵈ Dʳ Warton, who on first hearing this profession, remarked wᵗʰ much energy, putting his Spectacles upon his forehead 'we have in our Liturgy & in many parts of our Church service grand & Sublime passages but this composition leaves them all far behind.'"[60] So clear was Shakespeare's imprint on

---

56   Webb to Samuel Ireland, 30 June 1795, in BL Add. MS 30346, fol. 98ʳ.

57   Mackenzie to Chalmers, 11 April 1796, in Rosenbach EL3 f.I65i MS4 vol. 5

58   Webb to Samuel Ireland, 30 June 1795, in BL Add. MS 30346, fol. 98ᵛ.

59   Webb to Samuel Ireland, 30 June 1795, in BL Add. MS 30346, fol. 99ʳ.

60   BL Add. MS 30346, fol. 19ᵛ. The popularity of the Profession of Faith made it one of the most frequently reproduced items in Ireland's later self-forgeries, as he sold copies of

the papers that Webb "solemnly declare[d], that had not Shakspeare's handwriting or Name appear'd upon one single scrap of Paper; ... I should ascribe them to him."[61] This marks a noteworthy shift in the interpretation of Shakespeare in particular and literary genius more generally: where he had once been widely praised for his universality, for his ability to efface his own identity by entering the minds of his characters, in the 1790s he was being celebrated for his eccentricity, for the marks of personality that could not be concealed in anything he wrote.

This attention to Shakespeare not as a talented craftsman but as a unique genius, one who transcended the condition of mere mortals, is consistent with what we know about late-century conceptions of authorship—criticism was increasingly focusing on works as expressions of the personalities of their creators. As the eighteenth century turned into the nineteenth, works of art were increasingly understood as being the products of unique minds, and these works were assumed always to bear the marks of their makers. And it is the author's character, his or her own name, that gives to those works a satisfying organic form.

"The author's name," writes Michel Foucault in a famous essay, "serves to characterize a certain mode of being of discourse." This "certain mode" is paired with another, for it "must be received in a certain mode and ... must receive a certain status." This involved dynamic of author, work, and audience deserves close scrutiny, but Foucault does little more than gesture at the complexities of this relationship: "the word *work* and the unity that it designates," he admits, "are probably as problematic as the status of the author's individuality," but he ultimately confesses that "far from offering a solution" to these questions, "I shall only indicate some of the difficulties."[62] I add no solutions myself, but perhaps we can elucidate these "certain modes" by grounding them in specific cases. Since many critics who draw on Foucault's considerations of authorship are bogged down in the morass he has left, I hope to look for a more concrete illustration of the status of the author. Closer attention to an actual case history of composition and reception helps bring to light some of the more useful aspects of Foucault's work.

---

his forgeries to book collectors, billing them all as the "original forgeries." James Orchard Halliwell-Phillipps knew about Ireland's habit of mass-producing his forgeries—"Ireland did duplicate & triplicate copies *or more* of *some* of the forgeries, & several vols. of his forgeries are in all manner of places" (J. O. Halliwell-Phillipps to John Pearson, 25 Oct. 1883, in Folger Y.c.1265 1a, 1b)—but "duplicate & triplicate" hardly comes close to capturing Ireland's labors. I have now inspected 19 "original" copies of the Profession of Faith, and others certainly remain to be catalogued: see BL Add. MS 12051, fols. 43[r-v]; BL Add. MS 37831, no. 42; BL MS RP2345; Edinburgh Univ. Library H.-P. Coll. 321, fol. 3[r]; Edinburgh Univ. Library H.-P. Coll. 322, fol. 1[v]; Folger S.b.118, fols. 28–9; Folger S.b.119, fols. 22[r-v]; Folger S.b.157, no. 3; Folger S.b.159, pp. 9, 11; Folger W.b.496; Folger W.b.497; Harvard Theatre Collection TS 680.23.5F; Huntington 134037, pp. 60, 63; Huntington 287170; Hyde *Full and Explanatory Account* facing p. 75; Princeton MS RTC01 no. 176, p. 83; Princeton MS RTC01 no. 176, pp. 87–9; Rosenbach EL3 .I65 MS2; and Rosenbach EL3 f.I65i MS4 vol. 1, pp. 78–80.

61   Webb to Samuel Ireland, 30 June 1795, in BL Add. MS 30346, fol. 99[r].

62   Foucault, "What is an Author?" pp. 107, 104, 105.

Foucault holds that "There are a certain number of discourses that are endowed with the 'author function,' while others are deprived of it."[63] And the author's name is not a mere accessory piece of knowledge about a work, but an integral part of the work itself. The author himself, his personality and historical circumstances, are (at least in what Foucault calls an author-dominated age) as much a part of the work as what we call the "text itself." The division of a work into its "historical" and "aesthetic" components is convenient but ultimately indefensible, for the two are inseparably entangled: aesthetic value is contingent on historical circumstance. This is nowhere more evident than where the identity, even the existence, of the author is called into question.

The crime for which Macpherson was convicted as history's most perfidious literary faker was nothing more than the attribution of a group of poems to an author. The question is not whether the works had an author—since they were not the product of spontaneous generation, they obviously had either one (Macpherson or someone else) or several (Macpherson and someone else)—but whether they had a particular kind of author, one with power enough to conjure the Foucauldian "certain status," the "certain mode of being of discourse." The four possible answers to the authorship question—Ossian, Macpherson, anonymous balladeers, or some combination of them—seem to demand of an audience different and apparently irreconcilable reading strategies: Ossian's reception reveals that reading itself is impossible until one has been settled upon. With the rise of the author function, the formal features of texts (texts as artifacts) become insufficient to allow one even to begin reading: only when the historical identity of the author is settled can a text be read with confidence. Reading in the age of the Foucauldian author simply cannot take place until the reader has been informed which set of codes to employ, and these codes depend nearly inevitably on the identity of the author. The aesthetic lapses into abeyance, awaiting a verdict from history.

What effect has this author function on the audience's relation to the text? Foucault suggests it lends a work unity and coherence otherwise lacking, and this proves a key to the dispute over Ossian's poems. Macpherson's first Ossianic imposture in 1760 did not attract the vehement response the later epics drew. Though the work claims the authority of antiquity, its title—*Fragments of Ancient Poetry*—confesses its piecemeal nature. There is no unifying author, merely anonymous "bards." With this disclaimer, Hugh Blair's advertisement that "the public may depend on the following fragments as genuine remains of ancient Scotish poetry"[64] becomes somehow less egregious.

Even in the *Fragments*, though, Blair anticipates Macpherson's later course: "Though the poems now published appear as detached pieces in this collection, there is ground to believe that most of them were originally episodes of a greater work." Blair—no doubt acting on Macpherson's suggestions, since he knew no Gaelic and had no access to any "originals"—shows the aesthetic sliding into the historical as he expects historical circumstance to unify and therefore to authorize the fragments:

---

63   Foucault, "What Is an Author?" p. 107.
64   Blair, Preface to *Fragments*, p. 5.

Of the poetical merit of these fragments nothing shall here be said. Let the public judge, and pronounce. It is believed, that, by a careful inquiry, many more remains of ancient genius, no less valuable than those now given to the world, might be found in the same country where these have been collected.[65]

The "poetical merit," in other words, should remain in suspension until the "greater work" is "collected."

With the publication of the longer works (*Fingal* and *Temora*) under the name of a specific ancient author, though, the terms of the dispute change. Fiona Stafford makes clear the importance of the author *in propria persona* in the epics:

> The development of Ossian was perhaps the most important difference between *Fingal* and the *Fragments*. The earlier collection had been attributed to an anonymous body of "Bards," but when *Fingal* appeared, there was no question about the identity of the author: Ossian, the son of Fingal. An epic poem required an epic poet.... Despite its epic pretensions, *Fingal* is a sprawling work, held together not by unified action or theme, but by the presence of the narrator. As in Sterne's contemporary novel, *Tristram Shandy*, a baffling series of recollections is made coherent only through the development of the narrator as the focal point.[66]

This is clear in many early comments on the poems. When Hugh Blair defends the epics in his *Critical Dissertation on the Poems of Ossian, the Son of Fingal*, he does so in terms of a single personality: "His poetry," writes Blair, "more perhaps than that of any other writer, deserves to be stiled, *The Poetry of the Heart*. It is a heart penetrated with noble sentiments, and with sublime and tender passions; a heart that glows, and kindles the fancy; a heart that is full, and pours itself forth." It is not antiquity itself but an ancient personality that makes the difference. Literature, in the *Dissertation*, emanates spontaneously from personality, not artistry: "As their feelings are strong," he says of the ancient Scots, "so their language itself, of itself, assumes a poetical turn," and Ossian's artistic distinction is derived from his personal distinction: "This is such poetry as we might expect from a barbarous nation.... But when we open the works of Ossian, a very different scene presents itself." Here we see a work gaining authority not from its antiquity—that is dismissed as "barbarous"—but from the individuality of its author, his transcendence of his own antiquity. This origin in a unified personality produces that artistic unity we attribute to the author function: he speaks of "such a large collection of poems, without the least inconsistency," and for him this very uniformity testifies to its authenticity: "This representation of Ossian's times, must strike us the more, as genuine and authentick, when it is compared with a poem of later date.... in Ossian's works, from beginning to end, all is consistent."[67]

---

65 Ibid., pp. 5–6.

66 Stafford, *The Sublime Savage*, p. 141.

67 Blair, *A Critical Dissertation*, pp. 356, 345, 349, 355, 353. John Gordon made a similar point in 1762, praising the Ossianic poems: "Here the Poet sees and speaks with human eyes, and a human tongue" (Gordon, *Occasional Thoughts*, p. 90). See also James Boswell's comments of 8 Feb. 1763, where he notes that Thomas Sheridan and his wife "had fixed [Ossian's poetry] as the standard of feeling, made it like a thermometer by which they could judge the warmth of everybody's heart....'To be sure,' said he, 'except people have

The unifying force of a single personality was central, if largely unconscious, in the reception not only of the Ossianic verse, but of many texts of doubtful attribution. Foucault mentions Jerome's construction of the author as "a field of conceptual or theoretical coherence," and notes that in the author-dominated age "the author … serves to neutralize the contradictions that may emerge in a series of texts."[68] Authenticity is contingent on consistency, and only the individual author can produce the indivisible text. This search into a work's provenance—"We now ask of each poetic or fictional text: From where does it come, who wrote it, when, under what circumstances, or beginning with what design?"[69]—takes on a new significance with post-Renaissance reading practices. Antiquarianism now emphasizes the individuality and individualizing function of the author, an emphasis evident even before the appearance of the longer Ossianic epics, as in this letter of April 1760 from Thomas Gray to Horace Walpole:

> I am so charmed with the two specimens of Erse poetry, that I cannot help giving you the trouble to enquire a little farther about them, and should wish to see a few lines of the original, that I may form some slight idea of the language, the measures, and the rhythm.
>   Is there anything known of the author or authors?[70]

Ossian's *Fingal* was once confidently proclaimed equal, if not superior, to Homer and Virgil; Macpherson's *Fingal*, *literatim* the same poem, is now regarded as at best a curiosity of eighteenth-century taste. The aesthetic faculty begins not with the first page but with the title page: it is the author's name and circumstances that activate the strategies required for reading, and reading cannot proceed until it has a foundation in historicity.

Samuel Johnson thought Macpherson's book "an imposture from the beginning, [and] upon yet surer reasons an imposture still."[71] His first public declaration of disbelief gives his reason: "The editor, or author, never could shew the original,"[72] and to Boswell he acknowledged he would admit as contrary evidence "the sight of any original."[73] This appeal to *origin* as an authorizing and unifying agency is significant; it seems to be the factor that will settle whether Macpherson is "The editor, or author." Johnson's earlier work on the *Dictionary* and his edition of Shakespeare in the 1750s and 1760s—especially his effort to seek out early editions and contemporary testimonies—gave him an uncommon insight into the importance of origins and testimonial evidence in *belles lettres*. It is not surprising, therefore, that he sees something like the author function as a unifying principle more acutely than most of his contemporaries: "The poem of Fingal, he said, was a mere unconnected rhapsody, a tiresome repetition of the same images. 'In vain shall we look for the

---

genuine feelings of poetry, they cannot relish these poems'" (*Boswell's London Journal*, p. 182).

68 Foucault, "What Is an Author?" p. 111.
69 Ibid., p. 109.
70 Gray to Walpole, April 1760, in Gray, *Correspondence*, 2:664–5 (letter 310).
71 Johnson to Macpherson, 20 Jan. 1775, in Johnson, *Letters*, 2:168.
72 Johnson, Yale *Works*, 9:118.
73 Johnson to Boswell, 7 Feb. 1775, in Johnson, *Letters*, 2:177.

lucidus ordo, where there is neither end or object, design or moral.'"[74] Without an author, the poetry is unconnected, lacking an *ordo*. This explicit relationship of author and work shows up in Johnson's next great scholarly task, the *Lives of the Poets*, the original title of which—*Prefaces, Biographical and Critical, to the Works of the English Poets*—shows the interrelation of author and *ordo*.

Johnson was far from alone in his emphasis on origins. Blair, Gray, and Walpole seem to take the unification of the author function for granted, but Johnson makes it explicit. Johnson, a master of reading practices and possessed of a keen insight into the darker corners of psychology, recognizes the role of the author function in the creation of "end or object, design or moral." This recognition of the nearly unbreakable bond between origin and *ordo*, in its limited way, anticipates Foucault, and reveals the degree to which the reading process depends on the information about authorial identity that Johnson devoted so much energy to revealing.

Questions of fakery, then, allow us to see more sharply than before the ways in which the identity of an author—his or her unique personality, as expressed through his or her unique style—is assumed to lend an organic form to his or her works, and to provide a kind of unity across an entire oeuvre, one that works to keep that body of works free from contradiction. And the greatest authors are the ones whose force of personality is most evident in the works.

This is part of what made the fights over literary hoaxes so urgent: William Henry Ireland's plays would not have created such a stir had they been attributed to Marlowe or Massinger, but they presumed to tell us something about the towering genius at the heart of the canon. Even Macpherson's first venture into Ossianic poetry, the *Fragments*, was no great sin. Fragments do not call for any exceptional vigilance—even if they are bogus, they do not threaten to disturb our conception of poetic genius. But when they aspire to the condition of epics, when they begin to imply a unique mind, they demand a new attention. And violations of the implied contract between the individual author and the individual reader are supposed to deserve exceptionally harsh punishment.

---

74   Boswell, *Life*, 2:126.

Chapter 5

All Manner of Experience and Observation

"To bring a fact within the compass of possibility," Allan Ramsay scolded Henry Fielding, "there is nothing required but that it should not contradict itself; but to make it probable, it is likewise required that it should not be contradictory to ordinary experience."[1] Internal consistency, that is to say, makes an account possible in theory, but it takes consistency with the rest of the world to make it truly convincing.

Rash, Inconstant, and Ever Changing

Ramsay was writing about Elizabeth Canning, whose case fascinated London through 1753–54—a case that shows better than most of the episodes in this book how the varieties of contradiction could be used in debates over fraud. Through this year-and-a-half consistency was at the center of many of the debates. Londoners worked to sort out the "Multitude of very uncommon Circumstances, some of them directly contradictory to each other," wrote one contributor, and by the end many "different Opinions" were "formed from separate Parts of this Story."[2] But almost all of them came down to questions of consistency and inconsistency: those who found Canning's story to be consistent tended to believe her; those who found her story inconsistent sided against her.

Internal consistency, discussed in detail in the previous chapter, played a large role in the Canning case. The author of *Canning's Magazine* used this criterion in his challenge to Canning's credibility, facetiously employing the language of a criminal prosecutor: "The first Witness I shall call is *Elizabeth Canning*.... Her Testimony, instead of being *constant, uniform*, and *invariable*, ... seems to me *rash, inconstant*, and *ever changing*, and in its own Nature and Arrangement sufficient to discoutnenance any Belief of it."[3] And as we have seen already, there were several counter gambits for Canning's supporters. They could try to turn the charges of inconsistency against her accusers, as when the Canningite "Philologus"

---

1   Ramsay, *A Letter to the Right Honourable the Earl of* ——, pp. 5–6. Compare Geoffrey Gilbert: there are "Things whose Agreement or Difference is not known" solely on "Self-Evidence or Intuitive Knowledge." In such cases, Gilbert explained, we must "compare them by the means of some third Matter, by which we come to measure their Agreement, Disagreement or Relation" (*The Law of Evidence*, p. 2).

2   *Genuine and Impartial Memoirs of Elizabeth Canning*, p. iv.

3   *Canning's Magazine*, p. 34.

accused John Hill, "you say and unsay in one and the same Page"[4]—here it is the detector's narrative that is said to be inconsistent, leaving Canning's original story as the presumptive truth. Other Canningites ignored the accusations of their own inconsistency and, focusing only on the details that were internally consistent, they treated it as evidence of authenticity.

Not every dispute, however, was limited to internal consistency—to questions, in other words, of whether Canning contradicted herself. The Canning debates also depended on matters of external consistency—whether Canning's narrative contradicted other known facts. E. Biddulph, for example, draws up a catalogue of instances where Canning's testimony contradicts other known facts in the case:

> She could not mistake a Room above thirty-five Feet long and not ten Feet wide for a little square Room.
>   She could not swear, by Mistake, that she got out upon a Penthouse of Boards, when in Fact there is no such Penthouse....
>   She could not swear, by Mistake, that there was a Grate in the Chimney, because she says she took the Bed-gown out of it, and yet it is most certain that there was no such Grate.
>   She could not swear, by Mistake, that there were a few Pictures over the Chimney, and yet there never were any.
>   She could not swear, by Mistake, that there was nothing else in the Room except an old Table and an old Stool or two.[5]

In other words, even though Canning was consistent in calling the room of her confinement square, it was not really square; even though she was consistent in saying that she escaped on a penthouse, there was really no penthouse on which she could have escaped, and so on. Her story agrees with itself, but not with the rest of the world.

The anonymous author of the *Genuine and Impartial Memoirs* makes the same point in greater detail when he rehearses a list of arguments adduced by Canning's adversaries. He introduces what he calls "a Circumstance, that may possibly bring the Veracity of *Canning*'s Testimony into doubt":

> It was insisted by these [critics], that when *Canning* was before Alderman *Chitty*, she described the Place of her Confinement to be a *little, square, dark,* or *darkish Room*, with nothing in it but a *Grate* in a *Chimney*, out of which she took an *old Bed-gown*, and over which there were a few *old Pictures*; that the further Contents of the Room consisted only of an *old Table*, and a *broken Stool* of *two*; that she *lay* on the *bare Boards*; and that she *left* some *Water* in the *Pitcher behind her*, when she made her Escape, which she effected by *breaking down some Boards* that were *fastened* before the *Windows*, from whence she got out upon a *Shed*, or *Penthouse*, down which she slid, and jumped from the Edge of it upon a Bank. It is also said, that she swore, that after the two Men had robbed her, they carried her through *Bishopsgate-street*.—On the contrary, the Room she pitched upon did not in the least correspond with this Description; it appeared to be a *long, narrow Room*, near *three times as much* in *Length* as *Breadth*; that it had a *light Casement* in it, *without any*

---

4   "Philologus," *The Inspector Inspected*, p. 14.
5   Biddulph, *Some Account of the Case*, p. 56.

Fastening, big enough for a larger Person to get through with Ease; that it had *no Grate* in the Chimney, nor any Likelihood that any had been there for a long Time before, seeing the whole was covered with *Cobwebs* of no small Duration; that there were *no Pictures*, nor any Vestiges of any; but that, instead of them, there was an *old Glass Casement* over the Chimney, joined to the Wall by *Cobwebs*....[6]

The parallel constructions, with the opposed facts displayed in italics, allow the reader to go through Canning's assertions, as if on a checklist—and over and over again the conclusions are clear: Canning's story, in all its circumstantial details, cannot be reconciled with the real world.

The contradictions between Canning's testimony and the physical evidence of the room were not the only concerns of those who sought to disprove her story: many were eager to show that her testimony differed from the testimony of others. Ramsay admits that minor variations must be expected whenever two people tell the same story—"in accounts that are delivered with truth by two different persons concerning the same affair, there will be different circumstances constantly told by the different persons, according as their different memories and apprehensions suggest them to the relators"—but he insists that, "when the same facts occur to the relators, there never is, or can be, any thing material in the different manner of relating them." How, then, does Canning's testimony compare to Virtue Hall's? "In the Depositions of *Canning* and *Hall*," he insists, "the direct contrary appears. For *Hall* has not added one original circumstance from her own knowledge, ... while, on the other hand, she gives positive proofs of her ignorance, by blundering and disagreement." For him, this is the occasion for nothing less than "*an enquiry into the nature of moral evidence*, the axis upon which all human affairs turn."[7] And he was convinced that Canning failed the test, because her evidence often contradicted that of the other participants.

Once again, though, the Canningites tried to use the same principle to their advantage: they argued that the *consistency* of the testimony of several witnesses showed that the account must be true. It was a commonplace in law: "When, concerning a great number and variety of circumstances," wrote U.S. Supreme Court Justice James Wilson in the 1790s, "there is an entire agreement in the testimony of many witnesses, without the possibility of a previous collusion between them, the evidence may, in its effect, be equal to that of strict demonstration. That such concurrence should be the result of chance, is as one to infinite; or, to vary the expression, is a moral impossibility."[8] The Canningites thought they had this principle on their side, since—at least in many popular accounts—Canning's testimony was said to agree with Virtue Hall's. Biddulph thought "the Reader ought to be informed, that the Dates of Times when the Gypsey was proved to be at so many different Places by forty Witnesses, all exactly corresponded with each other, insomuch that where one Witness set her down another takes her up; that these Witnesses live remote from each other, and have no Connexions or Correspondence together; and, lastly, that, as they swear to three Persons all very well known to them, and fix

---

6   *Genuine and Impartial Memoirs of Elizabeth Canning*, pp. 9–10.
7   Ramsay, *A Letter to the Right Honourable the Earl of*——, pp. 40–41, 49.
8   Wilson, *Works*, 1:504.

the Time by Tokens which cannot err, it is impossible that they can be mistaken."[9] Fielding uses these facts to draw "the following syllogistical Conclusion":

> Whenever two Witnesses declare a Fact, and agree in all the Circumstances of it, either the Fact is true or they have previously concerted the Evidence between themselves:
> But in this Case it is impossible that these Girls should have so previously concerted the Evidence:
> And therefore the Fact is true.[10]

Hill, however, is more suspicious: "Now, Syllogist, where is your Argument! Can two Persons who swear the same thing agree in all Particulars, and yet that thing be false? Yes certainly, if one has heard the other's Story."[11]

Ramsay offered a similar explanation of why Canning's story had as much external consistency as it did: "those who know any thing of *Wells*'s house or its situation, asked her questions concerning it; to which, as she might plainly perceive they were asked with a friendly intention, and not with any design to entrap her, she always answered, Yes. By which means she might possibly have been furnished with some little knowledge of what she was before totally ignorant; and her neighbours, like the boobies who go to astrologers, were amazed to hear her relate in the afternoon, what their questions had taught her in the morning."[12] Biddulph explains the process in more detail: Canning's main interrogator admitted "that, in every one of his Questions, he mentioned some Particulars which he knew corresponded with the Situation of *Wells*'s House; that *Canning*'s Answer to every Question was constantly 'Yes'; that she did not say No to any one Question he asked her; that he did not ask her one general Question, but all leading ones; and that he never thought of asking her whether she had not observed things in the Neighbourhood of Mother *Wells*'s, which he knew were not to be found there, in order to discover whether she would not have said yes to them too."[13]

Credideris Nihil Temerè

Facts about the shape of the room in Mother Wells's house could be checked with comparative ease, but some arguments depended on "facts" that were harder to confirm. Canning notoriously claimed she was locked in a room for four weeks with only a quartern loaf and a gallon jug of water, prompting many of her critics to insist that she could not possibly have survived for so long on so little nourishment. One anonymous attacker pointed out that "this Girl, after she had subsisted for a Month upon a small Quantity of Bread and Water, and consequently must be reduced to the last Extremity of Weakness and Imbecility; yet she walked home that Night in six Hours."[14]

9   Biddulph, *Some Account of the Case*, pp. 10–11.
10 Fielding, *A Clear State of the Case*, p. 308.
11 John Hill, *The Story of Elizabeth Canning Considered*, p. 37.
12 Ramsay, *A Letter to the Right Honourable the Earl of ——*, pp. 28–9.
13 Biddulph, *Some Account of the Case*, p. 24.
14 *The Truth of the Case*, p. 6.

What seems irrefutable to us, though—surely no one could believe she survived a month on just a gallon of water—was not necessarily beyond the realm of credibility in 1753. James Solas Dodd thought of himself as admirably skeptical; his *Physical Account of the Case of Elizabeth Canning* opens with a title-page motto from Cato's *Distichs*, "Credideris nihil temerè"—"you should believe nothing rashly." Still he was prepared to believe that Canning survived a month on a gallon of water. "She was a hearty Girl," he writes, "sanguine, and of a florid Countenance; she had been accustomed throughout her Life, to a deficiency of liquid Aliment; having for many Years taken scarce half a Pint of Liquid in Twenty-four Hours." True, a gallon does not sound like much; still, "The Quantity of her Water, if proportioned to the Time she stayed there, was little less than her usual Quantity of Liquid."[15] He launches into an elaborate series of calculations to demonstrate that surviving on a gallon of water and four pounds of bread is not only possible, but perfectly consistent with her condition after she emerged from her month's absence:

> The Quantity of her Food was ... four Pounds, and near a half in Twenty-seven Days.... Now as she had no Stool, their [*sic*] could be no more Expence to be recruited, than what usually arises from insensible Perspiration.... The learned *Sanctorius* hath observed the Night and Day to carry off in Stool and by Urine thirty Ounces, and by Perspiration fifty Ounces. There should some Allowance be made for the difference of Heat in his Climate, and ours.... Now he says likewise, that Fear and Sorrow close the Pores, and hinder the freedom of Perspiration.... Reckoning therefore the Quantity of Bread and Water to weigh fourteen Pounds and a Half, by subtracting that from the sixty-seven Pounds eight, Ounces, expended, there will be a Deficiency of fifty-three Pounds. Now it must be allowed that the additional Quantity of Blood arising from this aforementioned Obstruction, must be almost forty-eight Ounces....[16]

And so on. Today's conventional medical wisdom tells us that the learned Sanctorius let Dodd down, and that his figures have little to do with reality. Dodd tries to offer more support from recorded cases—"But that these Things may not seem strange I'll give my Readers some authentic Accounts of Persons who existed Years without Food"[17]—probably all apocryphal.

Canning's critics were almost certainly right—she could not have survived so long on just a loaf of bread and a pitcher of water—and yet, even today, there are few hard facts about how long a healthy person can survive without water. We simply do not know with anything like certainty. Studies have been done on the ability of people to survive without water in extreme conditions (in deserts, on mountains, and so on), but no significant clinical study has ever determined how long a woman like Canning could stay alive on a gallon of water. The medical experts I consulted were all virtually certain that it would not be a month—but not one could back up this intuition with hard evidence, and not one was willing to remove the qualifier "virtually" from his or her declaration of certainty. And if there is still room for even slight doubt in the twenty-first century, can there be any wonder that people were

---

15 Dodd, *A Physical Account*, pp. 13–14.

16 Ibid., pp. 15–16.

17 Ibid., p. 21.

prepared to consider at least the possibility that the girl could survive on very little water? Even the assertions that "everybody knows" may prove to be false.

A very different episode of deception raises many of the same problems as the Canning case. Many of the most interesting fakes of eighteenth-century Britain dealt with a lost world—whether as recent Shakespeare's lifetime or as long ago as Ossian's—and the further we move into the past, the more difficult it becomes to be confident in supposed facts about the external world. Both accusers and defenders have fallen afoul of this problem, basing their arguments on historical "facts" they thought they knew. William Stukeley was famous in his day as a learned antiquarian. Eighteenth-century antiquarians were an eccentric lot; Stukeley, more than most of his contemporaries, probably deserves the epithet "crackpot." He used his knowledge of the origins of the ancient Britons—they were descendants of the Phoenicians, as he demonstrated by comparing archaeological remains—to authenticate the depiction of third-century Scotland that appeared in the Ossianic poems. Stukeley's work of seven years "in considering Abury & Stonehenge" had taught him much about the ancient Britons, especially their funerary customs. He excavated some "of the innumerable burrows, & *tumuli*, … & found such remains, as are mention'd in *Fingal*." The product of his investigation—*mirabile dictu*—was that "I found all the notions I have conceiv'd in my mind, concerning the great people, the old Britons, the *founders*; very much confirmed & illustrated by *Fingal*."[18] There is, of course, nothing to this; if the Ossianic poems really could be shown to reflect Phoenician practices, modern historians would not hesitate to reject them as fraudulent. But Stukeley was convinced the ancient Britons were Phoenician, and used this "fact" about the real world to authenticate a set of questionable documents.

Edmond Malone had a far sounder grasp of history than Stukeley, and his knowledge of the Elizabethan era was matched by few in the eighteenth century. He was able to put that knowledge to good use in his attacks on William Henry Ireland's Shakespeare fabrications. Consider his attack on the letter supposedly from Queen Elizabeth to "Master William Shakspeare atte the Globe bye Thames." He begins with a witticism about the imprecision of the direction—"on which side of the Thames it lay, whether north or south, the messenger was to find out as he could; if he did but perambulate he could not fail of stumbling upon it"—but then he delivers the *coup de grâce*, offering what he believes to be irrefutable evidence that the letter cannot be genuine: "Unluckily, however, the Globe theatre was not built at the time to which this letter must be referred."[19]

In arguing that the Globe was not constructed at the time Elizabeth's letter was written, he draws on a remarkable number of sources. His first task is to assign a date to the undated letter: "though the writer cautiously avoided putting a date to it, he has furnished us with a negative date by mentioning Lord Leycester as then living." Now able to compare the whereabouts of Elizabeth and Leicester month by month, he determines, "The Pretended Letter … must have been written either between the 23d of Nov. 1586, and the 25th of June 1587, or between the months of December

---

18   Stukeley, notes on Ossian, Bodleian MS Eng.misc.e.383, fols. 4ʳ–5ʳ.
19   Malone, *An Inquiry*, p. 84

1587 and Sept. 1588."[20] He then turns to a series of maps: Aggas's of 1568, Virtue's of 1560, and Braun and Hogenbergius's of 1573, none of which includes the Globe. A German visitor to London in 1579 left no record of its existence. From this, he concludes that the letter cannot be genuine.

But even claims like this are subject to dispute. They certainly did not stop Ireland's defenders from making unwarranted speculations to try to hold their ground against the enemy assault. Whalley Chamberlain Oulton, not satisfied with Malone's conclusion, tentatively offered a conjecture about what was referred to as the "*newly erected* Theatre": "if the NEW Globe was not erected till 1596, might not there have been an OLD Globe in 1585?"[21] Malone, as it happens, was right; so far, at least, no evidence of an Old Globe has turned up. The problem, however, remains a real one, at least in principle: Malone discredited Ireland's document by comparing it with the facts he knew about English theatre history, but if his own facts were wrong, the conclusions that followed from them were likely to be incorrect.

Of all the high-profile deceptions in the eighteenth century, the one most likely to provoke smirks today is the story of Mary Toft's giving birth to 17 rabbits. The story's prima facie absurdity means that many are surprised to hear that it could have provoked any significant dispute, any more than the most ridiculous headlines on down-market tabloid newspapers about the Mummy's Curse are taken seriously today. As Dennis Todd puts it, "There is, first and most vexing of all, the question of how such an improbable story could have held sway over so many people for so long." But a number of commentators usefully remind us that early eighteenth-century theories of reproduction still had room for such prodigies, and that even respectable physicians could entertain the possibility that Toft's having seen rabbits during her pregnancy could have left an impression on the child she was carrying. Todd answers his own question this way: "belief in Mary Toft's claims was not confined to the credulous at all. Those who perpetrated the hoax may have been knaves, but those who were taken in by it were not fools."[22] Lisa Forman Cody traces this possibility of belief in Toft's story to a shift in the institutional practices surrounding reproductive knowledge. She reminds us that male physicians before the 1720s had devoted little attention to questions of conception and childbirth, since most such lore was the province of people outside the institutional structures of "scientific" medicine: "knowledge about sex was largely in the hands of women and midwives."[23] Mary Fissell and Roger Cooter concur, alluding to "the natural knowledges shared by an illiterate peasant and a 'learned' medical man. Mary Toft created her story in accordance with those knowledges.... Toft's knowledge of reproduction had enough in common with that of learned medical men that she was able to fool at least some of them."[24]

---

20 Ibid., pp. 88, 89–90.
21 Oulton, *Vortigern under Consideration*, pp. 20–21.
22 Todd, *Imagining Monsters*, pp. 38, 39.
23 Cody, *Birthing the Nation*, p. 16.
24 Fissell and Cooter, "Exploring Natural Knowledge," p. 150.

Neither the Ignorance nor the Omission Seems Natural

External evidence poses one other significant problem, and it actually has to do with the lack of evidence. It is a truth universally acknowledged that it is impossible to prove a negative: "A Negative cannot be proved," writes William Nelson in *The Law of Evidence* (1717). That universal acknowledgment, however, has not stopped many people from trying. Several critics poked holes in Macpherson's account of the Ossianic poems because of things they did not contain. In 1771, Thomas Pennant finds it a "matter of suprize that no mention is made, in the Poems of *Ossian*, of our greater beasts of prey, which must have abounded in his days; for the Wolf was a pest to the country so late as the reign of Queen *Elizabeth*." Others made the same point. "We know from charters, &c.," wrote an anonymous commentator in 1786, "that wolves were quite frequent in Scotland…. Now Ossian does not once mention wolves; which is not to be supposed, had an animal so violent and mischievous been at all known to him. Boars are in the same predicament." "How comes Ossian to omit boars and wolves," asks John Pinkerton three years later, "so frequent in Scotland, down to the fifteenth century, in all his imagery?"[25]

This argument is more complicated than most of those based on external evidence. Nowhere do the Ossianic poems say there were no wolves in ancient Britain; they simply fail to say that there were. Implicit in his argument is the belief that *any* authentic third-century Scottish poetry—at least any sufficiently large collection of it—would have to reflect so important a fact about the real world. Its failure to do so should convince us that it was actually a product of a different world. The *Annual Register* noted another telling omission in the Ossianic poems: "We received such uncommon pleasure from the perusal of this performance … that we should be very glad if neither this, nor any thing else in the work, had given reason to doubt its being, at least in its present form, the genuine offspring of him to whom it is ascribed. But the total silence of the poem with regard to the grosser parts of the druidical religion, and the retaining what was most pure and poetic, … induce a suspicion of more art than simplicity in the poet."[26] Sound historical knowledge tells us the third-century Scots had to confront wolves and Druids; that Macpherson's poems failed to represent them was widely supposed to be evidence that they were inauthentic.

Thomas Warton applies a similar critique to the Rowley poems, cataloguing some of the things that do not appear in them. On successive pages of his *Enquiry* he notes three surprising omissions:

> In these poems there is no learning. I mean, Gothic Learning: such as the pedantry of a learned priest in the fifteenth century would have exhibited.

> In these poems we have no Religion…. I mean, they have no prolix devotional episodes, such as would have naturally flowed from a writer of Rowley's profession and character.

---

25 Pennant, *A Tour in Scotland*, p. 169 n; *Ancient Scottish Poems*, 1:xlvii; Pinkerton, *An Enquiry into the History of Scotland*, 2:84.

26 *Annual Register* (1761): 278.

We miss the marks of another sort of reading in these poems, and which a real Rowley would have shewn, I mean of old romances.[27]

As with the attacks on Macpherson, these critiques take it for granted that any fifteenth-century religious poetry would show "the pedantry of a learned priest," "prolix devotional episodes," and signs of reading in "old romances."

Absence of evidence, it was sometimes believed, could be evidence of absence. This was not simply a fallacy committed by thoughtless partisans in the give-and-take of debates, but a principle that actually became established in legal tracts. Jeremy Bentham made exactly the same kind of argument in his *Treatise of Judicial Evidence*: "The writing, or contract, in question, was not produced, nor any mention made of it, in circumstances where the party now using it would naturally have produced it, and taken advantage of it, if it had existed.... The writing in question makes no mention of facts and circumstances, which must have attracted the attention of the writer, and which he would not have omitted, had he known them; neither the ignorance nor the omission seems natural." He recognized that the conclusion did not follow in strict logic—"This indication is any thing but conclusive"—and yet he insisted that the lack of evidence we should expect "may lead to suspicion."[28]

Whatever Contradicts a Known Truth

All of these complexities reveal some of the practical difficulties of applying the standard of external consistency—difficulties which prove at least as formidable as those we confront when we apply the standard of internal consistency. And the practical problems are simply manifestations of the underlying philosophical problems, because every attempt to compare a questionable account against the known world raises many epistemological questions. Everyone agrees that inconsistency is evidence of inauthenticity—the task is figuring out what kind and what degree of consistency a questioned account should have with the rest of the world. The phrase "known facts" comes up often in these discussions, but these discussions make us reconsider just how many facts are really known.

To be fair, many tests for external consistency are fairly simple, at least in theory. Counterfeit banknotes, for example, can easily be checked against other banknotes, because the kinds of consistency we expect are easily understood. If one suspects a 20-dollar bill is a fake, for example, the best thing to do is to put it next to another 20-dollar bill known to be genuine. In this case spotting a counterfeit should be easy, at least in principle: if the questioned banknote differs in any material respect from the authentic one, it can be dismissed as fraudulent. Because all 20-dollar bills of the same series should look exactly alike—though we define "exactly alike" loosely enough to allow for different serial numbers, places of origin, and minute differences in ink density, paper quality, and so on—spotting an inconsistency is comparatively simple. If Andrew Jackson is looking to his right rather than his left, the bill is spurious. (One unfortunate would-be counterfeiter ran into this problem

---

27 Warton, *An Enquiry*, pp. 97, 98, 99.

28 Bentham, *A Treatise on Judicial Evidence*, p. 141.

on 29 September 1763: "A man who called himself *Holt*," reports the *Gentleman's Magazine*, "was apprehended at *Evesham* in *Worcestershire*, on suspicion of forgery, he having offered some bills drawn on *Smith* and co. bankers in *London*; on which, unluckily for him, was written the word *excepted* instead of *accepted*."[29]) And even though some variations will escape the untrained eye—minor differences in hatching in the engraving, for instance—they are still definitive when spotted.

Making such identifications, however, is not always an option. We are able to compare a questionable banknote with legitimate banknotes because we live in a fairly stable economy, where the number of issues in circulation is comparatively small: we have all seen countless genuine 10-pound notes and 20-dollar bills, and if need be we can easily produce another to make minute comparisons. Eighteenth-century merchants had far more difficulty, especially those in Britain's North American colonies. The variety of coins and notes circulating in eighteenth-century America could be stunning—not only English pence, shillings, crowns, guineas, and banknotes in many different issues, but also Spanish pieces of eight, Portuguese moidores, Dutch and German thalers, and so on. And the proportion of counterfeit currency in early America was surprisingly high. In such an environment, a merchant offered a half-moidore minted in 1722 may have never seen another, and may have no idea where to find a real one on short notice. How, then, is he or she to judge whether the one being offered is authentic?

The high degree of consistency associated with currency, moreover, cannot be expected in every situation and, even when it exists, it is not always evidence of authenticity. In handwriting, for instance, perfect consistency between two specimens, far from being evidence of authenticity, is evidence of fraud—a fact first systematically discussed in the late seventeenth century. A signature is rejected as spurious if it does not match a known authentic signature, but it should also be rejected if it matches it too closely: "Le form trop reguliere en vne escriture," notes Jacques Raveneau in an important early treatise on handwriting from 1666, "& particulierement en vne signature, peut estre suspecte, ... parce qu'il est impossible à qui que ce soit de faire deux signatures dans vne conformité si parfaite, si ce n'est pas vn contretirement."[30] The principle is now sufficiently well established that it shows up routinely in works of legal education: Katherine M. Koppenhaver's *Attorney's Guide to Document Examination*, for example, states clearly that "When one encounters two identical signatures, at least one of those signatures is not genuine."[31] A handwriting expert must learn how to look for essential similarities between the questioned and the known exemplars, but cannot expect perfect identity.

The same sorts of problems obtain in many investigations of literary fraud. Comparing a questionable third-century epic with an authentic example of the genre is nearly impossible, because no certain examples are known to exist: as Patrick Graham noted in 1807, "It is only from the internal evidence, furnished by the Poems themselves, that we can infer the period of their composition. But what other source

---

29   *Gentleman's Magazine* 33 (Sept. 1763): 461.
30   Raveneau, *Traité des inscriptions en faux*, p. 72.
31   Koppenhaver, *Attorney's Guide to Document Examination*, p. 204.

of evidence could we, in this instance, expect?"[32] And even when the genuine item can be found, knowing how to conduct the comparison is complex. Authenticating or rejecting a Shakespearean sonnet is much trickier than doing the same for a banknote. Looking exactly like another Shakespearean sonnet, far from being a confirmation of a poem's authenticity, would be clear evidence of either its inauthenticity or the mental imbalance—or perhaps Borgesian playfulness—of its creator. Instead, it would have to look sufficiently like other Shakespearean sonnets to be consistent with them, but sufficiently unlike them to be explicable as worth the time of their author. What exactly constitutes "sufficiently like" and "sufficiently unlike," though, is notoriously difficult to formulate with any precision, and threatens to cause us to fall back on the impressionistic judgments.

All of this suggests that the problems posed by tests for external consistency can be as complicated as those posed by tests for internal consistency. We have already seen William Adams arguing that "Truth is always uniform, and … whatever contradicts a known truth must be false."[33] The problem with invoking external consistency is that it depends on objective and reliable evidence about the real world against which a doubtful specimen can be measured—in Adams's terms, there must be such a thing as "a known truth." Is there? Einstein famously taught us in 1905 there is no fixed point in the universe; if you say object A is moving with respect to stationary object B, I can just as easily say B is moving with respect to a stationary A.[34] The metaphor from physics offers a few useful insights into the question of external consistency. Even if we spot a disagreement between a doubtful specimen and the "known" body of information, on what grounds do we award the prize of veracity to one side and dismiss the other as worthless?—which claim stays, and which goes?—what is stationary, what moving?

The Word "Oldsmobile"

Questions of this sort force themselves on our attention every time we measure a new assertion against an old one. What often happens in disputes over external consistency is an attempt to discern the limits of "known truths." How confident do we need to be before we can consider our knowledge certain, or at least certain enough to measure against a questionable new fact? Consider a comparatively straightforward eighteenth-century case, Malone's demonstration that William Henry Ireland's receipt from Lord Leicester must have been forged because it implies Leicester was alive in 1590, when we know he had died on 4 September 1588.[35] The principle of

---

32 Graham, *Essay on the Authenticity*, p. 10.

33 Adams, *A Test of True and False Doctrines*, p. 14.

34 See Einstein, "On the Electrodynamics of Moving Bodies," p. 2.

35 Ireland gives his account in *Confessions*, pp. 101–2. "Originals" of the receipt from Leicester can be found in Boston Public Library Msq.G.166.4; BL MS RP2345; Edinburgh Univ. Library H.-P. Coll. 321, fol. 12ʳ; Edinburgh Univ. Library H.-P. Coll. 322, fol. 14; Folger S.b.119, fol. 16ʳ; Folger S.b.159, p. 16; Folger W.b.496; Folger W.b.497; Huntington 134037, p. 113; Huntington 287170; Hyde *Full and Explanatory Account*, facing p. 103; Rosenbach EL3 f.I65i MS4 vol. 1, p. 59; and Shakespeare Birthplace ER1/50, fol. 85.

non-contradiction says these propositions cannot both be true—Leicester could not be both alive and dead in 1590—and at least one of the claims must therefore be rejected. But which? Because the epistemological status of the claim that Leicester died in 1588 is not inherently superior to the epistemological status of the claim that he was alive two years later, there is no easy *a priori* way to say. Ireland's defenders would have been happy to insist that Ireland was right and conventional wisdom was wrong.

In practice, we often approach documentary history in the same way we approach astronomy in an Einsteinian universe: we regard the bigger one as stationary. One document asserted Leicester was alive; dozens asserted he was dead: we can play the odds and suggest that the truth lies with the better-attested story. Suppose, however, that Ireland had been even more industrious than he was in real life—suppose he produced hundreds of documents that showed Leicester was alive, to balance out the dozens that showed he was dead. (To return to the example of a questioned banknote, one can imagine the difficulties of authenticating currency when a majority of the money in circulation is fraudulent.) Besides, not every "known fact" is backed up with as much evidence as Leicester's death. There is always at least the theoretical possibility that the new, controversial claim is right, and the old, widely accepted claim is wrong. This is the phenomenon that allows today's Marlovians to attribute the Shakespeare canon to Christopher Marlowe. The author of *Doctor Faustus* is "known" to have died in 1593, before most of Shakespeare's plays were written, but Calvin Hoffman, the twentieth century's leading Marlovian, insisted he could "prove Marlowe did not die in a British pub brawl in 1593 but lived on in hiding in Italy until 1627."[36] (Those who would attribute the canon to the Earl of Oxford usually prefer not to make Oxford's death later, but to adjust the chronology on about a third of Shakespeare's plays to make them come before 1604.)

Just as tests for internal consistency can prove to be unreliable when they are not applied with philosophical rigor, so tests for external consistency are likely to fail when they are not explicit about the grounds on which they are made. Apparent inconsistency, after all, is not always *de facto* evidence of inauthenticity. Consider the *Gentleman's Magazine*, which wrestled with this problem in Chatterton's works. "In these poems," the writer points out, "it has been observed, many words occur which are not elsewhere to be found."[37] Rowley's language, in other words, was inconsistent with that of the fifteenth century. Were these otherwise unattested words therefore evidence of forgery? The twentieth-century textual scholar Paul Maas, in a technical discussion of transmission and corruption, pauses to caution would-be textual critics: "We must distinguish sharply between anomaly and *singularity*. What is unique is not for that reason alone to be regarded with suspicion."[38] This is a salutary lesson even for those with no interest in Lachmannian stemmata and *lectiones difficiliores*, for if we judge the plausibility of a phenomenon solely on its conformity with what we already know, how can we be receptive to new knowledge?

---

36   Matt Wolf, "Marlowe Was Shakespeare." See also Hoffman, *The Murder of the Man Who Was "Shakespeare,"* for more extensive documentation of his claims.

37   *Gentleman's Magazine* 47 (June 1777): 277.

38   Maas, *Textual Criticism*, p. 12.

The textual critic rejects anomalies by drawing on his or her knowledge of language, style, the history of the transmission, and so on: Homer never used the genitive here; the line is therefore corrupt. But what to do with a single instance of the genitive when there is no particular reason to suspect corruption? Is it actually authorial, a unique usage—a *hapax legomenon*—or is it the product of textual corruption? And what about metaphorical *hapax legomena*? If we admit as true only what is plausible, and draw our standard of what is plausible only from what we have already experienced, we foreclose the possibility of encountering anything new, anything outside our experience. This poses a problem for any system of epistemology, but for empiricism, in which experience is the foundation of all knowledge, it is uncommonly acute.

This situation offers a fine example of the hermeneutical circle: we recognize anomalies because they differ from the norm, but we come to know the norm only by rejecting the anomalies. Hermeneutical circles are frustrating, but in practice not necessarily inescapable. We can look for an abundance of apparent anomalies, and let the laws of probability take over—laws first formulated, as it happens, in the late seventeenth and eighteenth centuries.[39] A single inconsistency in a long document will likely be dismissed, perhaps called either a legitimate *hapax* or a minor textual corruption. Two hundred fifty errant forms, however, will probably make us reject the entire document as a fraud. Ditto outrageous departures: one of Woody Allen's stories mentions a newly discovered set of Dead Sea Scrolls whose "authenticity ... is currently in great doubt, particularly since the word 'Oldsmobile' appears several times in the text."[40] But even when such judgments are simple enough in practice, making a sound *theoretical* case for rejecting Nag Hammadi Oldsmobiles but admitting Homeric genitives is complicated. The word *genocide* appears in no sixteenth-century document: if a text purporting to be from that period *does* contain the word, is it evidence of fakery, or evidence that the form existed earlier than we thought?[41]

Walk on Water

Problems like these occupied many eighteenth-century minds, and in many different fields. Jurists, as we have seen, tried to lay down ground-rules for sorting through testimony; natural philosophers tried to systematize their own rules of evidence; historians debated the kinds of evidence on which historical narratives could be built; travelers hoped to distinguish real from fabulous accounts of faraway lands; philosophers considered the kinds of claims that demanded assent; theologians worked to find their own principles that would authorize the claims of their own

---

39   "It would appear that the mathematical theory of probability came into being in only about 1660.... the decade of the 1660s remains a turning point in mathematical history. Mathematical probability requires only the most rudimentary arithmetic; its invention thus appears to be a conceptual development rather than simply an elaboration of formal methods" (Patey, *Probability and Literary Form*, p. 266).

40   Allen, "The Scrolls," in *Without Feathers*, p. 21.

41   See Mumford, "Clara Miccinelli's Cabinet of Wonders."

religion without authorizing the supposed absurdities of other faiths. Although these fields of inquiry differed in the details of their approaches, all were engaged in the same collective enterprise, and they often borrowed from one another.

As Steven Shapin argues, "The order of society depends on ... a complex of normatively ordered expectancies. How could coordinated activity of any kind be possible if people could not rely upon others' undertakings?"[42] The result is that our usual mode is to assume an assertion about the world is true unless we have reason to believe it false, and to assume that a speaker is honest unless we have reason to assume he or she is a liar. This is how Charles de Brosses approaches the fantastic travel narratives that described Patagonian giants in 1768: "But what shall we say on the other hand to the testimony of those, who assert they have seen the giants on the *Patagonian* coast? Shall we reject the concurring evidence of *Magellan*, *Loaisa, Sarmiento, Nodal*, among the *Spaniards*; of the *Dutch, Sebald de Weert, Noordt, Maire*, and *Spilberg*, and of *Candish; Hawkins* and *Knivet* among our own countrymen; not to mention the late accounts of this people, we have from those who made the voyage of the Straits with Commodore *Byron*? Shall we reject, I say, the concurring testimony of so many, who affirm, that they not only saw these extraordinary men, but that they eat and drank with them, had them on board their ships, and exchanged goods and toys with them?"[43]

Yet, even as many cultural interactions depend on taking things on trust, one of the most important cultural developments of the seventeenth and eighteenth centuries was the rejection of traditional authoritative testimony in favor of new observation. The authorities of the past were increasingly being disdained—*nullius in verba*, proclaimed the Royal Society—as experimental science was overturning more and more things that "everyone knew." Everyone knew that white light was pure, but Newton showed that it comprised all the colors of the rainbow; everyone knew that phlogiston accounted for combustion, but Lavoisier showed the theory was both unnecessary and incoherent. These spokesmen for new truths recognized the difficulty of the task they faced: as Shapin demonstrates, "Such modern practitioners as William Gilbert instructed doubting readers not to distrust experimental relations simply because they went against common experience or traditional textual authority: 'Men are deplorably ignorant with respect to natural things, and modern philosophers, as though dreaming in the darkness, must be aroused.'"[44]

As a result, seventeenth- and eighteenth-century writers and experimentalists increasingly came to demand what Shapin calls "ontological openness," the willingness to believe in the newly established facts even when they contradict conventional wisdom, and they were therefore obliged to prepare the ground for many new and counterintuitive understandings of the world. The institutionalization of scientific practice went a long way toward eliminating the questions about the

---

42   Shapin, *A Social History of Truth*, p. 8.

43   Brosses, *Terra Australis Cognita*, 3:728. The reference to the Patagonian giants was in the eighteenth century "a kind of talisman or touchstone of the marvellous" (Baines, *The House of Forgery*, p. 114).

44   Shapin, *A Social History of Truth*, p. 198, citing William Gilbert, *De Magnete* (1600), p. 47.

personal credibility of the reporter: we need not always trust the word of other scientists implicitly, since published descriptions of methods give us the opportunity to reproduce the results for ourselves. But how many contrary results do we need before we can overturn widely acknowledged truths? The modern science of statistics has tried to describe more carefully the degree of confidence we can place in generalizations made from observations—standard deviations, standard errors, p-values, and confidence intervals are all ways of quantifying the degree of certainty that one can accord to a proposition that cannot be known *a priori*. It is surely significant that the rudiments of our understanding of probability and statistics date from just this period.

The practical problems involved in using observation to overturn conventional wisdom prompted not only developments in scientific method and statistics, but also much ontological and epistemological speculation, particularly on the difficulties of believing in things one had not experienced firsthand. In 1690, John Locke considered the grounds on which we accept or reject testimony about a fact inconsistent with our previous experience, and in the process, he originated a thought experiment widely quoted throughout the eighteenth century. He begins by noting that, if someone "tells me he saw a Man in *England* in the midst of a sharp Winter, walk upon Water harden'd with cold; this has so great conformity with what is usually observed to happen, that I am disposed by the nature of the thing it self to assent to it." Locke was, after all, a resident of northern Europe, and had therefore experienced ice himself. A testimony of its existence in a particular case, therefore, is plausible, and should be rejected only if there is good reason to doubt the witness. To "one born between the Tropicks," however, "who never saw nor heard of any such Thing before, there the whole Probability relies on Testimony"—and in such cases the testimony would need to be much stronger, since the witness was seeking to persuade him of something entirely outside of his experience. "To a Man," writes Locke, "whose Experience has always been quite contrary, and has never heard of any thing like it, the most untainted Credit of a Witness will scarce be able to find belief." He then introduces the story of the Dutch ambassador to Siam:

> And as it happened to a *Dutch* Ambassador, who entertaining the King of *Siam* with the particularities of *Holland*, which he was inquisitive after, amongst other things told him, that the Water in his Country, would sometimes, in cold weather, be so hard, that Men walked upon it.... To which the King replied, *Hitherto I have believed the strange Things you have told me, because I look upon you as a sober fair man, but now I am sure you lye.*[45]

---

45 Locke, *An Essay concerning Human Understanding*, pp. 656–7 (4.15.5). The example was often repeated: see Benjamin Bennet, writing in 1730: "It was once thought impossible there should be *Antipodes*; and yet now no body questions it. The King of *Siam*, 'tis said, thought himself affronted by the *Dutch* Ambassador, when he told him that in *Holland* the Water would become so hard in cold Weather, than Men or Elephants might walk upon it. We believe a great many Things we do not understand, cannot account for, and have Reason to think as impossible as any of the Things the Objection refers to in Scripture" (Bennet, *The Truth, Inspiration, and Usefulness of the Scripture*, p. 317). Daniel Cox quotes this very passage from Locke in *An Appeal to the Public, in Behalf of Elizabeth Canning*, p. 50.

We can laugh at the Siamese king who thought his experience of water ruled out the possibility that it might turn solid: we know that he simply had not experienced it in the right climate. To the king, though, such a thing was beyond the limits of plausibility. Might we not be similarly naive when we consider things beyond our experience? And the question could be exceedingly urgent, since not long before Locke wrote, arguments like those of the Siamese king sent innocent men to the gallows. Roger L'Estrange found some testimony in the Popish Plot contrary to his experience, and was sure they lied: "Suppose my Boy should come in and tell me that it rains *Butter'd Turnips*, I should go near to open the Window to see whether it be so or no: and you would not blame me for Doubting neither. For *That* is *firmest Faith* that is *introduced* by *Reason*, and *established* by *Experience*."[46]

In *An Essay concerning the Use of Reason in Propositions, the Evidence Whereof Depends upon Human Testimony*, the philosopher Anthony Collins took up a related question in 1709, when he recognized that the claims of witnesses had to be balanced against our knowledge of the world. "Testimony of it self," he said, "is not sufficient to procure Faith or Assent, unless accompanied with these two Circumstances, credibility of Persons, and Credibility of the Things related." This amounts only to an assertion that a statement must be internally consistent, but he goes on: "for let a Proposition be ever so improbable, if it amounts not to a repugnancy to another Proposition in the Historical Relation, or to one which is self-evident, … it may be receiv'd as a Truth from a credible Author."[47] Collins's reservations and qualifications, however, are most interesting: we are inclined to accept a proposition, he says, even an improbable one, as long as it "amounts not to a repugnancy to another Proposition." True. But what happens when a new claim *does* contradict a known fact? Collins offers no satisfying answer, but the question is clearly on his mind. He considers the argument that an oak should grow from an acorn "up to the size and stature of a Tree … in less than an hour," a clearly implausible claim. But impossible? That we have never seen it happen is not enough to contradict the testimony of a trustworthy eyewitness, and so we must allow the possibility that our knowledge about the speed at which trees grow may be false. If the witness is credible, "all difficulties whatever, as to the thing testify'd, that come short of a Contradiction of one part of the *Relation* … to what we know otherwise to be true, hinder not the thing related from being credible."[48] Collins leaves the question unanswered. Similar concerns showed up in eighteenth-century legal theory, and jurists did not have the luxury of ignoring such problems when they arose. Many writers addressed the problem of testimony that contradicts known facts. Geoffrey Gilbert insists that a single witness is insufficient to overturn universal experience, "for if the Fact be contrary to all manner of Experience and Observation, 'tis too much to receive it upon the Oath of one Witness; or if what he says be contradictory, that removes him from all Credit, for Things totally opposite cannot receive Belief from the Attestation of any Man."[49] Fair enough. What, though, about the oaths

---

46 L'Estrange, *A Further Discovery of the Plot*, p. 3.
47 Collins, *Essay concerning the Use of Reason*, pp. 6, 8–9.
48 Ibid., p. 9.
49 Gilbert, *The Law of Evidence*, p. 150.

of two witnesses?—or ten?—or a thousand? And what if it is not "contrary to all manner of Experience," but merely the experience of most?—or something that seems probable to those who have bothered to think about it? At what point should a doubtful new claim be enough to overturn conventional wisdom?

Locke and Collins never found a really satisfactory answer to the question of how to reconcile contradictions between experience and testimony—in fact they seem uncomfortable with the very prospect that widespread credible testimony may not be reliable. One author, though, was willing to confront the disturbing implications of the possibility that widespread testimony by apparently credible witnesses may well be wrong. David Hume makes this the center of "Of Miracles," section 10 of *An Enquiry concerning Human Understanding* (1748). After asserting that "Our evidence … for the truths of the *Christian religion* is less than the evidence for the truth of our senses," and that "a weaker evidence can never destroy a stronger,"[50] he goes on to assert that no amount of testimony is enough to overturn the laws of nature—and yet he never clearly describes the criteria that allow us to distinguish our own experience with everyday phenomena from the true and inviolable laws of nature. Many modern philosophers have worked to save Hume from tautology on the one hand and absurdity on the other.[51] It should not be surprising to discover that Hume's answer has failed to satisfy many readers in his own day, largely because, as Shapin observes, he was far outside the intellectual mainstream: "David Hume's treatment of miracles," he writes, "turned upside down the preferred solution arrived at by most of these authors" who had earlier considered the problem.[52] His skepticism sought to render supernatural events implausible, leaving natural ones as the only possibility. Skepticism, though, once released, has a habit of corroding all the truths with which it comes into contact. Distinguishing events that are truly supernatural—in other words, those that defy natural laws—from those that are merely unusual poses difficulties Hume never solved.

Humean skepticism and the dangers of Pyrrhonism will be one of the subjects in Chapter 9. For now it is enough to note that these problems posed by any comparison of a questioned fact with knowledge about the world—whether about history, biology, or the laws of physics—are often very difficult to ignore. It should then be no surprise that the eighteenth century saw sometimes heated debates over the plausibility of testimony we now would reject out of hand. One extreme example came in the nineteenth century, and it shows that some dupes have missed even the most obvious clues. Perhaps the most remarkable case of an inept forger going far is Vrain-Denis Lucas, who sold many thousands of forged autograph letters from historical figures. Most meet the minimal requirements for internal consistency, but splendidly fail even the simplest tests for external consistency, as is obvious on even a superficial glance. Lucas's letters from Sappho and Julius Caesar were written in French on paper; it requires no recondite critical knowledge to know that Sappho

---

50   Hume, *Enquiries*, p. 109 (*Human Understanding*, 10.1.86).

51   There is a substantial literature on Hume's discussion of miracles. A useful brief summary of some of the more important attempts to make sense of it is David Johnson, *Hume, Holism, and Miracles*.

52   Shapin, *A Social History of Truth*, p. 212.

and Caesar both died long before either the language or the medium came into being. And yet Lucas found buyers willing to pay for even the most farcical lies.

Few went to such absurd extremes, but it is not surprising that a few did. Nor should it be at all surprising that otherwise serious people were prepared to believe that a woman could live for a month on a jug of water, that a third-century epic could be passed down intact by oral tradition, that Shakespeare could be responsible for *Vortigern*, or that a woman could have given birth to rabbits. In the last few centuries a considerable array of institutions—scientific academies, refereed publication, prestigious university press imprints—have helped to clarify the boundaries of what counts as knowledge, and to allow us to be far more confident in repeating things we "know." Yet even today there are many facts taken largely on faith, which have never received the sort of scrutiny that we supposedly demand of knowledge. And the more philosophical quandaries are just as bothersome today as they were in the eighteenth century. Our own remaining insecurities surrounding the things we think we know should be another reminder of why it is prudent to take these eighteenth-century debates seriously, and not to laugh at the past for being foolish.

Chapter 6

The Mention of Posterior Facts

One of the most important varieties of external contradiction—so important that Jeremy Bentham calls it the "first indication of forgery"—is the anachronism. "The falsehood of a writing will often be detected," he writes, "by its making direct mention of, or allusions more or less indirect to, some fact posterior to the date which it bears.... *The mention of posterior facts*;—first indication of forgery."[1] The power of an anachronism to disqualify a questionable document is now widely taken for granted, so much so that the principles underlying such investigations are often assumed to be self-evident, but they deserve to be spelled out. An anachronism seems a violation of consistency only when it is believed that a work of art derives its authenticity not only from coherence with the real world in general, nor simply from the unifying power of a single intelligence, but also from the historically specific conditions under which it was created.

Sacrilegious Boldness

The most famous example of a forgery detected through anachronism lies well outside the eighteenth century: in 1440, Lorenzo Valla debunked the Donation of Constantine. The Donation purported to be a grant from the emperor Constantine to Pope Sylvester I, and the Church had long used it to justify its temporal power. Valla's suspicion was aroused by some apparent inconsistencies that, to him, ruled out the possibility that the Donation could be genuine. The inconsistencies were various—some had to do with the plausibility of Constantine's motives, and others with errors in geography—but the most telling were references to historical events that happened after the fourth century. The supposed emperor, for example, refers to his city as "Constantinople," even though it did not receive that name until after his death: "How in the world—this is much more absurd, and impossible in the nature of things—could one speak of Constantinople as one of the patriarchal sees, when it was not yet a patriarchate, nor a see, nor a Christian city, nor named Constantinople, nor founded, nor planned!" Valla challenges the anonymous forger: "O scelerate atque malefice!"—"O thou scoundrel, thou villain!"—and then points out that the document refers to *satrapes*, provincial governors not found in the real world of the fourth century. "What! How do you want to have satraps come in here? Numskull, blockhead! Do the Caesars speak thus; are Roman decrees usually drafted thus? Whoever heard of satraps being mentioned in the councils of the Romans?" And the Donation speaks of churches devoted to Peter and Paul, but Valla demands,

---

1   Bentham, *A Treatise on Judicial Evidence*, p. 140.

Who had constructed them? Who would have dared to build them, when, as history tells us, the Christians had never had anything but secret and secluded meeting-places? And if there had been any temples at Rome dedicated to these apostles, they would not have called for such great lights as these to be set up in them; they were little chapels, not sanctuaries; little shrines, not temples; oratories in private houses, not public places of worship.

In referring to the provinces that were being given to Sylvester, "this forger, of course, did not know which provinces were under Constantine, and which were not." And so on, through dozens of anachronisms. His conclusion: "Who then does not see that the man who wrote the 'privilege' lived long after the time of Constantine?"[2]

What is remarkable about this detection is not that it happened, but that it did not happen much sooner. No one in the previous seven centuries—even those who had good reasons to challenge the authenticity of the Donation—thought to examine its relation to its historical moment. What now seems obvious was a breakthrough in the fifteenth century: it depended on a nascent sense of historicism, a hallmark of the new humanism. Paul Ricoeur calls this episode "the birth of historical criticism."[3] The rise of a historicist consciousness is a defining characteristic of early modern intellectual life.

We find few traces of this kind of consciousness earlier. Chaucer populates his ancient Troy with people who dressed and acted like his own contemporaries. It seemingly never occurred to him that the world of 1100 B.C. was fundamentally different from that of A.D. 1375. Even Shakespeare, living in a much more historically aware age, makes the same blunder about the same historical moment; characters in his *Troilus and Cressida* notoriously quote Aristotle centuries before Aristotle was born. In other works, Richard III compares himself to Machiavelli, who published nothing until 14 years after Richard's death; clocks toll in *Julius Caesar* before the first tolling clock was built; and Douglas, in *1 Henry IV*, fires a pistol long before pistols had been invented. Anachronism abounded, and no one cared. Historical periods were more or less interchangeable.

But not for Valla. Although the Church long resisted his claims, most scholars came around, and by the eighteenth century, his innovations were widely accepted— so much so that the less historically aware ages came to seem positively benighted. For instance, in 1753 Protestant propagandist John White calls the original writer of the Donation "one of the greatest Bunglers in Forgery that ever took up that trade," who was able to succeed only "by Reason of the Ignorance of those Times."[4] Edward Gibbon similarly marvels at the "ignorance and credulity of the times" that left so many in the Middle Ages "incapable of discerning a forgery." Things improved in the next age:

> In the revival of letters and liberty this fictitious deed was transpierced by the pen of Laurentius Valla, the pen of an eloquent critic and a Roman patriot. His contemporaries of the fifteenth century were astonished at his sacrilegious boldness; yet such is the silent and

---

2   Valla, *The Treatise of Lorenzo Valla*, pp. 95, 84–5, 97, 125, 95–7.

3   Ricoeur, *Memory, History, Forgetting*, p. 172.

4   White, *The Protestant Englishman*, p. 217.

irresistible progress of reason, that before the end of the next age, the fable was rejected by the contempt of historians and poets.[5]

But what struck the mid-eighteenth century as inconceivable ignorance was simply the lack of a single faculty, an awareness that every age has its own character. After Valla, this kind of historicism became increasingly widespread, and forgers were effectively put on notice that their works had to reflect the age from which they purported to come.

A Foundation of Truth and Superstructure of Fable

Since many of the high-profile forgeries of the eighteenth century were supposed to be historical documents—think of Ossian, ostensibly of the third century; Rowley, of the fifteenth; and Ireland's Shakespeare, of the sixteenth and early seventeenth—the techniques developed by Valla often came into play. It is this historical distance that makes the imitation of the past so difficult, because no one can be conscious of every possible shibboleth that might reveal his or her true identity. A spy operating in a foreign country is found out by his accent, his idiom, his table manners. A forger operating in the foreign country of the past is similarly exposed by his or her inability to capture the tenor of a lost age—they do things differently there. Anthony Grafton explains the value of this historicist insight for investigations of authenticity: "If any law holds for all forgery," he writes,

> it is quite simply that any forger, however deft, imprints the pattern and texture of his own period's life, thought, and language on the past he hopes to make seem real and vivid. But the very details he deploys, however deeply they impress his immediate public, will eventually make his trickery stand out in bold relief, when they are observed by later readers who will recognize the forger's period superimposed on the forgery's. Nothing becomes obsolete like a period vision of an older period.[6]

So Thomas Warton says of Chatterton: "A builder of ruins is seldom exact throughout, in his imitation of the old-fashioned architecture…. Some member of the Chinese Gothic will unavoidably peep out, and betray the fraud."[7]

Detectors therefore looked for modern touches in the ostensibly old works they hoped to discredit. Anachronisms were at the heart of Edmond Malone's exposure of Ireland's Shakespearean forgeries. When Ireland's Shakespeare observes "Each titled dame deserts her rolls and tea," Malone catches him out for "introducing our fragrant Chinese beverage" decades before it was introduced to England—Thomas Garway first offered "China Tcha, Tay or Tee" for sale in 1657. Ireland's Shakespeare, moreover, writes, "thou arte ass a talle Cedarre stretchynge forthe its branches ande succourynge smaller Plants." Malone's reply shows him resorting not strictly to literary and historical evidence, but even to botanical: "As Shakespeare is known to have been a curious observer of nature, we might suppose that his description was

---

5   Gibbon, *Decline and Fall*, 3:115–16.

6   Grafton, *Forgers and Critics*, p. 67.

7   Warton, *An Enquiry*, p. 11.

suggested by what he had himself seen: but ... there were no Cedars in England till after the Restoration."[8]

Anachronisms as conspicuous as tea-drinking Elizabethans may be dead giveaways, but not all anachronisms are so easily spotted. Many require a specialist's knowledge of unfamiliar events, customs, or facts about a long-forgotten world. This knowledge can range widely, taking in history, archaeology, numismatics, even zoology. Consider just one field of knowledge, the history of finance. Ireland worried about "a false report having gone abroad that ye word guineas was mentioned in some of the deeds"—in fact the word appears nowhere in the Shakespeare papers—but the papers do give a suspicious number of monetary amounts in multiples of 21 shillings, as when Shakespeare promises to pay "my good and Worthye Freynd John Hemynge the sume of five Pounds and five shillings English Monye." Samuel Ireland therefore consulted his friend Henry James Pye, who put his mind at ease: "I have this moment met with a passage in Mr Anderson's History of England which I transcribe as it fully accounts for the sum of *pounds* & *shillings* which were objected to by some of your *candid* critics[:] 'Henry VII was the first English king who coined the golden sovereign of forty two shillings & the half sovereign of half that value.'"[9] In fact, the half-sovereign's value varied throughout the sixteenth century, but the 21-shilling coin was definitively established only in December 1717. Malone spotted that one, as he did the similarity between supposedly Shakespearean promissory notes and those of his own day: "We have here fortunately a date," he remarks caustically, "which beside the other uses it may serve, may prevent your lordship from supposing that you are reading some tradesman's promissory note of the year 1796." He includes a long appendix to his *Inquiry* on the "Origin and History of Promissory Notes and Paper Credit."[10]

Similar financial concerns were common in the Chatterton case. Warton was made suspicious by Rowley's reference to a *repayring lease*: "I very much question, whether this technical law-term, or even this mode of contract, existed in the year 1400."[11] Malone was also wary about Cannynge's "possessing a *Cabinet* of coins and other curiosities, a century at least before any Englishman ever thought of forming such a collection."[12] These accusations were answered, but not very convincingly. Edward Burnaby Greene challenges Malone's criticism: "To speak fully upon 'Cannynge's alleged *collection* of coins,' the *word* may possibly sound too high in modern ears, when applied to the fifteenth century: but as Cannynge might certainly, as it is surmised, have *collected* pictures and books; why should coins be eradicated as objects of his curiosity?"[13] Jeremiah Milles, unable to explain some of the inconsistencies in Cannynge's numismatic knowledge, suggested that

---

8   Malone, *An Inquiry*, pp. 102 n, 162.

9   Henry James Pye to Samuel Ireland, 7 April 1795, in BL Add. MS 30346, fol. 89^r.

10   Malone, *An Inquiry*, pp. 134, 369–401. For his detection of the 21-shilling guinea, see p. 136.

11   Warton, *The History of English Poetry*, 2:164 n.

12   Malone, *Cursory Observations*, pp. 24–5.

13   Greene, *Strictures upon a Pamphlet*, p. 16.

the apparent errors were intentional and, far from proving the documents forgeries, were actually further proof of their authenticity: Cannynge's

> history of coinage, contained in the yellow roll—His drawings and descriptions of ancient coins and inscribed stones, said by him to have been dug up in the city and neighborhood of Bristol, and calculated to do honour to the place, (though no such genuine coins or inscriptions could have existed) contain such a mixture of probable and improbable facts, such a foundation of truth and superstructure of fable, as shew the author to have been well acquainted with the antiquities of the kingdom, and capable of misleading the generality of readers; who, in that illiterate age, were very incompetent judges of historical truth.[14]

And Rayner Hickford, who saw in Rowley nothing but a confused mess of numismatic knowledge—"the *Mark* is spoken of as a *gold coin*, which was no coin at all, but only a sum in accounts ... and the *Noble* is mentioned as a *silver coin*, which was a gold one"—concluded, therefore, that "Chatterton must have made an alteration" in transcribing authentic fifteenth-century sources "to render them suitable to his own ideas of Marks and Nobles."[15]

Some anachronisms were more subtle still, requiring knowledge not of, say, the history of financial instruments, but of the language itself. These, too, go back to Valla, whose *Treatise* devotes much of its space to criticism of linguistic anachronisms. The forged Donation uses the late Latin word *banna* ("flag") instead of the fourth-century *vexillum*; it uses the verb *clericare* ("to ordain") even though there is no other evidence of the word until long after Constantine's day. Grammatical forms were likewise characteristic not of the fourth century but of the eighth. Even the style was inconsistent with fourth-century "purity," and more characteristic of what the fifteenth-century Valla saw as medieval barbarism: "What? Does not that barbarous way of talking show that the rigmarole was composed, not in the age of Constantine, but later; 'decernimus quod uti debeant' for the correct form 'decernimus ut utantur'? Boors commonly speak and write that way now; 'Iussi quod deberes venire' for 'Iussi ut venires.'"[16] Valla was therefore able to make a convincing case that the document was an eighth-century forgery. And this attention to linguistic anachronism has proven exceptionally valuable in spotting forgeries, because every document makes countless claims that are invisible even to its creator.

Suppose someone were to set out to repeat William Henry Ireland's imposture today, and to try to pass off original works as Shakespeare's. It would not be difficult for him or her to learn the basics of early modern English grammar—the inflections, the syntax, perhaps even the phrasal verbs. A sprinkling of obsolete words and some judicious archaizing of the spelling would be necessary. Today a would-be forger could turn to concordances and historical dictionaries to avoid the more egregious lapses in vocabulary and spelling—something not available to Ireland in 1795. But even these resources are far from comprehensive, and some things do not lend themselves to easy cataloguing in a dictionary. How many would-be fakers of early

---

14   Milles, "Additional Evidence," in Chatterton, *Poems Supposed to Have Been Written at Bristol*, ed. Milles, p. 517.

15   Hickford, *Observations on the Poems Attributed to Rowley*, p. 31.

16   Valla, *The Treatise of Lorenzo Valla*, p. 121.

modern English, for instance, would know that the modern passive progressive form (*is being done*) is not to be found before the late eighteenth century? A clever faker could fool most amateurs, but only an expert in historical linguistics would be able to concoct pseudo-Shakespearean language that would deceive other experts. And even if that expert got the language exactly right according to the current state of the art, he or she would have to fear detection from future generations of historical linguists, who will likely discover features of early modern English invisible even to the keenest modern eyes. This is why the anachronism has become one of the most important weapons in any detector's arsenal.

Some Words Go Off

Although Continental humanists learned the historicist lesson from Valla, it took some time for his methods to reach Britain. One of the first prominent and extended uses of this kind of historicism to challenge authenticity in England was Richard Bentley's *Dissertation upon the Epistles of Phalaris* (1699). The broad outlines of the story are now familiar: Bentley, convinced the *Epistles* were late forgeries, marshaled his impressive classical knowledge to lay waste to the arguments of Sir William Temple and the other supporters of their authenticity. His *Dissertation* covered the full range of *Altertumswissenschaft*, but most of his arguments dealt with the language of the *Epistles*. His attacks proved most effective, and most memorable, when they demonstrated that the ostensibly sixth-century-B.C. Phalaris could not have used forms of the language that came into being after his death.

Before he could offer any specific arguments, though, Bentley had to lay the theoretical groundwork by convincing his readers that language can provide an insight into history. His case depends on three related facts: that languages change over time; that each age therefore has its own characteristic linguistic forms; and that works bear the marks of the age in which they were written. As he puts it:

> Every living Language, like the perspiring Bodies of living Creatures, is in perpetual motion and alteration; some words go off, and become obsolete; others are taken in, and by degrees grow into common use; or the same word is inverted to a new sense and notion, which in a tract of time makes as observable a change in the air and features of a Language, as Age makes in the lines and mien of a Face.[17]

This argument was in principle no longer surprising when Bentley advanced it; some kind of linguistic historicism was widespread, and any late seventeenth-century Englishman who had read Spenser or Shakespeare could easily see how much English had changed in just a few decades. Even Charles Boyle, the Earl of Orrery, one of Bentley's most vocal opponents, was prepared to admit that English has changed: "I can easily grant, that the *English* Tongue has undergone very considerable and surprizing Changes, especially in this Last Century."[18]

---

17   Bentley, *A Dissertation*, pp. 392–3.
18   Boyle, *Dr. Bentley's Dissertations*, p. 69.

But though a modern, debased language like English may be mutable, Boyle insists, Greek was different. "If Dr. *Bentley* pretends to point out as *Real and Sensible Differences* in the several Ages of the *Greek*, as a moderate Critic may in the *English*, I'm afraid his *Subtilty of Tast* will fail him. Does he take the *Greek* of *Lucian* to be as different from that of *Plato*, as our *English* Now is from that which was spoken soon after the Conquest?" Greek writers, after all, unlike their inferior English counterparts, cared about the purity of their language; their "Contempt of the Barbarity of other Countries" kept their tongue free of foreign corruptions. The result is that "we have *Greek* Books writ by Authors at almost Two thousand Years distance, who disagree less in their Phrase and Manner of Speech, than the Books of any Two *English* Writers do, who liv'd but Two hundred Years asunder."[19] What seem to be late forms in Phalaris had been there all along. The privileged cultures of antiquity had transcended historicism, Boyle insists, and presented unchanging images of perfection.

Not so Bentley. "The *Attic*," he lectures, "was no more privileged from change than the other Languages of the World are." He offers some examples: "There were only two Centuries between *Solon* and *Lysias*," he says, "and the Alteration seems to be almost as great, as what has happen'd in our own Language within the same space." Having laid the groundwork, he is able to use his specific philological evidence to devastating effect. "In the very first Epistle," he writes, "ὧν ἐμοὶ προτρέπεις, *which you accuse me of*, is an innovation in language, for which the Ancients used προφέρεις."[20] And so on, through more than 500 pages of linguistic anachronisms, all of which demonstrated that the *Epistles* used linguistic forms—vocabulary, accidence, grammar, idioms—that were inconsistent with the historical Phalaris. Temple, Boyle, Atterbury, and Swift continued to fight against Bentley and his kind for some years, producing along the way masterpieces of satirical invective, including Swift's *Tale of a Tub* and Pope's *Dunciad*. But it is now impossible to doubt that Bentley had the better arguments and, once the Scriblerian generation had passed, his reputation—as a scholar, if not as a gentleman—grew. After mid-century, virtually no one took the *Epistles* of Phalaris for genuine sixth-century works.

Once this kind of historicist reading had been introduced into English criticism, it became a standard part of any investigation of the authenticity of ostensible antiques. Bentley's model, for example, seems to have been present to those who challenged the authenticity of Chatterton's Rowley poems. Rowley supposedly lived in the fifteenth century, and therefore should have written the language of the fifteenth century. If his language is not consistent with that of his time—especially if it bears the marks of a later age—it follows that it cannot be genuine. Warton therefore offers a list of "modern words, and modern formularies of expression," including *puerilitie*, *bred* (in the sense of "educated" or "brought up"), *optics*, *Latinised*, *piece* (for a work of literature), *tragedy* (for a play), the tag *thus he* (as a speech prefix), and so on, all of which prove that the poems could not have been written in the fifteenth century.[21] Thomas Tyrwhitt states the principle clearly in his edition of the Rowleian

---

19   Ibid., pp. 69–70, 71.
20   Bentley, *Dissertation*, pp. 399, 394.
21   Warton, *An Enquiry*, pp. 23–4.

poems: "I shall premise only one *postulatum*, which is, that Poets of the same age and country use the same language, allowances being made for certain varieties, which may arise from the local situation, the rank in life, the learning, the affectation of the writers, and from the different subjects and forms of their compositions." That *postulatum* being granted, he is only a few steps away from his conclusion: "I have nothing to do but to prove, that the language of the poems attributed to Rowley ... is totally different from that of the other English writers of the XV Century."[22] Rowley, therefore, is not of the fifteenth century: Q.E.D.

Tyrwhitt often speaks with conviction, even a certain degree of swagger. He appears to admit no doubt in his indictment of Chatterton: "I shall only take notice of such as can be referred to three general heads; the *first* consisting of words not used by any other writer; the *second*, of words used by other writers, but in a different sense; and the *third*, of words inflected in a manner contrary to grammar and custom."[23] But although this kind of attention to historically specific forms of the language is now universally accepted, we should not assume it was always a simple matter. We have grown accustomed to tools like the *Oxford English Dictionary* that allow us to date with reasonable precision the entry of words into the written language, to say nothing of full-text electronic databases that make such searches simple. It requires a stretch of the imagination to recover the uncertainty of the eighteenth century, when that information had not been collected and each author had to rely on nothing more than his or her memory. Tyrwhitt offers pages of observations like this: "I do not believe that *champion* was used as a *verb* by any writer much earlier than Shakespeare." In this instance, he is probably right; the *Oxford English Dictionary* credits Shakespeare with the first use. On other matters, though, his recollections are not so happy. He insists *almer* was not used in the fifteenth century, but the *OED* does not bear him out. "*Swarthe*, used as a noun," says Tyrwhitt, "has no sense that I am acquainted with,"[24] and Johnson's *Dictionary* agrees; but we now know that *swarth* (in its various spellings) meant "skin" beginning in the eighth century and "turf" beginning around 1400. Although Tyrwhitt's conclusion is correct, he makes quite a few mistakes along the way about the history of the language—and this despite what he called the "the *intense application* which I have been obliged to bestow" on the work.[25]

Edmond Malone's own application was intense enough when he entered the debates over Chatterton; it was more intense still when he turned his attention to Ireland. Malone's scholarly energy was prodigious, and he enjoyed trotting out ostentatious citations to back up his assertions: "Now unfortunately no such verb active as to *complement*, in this sense, was known in [Shakespeare's] age, nor for some time afterwards," he insists: "and when it did come into use, it was always coupled with a preposition, not found here."[26] He backs up this generalization with quotations from 16 works, mostly dictionaries, but also several of Shakespeare's

22   Chatterton, *Poems*, ed. Tyrwhitt, p. 312.
23   Ibid., pp. 312–13.
24   Ibid., p. 317.
25   Tyrwhitt to Burgess, 29 July 1782, in BL Add. MS 46847, fol. 59ʳ.
26   Malone, *An Inquiry*, p. 76.

works, with the dates carefully noted. And yet the *OED* finds an example of a transitive *complement* without a preposition from 1617, making a Shakespearean example not out of the question. Without the benefit of authoritative reference works, it was too easy to make errors like this.

Malone has never been accused of excessive modesty, but the lack of authoritative sources often prompted others to phrase their suspicions in very tentative terms: *I do not recall seeing this form, I am unacquainted with any occurrence of this word, I believe the reader will find few examples*, and so on. But even if a reference work like the *OED* had existed in the eighteenth century, it would not necessarily settle all questions of authenticity, simply because someone must have been the first to use each new word, and the newly discovered document could be the earliest source. If an author speaks of a guinea before guineas had been coined, or of tea before tea was introduced into Europe, we can be fairly certain that the source is a fake: it is the thing, not merely the word, that constitutes the anachronism. Authors speak and write the language of their age, but that language is always changing, and the authors in question may well be the source of some of that change. If a questioned poem uses a word that had never been used before its supposed date, does it necessarily follow that the poem is a fake? Yes, says Malone: "no manuscript alleged to have been written in the age of Queen Elizabeth," he writes of the Ireland papers, "can be genuine, in which a single word is found which was not in use till several years, or perhaps an age, after her death." When he spots the word *accede* in an ostensibly Shakespearean document, therefore, he is confident: "We have here therefore a word unknown to our language for near a century after the death of the person by whom it is pretended to have been used. If this be not a decisive proof of forgery, I know not what has a title to be considered as one."[27] The same conviction led Tyrwhitt to compile a list of words in Rowley's poems that appear nowhere else in the fifteenth century—a single word that was not in use, he insists, should disqualify the whole Rowleian corpus. The list is ostentatiously alphabetized and numbered, with 20 words just from *abessie* to *astende*.

We should pause to remember, though, that Shakespeare would fail such a test: it is easy to produce long lists of words he used that are found in none of his predecessors or contemporaries. (*OED* records at least 96 new coinages in *Hamlet* alone.) And although Shakespeare's linguistic inventiveness is the stuff of legend, most of his contemporaries also coined many words, or at least were the first to record words that had circulated in oral culture; it does not follow that their works are forgeries. F. G. Waldron, therefore, admits to his own doubts about a possible anachronism in Ireland's papers: "the only doubt that struck me … was of the word *whymsycalle*; which, I then observed, I did not remember to have met with at so early a period: this objection was soon overruled by the supposition that, as the word must have been produced at some period, Shakspeare might have then coined it."[28]

Despite the nagging doubts about circularity, though, by the early nineteenth century the argument about linguistic anachronism had won the day, and even appeared in Bentham's discussion of legal evidence. "In a living language," he

---

27 Ibid., pp. 76, 204.
28 Waldron, *Free Reflections*, pp. 6–7.

explains, "there are always variations in words, in the meaning of words, in the construction of phrases, in the manner of spelling, which may detect the age of a writing, and lead to legitimate suspicions of forgery.... This principle of criticism, when applied to literary works, has often led to difficult and doubtful researches; but its results are more certain, and sometimes decisive, in legal deeds."[29]

The Charm of Old Spelling

Language is more than vocabulary: accidence can provide further evidence for those who question authenticity. Tyrwhitt says as much of Chatterton, whose grasp of fifteenth-century syntax is imperfect: "In a language like ours, in which the inflections are so few and so simple, it is not to be supposed that a writer, even of the lowest class, would commit very frequent offences of this sort. I shall take notice of some, which I think impossible to have fallen from a genuine Rowley." These "offences" are numerous, but "the capital blunder" is "the termination of *verbs in the singular number* in *n*,"[30] of which he adduces pages of examples. Orthography, too, has often aided skeptics. Chatterton obviously hoped his faux-antique spelling would make his works seem older; in Thomas Warton's words, "In the Pseudo-Rowley, we are imposed upon by the charm of old spelling."[31] In addition, many casual inspectors of their works seem to have been taken in simply by their antiquated-looking spellings, so much so that Hardinge and a few others hoped that "some future editor of Rowley's poems may print them *unbristled*, as it were, with this strange spelling."[32] Yet for many of the detectors, his spellings were proof that the works were not written in the fifteenth century.

Rowley's defenders tried to argue that these arguments from spelling were not definitive. Even conspicuous anachronisms did not always convince everyone. George Catcott, one of Rowley's most vocal supporters, reacts to his critics with simple incomprehension: "I don't find they bring any other proof to invalidate the originality of the MSS., but that the characters are not precisely reducible either to the era of the poems, or any other preceding or subsequent to them."[33] What seems an obvious argument against the poems' authenticity—that they are in the language of no age—is reduced to a minor cavil. Samuel Seyer likewise works to suggest orthography is unimportant, since such picayune matters are rarely transmitted from age to age intact: "Homer's works have never been suspected," he writes not many years before Homer's works were first suspected; "& yet we can prove that these writings are totally different from the language & orthography of Homer's time."[34] Jeremiah Milles too dismisses orthographical objections as "trifling

---

29 Bentham, *A Treatise on Judicial Evidence*, p. 140.

30 Chatterton, *Poems*, ed. Tyrwhitt, pp. 320, 321.

31 Warton, *An Enquiry*, p. 91.

32 Hardinge, *Rowley and Chatterton in the Shades*, p. viii n. Walter William Skeat took Hardinge's advice in 1871, when he published a two-volume edition of Chatterton's works in modern spelling.

33 Catcott to Charlemont, 5 Nov. 1773, in BL Add. MS 47865, fol. 141[r].

34 Seyer, *Mr. Seyer's MSS*, in Bristol Central Library MS B4533, facing fol. 117.

verbal Criticisms," and if the spellings are in fact inconsistent, "the only ground was the modern spelling of the Words by *Chatterton*, who might be inattentive to the Orthography of the Original."[35] This argument about imperfect transmission would be much more convincing if we did not have documents that purported to be autograph manuscripts by Rowley himself.

More complicated than even accidence and orthography, though, was prosody, which often featured in the debates over Chatterton and Ireland. "I communicated the poems to Mr Gray and Mr Mason," writes Horace Walpole, "who at once pronounced them forgeries, and declared there was no symptom in them of their being the productions of near so distant an age; the language and metres being totally unlike anything ancient."[36] His interest in the "metres" of the Rowleian poems was characteristic of his age: for eighteenth-century critics, prosody was a surprisingly important marker of the age of a composition. Many eighteenth-century readers had a clearer notion of the progress of versification than they had of the history of any particular word.

Sometimes a particular poetic form tipped off the skeptics. Thomas Warton objects to the 10-line stanza ending with an Alexandrine as being derived from Prior (and in turn from Spenser); the caesura after the third foot in his Alexandrines; the double rhymes used to comic ends (*baskette—aske ytte*); and the natural accent on polysyllables.[37] Edward Burnaby Greene cries foul, accusing Warton of a double standard: "'Double rhimes' are particular objects of censure," he says, "as arguing modernism of date. In Chaucer what is pronounced '*accidental*' is attributed, as to the author of these Poems, to *design*."[38] Warton notices that "The Songe to Ella is composed in that devious and irregular measure, which has been called the Pindaric. What shall we think of a Pindaric ode in the reign of Edward the fourth?"[39] Greene replies: "The truth is, that odes, call them balads [*sic*], call them songs, call them poems, without the metre of *heroick* complection, displayed the lyrick spirit in very early times."[40]

But even more important than particular poetic forms was a subjective sense of the regularity of the meter. In examining Chatterton's poems, the "smoothness of the versification" is for Malone the "first and principal objection to the antiquity of these poems." The modernity of the prosody, he explains, is clear even through the antiquated orthography: "A series of more than three thousand lines, however disfigured by old spelling, flowing for the most part as smoothly as any of Pope's— is a matter difficult to be got over."[41] The *Monthly Review* likewise noted that the excellence of the versification was the first indication of fraud: "On our first opening these Poems, the smooth style of the harmony, the easy march of the verse, the regular

---

35 Catcott's transcription of Jeremiah Milles to Catcott, 3 Nov. 1774, in Catcott, *Chattertoniana*, Bristol Central Library MS B5342, p. 250.

36 Walpole to William Bewley, 23 May 1778, in Walpole, *Correspondence*, 16:126.

37 Warton, *An Enquiry*, pp. 35–42.

38 Greene, *Strictures upon a Pamphlet*, p. 60.

39 Warton, *An Enquiry*, p. 33.

40 Greene, *Strictures upon a Pamphlet*, p. 58.

41 Malone, *Cursory Observations*, p. 3.

station of the cæsura, the structure of the phrase, and the case and complexion of the thoughts, made us presently conclude they were *Mock Ruins.*"[42] When Walpole read the opening of *The Battle of Hastings II*—"Oh Truth! immortal daughter of the skies,/Too lyttle known to wryters of these daies"—he scribbled in the margin of his copy, "Is it credible that these shou'd not be modern lines?"[43]

Jacob Bryant, Rowley's most indefatigable defender, devoted much of his energy to insisting on at least the possibility of a fifteenth-century poet's mastery of versification. After observing that many critics "object to the rythm [*sic*] of Rowley, and to the harmony of his numbers, which they think too good and accurate for so early a date," he confesses "that I have had my scruples upon this head." After all, those who advanced these arguments "were gentlemen of uncommon learning, to whose opinion I could not help paying a very great regard." After further thought, though, evidence outweighed deference to authority, and "I was obliged to suppress my scruples." True, Rowley's meter was far superior to anything else in the fifteenth century; still, "In every age there will be a difference among writers; and whatever number of poets there may be found, it is a great chance, but there will be some one person more eminent than the rest." Ergo, all this evidence from metrical development is unreliable: "though from the texture of a poem, and the mode of composition, and more especially from the language, a notion concerning its age may be formed; yet nothing certain can be determined: and we are liable to be greatly deceived."[44]

Bryant's more candid critics may have been prepared to admit that arguments from versification fell short of the standard of demonstration—it was, after all, just possible that a lone fifteenth-century genius might have independently developed one verse form before it became familiar. Perhaps someone wrote something as complex as a Spenserian stanza before Spenser. For these critics, though, it was the sheer volume of evidence that tipped the balance, for no poet could have been happy enough to develop multiple verse forms otherwise known only after his death. A correspondent to the *Gentleman's Magazine* in 1777 marveled that a "writer must, surely, have possessed an unparalleled portion of genius, who, at a time when the structure of no one species of versification now in use was so much as formed, could compose several of those species in the greatest perfection."[45]

Sometimes it is not any particular word, meter, or even genre, but the texture of the language as a whole that seems alien. This is what Samuel Badcock argues in his review of Milles's edition of Rowley's poems (1782): "although it was easy for Chatterton to copy antient *words*, it was, however, by no means so easy for him to copy the antient *stile*. Here lies the main defect in the imposition; and by *this*, and this *alone*, the controversy may, we think, be fairly decided."[46] Warton says much the same thing: "Antiquated expressions are engrafted on present modes of speech … and the tinsel of a polished phraseology is but thinly tinged with the rust of antiquity. The diction and versification are at perpetual variance. Our author is smooth and

---

42   *Monthly Review* 56 (April 1777): 256.
43   Walpole's annotations to Chatterton's *Poems*, p. 97.
44   Bryant, *Observations*, pp. 425–6.
45   *Gentleman's Magazine* 47 (Aug. 1777): 361.
46   *Monthly Review* 66 (May 1782): 324.

mellifluous as Pope and Mason, yet more obscure and inexplicable than Gower or Chaucer." The result is that "many entire lines, and often prolix paragraphs, cannot be distinguished from the compositions of the present day."[47]

The apparent modernity of Rowley's style features in many discussions of the poems. The *Monthly* reviewer quotes from *Ælla*, "Oh thou, whereer (thie Bones att reste)," and adds, "Those who can suppose that this stanza was written in the fifteenth century must be very little acquainted with the style and manners of our poetry in that period. Only change the orthography and it is perfectly modern.... Compare this with the odes of Gray and Collins, and the marks of imitation will be sufficiently obvious."[48] The reviewer for the *Gentleman's Magazine* spotted the same parallel, though he hedges his objection with some qualifications that it may be mere coincidence: "There is, perhaps, nothing more difficult than positively to distinguish accidental coincidence from designed imitation. The following exquisite lines, however, bear a very strong resemblance to a justly-admired stanza of Gray."[49]

Warton is willing to suppose for a moment that Rowley was a singular genius in the fifteenth century, but at once states this objection: "But how comes it to pass, that this great genius should have *precisely* copied the style of the eighteenth century? Rowley might have formed a style: but it would not have been the same as that now existing." All of his objections to Rowley's authorship of the works attributed to him add up to this: they are incompatible with the story of progress he has learned. He sees in the poems "a facility of combination, a quickness of transition, a rapidity of apostrophe, a frequent variation of form and phrase, and a firmness of contexture, which must have been the result of a long establishment of the arts and habits of writing." Having studied English literary history for years, he was nearly certain that no work of the fifteenth century could have the degree of polish he found in the Rowleian poems: "Poetry, like other sciences, has its gradual accessions and advancements. The united labour of past ages contributes to its maturity." Poetical maturity, he argues, consists in abstraction and generality: "Our old English poets," he observes, "are minute and particular. They do not deal in abstraction and general exhibition, the effects of affectation and a restless pursuit of novelty. They dwell on realities."[50]

How does Rowley fit into this pattern? He was an uncomfortable exception to the rule. To those who suggested that Rowley's superiority to his contemporaries was consistent with his fifteenth-century date, because he possessed genius, Warton replied: "But superiority of genius, in the infancy of composition, never yet produced a perfect model. A great genius, at such a period, in the boldness of native conception, will strike out sublimities and beauties never before seen. But these will be vague, extravagant, and undigested. The truth is, such a delineation as this before us, is not the work of genius but of art."[51]

---

47 Warton, *An Enquiry*, pp. 42, 27.
48 *Monthly Review* 56 (June 1777): 447.
49 *Gentleman's Magazine* 47 (Aug. 1777): 361.
50 Warton, *An Enquiry*, pp. 18, 9, 17, 10.
51 Ibid., p. 17.

In one of the most curious twists on the charge of anachronism, Warton insists the Rowley poems cannot be real because they are anachronistic in their exclusion of anachronism. "Our antient English bards," he argues, "abound in unnatural conceptions, strange imaginations, capricious extravagances, and even the most ridiculous inconsistencies. But Rowley's poems present us with no incongruous combinations, no mixture of manners, institutions, usages, and characters. They have no violent or gross improbabilities." More important, early poets had no historical sense: his own historical sense tells him we should see such errors in medieval works. "In our old poets," he explains, "Ovid and saint Austin are sometimes cited in the same line. Our old poets are perpetually confounding Gothic and classical customs, knight-errantry and antient history, scripture and romance, religion and chivalry."[52] Warton paradoxically accuses Chatterton of lacking historical sense because he has historical sense: had Rowley been an authentic barbarian, he would inevitably confuse manners and customs from different periods, but Chatterton was too consistent to be genuine. Badcock's conclusion was similar: as he wrote in the *Monthly Review* in 1782, "Aukward attempts at something which looks like metre and rime; affected conceits of expression; dull and trite reflections; or tedious and unadorned narratives, make up the general sum of what was called poetry in the age in which Rowley is supposed to have written with the spirit of Dryden and the judgment of Pope! The Poems of Rowley are uniformly good. They are the productions not only of genius but of taste;—a taste which could not possibly have been acquired on a sudden."[53]

The History of the Times

The notion that "taste"—what eighteenth-century critics would call "true taste"—arrived not suddenly but over a long period is consistent with one of the dominant narratives of cultural progress. Samuel Johnson conveniently summarizes a widespread belief: "Nations, like individuals, have their infancy."[54] And in this infancy, writes Thomas Warton—he calls it "the unpolished ages"—"the muse was too awkwardly or too weakly courted to grant many favours to her lovers." Although the later eighteenth century would see a fascination with many of the products of the "Gothic" ages, most mid-century critics were confident that medieval literature lacked the polish that had arrived in the seventeenth century. "Of old English poetry," Thomas Warton explains, "one of the striking characteristics is a continued tenour of disparity, not so much in the style as in the sentiment. But the bad predominates. In this sort of reading, we are but rarely relieved from disgust, or rouzed from indifference. We are suddenly charmed with a beautiful thought in the midst of an heap of rubbish."[55]

---

52 Ibid., p. 21.

53 *Monthly Review* 66 (May 1782): 325.

54 Johnson, Yale *Works*, 7:82. I discuss this metaphor and its applications at greater length in *The Age of Elizabeth in the Age of Johnson*, chap. 2.

55 Warton, *An Enquiry*, p. 19.

At the time of his *Enquiry into the Authenticity of the Poems Attributed to Thomas Rowley* (1782), Warton was still hesitant to say definitively that Rowley was a fake, but he was clear about the consequences for his story of literary progress should the poems prove genuine: "If it should at last be decided, that these poems were really written so early as the reign of king Edward the fourth, the entire system that has hitherto been framed concerning the progression of poetical composition, and every theory that has been established on the gradual improvements of taste, style, and language, will be shaken and disarranged."[56] The reviewer for the *Gentleman's Magazine* said the same about Rowley's contemporaries: "Our old poets were not remarkable for sentiments of humanity and chastity; on the contrary, they applauded barbarous ferocity, and were delighted with merry jokes and lascivious stories: our author's sentiments are almost uniformly humane, chaste, and moral."[57] The critics' conviction that the forgers violated this narrative of poetic progress led to one of the more paradoxical charges leveled against Chatterton: he was bad because he was too good. In other words, his very excellence proved the poems were not of their supposed age; since they were not of their supposed age, they must be fraudulent; since they were fraudulent, they did not deserve the kinds of praise lavished on them by those who thought them genuine.

Historicist criticism, that is to say, could be applied not only to technical features like orthography and prosody, but to excellence itself, and this depended on a shared narrative of cultural progress from age to age. The greatest writers must write in an era suitable to their genius. Participants on either side of any dispute sought to characterize the "spirit of the age," whether to show that a questionable work is compatible with that age or to show that it is not. And these debates were at their most heated in the case of Ossian, because his great antiquity made it difficult for critics to speak with authority on the character of ancient Britain. This difficulty, though, did not stop people on either side from trying, and it was problems of anachronism more than anything else that served to discredit Macpherson.

Macpherson sometimes resorted to historicist arguments himself, but he more often depended on one of the most prominent historicist critics of his day, Hugh Blair, to make them for him. Blair suited Macpherson's purposes well, because his passions were often more historical than literary, and much of the poems' appeal for him lay in the information they offered about third-century Scotland. As soon as the Ossianic poems appeared, he speculated that "it might serve to throw considerable light upon the Scottish and Irish antiquities." This is for Blair the best reason for reading the poems: we should care about them because "the most natural pictures of ancient manners are exhibited in the ancient poems of nations." He agreed with Macpherson's assertion that "What renders Temora infinitely more valuable than Fingal, is the light it throws on the history of the times."[58]

---

56 Ibid., pp. 7–8.

57 *Gentleman's Magazine* 47 (Aug. 1777): 363.

58 Blair, Preface to *Fragments*, p. 6; *A Critical Dissertation*, p. 345; "A Dissertation," p. 215. Compare another early commentator, who was convinced that "the many Fragments still preserved amongst our Highlanders of their antient Poetry, may be of great Use in settling the History, and ascertaining the Meaning of several Antiquities dispersed over the

Blair made the case that the poems Macpherson published were such an accurate portrait of the age that there was not a trace of anachronism: "In Ossian's works, from beginning to end, all is consistent; no modern allusion drops from him."[59] The signs of anachronism Blair claimed to be looking for, though, were not the same as those Bentley had explored decades earlier. Bentley drew attention to linguistic change to disprove the authenticity of the letters attributed to Phalaris; Blair shared the theoretical principles, but was not proficient in Gaelic, and was therefore unable to comment on the vocabulary or syntax of the "original." He did, however, believe that historically specific stages of the language would demonstrate the Ossianic poems genuine. The figurative language of the poems was evident even in translation, and Blair was convinced it bore the marks of the age in which the poems were supposedly written.

For Blair, as for Thomas Blackwell and other "primitivists," language change is a function of cultural change. "In the infancy of societies," he explains, "men live scattered and dispersed, in the midst of solitary rural scenes, where the beauties of nature are their chief entertainment. They meet with many objects, to them new and strange; their wonder and surprize are frequently excited." This "wonder and surprize" shape their language: "As their feelings are strong, so their language itself, of itself, assumes a poetical turn." This contradicts what Blair took to be conventional wisdom in his day: "Figures," he says, "are commonly considered as artificial modes of speech, devised by orators and poets, after the world had advanced to a refined state." In fact, he tells us, "The contrary of this is the truth," because primitives speak more figuratively than decorous moderns. Evidence is available not only in the past, but in the primitive societies that survive: "An American chief, at this day, harangues at the head of his tribe, in a more bold metaphorical style, than a modern European would adventure to use in an Epic poem."[60]

For Blair, then, the "bold metaphorical style" of the Ossianic poems was itself evidence of their origin in a primitive society. Beyond the question of style, the

---

mountainous Parts of *Scotland*" (J. M——— G——— to William Shenstone, 21 June 1760, in Hull, *Select Letters*, 2:169).

59 Blair, *A Critical Dissertation*, p. 353.

60 Ibid., pp. 345–6. The association of primitives with figurative language was widespread at mid-century, especially among Scots; Adam Ferguson, for example, argues that "When we attend to the language which savages employ on any solemn occasion, it appears that man is a poet by nature" (*An Essay on the History of Civil Society*, p. 172). Charles M'Kinnon makes a similar point on the "similies and figured expressions" of primitives, noting that "the oratory of the North Americans shows them to be not unnatural to savages." The conclusion he draws shows the less savory attitudes with which primitivism has long struggled: "as the Whites are superior to any other breed of human creatures, it is no violent supposition, that the oratory of at least some varieties of Whites has been also much figured" (M'Kinnon, *Essays on the Following Subjects*, p. 73). Howard Gaskill notes that "The decade preceding the appearance of the Ossianic poems had shown numerous signs of a growing interest in the (non-classical) ancient and the primitive: for instance, the 'oriental' style of Biblical poetry (Lowth), scaldic literary monuments (Mallet), the figure of the 'Bard' (Gray)" (Gaskill, "Ossian in Europe," p. 661). See also Pittock, *Inventing and Resisting Britain*, pp. 156–7, and Dafydd Moore, *Enlightenment and Romance*, pp. 140–141.

manners depicted in the poems were also supposed to be consistent with the primitive world that created them, though, again, it was contrary to common sense. Savages, he argues, can in fact be more tender than their more sophisticated descendants. Ossian himself, to be sure, was exceptional, "endowed by nature with an exquisite sensibility of heart." But he was not unique, for "The manners of Ossian's age, so far as we can gather from his writings, were abundantly favourable to a poetical genius." These manners produced not only tenderness but also the other characteristic quality of the Ossianic poems, sublimity: "Amidst the rude scenes of nature, amidst rocks and torrents and whirlwinds and battles, dwells the sublime. It is the thunder and the lightning of genius. It is the offspring of nature, not of art." He was even convinced that "The compositions of Ossian are so strongly marked with characters of antiquity, that although there were no external proof to support their antiquity, hardly any reader of judgment and taste, could hesitate in referring them to a very remote æra."[61]

Blair was not the only believer to defend the authenticity of the poems on historicist grounds. In *Galic Antiquities*, John Smith follows him, sometimes repeating his arguments verbatim, insisting "the train of ideas are every where so much out of the common line of modern composition, that nothing but the real circumstances which they describe could possibly have suggested them." Like Blair, he draws on Ossian's language ("bold, animated, and metaphorical; such as it is found to be in all infant states") and manners (which "uniformly relate to a very early stage of society").[62] William Stukeley too makes a similar argument about how "much may be collected" from the Ossianic poems "to inlarge our most antient Brittish history."[63] His bizarre antiquarian theories served to back up the poems' authenticity. When he saw that *Fingal* was consistent with his notions that the ancient Britons were descended from Phoenicians, he wrote an open letter to Macpherson, "your history has confirm'd my mature thoughts about them."[64]

Many of Stukeley's more revealing comments were unpublished, but the tenor is similar. "I discerned sufficiently," he wrote, "our *Ersk* hero's, to be the remains of the most antient Britons; & I doubt not but their language & customs [are] the same. So that whatever is great & excellent in these highlanders & old Irish, we may justly suppose to have been more great & excellent, in the first inhabitants of Wiltshire, Dorsetshire, & those Southern countrys. there [*sic*] they first dwelt, coming by sea, from Asia, in the very first, & most heroical ages." "Whoever reads these poems," insists Stukeley, "cannot but judg, they needs must be antient, abounding altogether, with those ideas, wh only belong, to the most early State of Society."[65]

Ossian's supporters opened the historicist door; Ossian's critics rushed through it. Once it was suggested that the epics afforded verifiable historical information about the real world, those who doubted Macpherson's story could use historical information to discredit the poems. "In Truth," writes Charles O'Conor in 1766, "the

61   Blair, *A Critical Dissertation*, pp. 352, 394–5, 353.
62   John Smith, *Galic Antiquities*, pp. 88–90.
63   Stukeley, notes on Ossian, in Bodleian MS Eng.misc.e.383, fol. 16ʳ.
64   Stukeley, *A Letter from Dr. Stukeley to Mr. Macpherson*, p. 7.
65   Stukeley, notes on Ossian, in Bodleian MS Eng.misc.e.383, fols. 5ʳ, 20ʳ.

Absurdity of inserting into these Poems of *Fingal* and *Temora*, Customs, unknown in *Ireland*, or *North-Britain*, until long after the Decease of the supposed Author, brings a Proof not to be invalidated, that the Exhibiter of these *modern* Customs, is a mere *modern* Poet."[66] Although a late entry into the Ossianic wars, Edward Davies's *Claims of Ossian* (written shortly after the turn of the century, but not published until 1825) was one of the most brutal with regard to highlighting till the anachronisms in Macpherson's works. "The first objection, that forcibly presents itself upon the face of the work," he argues, "is the glaring appearance of anachronism; or the incongruity of the events related with the age in which they are placed, or with any one historical age whatsoever."[67] And some of the anachronisms he identified could sometimes be glaring indeed. "Oscar, the son of the Bard," writes Davies, "falls in the Battle of *Gabhra*, A.D. 296.... Yet the same Fingal, and his sons, and his grandson, are repeatedly brought into the field, to oppose the invading Danes, ... in the very close of the eleventh century."[68] It is impossible that a third-century poet could describe eleventh-century battles: "The general subjects of these poems are ... either not synchronous with the supposed æra of Ossian; or else wholly unfounded in history and real fact." He therefore argues sarcastically, "Ossian is elevated into the rank of an authentic historian, the first that exists, among the natives of the British Isles, and even, the north of Europe. By his sole aid Mr. Macpherson overturns the long established account of the colonization of Britain and Ireland."[69]

And just as Blair and Stukeley could draw not on objective facts about the ancient Britons, but a more subjective sense of the character of the age, so could Ossian's critics. Davies points out not only the absurdity of eleventh-century Danes in a poem supposedly written seven or eight centuries earlier, but the incompatibility of Ossianic manners with what he believes must have been the case in Scottish antiquity: "The characters ... do not appear to have been immediately drawn from real life. ... They are the ideal sketches of a man who contemplates human nature, *as it ought to be*; not the faithful touches of him, who observes it, *as it is*. They resemble those sublime figures, which the imagination has often delineated, on the canvass of poetry and romance." He discerns "the *Gothic*, rather than the Celtic style," in the Ossianic poems, but the manners are not even consistently Gothic: "the manners and sentiments which present themselves in the poems of Ossian, were not fully appropriate, either to the Celts or the Goths. The painting is far above nature, and can by no means be considered as verified, in the age and country in which Ossian is supposed to have lived." From this, Davies draws what he sees as the inevitable

---

66 O'Conor, *Dissertations on the History of Ireland*, 2:29.

67 Davies, *The Claims of Ossian*, p. 15.

68 Ibid., pp. 17–18. Sylvester O'Halloran made the same point in 1772: "to synchronize warriors who flourished at very different periods, such as Cucullin, Conall Cearnach, &c. of the first century, with Fingal, or Fione Mac Cumhal, who lived in the third; and to unite all these in a war against the Danes, who were not even heard of in Europe till the ninth; demanded all the finesse imaginable!" (O'Halloran, *An Introduction to the Study of the History and Antiquities of Ireland*, p. 312). Compare this objection to Chatterton's poems: "we are told ... that the battle of Hastings was written by Turgot the monk, a saxon in the tenth century, ... that is, one hundred years before the event" (*Gentleman's Magazine* 47 [May 1777]: 206).

69 Davies, *The Claims of Ossian*, pp. 19, 9.

conclusion: "The poet, therefore, has not sketched his sentiments from nature, and observations of the scenes which passed before him; but from a contemplative imagination—from the tablet of romance, or the prevailing taste of his age. He has not informed our judgments, with the colouring of history, but amused our fancy with that of poetry. It follows that the work cannot be ascribed to Ossian."[70]

The confidence with which he makes that assertion is important: it reveals that the principles that were controversial in the fifteenth century had become commonplaces in the eighteenth. Even Bentley's use of linguistic evidence had become a mainstream part of the detection of fraud. By the middle of the eighteenth century, British criticism had become solidly historicist, and "the mention of posterior facts" had indeed become the "first indication of forgery." All the problems that make any discussion of external evidence difficult still apply; one needs to know with some confidence that supposed facts can be relied on, and that made many of these discussions more complicated than they would seem to be necessary for us. But few of the century's most high-profile literary hoaxes could have been debated without a firm historical sense, and the debates themselves show just how much that historicist awareness had penetrated eighteenth-century literary thought.

---

70 Ibid., pp. 24, 35.

Chapter 7

False Recollections

Evidence must be consistent with itself; it must be consistent with the real world; it must be consistent with the age in which it was created—but above all it must be true. Many plausible stories may seem convincing, but not all of them are trustworthy. One of the recurring concerns of those who investigate cases of deception is whether the evidence adduced by the combatants on either side can be counted upon.

Confusions of Memory

As we have seen, the most common form of evidence has long been testimony—for much of Western legal history it was the only admissible form of evidence. Yet testimony is also one of the least trustworthy forms of evidence because it depends not only on the honesty of witnesses, but also on the accuracy of their perception, the reliability of their memories, and the soundness of their understanding. The threats to the accuracy of testimony therefore come from two sides: conscious liars pose an obvious set of problems, but unconscious liars pose another and perhaps more insidious one. Even those who are not seeking to dupe the gullible may be gullible themselves; they may be prey to hazy memory or easy suggestibility. Granted, seventeenth- and eighteenth-century trials moved quickly—"Most of the crimes tried at the December [1678] sessions," John Langbein writes, "had been committed in November or October"[1]—and witnesses would therefore have had little time to forget important details. Still, as Geoffrey Gilbert noted in his *Law of Evidence*, "the Testimony of an honest Man, however fortified with the Solemnities of an Oath, is yet liable to the Imperfection of Memory."[2] And when they begin giving testimony that bolsters a case they honestly but inaccurately believe, simple credulity may turn into deception. Error can be contagious. The deceived can easily become deceivers.

False memory is not simple forgetfulness: as Jeremy Bentham explains, "Forgetfulness is not the only defect to which memory is susceptible; there is another—erroneous recollections, *false recollections*, if we may give them that name. Without the least intention to depart from truth, without the slightest consciousness of his error, a person may have a supposed recollection, false not only in some circumstance, but false throughout." In recent years, psychologists have begun studying the phenomenon in more detail, a task that has grown more urgent as "recovered memory" has been introduced into many legal proceedings.[3]

---

1 Langbein, "The Criminal Trial before the Lawyers," p. 280.
2 Gilbert, *The Law of Evidence*, p. 6.
3 Bentham, *A Treatise on Judicial Evidence*, p. 25. A review of modern research on "false memory" is Brainerd and Reyna, *The Science of False Memory*, especially Chapters 1 and 2.

Sometimes these "false recollections" are the result of serious psychological disturbance. It is likely, to take a modern example, that Binjamin Wilkomirski sincerely believes he passed his early childhood in a series of Nazi concentration camps, as he described in his powerful Shoah memoir of 1995, *Fragments*. His story, though, has been shown to contradict the historical record in countless particulars, and it now seems to be little more than a harrowing fantasy.[4] The evidence suggests he is not a liar in any traditional sense, since he does not seem to have consciously chosen to fool people—and yet his testimony, for all the light it sheds on his psyche, tells us nothing about what happened in the 1940s. Not every inaccurate recollection, though, is as pathological as Wilkomirski's. Stephen Jay Gould, always concerned with the reliability of evidence in his scientific work, notes with only slight exaggeration that "Probably a quarter of a million people will swear they saw" Mickey Mantle's legendary line drive of 1963 "in the flesh (though Yankee Stadium then held but a quarter that many)."[5] And such confused recollections are not a twentieth-century phenomenon. Samuel Johnson noticed it even in himself: in his *Annals* he relates an operation that he underwent as a child, and then adds, "I always imagined that I remembered it, but I laid the scene in the wrong house. Such confusions of memory I suspect to be common."[6]

Repeated by His Father and Grandfather

These "confusions of memory" were indeed so common that the reliability of testimony was often questioned in eighteenth-century arguments over authenticity—in the Ossian case above all. Because of the famous "manuscript problem" discussed in Chapter 1—Macpherson refused to show whatever manuscript records he may have used in preparing the Ossianic poems—the investigation of *Fingal* and *Temora* depended largely on the testimony of people who could recall hearing the poems before they were published. If their claims were true—if someone could demonstrate convincingly that *Fingal* was heard in its entirety in something like the form Macpherson gave it in, say, the 1740s—the Ossianic question would be at an end, and even Macpherson's harshest critics would have to admit the poems he published were "genuine." Many of the recollections of those who testified, however, were hazy, even if not genuinely mendacious.

Since he could not (or would not) submit manuscripts or other physical evidence to examination, the only kind of external verification available to Macpherson and

---

4   See Maechler, *The Wilkomirski Affair*, for a thorough account of Wilkomirski's errors.

5   Gould, *Triumph and Tragedy in Mudville*, p. 96.

6   Johnson, Yale *Works*, 1:4. Compare another of his childhood recollections: "I always retained some memory of this journey, though I was then but thirty months old. I remembered a little dark room behind the kitchen, where the jack-weight fell through a hole in the floor, into which I once slipped my leg. I seem to remember, that I played with a string and a bell, which my cousin Isaac Johnson gave me; and that there was a cat with a white collar, and a dog, called Chops, that leaped over a stick: but I know not whether I remember the thing, or the talk of it" (Yale *Works*, 1:8–9).

his supporters was the testimony of others. His claims for the authenticity of the poems depended on the belief that the materials were traditional and widespread in the Highlands of Scotland. Ossian's supporters were therefore keen to point to Highlanders who remembered hearing the poems long before Macpherson published them. "There is not an old man in the Highlands," wrote John Smith in *Galic Antiquities* (1780), "but will declare that he heard such poems repeated by his father and grandfather."[7] Macpherson's critics, on the other hand, admitted there were traditional Highland ballads on Ossianic themes, but they were eager to deny that these ballads corresponded in any significant way to *Fingal* and *Temora*. Some of these critics were prepared to admit that fragments superficially similar to the Ossianic poems may have circulated before the 1760s, but they adamantly denied that Macpherson's poems and these traditional poems were the same thing.

The discussion began early. In September 1760, just a few months after the appearance of the *Fragments*, a correspondent known as Caledonius addressed a letter to the *Gentleman's Magazine*: "As many doubts have been started concerning the *Erse* odes," he wrote, "be pleased to assure the public that their originality and authenticity may be fully proved; that the piper of the *Argyleshire* militia can repeat all those that are translated and published, and many more; and that several other persons can do the same in the highlands, where they are traditionally remembered."[8] Had an investigation begun in earnest in the 1760s, the question might have been settled quickly. But there was no serious inquiry into the testimony of this Argyleshire piper and, by the time investigators got up the energy to begin questioning people in a systematic way, decades had passed. And so the Highland Committee, charged in the late 1790s with ascertaining the truth of Macpherson's claims, devoted most of its energy to trying to pin down unreliable and sometimes contradictory memories. The questionnaire the Committee sent to a large group of older Highlanders begins:

> Have you ever heard repeated or sung, any of the poems ascribed to Ossian, translated or published by Mr. Macpherson? By whom have you heard them so repeated, and at what time or times? Did you ever commit any of them to writing, or can you remember them so well as now to set them down? In either of these cases, be so good to send the Gaelic original to the Committee.[9]

The Appendix to their *Report* includes copious extracts from the responses. No doubt with Macpherson's refusal to show the manuscripts in mind, the authors included a note, "the papers themselves are open to the inspection of any person wishing to examine them more thoroughly."[10]

Many of the answers to the questionnaire suggest the poems published as Ossian's existed in some form before Macpherson's publication. Andrew Gallie wrote to the Committee on 4 March 1801, "Before Mr Macpherson could know his right hand from his left, I have heard fragments of them repeated, and many of those fragments

---

7 John Smith, *Galic Antiquities*, p. 93.

8 *Gentleman's Magazine* 30 (Sept. 1760): 421.

9 Mackenzie, *Report*, p. 2.

10 Ibid., p. iv.

I recognized in Mr Macpherson's translation."[11] Neil Macleod, likewise, reported on "Mr Campbell of Octomore, an aged gentleman," who "knows of these poems of Ossian.... in his younger days, he heard Fingal repeated very frequently in the original, just as Mr Macpherson has translated it."[12] Macleod himself insisted he head heard all the Ossianic poems

> in the Island of Sky, when I was a little boy, from an old man who used to repeat them to me for some tobacco.... This man died when I was but very young, and I could never since meet with any person that could repeat so many of the poems of Ossian, or so perfectly.... Had such an enquiry been made fifty years sooner, I am persuaded hundreds could attest that Mr Macpherson's translations are really what they pretend to be.[13]

Oral literature, though, is necessarily evanescent; sounds leave no traces. Henry Mackenzie and the Committee were working 40 years after the Ossianic poems were published, so their attempt to reach a definitive verdict on transitory oral literature was inevitably compromised even before it began. An old man's memories of stories he heard as a child are likely to be even more suspect. People who honestly and accurately remembered hearing traditional ballads on similar stories were willing to testify that they had heard the Ossianic poems as Macpherson published them—and on that matter the doubters could be brutal.

Samuel Johnson recognized that Highlanders were familiar with stories about Fingal and Ossian, but he distrusted those who said the stories they knew were the same as *Fingal* and *Temora*. He thought he understood what had happened: familiarity with the broad outlines of the legends was being misinterpreted as familiarity with the poems as delivered by Macpherson. And though he enjoyed ridiculing those North Britons who "love Scotland better than truth,"[14] he recognized that his own countrymen were equally liable to misremember what they had heard. He boasted he could "write an epick poem on the story of *Robin Hood*, and half England, to whom the names and places he should mention in it are familiar, would believe and declare they had heard it from their earliest years." He made a similar point to Donald Macqueen, who told Johnson that "he could repeat some passages in the original; ... but that he could not affirm that Ossian composed all that poem as it is now published." Johnson was not surprised. He "contends that it is no better than such an epick poem as he could make from the song of Robin Hood; that is to say, that, except a few passages, there is nothing truly ancient but the names and some vague traditions."[15] Besides, Johnson asserted that many of the people claiming to have heard the Ossianic poems were unfamiliar with the language in which they were delivered. When a supporter of Ossian declared "that *Fingal* was certainly

---

11   Ibid., p. 39.

12   Ibid., Appendix, p. 21.

13   Ibid., Appendix, p. 22.

14   Johnson, *A Journey to the Western Islands of Scotland*, ed. Fleeman, p. 119.

15   Boswell, *Life*, 5:389, 164. He made the same point in a passage he ghostwrote for William Shaw: "if I were to read Fingal in the Highlands, multitudes who never heard the original, would believe that they had heard it; and deliver their belief upon oath, without consciousness of falsehood" (Shaw, "Appendix," p. 74).

genuine, for that he had heard a great part of it repeated in the original," Johnson "indignantly asked him whether he understood the original"—which he did not. "I mention this," writes Boswell, "as a remarkable proof how liable the mind of man is to credulity, when not guarded by such strict examination as that which Dr. Johnson habitually practised."[16]

Although Johnson's enemies attributed these arguments to his famous anti-Scottish bias,[17] even some of Macpherson's countrymen made the same point. Walter Scott suspected that the Highlanders' memory was playing tricks: "How many people not particularly addicted to poetry who may have heard Chevy Chace in the nursery or at school & never since met with the ballad might be imposed on by a new Chevy Chace bearing no resemblance to the old one save in here & there a stanza or an incident."[18] David Hume was worried about unreliable memories from the beginning, although at first his concerns had to do not with the authenticity of the Ossianic poems, but with their national origins. In 1763 he wrote, "on the first publication of Macpherson's book, all the Irish cried out, *we know all these poems, we have always heard them from our infancy*. But when he asked more particular questions, he could never learn, that any one had ever heard, or could repeat the original of any one paragraph of the pretended translation."[19] And James Macdonald, who spent his youth in the Hebrides, insisted that "among all the pieces I have heard recited or have learned myself in my infancy I never heard any that had the smallest analogy with an epic poem."[20] Malcolm Laing thought it mysterious that "No sooner were the translations published than the traditionary existence of the poems disappeared."[21]

Some attempted to answer these objections. John Clark was careful, in his reply to William Shaw, to state precisely what he did hear: "The epic poems of Fingal and Temora I have never heard rehearsed by any *single* Highlander, in the same arrangement in which Mr Macpherson had published them. By *different* persons I have frequently heard almost every passage in these two poems."[22] For some, remember, this was enough for Macpherson's claims to be true; for others, evidence that two supposed epic poems had existed as fragments known by different people contributed nothing toward the authenticity of the Ossianic epics.

Given not only the imperfect memories, but also the different standards of what constituted authenticity, it is no surprise that the Highland Committee got widely varying answers. Mackenzie summarized the frustrating state of affairs:

---

16 Boswell, *Life*, 5:388.

17 See Donald M'Nicol, who acknowledges that "It is true, there is no man now living, and perhaps there never has existed any one person, who either can or could repeat the whole of the Poems of *Ossian*. It is enough, that the whole has been repeated, in detached pieces, through the Highlands and Isles.... But arguments are lost, and facts are thrown away, upon men, who have *predetermined* to resist conviction itself" (M'Nicol, *Remarks*, pp. 350–351).

18 Scott to Seward, Sept. 1806?, in *Letters of Sir Walter Scott*, 1:322.

19 Hume to Blair, 19 Sept. 1763, in Hume, *Letters*, 1:400 (letter 215).

20 Gillies, *A Hebridean in Goethe's Weimar*, p. 64.

21 Laing, *The History of Scotland*, 2:389.

22 Clark, *An Answer to Mr Shaw's Inquiry*, p. 17.

A few of the Committee's correspondents sent them such ancient poems as they possessed in writing, from having formerly taken them down from the oral recitation of the old Highlanders who were in use to recite them, or as they now took them down from some person ... but those, the Committee's correspondents said, were generally less perfect, and more corrupted, than the poems they had formerly heard, or which might have been obtained at an earlier period.[23]

The investigators therefore sought more reliable evidence. People, after all, lie and forget; things do neither. In the Ossianic dispute no documents were offered to inspection. In other cases, though, such as those of Chatterton and Ireland, there were manuscripts aplenty. And because the physical world does not suffer from the unreliability of human witnesses, many disputes tried to turn from testimony to documentary evidence.

La Science de la Diplomatique

This is in keeping with the age's increased interest in the reliability of material as opposed to testimonial evidence in legal proceedings, and it seems the legal and the literary investigations may have been mutually influential. In Jeremy Bentham's work at the turn of the nineteenth century, notes Paul Korshin,

> for the first time, we find strong doubts about the accuracy of memory and the usefulness of eyewitness testimony. Bentham attaches great importance to documents (which he calls pre-appointed evidence) and to makeshift evidence, that is, evidence that is secondhand, like hearsay, which he values less than he does documents. He devotes a whole book of his treatise to the manner of authenticating evidence, a procedure for which he employs approximately the same tests that the scholars of the eighteenth century were using to determine whether works of literature were genuine or forgeries.[24]

Bentham's "manner of authenticating evidence" necessarily differed from our own. Few of the forensic techniques with which we are now familiar, after all, were available in the eighteenth century. DNA was unknown; radiocarbon dating was not an option; even the simplest chemical tests on ink and paper had to wait for the nineteenth century.[25] They were, however, able to make some basic investigations of paper, watermarks, and especially handwriting. One commentator in 1711, for example, was convinced that an ecclesiastical document ostensibly from 1562 was a forgery became "the Manuscript is on Paper, which 'tis not usual for the perfect Acts of Convocation to be Writ on. And there are frequent putting in of Words, and lines

---

23   Mackenzie, *Report*, pp. 78–9.

24   Korshin, "Evidence," p. 141.

25   "The earliest example of the scientific examination of a document," writes Henry T. F. Rhodes, "was that of the Königinhofer Handschrift in the early part of the nineteenth century. In this example a chemical examination revealed the presence of prussian blue, a pigment not in use at the date the document purported to bear" (*The Craft of Forgery*, p. 236). Bentham discusses the physical examination of paper or parchment in *Rationale*, 3:614–15.

in a different hand; and many crossings out of Words, Lines, Sentences, and some times whole Articles."[26]

It is reasonable to assume that an informal sizing-up of manuscripts must have always played some part in judging whether they were genuine, but the systematic study of documents as physical objects took a long time to develop. Exactly when the breakthrough came is the subject of some disagreement. Luciana Duranti finds one turning point in late antiquity: "The problem of distinguishing genuine documents from forgeries was present in the earliest periods of documentation, but until the sixth century no attempt was made to devise criteria for the identification of forgeries."[27] John H. Wigmore, on the other hand, the early twentieth century's most distinguished scholar of evidence, placed the real revolution somewhere in the middle of the nineteenth century, writing in 1910 that "A century ago the science of handwriting-study did not exist. A crude empiricism still prevailed."[28] But the most common date offered for the paradigm shift is that described by Arthur Giry: "La science de la diplomatique naquit elle-même en France à la fin du XVIIᵉ siècle."[29] The late seventeenth century, that is to say, saw the birth of "diplomatics," which came to assume ever greater importance in discussions of authenticity over the eighteenth and nineteenth centuries.[30]

Diplomatics was born in religious controversy: as Duranti points out, "the impetus for articulation of a method of proving the authenticity of documents came from doctrinal conflicts of the Reformation and Counter-Reformation."[31] And the seventeenth century was the time of the *bella diplomatica*, or "diplomatic wars," when in 1643 the followers of the Jesuit Jean Bolland began publishing the *Acta sanctorum*. Their goal was to separate fact from fiction in the centuries-old *vita* tradition, but they were forced to proceed without any reliable principles to guide them. Daniel Van Papenbroeck spelled out one set of heuristics in his preface to the second volume but, by establishing very stringent standards for accepting documents as true, he inadvertently ruled out virtually everything from the Merovingian period. The result was chaos.

The most important figure in the history of diplomatics is Jean Mabillon, whose *De re diplomatica libri VI* is a response to Papenbroeck and the Bollandists. Mabillon, a scholar so distinguished that the Archbishop of Reims introduced him to the king as "the *most learned* man in your realm,"[32] published his work in 1681—a year, says Marc Bloch, that "was truly a great one in the history of the human mind,

---

26 *Lay-Craft Exemplified*, pp. 7–8.

27 Duranti, *Diplomatics*, p. 36.

28 Introduction to Osborn, *Questioned Documents*, p. vii.

29 Giry, *Manuel de diplomatique*, p. 61.

30 René Prosper Tassin and Charles Toustain offer an eighteenth-century definition of *diplomatique* that provides a useful starting point: "Elle ne se borne pas à fournir des moyens surs, pour reconnoitre la vérité ou la fausseté des pièces … elle étend encore ses droits jusqu'à régler les différens degrés de certitude ou de suspicion, dont elles sont susceptibles" (Tassin and Toustain, *Nouveau traité*, 1:1).

31 Duranti, *Diplomatics*, p. 38.

32 Sandys, *History of Classical Scholarship*, 2:296.

for the criticism of the documents of archives was definitely established."[33] Other critics see that year and that work as similarly epochal. Giry separates "l'étude des sources diplomatiques avant Mabillon" from "la science de la diplomatique depuis Mabillon,"[34] and Duranti says *De re diplomatica* "marks the birth date of diplomatics and paleography."[35]

Mabillon, as Christopher N. L. Brooke observes, "gave the study of documents a comprehensive frame of sensible rules, and established certain criteria of judgement; and the tradition of scholarship which he passed on to his disciples set the pattern for the study of medieval forgery for several generations."[36] But while Mabillon's work offers plentiful advice on distinguishing the genuine from the false, it also deserves credit for refusing to offer a simple checklist of criteria for authenticity: everything has to be weighed with care, and even apparent contradictions should not be considered *de facto* evidence of fraud. His book, writes David Knowles, "provided at once a description, a critique and a text-book of the new expertise. Mabillon frankly admitted that the authenticity of a charter could not be proved by any metaphysical or *a priori* argument; a decision could be reached only after the expert had examined a whole series of different indications.... In consequence, the certainty attainable in a favourable case could be no more than a moral certainty, but this was very different from doubt or complete scepticism."[37]

We should not overstate the extent of the victory of the diplomatic revolution. Although a new language and a new set of criteria became available for examining questioned documents in the late seventeenth century, the grossest and most childish forgeries could continue to circulate, even among the educated. The collectors who gladly paid good money in the 1860s for tens of thousands of crude forgeries by Vrain-Denis Lucas, with ancient Greeks and Romans writing notes in French on modern paper, clearly never exercised a moment's thought on what strike us as obvious impossibilities. And things may not have improved much even by the 1980s, when Konrad Kujau sold what he claimed were Hitler's diaries to *Stern*, even though they were written with demonstrably post-War inks in demonstrably post-War notebooks. But even if there was still a long way to go, the nascent science of diplomatics came to play an important part in a number of eighteenth-century British considerations of fraud.

The most important developments in diplomatics took place on the Continent—in France above all, but later in Germany as well. No significant treatise on diplomatics was written in English before 1800. Several Continental sources were, however, translated into English after mid-century: Jean-Henri-Samuel's *Principes élémentaires des belles lettres* (1760) appeared as *Elementary Principles of the Belles Lettres* in 1766, and it included a section of several pages spelling out the foundations of the science. It was also, apparently, the first discussion to

---

33 Bloch, *The Historian's Craft*, p. 81.
34 Giry, *Manuel de diplomatique*, p. 51.
35 Duranti, *Diplomatics*, p. 37.
36 Brooke, "Approaches to Medieval Forgery," p. 378.
37 Knowles, *The Historian and Character*, pp. 222–3.

introduce the word *diplomatics* into an English context,[38] and the first to define the new term: "*Diplomatics* explains the ancient Documents, and apply [*sic*] them to history, in discerning the false from the true ones. There is a vast number, of which the certitude cannot be ascertain'd but by that help."[39] More influential was Jakob Friedrich Bielfeld's *Premiers traits de l'erudition universelle* (1767), Englished in 1771 as *The Elements of Universal Erudition*: its slightly more extended treatment of diplomatics formed the basis of the entry on *diplomatics* in the second edition of the *Encyclopædia Britannica* (1778–83), making the basic principles available to a general Anglophone audience for the first time. By the beginning of the nineteenth century, Continental principles of document examination had led to great confidence in Britain. Thomas Astle, a careful reader of Mabillon, made grand claims for diplomatics in 1803: "The DIPLOMATIC SCIENCE ... may be considered as a guide to all the others." He was convinced that "The DIPLOMATIC SCIENCE ... treats of matters which are capable of certainty: truth and falsehood are often manifestly distinguished by it."[40]

The value of diplomatics in the cases of Chatterton and Ireland should be obvious: it was almost as if the science was developed for the purpose of showing their manuscripts to be false. Chirography, the study of handwriting, was the most important aspect of diplomatics in Britain, and many critics provided expensive engraved facsimiles of both authentic and questioned handwriting in the attempt to demonstrate the works of Rowley or the pseudo-Shakespeare were forged. Edmond Malone led the way in this respect. One of the plates in his investigation into Ireland's forgeries compares, letter by letter, Elizabeth's known hand with Ireland's forgeries: he places Elizabeth's lowercase *a* above Ireland's imitation of it, then *b*, and so on through the alphabet. The accompanying text provides further discussion. At times the details can become dense and hard to follow, as when an entire paragraph is devoted to the changing habits in Elizabeth's writing the letter *a*: "In the early part of her reign she formed the direct stroke of that letter like other persons: but by degrees it became higher than the circular part."[41] However difficult to follow, though, the case was made by its overwhelming amount of detail.

The True Basis of Security

The handling of textual evidence, though, was almost always more sophisticated than that of physical evidence. Even in the late eighteenth century, the study of paper and other writing materials was still rudimentary. Malone paid attention to watermarks—"I ought not to pass over without remark the manner in which this and the other pieces in this volume have been published, without the slightest notice of the water-mark on each paper"[42]—but few others thought about books or

---

38   The *OED* gives the first English citation of *diplomatics* in a work of 1803–19, but the English translation of Formey's work antedates that by several decades.

39   Formey, *Elementary Principles of the Belles Lettres*, p. 214.

40   Astle, *The Origin and Progress of Writing*, pp. iv, v.

41   Malone, *An Inquiry*, p. 105.

42   Ibid., p. 115.

manuscripts as physical objects. When, in 1770, Edward Burch and Matthew Martin were accused of forging a will of Sir Andrew Chadwick, the Crown questioned the younger James Whatman, one of the leading paper makers of the day, whose firm had made the paper on which the will was written. The disputed will was dated 1764; Whatman, however, testified that the paper on which it was written was sold only after 1768. Evidence of this sort was still a novelty: "Are you able," asked the prosecuting attorney, "to know whether that paper was manufactured at your mill, and at what time manufactured?" Whatman insisted he could, and offered "convincing proof": the "J W" watermark assumed that particular form only after 1764; Whatman "improved the manufactory" of the paper "by throwing blue into it, as people do in washing into linen, in order to take off the yellow cast," a method developed in April 1765; the paper was "made on a mould which is the first mould in which two sheets of this kind of paper was made at once," a technique dating to January 1768; and the firm's records indicated that "the first [paper] made from these moulds that was ever sent to London was the 11th of March 1768."[43] It was the first time such evidence had proven determinative in a legal proceeding, and the line of questioning suggests people were struck by its novelty.

Perhaps with similar cases of deception in mind, many paper makers of the late eighteenth and early nineteenth century began putting the date of manufacture in the watermark itself, making it available even to the untrained eye. These watermarked dates remain a valuable source of information today in dating editions of printed books and in spotting forgeries of various sorts. The Hyde copy of William Henry Ireland's manuscript *Frogmore Fete*, for instance, though clearly dated June 1808, is on paper watermarked 1824.[44] Ireland was the victim as well as the perpetrator of such a hoax: his *Authentic Account* was published in 1796, but an unauthorized reprint appeared several years later. The pirated copies can be distinguished from their legitimate originals most easily by looking for the "1803" and "1804" watermarks on some sheets.

In writing his *Frogmore Fete* Ireland could not be bothered to find or fabricate paper from 1808 or earlier; in reprinting *An Authentic Account*, the anonymous pirate saw no need to secure paper that might have been used in an actual book from 1796. In both these cases, though, the stakes were small, and the effort and expense the deceivers were willing to put into recreating older paper were correspondingly small. When it came to printing false money, though, the potential rewards obviously became much greater, and many counterfeiters were willing to take the trouble of reproducing the proper sorts of paper, ink, and engraving. As Johann Wilhelm von Archenholz recorded in his description of England, "Notwithstanding it is extremely

---

43   Balston, *James Whatman Father & Son*, pp. 147–8. For another case in which Whatman's testimony was introduced, see *Authentic Memoirs of William Wynne Ryland*, pp. 25–6. Another instance of watermarks leading to the identification of a forged banknote appears in *Memoirs of the Life of John Matthieson*, p. 22.

44   The title page reads "Frogmore Fete | As written & composed by me | Wm H^y Ireland. | At the Request of Princess Elizabeth | In 1802 | Thus Fairly Transcribed. | 1808," and the preface, which leaves no doubt that the comments refer to this copy, is dated "June 1808" (Ireland, *Frogmore Fete*, fol. v).

difficult to counterfeit a bank-note, more especially on account of the water-mark, which is imprinted on the paper while making, yet the allurements arising from success have induced many to make the attempt."[45] Coinage had long been subject to counterfeiting, and the problem remained acute in the eighteenth century. As William Symons pointed out in 1770, "a Piece of Coin may be full Weight when weighed in Air, ring well, appear to the Eye to be pure Gold, and even answer the Touchstone, and yet be adulterated to that Degree, as to have little or no Gold in it at all."[46] But if coins were troublesome, paper money—still a relative novelty in the eighteenth century—was much more so, partly because the disparity between its "intrinsic" and its conventional worth was so wide, but mostly because it was easier to fake. Yet the increasing popularity of paper money over the course of the century made the stakes ever higher. This led to a strange arms race between the legitimate issuers of banknotes and the counterfeiters.

The problem is easily understood. In theory, at least, a would-be counterfeiter can replicate any technique that can be used to produce a legitimate banknote—a situation as true today as it was in the eighteenth century. Counterfeiting can therefore never be prevented entirely. It can, however, be made difficult, in the hopes that would-be forgers will find the trouble not worth the financial benefit. As Sir William Congreve put it in 1820, "the *true basis of security*, as far as concerns the engraving and printing upon a Bank Note, is to achieve some description of work which can *only* be imitated in the *same way* in which it was originally produced; for then, *whatever of* DIFFICULTY *is given to the original plate, that same difficulty must attach to the forger who copies it*." Congreve therefore warned his countrymen that the monochrome engraving techniques that were universal in American banknotes were inadequate: "*there is no real security against forgery to be achieved in* ONE *colour*, to which the American Note is limited." His suggestion: security "must be sought for *in the use of two or more colours*; and indeed the extension of field thus obtained, for the *exercise* of *variety*, *ingenuity* of *combination*, and *difficulty* of *execution*, especially *in printing*, is evident."[47]

The Best Engraver in the Universe

But using "two or more colours" made counterfeiting only slightly more difficult, not impossible. Similar experiments had been tried throughout the eighteenth century. Benjamin Franklin held the contract for printing paper money in several of the American Colonies in the 1730s, and tried a number of techniques for making it harder to counterfeit. He began with the idea of using multiple typefaces: this would increase the difficulty with which a potential counterfeiter could secure the needed materials. Typefaces, though, were standard, and if one printer could obtain them, so could another. Type ornaments were more difficult to reproduce, especially when they were complicated; Franklin therefore cut some new ornaments himself to ensure they would not be available for sale. Still, this was not enough. Carvers of

---

45 Archenholz, *A Picture of England*, 1:207.
46 Symons, *An Essay on the Weighing of Gold*, p. ii.
47 Congreve, *An Analysis of the True Principles of Security*, pp. 1, iii.

type ornaments and intaglio engravers were trained to reproduce others' images very closely and, although they may be comparatively difficult to copy, they were not beyond the power of the more devoted counterfeiters.

Franklin therefore tried an unusual experiment, one that sought to produce an image beyond the power of even the most skilled engravers to reproduce. In August 1739, he issued a 20-shilling note bearing the imprint of three blackberry leaves on a sprig and a willow leaf with stipules. Numismatists have long been aware of these leaf prints on the pre-Revolutionary and Revolutionary currency of Delaware, Maryland, New Jersey, Pennsylvania, and the Continental Congress. No one, however, understood the logic behind them or the process by which the delicate prints were made, and most regarded them as little more than decorative. Only in 1964 did Eric P. Newman publish a multi-part article on Franklin's use of "nature printing," revealing for the first time the way the images served to foil counterfeiters.

Franklin's secret process allowed him to reproduce the complicated pattern of the veins of a leaf on paper—not by recreating it manually, but by allowing the leaf to impress its image directly onto the page without human intervention. The pattern, that is to say, was not the work of an engraver, but the direct impression of the leaf itself. As a result, it had a degree of complexity that no human engraver could hope to reproduce—and no one would be able to reproduce at all, as long as Franklin's process remained a secret. As Newman observes, "leaves not only had exceedingly complex detail but ... their internal lines were graduated in thickness. This would make virtually impossible a fine reproduction by engraving. If, therefore, Franklin could keep his nature printing process concealed, he would have a very effective weapon against counterfeiting." And Franklin's success in keeping the process concealed is evident because Newman was the first to understand what had been clear to Franklin more than two centuries earlier: that organic form is much more difficult to imitate than any artificial form. A skilled craftsman can reproduce a typeface or a type ornament made by another craftsman, but only God can make a leaf. As Joseph Breintnall put in the caption to his own nature prints, they were "Engraven by the Greatest and best Engraver in the Universe."[48]

Organic form became an important part of many discussions of the reliability of evidence, because it was so difficult—perhaps even impossible—to fake convincingly. This applies not only to images of natural things, but to the things themselves. Nature's complexity was central to the Canning case. "Human testimony in a thousand instances, as well as this, has been found erroneous, varying and fallacious," noted one commentator; "whereas, the testimony of nature, is constant, uniform, and unvariable; and whatever we think it otherwise, we shall always find it was owing to our ignorance of the powers of nature, and not to the inconstancy of nature herself.... When therefore, the testimony of nature, and human testimony, seem to contradict one another, ... then the last ought to be entirely rejected, and to have no regard paid to it."[49] People lie; people forget; nature does neither.

The difficulty of imitating organic complexity shows up in many discussions of the Canning abduction. Canning described a chimney with a grate in the room in

---

48   Newman, "Nature Printing," pp. 154, 149, 153.
49   *The Imposture Detected*, pp. 50–51.

which she was locked; when she led a party to the room in Wells's house, however, they found a chimney but no grate. The obvious objection is that the grate had been removed after Canning's escape—and yet an extensive network of cobwebs filled the fireplace, making it inconceivable that anything had been removed in recent weeks. "It is palpable," insisted John Hill, "there could have been no Grate on the Chimney of a long Time; for the whole Expanse of it was found covered and overspread with Cobwebs, the Work of many Generations of unmolested Spiders. Oh Providence that assists in these Discoveries!"[50] No human spinner could hope to reproduce authentic-looking webs; it follows, therefore, that there had been no grate. One of Canning's partisans dismissed the objection—"This Cobweb Story ... seems like *Arachne*'s, to be spun from yourself"[51]—but he had no substantive answer, only sarcasms.

The most complicated organic form of all, though, was not a leaf, not a cobweb-filled chimney, but the human body itself—Victor Frankenstein's achievement notwithstanding, it is impossible to produce a convincing replica of a body. Human bodies, therefore, in all their organic messiness, feature in a number of eighteenth-century discussions of authenticity. Moreover, it is significant that most of these bodies are female. Women's testimony had long been distrusted, both in popular misogynist culture and in official legal practice. Legal theorist Giles Jacob puts it bluntly: "By the Civil Law the Testimony of a Man is preferred to that of a Woman."[52] Those who would discover the truth about women therefore often ignored their lying tongues, and turned instead to their ostensibly truthful bodies.

Many of the greatest difficulties raised by Canning's abduction, as we saw in Chapter 5, came from her account of living for four weeks on a few pieces of bread and a small jug of water. These difficulties were exacerbated by her further claims: "Being asked whether, during that Time, she had any *Evacuation* by *Stool* or *Urine*, repeated, that she had no Stool during her Confinement, and had only made Water."[53] "I cannot help thinking," wrote one investigator, "her story is contradicted by the testimony of nature, and where no miraculous interposition is supposed, that must always overballance any human testimony whatever."[54] And "the testimony of nature" almost always meant human biology. Another skeptic recorded that "during the whole Month of her Confinement she had no Passage thro' her." It may be possible, he admits, that "for Life to subsist so long without the natural Evacuations of the Body," though the question "must be left to the learned Physicians to determine." But on "the Night she was seiz'd, she was just come from visiting her Uncle and Aunt, with whom no doubt she had eat and drank plentifully. Now, can it be imagined that this Food, then taken, did not make its Passage thro' her Body in twenty-four Hours or thereabouts even tho' she took no more for several Days afterwards?"[55] Canning may have been able to tell a story about her confinement, but her body would tell another, and bodies do not lie.

---

50 Hill, *The Story of Elizabeth Canning Considered*, p. 26.
51 "Philologus," *The Inspector Inspected*, p. 32.
52 Jacob, *A Treatise of Laws*, p. 396.
53 *Genuine and Impartial Memoirs of Elizabeth Canning*, p. 24.
54 *The Imposture Detected*, p. 7.
55 *The Truth of the Case*, p. 5.

Not everyone was convinced by these arguments. The physician Daniel Cox found nothing remarkable in Canning's story of a surviving a month on a loaf of bread and a jug of water. He admitted that "her costiveness has been made one objection to the truth of her story," but gave his professional opinion "that this state of her intestines was quite natural to her case, as she relates it—a kind of providence of nature, ever solicitous to support the body under every emergency of danger." He elaborates: "I remember the case of a woman about a dozen years since, who had no intestinal or any other capital evacuation for at least five or six months before she died."[56] "Are there not on record," asks another defender, "in the transactions of the royal society, and in authentic history, unquestionable instances of persons fasting ... much longer than one month?"[57] Another physician offers learned disquisitions on bodily functions, all of which serve to support Canning's unlikely story: "in the Body there are two chief Springs, or principal Instruments of Motion, *viz.* the *Dura Mater* ... and the *Heart*, they both agree in this, that by alternate Dilitations and Contractions, they take in and throw out again certain Liquids ...." Such considerations allow him to account for Canning's survival by her five-month obstruction of "the common Female Benefit," which was "one chief Means of her Support, by affording her an additional Quantity of Blood and Spirits."[58]

A Very Painful Experiment

In the age before controlled medical experiments and the systematic collection of clinical data, fantastic accounts of medical prodigies abounded and circulated as true. Even those who should have known better could easily be taken in by traditional accounts of medical oddities, which served to undermine confidence in what was medically possible. James Solas Dodd, a physician who defended Canning, credulously relates "some authentic Accounts of Persons who existed Years without Food," including the history of "A young Girl, somewhat above nine Years of Age," who "was never known to eat any Victuals whatsoever, for the Space of three Years successively," and another of "*Katharine Binder*, Native of the *Upper Palatinate* in *Germany*, [who] received no Nourishment for nine Years." He also tells us of a bout of constipation that makes Canning's 28 days seem like nothing: "*Fernelius* relates, that an Embassador of King *Charles* the Fifth was discomposed in his Bowels for six Years, but by proper Clysters voided an hard concreted Substance of Excrement twelve Inches long, and resembling the Shape of the Intestine."[59] The circumstantial details and citations of authorities in these stories seem to provide a kind of verification, and yet modern medicine recognizes them as far beyond the boundaries of possibility.

A similar lack of reliable evidence about the body was even more prominent in the case of Mary Toft's supposed delivery of rabbits. One participant in the debates reported that "Countess *Margaret*, Daughter to an Earl of *Holland*, ... brought forth

---

56 Cox, *An Appeal to the Public*, pp. 20–21.

57 *A Collection of Several Papers Relating to Elizabeth Canning*, p. 8.

58 Dodd, *A Physical Account*, pp. 38–9, 14, 20.

59 Ibid., pp. 21, 25–6, 44.

at once 365 Children,"[60] suggesting that a mere seventeen rabbits is nothing too outrageous—and reminding skeptical readers that not only uneducated women from Godalming made such claims, since we find prodigies even among countesses. Once again, the unreliable empirical medical record encouraged what seems to us reckless theorizing. Besides, there were good religious reasons to believe Toft's account: "I surely believe [the story] to have been undeniably real," wrote William Whiston a quarter-century after the affair had ended, "and no other indeed than one direct completion of the emminent Signal before us, that towards the end of the world, '*Monstrous Women should bring forth Monsters.*'" Of course it is contrary to daily experience, but the Scriptures are filled with things contrary to daily experience. "I have very long, and very successfully accustomed myself to be guided wholly by another rule," writes Whiston: "by the real evidence of facts and testimonies … as do all wise and upright Judges in their courts of justice, without any regard to the vain amusement of our present merry and profane scribblers."[61]

But it was not merely millenarian enthusiasts or those who believed in human litters of 365 children who at least considered the possibility that Toft's story might be true. As Dennis Todd and Lisa Forman Cody have demonstrated, some of the best obstetric thinking of the day at least left room for the possibility. Even the more skeptical commentators sometimes fell for traditional beliefs without any modern scientific support: a physician who considered Mary Toft's story was convinced that the mother's thoughts alone were not enough to change the species of the offspring, though he was willing to admit they can be impressed upon the fetus in other ways.[62]

Against this background, then, it is noteworthy that James Douglas was able to state his opinion so firmly: "I begin by declaring it to have always been my firm Opinion, that this Report was false; because I never could conceive the Generation of a perfect Rabbit in the *Uterus* of a Woman to be possible, it being contradictory to all that is hitherto known, both from Reason and Experience."[63] An anonymous commentator was even more confident in the state of his knowledge: "a true Surgeon," he insisted, "would never have suffer'd his Curiosity to be at all alarm'd by seeing a Letter from *Guildford*, which mention'd a Woman's *being deliver'd of five Rabbits*: Suppose one were to see a Letter from *Battersea*, importing that a Woman there had been delivered of five Cucumbers, or indeed a hundred Letters, would that lead a Man of Sense to believe any Thing, but, either that the People who wrote these Letters had been grossly impos'd upon themselves, or intended to impose upon him."[64] What seem like unproblematic statements of fact to us were in fact controversial assertions in 1726.

For both the believers and the skeptics, the state of Toft's body was the best sort of evidence that could be introduced: the expert testimony of a man who had examined her should be trusted before her own firsthand testimony about her experience. As

---

60 *The Wonder of Wonders*, p. 9.

61 Whiston, *Predictions*.

62 See *A Letter from a Male Physician in the Country*, p. 75.

63 James Douglas, *An Advertisement Occasion'd by Some Passages*, p. 3.

64 "Gulliver," *The Anatomist Dissected*, pp. 5–6.

a result, many of the discussions of the Toft affair are filled with copious medical details that may have aroused a prurient interest in many readers. Manningham gives this account of his examination of Mary Toft:

> I proceeded to examine her Breasts, wherein was a small Quantity of thin *Serous Matter* like *Milk*.... I afterwards diligently search'd the whole *Vagina*, and being well assured that that time all was clear from Imposture, I touched the *Os Uteri*, which was close and contracted in such manner that it would not receive so much as the point of a Bodkin into it's Orifice; the Neck of the *Uterus* was somewhat long; I then press'd against the *Uterus* with my Fingers opened in such a manner as to receive as much of the Body of the *Uterus* into my Hand as possible, which seem'd to me to contain something of Substance in its Cavity.[65]

The intimate gynecological details are unexpected in a cheap pamphlet, and the comparison with bodkin's point introduces a sinister note into the discussion, suggestive of sexual violence. The threat of violence becomes even clearer when Manningham decides to bluff in the hopes of throwing Toft off her game: "I urged her very much to confess the Truth; and told her, I believ'd her to be an Impostor, ... therefore I resolved to try a very painful Experiment upon her."[66]

Toft's body also undergoes much public scrutiny and discussion in Cyriacus Ahlers's account: "I ... examin'd her Breasts, which I found relax'd, a without any Hardness in the Glands, and no Milk in them; only upon squeezing, a little clear Serum came out.... when I laid hold of it [the mangled rabbit], the *Vagina* contracted itself so strongly, that it snapp'd back again the full Breadth of a Finger." Ahlers, however, seems more compassionate than Manningham: "By this Time I began to conceive a violent Suspicion of the whole Matter; but thought fit to conceal it.... I forged a great Compassion for the Woman's Case."[67] And a few commentators were able to go beyond forged compassion, offering genuine sympathy. Nathanael St. André's comments are pleasingly refreshing. In his *Short Narrative* he is more honest than most of the controvertists in the case: his own pamphlet is a record of doubtful evidence. He frankly presents the results of his investigations, even when they do not support his argument. He was even honest enough to reproduce all the best evidence his enemies used against him, and he rarely loses sympathy with Toft who, despite her imposture, was still subjected to what must have been some harrowing experiences. His judgment is still questionable: he is too credulous, and often accepts on faith things for which a more skeptical investigator would demand proof. But this makes him merely a bad doctor—he remains a thoroughly decent person.

The Identity of Consciousness

Even the physical evidence of the body, though, remains open to question. Physicians lacked knowledge about how long a person could live without food or water;

---

65   Manningham, *An Exact Diary*, pp. 7–9.
66   Ibid., pp. 31–2.
67   Ahlers, *Some Observations concerning the Woman of Godlyman in Surrey*, pp. 5, 11, 13.

obstetricians disagreed on the biology of reproduction. The physical world seems to be free of so many of the problems of testimony, but ultimately we are too often forced to depend on testimony about the physical world. And when that testimony is incomplete or unreliable, we face all the same problems we tried to avoid.

Perhaps the strangest body in eighteenth-century Britain, and the one that raises the most vexing issues with regard to the connections between biology and identity, is that of George Psalmanazar. No documents or other physical evidence could serve to authenticate him—had he produced the seventeenth-century Formosan equivalent of a driver's license or a passport, how could anyone check their accuracy? The only hard evidence about his identity, apart from his own narrative, was his person. And yet that person was notoriously difficult to interpret. We can begin with what strikes us as the most obvious evidence that Psalmanazar was a liar: that a fair-skinned European could pass himself off as an East Asian strikes us at once as absurd. Michael Keevak, in the most insightful published account of the Formosan imposture, makes the point well:

> What critics find so hard to imagine, and particularly from a modern, postcolonial perspective, is the apparent ease with which a white, blond Frenchman was able to pass himself off as a Japanese Formosan, and even to publish a book about the island replete with what now appear as utterly ridiculous illustrations and a phony language. How could such educated and highly cultured people have believed him? How could he have gotten away with it?[68]

But we should remember that very few Europeans had any direct contact with such exotic natives. Empirical evidence was lacking, and even the racial theories of Johann Friedrich Blumenbach lay nearly a century in the future: as Keevak once again points out, "neither race nor racial thinking as such could be said to exist in the early eighteenth century."[69] There was widespread belief that a torrid climate would produce dark-skinned inhabitants, though even on this point the experts were divided over whether the darker pigmentation was permanent or would come and go with more or less exposure to the sun. Psalmanazar, anticipating the objection, had a ready answer: "My complexion, indeed, which was very fair, appeared an unanswerable objection against me," he admitted. Therefore he "soon hatched a lucky distinction between those whose business exposes them to the heat of the sun, and those who keep altogether at home, in cool shades, or apartments under ground, and scarce ever feel the least degree of the reigning heat."[70] Poor Formosans were dark-skinned, but the wealthy Formosans who lived in underground cities were every bit as fair as a northern European. Once again, there was no clinical evidence to disprove his story.

Much of the interest of Psalmanazar's story is owing to when it was set. He arrived in England just a few years after the publication of the most influential philosophical work of the long eighteenth century, John Locke's *Essay concerning Human Understanding* (1690), which in a section called "Identity and Diversity"

---

68 Keevak, *The Pretended Asian*, p. 11.

69 Ibid., p. 12.

70 Psalmanazar, *Memoirs*, p. 197.

takes up the question "Wherein Identity consists." He arrived, in other words, at a time when notions of identity were in flux, receiving a basis in the new empiricist epistemology. This is not to justify him; his charade would have been offensive under both the old dispensation and the new. But considering his adventures in the context of these new Lockean conceptions of identity may help us to understand how his contemporaries regarded him, and why his seemingly transparent deception caused such a stir at the beginning of the eighteenth century.

Locke's conception of the basis of personal identity is worth quoting:

> Since consciousness always accompanies thinking, and 'tis that, that makes every one to be, what he calls *self*; and thereby distinguishes himself from all other thinking things, in this alone consists *personal Identity*, *i.e.* the sameness of a rational Being: And as far as this consciousness can be extended backwards to any past Action or Thought, so far reaches the Identity of that *Person*; it is the same *self* now it was then; and 'tis by the same *self* with this present one that now reflects on it, that the Action was done.[71]

Personal identity, that is, consists in consciousness, and nothing else. Personal identity extended across time is nothing more than consciousness extended across time, apparently through the mechanism of memory.

Locating identity in consciousness has the significant effect of shielding it from third-party scrutiny. Modern scientific ideas about what constitutes an identity—a unique DNA structure, perhaps—do not make for easy tests in casual conversation, but identity is at least theoretically something objective, something that can be verified by a third party, something *material*. Lockean identity, though, is by definition subjective; it is subjectivity itself. As Locke explains, "The *Substance*, whereof *personal self* consisted at one time, may be varied at another, without the change of personal *Identity*." Matter does not matter. And here Locke begins to entertain some apparently paradoxical ideas about personal identity: "*Personal Identity* consists, not in the Identity of Substance, but ... in the Identity of *consciousness*, wherein, if *Socrates* and the present Mayor of *Quinborough* agree, they are the same Person: If the same *Socrates* waking and sleeping do not partake of the same *consciousness*, *Socrates* waking and sleeping is not the same Person."[72] Identity, he says, may not be bound to physical bodies. As one modern philosopher muses, "With personal identity thus placed in consciousness, we have the possibility that one and the same man should be two persons,"[73] and vice versa.

---

71 Locke, *An Essay concerning Human Understanding*, p. 335 (2.27.9).

72 Ibid., pp. 337 (2.27.11), 341 (2.27.19).

73 McCann, "Locke on Identity," p. 73. See also Isaac Watts, who explored some of the paradoxes of Locke's ideas in 1733: "according to this Doctrine of *personal Identity*, many Men may successively or simultaneously be one Person; and thus every private Soldier in the Army of *Lewis* the XIVth may become the same Person as *Alexander the Great*.... And so any one Man may become many Persons: For if M. *N. Lee* the Tragedian hath a strong Impression on his Fancy, that he taught *Plato* Philosophy, then he is the same Person with *Socrates*; or that he pleaded in the *Roman* Senate against *Mark Antony*, then he is *Cicero*; or that he subdued *Gaul*, and made himself Master of *Rome*, then he is *Julius Cæsar*; that he wrote the *Æneid*, then he is *Virgil*; that he began the Reformation from Popery, then he is *Martin Luther*; and

Here we may seem to lose touch with reality: this is certainly unfair to Locke, who was not writing a how-to manual on recognizing people.[74] Locke in fact distinguishes the identity of the *person*, which consists in continued consciousness, from the identity of the *man*, which consists in the continuance of a physical body, and such physical identity is obviously an important part of our ability to recognize people. On Tuesday morning I recognize my students I last saw on Thursday not because I have access to their consciousness, but because they look more or less like the people I saw last week, and that is good enough for most purposes. Psalmanazar, though, takes us beyond "most purposes," for the *man* was of no use to Londoners in 1703: no one had seen him before, or indeed anyone like him. This is where his specifically Oriental identity comes into play, for Locke's most important contribution to eighteenth-century epistemology was a thoroughgoing empiricism. Ideas, said Locke, come from perception and reflection, and judgment comes from the comparison of ideas. But how are we to make any judgments about Psalmanazar's claim without empirical data, without having perceived a Formosan?

There is a playfulness in many of Psalmanazar's stories, a delight in spinning yarns, which sometimes makes him sound like Baron Münchhausen. As his confession makes clear, the Formosan imposture had a greater attraction than mere ease of passage through Europe: "I thought [it] afforded a vast scope to a fertile fancy to work upon, and I had no mistrust of myself on that head." The opportunity to exercise his fancy is the real enticement, and he soon discovers he is good at it: "When any question has been started on a sudden, about matters I was ever so unprepared for, I seldom found myself at a loss for a quick answer, which, if satisfactory, I stored up in my retentive memory."[75]

And here we can see Psalmanazar, probably unconsciously, toying with Lockean epistemology: he knew that by locating his identity outside the horizon of European perception, he shielded his story from inspection. He at first tried to pass as an Irishman, but an Irish identity might be compared with other identities. A claim to Oriental identity, on the other hand, was unimpeachable because inscrutable. His imagined Formosa became a sort of intellectual playground, or a screen onto which this uncommonly inventive youth could project his fantastic magic-lantern shows. "I flattered myself," he confessed, "I might succeed the more easily, as I supposed they were so little known by the generality of Europeans, that they were only looked

---

that he reign's in *England* at the latter End of the sixteenth Century, and then he is the same Person with Queen *Elizabeth*" (Watts, *Philosophical Essays*, p. 299).

74 This has not kept some critics from making perverse interpretations of Locke's text. Margaret Atherton scolds philosophers for such misreadings: "Locke's theory has generally been assumed to be offering a way of telling how one ought to go about reidentifying other people. Conceived as a practical suggestion about how to reidentify people, it has been thought to be problematic because it relies exclusively on a psychological rather than a physical criterion.... [But] The criterion of personal identity that Locke is establishing is not meant to solve third-person problems about whether our friends or Perkin Warbeck or the Princess Anastasia are the same when encountered today as someone encountered earlier" ("Locke's Theory of Personal Identity," pp. 274–5).

75 Psalmanazar, *Memoirs*, pp. 135–6, 138.

upon, in the lump, to be Antipodes to them."[76] Keevak summarizes the situation: "Formosan or any non-European culture was both undefined and indeed indefinable in 1704—or, rather, definable only by means of traits that could easily be faked, and thus easily appropriated."[77]

Psalmanazar's story shows that the attempt to escape the problems posed by testimony, to turn from unreliable words to trustworthy things, could never be wholly successful. Over and over again the physical world refuses to speak, and demands interpretation—and we are therefore forced to turn back to fallible minds. Documents can be reproduced by skilled craftsmen; the peculiarities of human bodies depend on testimony about other human bodies; and ultimately personal identity is something different from physical being. These problems give a restless quality to much eighteenth-century discussion of authenticity—no attempt to ground the debates in something stable has ever been entirely successful. Detectors who turn to things rather than people can make life more difficult for liars, but they can never make deception impossible—a devoted faker can, with enough effort, imitate anything genuine. And, as we will see in the next chapter, there have been fakers willing to make that effort, for what sometimes seems to be minimal rewards.

---

76 Ibid., p. 135.
77 Keevak, *The Pretended Asian*, p. 13.

Chapter 8

Motivated Malignity

"The labour of invention," writes Jeremy Bentham, "is more painful than that of memory."[1] Lying, in other words—at least lying well—is not easy. A credible deception takes time and effort. In a literary forgery, for example, appropriate writing materials must be secured; historical forms of the language must be scrutinized; private time must be set aside; cover stories must be prepared; tracks must be covered. Fabricators have to remember the details of their fabrications to avoid being caught in a contradiction: as Montaigne writes, "he who has not a good Memory should never take upon him the Trade of Lying."[2] In an imposture such Psalmanazar's, every waking moment must be devoted to sustaining an elaborate illusion. And would-be hoaxers must be prepared for prolonged attacks on their character: many of the fakers discussed in this book ended up the targets of bitter ridicule in scurrilous pamphlets, insulting caricatures, even obscene ballads.

Since deceit requires so much expenditure—of time, energy, and reputation, if not always of money—many have wondered what the fakers stand to gain in return. *Why* may be the most often asked, albeit the least satisfactorily answered, of all the questions regarding forgery. Such has been the case since these deceptions were still current events. In 1764, Alexander Mac Aulay wondered why Macpherson should "chuse, without temptation or necessity, to expose himself to the hazard of being detected of an imposture ... rather than to acknowledge them for his own." "What," asked Herbert Croft, "could induce C[hatterton] to lay such a plan?" Psalmanazar boasted that "my case was so intricate and perplexing, that it was next to impossible for the ablest heads to have guessed what my motives were, or for what, or by whom, I was induced thus to impose upon mankind." Some critics asked questions about motives, only to admit that they were unable to provide an answer: John Douglas confessed he was "at a Loss to conceive what cou'd tempt [Lauder] to make an Interpolation that cou'd so little serve his Cause," and in exposing the Ireland forgeries Edmond Malone mused that "It might have arisen from caprice.... Whatever the cause or motive may have been, the forgery is proved by the *fact*."[3] Still, even when it goes unanswered, the question about motivation forces itself on our attention. What could possibly have led a Scottish poet to say his poems were by a third-century bard, a mild-mannered editor to assert that Milton was a plagiary, or a poor woman to try to convince the king's physician that she had given birth to rabbits?

---

1   Bentham, *A Treatise on Judicial Evidence*, p. 30.

2   Montaigne, "Of Lyars," in *Essays of Michael Seigneur de Montaigne*, 1:43.

3   Mackenzie, *Report*, Appendix, p. 26; Croft, *Love and Madness*, p. 209; Psalmanazar, *Memoirs*, p. 204; John Douglas, *Milton Vindicated*, p. 45; Malone, *An Inquiry*, p. 147 n.

Mortal Antipathy

Money is often suggested as a possible motive for deception, and it should be taken seriously as such. Avarice certainly drives most of those who counterfeit currency or forge bonds, and it explains many of the mass-produced faux-antique artifacts supposedly found in Herculaneum and the counterfeits of Old Masters paintings sold to gullible grand tourists. Rumors of illicit income swirled around many of the supposed forgers; Elizabeth Montagu, although she confessed that "I find great difficulty in believing or disbelieving the authenticity of [Ossian's] poems," did report that "the Bishop of Ossory tells me, Mr. Macpherson receives an £100. per annum, subscription, while he stays in the Highlands to translate the poems; if he is writing them, he should have a thousand at least."[4] Few of the fakers in this book, though, did anything that was obviously for financial gain—many, in fact, stood to gain much more by claiming their works as their own than by attributing them to others. As one of Chatterton's schoolmates asserted, "had Chatterton been the author of the poems attributed to Rowley, so far from secreting such a circumstance, he would have made it his first and his greatest pride," and Macpherson himself insisted "It would be a very uncommon instance of self-denial in me to disown them, were they really of my composition."[5] It is easy to understand what prompts a plagiary to claim others' work as his or her own; it is far more difficult to understand why someone should insist his or her work had been written by someone else. Something other than money—something less tangible—must also be operating.

Some of these less tangible motives seem clear enough. The degree of anti-Catholic zeal that prompted Titus Oates to "conduc[t] the Reader through this dark and intricate Labyrinth of Confederated Roguery"[6] was certainly pathological, but it was no different in kind from the sectarian sentiments of many other Protestants in the 1670s and '80s. The links between forgery and religious bigotry seem to be perennial: the bogus *Protocols of the Elders of Zion* was used to justify anti-Semitic violence a century ago, and the work continues to circulate among hate groups today—an Internet search for the *Protocols* turns up some harrowing results. A similar kind of bigotry drove Mark Hofmann to forge documents to embarrass the Mormon Church in the 1980s, although the money he received from blackmailing the Church elders was certainly another motive.

These religious cases point toward another prominent motive among forgers of historical artifacts and documents: the opportunity to rewrite history. The *Protocols* rewrote history, blaming Jews for many of Europe's ills. Such an opportunity to determine the shape of the past can be a strong temptation. James Macpherson never declared the reasons for his chicanery, but it is not difficult to imagine some of the attractions the Ossianic story held for him. He grew up in the demoralized Highlands after the '45, when Scottish customs were being systematically snuffed out. The Ossianic poems showed that Scotland had a literary tradition every bit as

---

4   Elizabeth Montagu to Lord Lyttelton, 31 Oct. 1760, in Montagu, *Letters*, 4:320.

5   Reported in Mathias, *An Essay on the Evidence*, p. 48; Macpherson, Preface to the first edition of *Fingal*, in *The Poems of Ossian*, p. 35.

6   Oates, *An Exact and Faithful Narrative*, p. 35.

distinguished as England's; the great antiquity of the poems demonstrated, moreover, that the Scottish tradition was even older than the English. Promoting Scotland's cultural heritage was a widespread concern among the Edinburgh literati around mid-century, and the generally pro-Scottish *Critical Review* praised Macpherson for his "diligence exerted in rescuing from oblivion those beautiful fragments of antiquity, and monuments of the valour and genius of the ancestors of that warlike people, who have lately bled so freely in the service of their country."[7] Fiona Stafford, Howard Gaskill, Richard Sher, and others have convincingly set Macpherson's activities in the context of post-Culloden Scotland, where the need to recover some national pride and distinctiveness was keenly felt among many intellectuals of the day.

Some attempts to rewrite history may be less national and more personal. William Lauder's "mortal antipathy to the name and character of Milton," wrote Hester Thrale Piozzi, caused him to "collec[t] from several Latin poets ... all such passages as bore any kind of resemblance to different places in the Paradise Lost." Milton, in turn, "was supposed to be guilty of plagiarism from inferior modern writers."[8] Exactly where this "mortal antipathy" came from is unclear, and Lauder's attempts at self-justification were inconsistent. In one account he gave, he was angered by Alexander Pope's caustic ridicule of his beloved Arthur Johnston and praise of Milton in *The Dunciad Variorum*: "On two unequal crutches propt he came," wrote Pope of William Benson, "Milton's on this, on that one Johnston's name." This insult, said Lauder, drove him to besmirch Milton's reputation.[9] On another occasion, he insisted his "offence proceeded from no design to impose upon the publick, as no one ever had a better cause than mine": it arose

> rather from a well-meaning zeal to undeceive mankind, in a very curious particular, relating to a book, concerning the true Author, whereof much noise has been made in the world, by disclosing a master-piece of fraud and forgery committed by Milton against the memory of King Charles the First, which very few persons seem to be acquainted with.[10]

In *Eikonoklastes*, rebellious Milton had attacked saintly Charles for incorporating Pamela's prayer from Sidney's *Arcadia* into his *Eikon Basilike*; Lauder thought it his duty to inform the world that Milton had doctored his evidence by interpolating the prayer into Charles's text, committing an "unparallel'd Scene of Villainy."[11] When Lauder was convicted of exactly the same offense, his enemies delighted in quoting his words back at him.

---

7   *Critical Review* 15 (March 1763): 200.

8   Piozzi, *Anecdotes*, pp. 393–4.

9   Pope, *The Dunciad (B)*, 4.111–12, in *Poems*; Nichols, *Literary Anecdotes of the Eighteenth Century*, 2:137 n.

10   Lauder to Mead, 9 April 1751, in Nichols, *Illustrations*, 4:428–9. See also two works by Lauder: *A Letter to the Reverend Mr. Douglas*, pp. 13–14, where he explains his enmity toward Pope; and *King Charles I. Vindicated from the Charge of Plagiarism*, pp. 2–3, where he minimizes the extent of his transgressions.

11   Lauder, *King Charles I. Vindicated*, p. 23.

A Pleasure of Deceiving the World

Another forger's motives seem to have been largely personal: whatever else prompted him to "discover" lost works of Shakespeare, William Henry Ireland hoped by doing so to earn the affection of his bardolatrous father. In an unpublished autobiographical account, Ireland explains what first led him to begin the forgeries: "I had sought to give Mr Ireland pleasure—I accomplished my plan without the smallest intention of evil nor ever intended to write one Syllable more on the Subject."[12] His story is similar in a letter to his father, shortly after his first private confession: "I thought at last that it might be received & turn to the advantage of my family[.] this was my first my principal wish—besides the pleasure I thought you woud receive in thinking yourself possess'd of the papers."[13] Ireland père, however, was rarely pleased, and the son's efforts were not repaid with the affection he sought. The remarkable letters between Ireland's father and his imaginary benefactor, "H," are among the most pathetic ever written, as Ireland praises himself in the third person to his own unaffectionate father. "Without flattery," writes the enthusiastic H, William "is the young Man after *my own Heart* in whom I wou'd confide & even consult on the nicest affairs"[14]—a degree of confidence he never received from his real father. H praises "a *Play* written by *your Son* which for stile & greatness of thought is equal to any one of *Shakspeares.... No man* but your *Son* ever wrote like *Shakspeare....* upon my honour & soul I woud not scruple giving £2,000 a year to have a son with such extraordinary faculties."[15] (Samuel, it seems, would just as soon have the £2,000.) H writes that William "never utters a syllable unbecoming a dutiful & loving Son."[16] The culmination of young Ireland's pathological psychodrama appears in an unpublished autobiography, *A Full and Explanatory Account*, where a reconciliation takes place between repentant, dying father and forgiving, loving son:

> I attended him—unremittingly attended him for the space of four months during which period he stated that I constituted all his happiness[.] I even indulged him in his pursuits to the last and a thousand times he declared with tears in his eyes that my presence constituted his sole happiness——At length Nature worn out yielded him into the bosom of peace——He died in my arms.[17]

The scene is almost certainly imaginary—according to every other account, father and son never had a reconciliation—but William's longing to be his father's "sole happiness" is both poignant and telling.

Ireland's motives, though, go beyond pleasing a recalcitrant father, for at times he actually seemed to get a thrill from flirting with discovery. A turning point in his story comes when his friend and colleague Montague Talbot caught him red-

---

12   Ireland, *A Full and Explanatory Account*, pp. 71–2.

13   W. H. Ireland to Samuel Ireland, 14 June 1796, in BL Add. MS 30346, fol. 241^v.

14   "H" [i.e., W. H. Ireland] to Samuel Ireland, [c. 20 July 1795], in BL Add. MS 30346, fol. 47^v.

15   "H" to Samuel Ireland, 25 July 1795, in BL Add. MS 30346, fols. 54^r–55^r.

16   "H" to Samuel Ireland, 30 July 1795, in BL Add. MS 30346, fol. 57^v.

17   Ireland, *A Full and Explanatory Account*, pp. 245–6.

handed. Most readers, in reviewing Ireland's comments on the scene, have assumed he genuinely hoped to escape detection, especially when he refers to the "infinite difficulty" with which he tried to conceal his forgeries from his office-mate. But the effort seems far short of "infinite," especially since Talbot had already declared his belief that Ireland was the forger, and since he had several times tried breaking in on Ireland hoping to catch him in the act:

> Mr. Talbot found means to elude my observation, by bending himself double, and in that position creeping beneath the window at which I was accustomed to write: thus unobserved he suddenly darted into the chambers, and ere I could find means to conceal the document whereon I was then occupied, he arrested my arm, and by this stratagem became at once acquainted with the whole mystery.[18]

Had Ireland really hoped to avoid detection, he might have considered whether it was wise to set up his counterfeiter's atelier in the same office as his suspicious coworker—the mysterious inks and scraps of old paper would have been difficult to conceal, even in a legal office. More curious still, his performance before his laundress positively begs for discovery:

> the female who attended at the chambers where I was articled was present during the whole of my fabrication of Elizabeth's supposed letter; which, when completed, I gave into her hands, and requested to know whether she would not have conceived it very old; to which she replied in the affirmative; adding, with a laugh, *that it was very odd I could do such unaccountable strange things.*[19]

He knew perfectly well that "Had this circumstance been generally known, it would unquestionably have led to the developement of the whole Shaksperian forgery."

Other evidence of his desire to be caught, or at least to flirt with the danger of discovery, appears in a series of bizarre inside jokes. His discovery of a letter from Shakespeare to one "William Henry Ireland," an ostensible ancestor who saved the playwright from drowning, struck critics as so improbable that they found it laughable. One of Ireland's supporters, Francis Webb, could offer only the half-hearted defense that the story was too good to be false: "Can it be supposed," he asked, "that any man ... would ever have risqued issuing such coinage as this, and ventured at fabricating such a story, of which there had never been the slightest report? Imposture, in general, keeps within the bounds of probability."[20] There are also odd passages in the letters from H: "If your *Son* is not a second Shakspeare," for instance, "I am not a *man*"—which, of course, he was not, being at best an imaginary friend. And when H calls Ireland "the only Man that ever walkd with [Shakespeare] hand in hand," he seems to be alluding not only to a hand offered in affection, but also to the handwriting he was accused of imitating.[21]

---

18 Ireland, *Confessions*, pp. 122–3. The story is also told, with few significant differences in details, in *A Full and Explanatory Account*, p. 148.

19 Ireland, *Confessions*, p. 77.

20 Webb, *Shakspeare's Manuscripts*, p. 16. Michael McKeon refers to this gambit as "the 'strange, therefore true' paradox": *The Origins of the English Novel*, p. 111.

21 "H" to Samuel Ireland, 25 July 1795, in BL Add. MS 30346, fol. 55ʳ.

There can be no doubt that Ireland reveled in deceiving his intellectual betters; it clearly did much for his self-image to think that the smartest people of the day were fooled by his games. His barely competent drawing, the "Witty Conundrum," had been dismissed as "ridiculous" by Samuel Ireland, but when William produced a letter from Shakespeare to Cowley to back it up, the critics were more favorable:

> This immediately threw a great value on the Conundrum and all the *sage* Book worms gave their various ideas & even pretended to explain the curious enigma—Which to speak positive matter of fact I myself was a total stranger to—Having written [it] ... without any meaning whatever (so much for the Learned in antiquities &c.).[22]

"So much for the learned" forms a kind of refrain in many of his manuscript accounts of his forgeries, and he always seemed to beam when he made serious antiquarians look ridiculous. It is impossible to miss the sarcasm in the description of his supposed offenses in his pseudonymous *Chalcographimania* (1814):

> To parent now the *son* let's add,
> Of ancient lore, *impostor lad*
> Who guilty was—accursed sin,
> Of taking all the old ones in!
> A crime I swear to pardon never,
> Or even grant the forger clever.[23]

Thus the vitriol he directed at those antiquarians who failed to fall for his trickery. His "Lines which I wrote Extempore on Malone's Notes to Shakspear" are remarkable for their acrimony:

> An Irish Critic stor'd with brains of Wool
> Produc'd an Irish Brat—An Irish *Bull*
> Made Notes on him whose Genius we adore
> With leaden Pen bespatter'd Shakspear's lore.
> Prov'd by his labours what he was at once
> A God like Bard—Himself an Irish *Dunce*.[24]

He can smirk at the critics who blundered; he can only fulminate at those who were right.

A similar delight in fooling the literary establishment seems to have operated nearly as strongly on Ireland's most important precursor. Although E. H. W. Meyerstein doubts that "Chatterton's 'originals' ... were ever seriously intended to deceive,"[25] many scholars, then and now, have noticed in Chatterton a thrill at pulling wool over antiquarian eyes. Thomas Warton considers Chatterton's motives, beginning with the obvious financial interest: "It will be asked, for what end or purpose did he contrive such an imposture? I answer, from lucrative views." He then

---

22 Edinburgh Univ. Library H.-P. Coll. 321, fol. 10ʳ.
23 Ireland, *Chalcographimania*, pp. 102–3 n.
24 Ireland, *A Full and Explanatory Account*, p. 121.
25 Meyerstein, *A Life of Thomas Chatterton*, p. 121.

pauses, however, and changes course: "or perhaps from a pleasure of deceiving the world, a motive which, in many minds, operates more powerfully than the hopes of gain.... he might have sacrificed even the vanity of appearing in the character of an applauded original author, to the private enjoyment of the success of his inventions and dexterity."[26] A similar "pleasure of deceiving the world" seems to have motivated George Psalmanazar, whose posthumous *Memoirs* detail "the various ways by which I was in some measure unavoidably led into the base and shameful imposture of passing upon the world for a native of Formosa." It was his youthful academic distinction that "unavoidably led" him to his hoax: "what did me in particular the most hurt ... was the great admiration which my more than common readiness at learning whatever came in my way had gained me, and the imprudent fondness and partiality which my masters shewed to me on that account."[27] In the cases of Ireland, Chatterton, and Psalmanazar, we can attribute much of the appeal to the pleasures of engaging in a virtuoso performance and the delight in deceiving their intellectual and social betters.

Excited by Some Motive

The various motives proposed for the deceivers—and this list of possibilities is far from comprehensive—are interesting in their own right, but perhaps even more interesting is the notion that we expect to find a motive at all. We take it for granted that the *why* question must have an answer that will make sense to us. This conviction seems to be related to a significant eighteenth-century shift in the understanding of human motivation. Many early eighteenth-century Britons were content with a model of a single "ruling passion": Alexander Pope boasted to Joseph Spence about his "New Hypothesis, That a prevailing passion in ye mind is brought wth it into ye world, & continues till death."[28] As suggested by the original etymological meaning of the word *character*—a stamp or inscription—one's nature was fixed, and dominated all of one's actions:

> The ruling Passion, be it what it will,
> The ruling Passion conquers Reason still.[29]

This passion, once discovered, would be enough to explain even seemingly inconsistent behavior:

> Search then the Ruling Passion: There, alone,
> The Wild are constant, and the Cunning known;
> The Fool consistent, and the False sincere;
> Priests, Princes, Women, no dissemblers here.[30]

---

26 Warton, *History of English Poetry*, 2:158.
27 Psalmanazar, *Memoirs*, pp. 5, 73.
28 Pope, reported by Spence, May 1730, in Pope, *Poems*, 3.2:xxii.
29 Pope, "Epistle to Bathurst," 155–6, in *Poems*.
30 Pope, "Epistle to Cobham," 174–7, in *Poems*.

Even as Pope was writing, though, conceptions of the passions were shifting. For many economic and political thinkers, the number of possible ruling passions was too messy, and over time the range was narrowed to only material acquisitiveness—now, in an increasingly commercial society, distinguished from the traditional sin of avarice, and assumed to be a universal human trait. This reconception made possible the nineteenth century's ideal of the rational economic actor, who always sought to maximize his own self-interest.[31] Adam Smith put it simply in *The Wealth of Nations*: "An augmentation of fortune is the means by which the greater part of men propose and wish to better their condition. It is the means the most vulgar and the most obvious."[32]

Other moral philosophers, though, were not convinced this was always so; they saw far more complexity in human motivation than simple "augmentation of fortune," and therefore gave increasing attention to competing desires within the mind. As Samuel Johnson pointed out in one of his sermons, mere acquisitiveness is not enough to explain the variety of human wishes. "There is a kind of mercantile speculation," he writes, "which ascribes every action to interest, and considers interest as only another name for pecuniary advantage. But the boundless variety of human affections is not to be thus easily circumscribed. Causes and effects, motives and actions, are complicated and diversified without end." So complicated are they, in fact, that Johnson elsewhere admits "We are sometimes not ourselves conscious of the original motives of our actions."[33] The Earl of Shaftesbury makes a similar point: he alludes to the "common saying," "interest governs the world," but insists that more thoughtful people "will find that passion, humour, caprice, zeal, faction and a thousand other springs, which are counter to self-interest, have as considerable a part in the movements of this machine. There are more wheels and counterpoises in this engine than are easily imagined."[34]

However complicated, however diversified, however unconscious the basis of motivation, though, it was still taken for granted almost universally in eighteenth-century Britain that there *were* motives for every action, at least among the sane. "Every man is conscious," writes Johnson in another of his sermons, "that he neither performs, nor forbears any thing upon any other motive than the prospect, either of an immediate gratification, or a distant reward."[35] "To act without a Motive," writes Thomas Morgan in 1725, "would be the same thing in effect as not to act at all."[36] Henry Home, Lord Kames, makes the point as explicitly as can be:

> It is admitted by all men, that we act from motives.... If we are uncertain what part a man will act, the uncertainty arises, not from our doubting whether he will act from a motive; for this is never called in question: it arises from our not being able to judge, what the motive is, which, in his present circumstances, will prevail.[37]

---

31   See Hirschman, *The Passions and the Interests*, esp. pp. 31–48.

32   Adam Smith, *An Inquiry into the Nature and Causes of the Wealth of Nations*, 1:363.

33   Samuel Johnson, *Sermon* 23, in Yale *Works*, 14:241; *Rambler* 87, in Yale *Works*, 4:95.

34   Shaftesbury, *Characteristics*, pp. 53–4.

35   Samuel Johnson, *Sermon* 14, in Yale *Works*, 14:149.

36   Morgan, *Philosophical Principles of Medicine*, p. 367.

37   Kames, *Essays on the Principles of Morality*, pp. 159–60.

So too Jonathan Edwards: "every Act of the Will whatsoever, is excited by some Motive." Edwards here is challenging the anonymous author of *An Essay on the Freedom of the Will*, who, in Edwards's summary, "supposes the Will in many Cases to be determined by *no Motive at all*." Edwards's verdict: "The very Supposition which is here made, directly contradicts and overthrows itself."[38]

By mid-century, mechanistic conceptions of moral philosophy were being developed to match the increasingly mechanistic natural philosophy of a post-Newtonian age. Helvétius insists that "interest is always obeyed.... If the physical universe be subject to the laws of motion, the moral universe is equally so to those of interest. Interest, on earth, the mighty magician, which to the eyes of every creature changes the appearance of all objects."[39] The most extended eighteenth-century British discussion of the ubiquity of motivation comes in Joseph Priestley's similarly materialist *Doctrine of Philosophical Necessity Illustrated* (1777). "The more I examine my own actions, or those of others," writes Priestley, "the more reason I see to be satisfied that all volitions and actions are preceded by corresponding motives." His notion of *motive* is related to mechanistic conceptions of motive forces:

> whenever we either reflect upon our own conduct, or speculate concerning that of others, we never fail to consider, or ask, what would be the *motive* of such or such a choice; always taking for granted that there must have been some motive or other for it; and we never suppose, in such cases, that any choice could be made without some motive.[40]

Motives may be complex; they may be hidden; they may even be contradictory. But they are always there, and human action can always be understood with reference to them.

This is the gist of the introduction to William Richardson's *Philosophical Analysis ... of Shakespeare's Remarkable Characters* (1780), which borrows extensively from Lord Kames and the philosophers of the Scottish Common Sense school. Human minds, he insists, behave according to principles that, however difficult to sort out in practice, are always comprehensible in theory. The weather, he reminds his readers, is difficult to predict—in today's terms, it is chaotic—but it is not random. We know that all meteorological effects proceed from strict natural causes; they may seem random to the casual observer, but they are guided by art unknown to us, and direction that we cannot see. "Thus," Richardson goes on, "even external phenomena, to an uninstructed person, will seem as wild and incongruous as the motions and affections of the mind. On a more accurate inspection, he finds that harmony and design pervade the universe; that the motions of the stars are regular, and that laws are prescribed to the tempest." So too with human motivation: he ridicules those who "maintain that the mind is in a state of anarchy and disorder," and insists that it appears that way only because of the "Difficulty in making just experiments."[41]

---

38 Edwards, *A Careful and Strict Enquiry*, pp. 117, 79.
39 Helvétius, *De l'Esprit*, p. 27.
40 Priestley, *The Doctrine of Philosophical Necessity Illustrated*, pp. 28, 48–9.
41 Richardson, *A Philosophical Analysis*, pp. 16, 17–18.

We cannot make those experiments on real human beings, Richardson admits, but we do have at our disposal the most extensive laboratory of characterological specimens ever assembled—they can be found in the works of Shakespeare. Britain's great dramatist was at the center of the developing conceptions of consistent motivation, for his were the first modern literary characters to receive any extended analysis. One author, convinced that "The knowledge of human nature has been, and still is, universally allowed the most proper study of man," knew that he would find rich materials in the Bard, for "so great a master as SHAKESPEARE has left to the world, if I may so term it—the soul anatomized."[42] Whether or not he was, as Harold Bloom has argued, the creator of modern subjectivity, he certainly provided the first few generations of literary critics who examined vernacular English works with their most important models of that faculty.

Of course, the idea of character motivation was not entirely new in the eighteenth century. Achilles was angry because he was slighted in the division of spoils; Odysseus wanted to return home—from these two motives spring two of the founding plots of Western literature. The epic and romance traditions generally, though, gave little extended attention to psychological complexity and competing desires. A character like Thersites can be summed up in a single Popean couplet: "Spleen to Mankind his Envious Heart possest,/And much he hated All, but most the Best."[43] Nothing more needs to be said. In most earlier epic, romance, and drama, eighteenth-century critics saw only the broadest kinds of characters, motivated only by the simplest of drives and passions.

Not so in Shakespeare. "Other dramatists," writes Johnson in 1765, "can only gain attention by hyperbolical or aggravated characters," but Shakespeare gives us figures "who act and speak as the reader thinks that he should himself have spoken or acted on the same occasion." His characters are "consistent, natural and distinct"; they "act and speak by the influence of those general passions and principles by which all minds are agitated, and the whole system of life is continued in motion"; they are, in short, plausibly motivated.[44] And what appeared in Shakespeare had a strong influence on the most important developing genre of eighteenth-century Britain, the novel. The rejection of the supernatural is one of the features most often noted in accounts of the "realistic" novel's development out of the earlier romance, but consistent and comprehensible character motivation may be just as important. Johnson's emphasis on "accidents that daily happen in the world" in *Rambler* 4 is famous, but the same sentence notes that novels "exhibit life … influenced by passions and qualities which are really to be found in conversing with mankind."[45]

This conception marks an important difference from earlier modes of prose fiction. The heroes of romances spent their time slaying dragons and rescuing damsels because that is what heroes did; the villains were driven by nothing more than a delight in evil. The heroes (and, at least as important, heroines) of eighteenth-century novels do things for reasons that are supposed to make real-world sense. A

42 *Shakespeare: Concerning the Traits of His Characters*, p. 3.
43 Pope, *Iliad*, 2.267–8, in *Poems*.
44 Johnson, Preface to Shakespeare, in Yale *Works*, 7:64, 75, 62.
45 Johnson, *Rambler* 4, in Yale *Works*, 3:19.

villain's actions in a novel may spring from obvious causes like avarice or ambition; they may emerge from an insult that has rankled for years; by century's end, they may even be the product of a misguided upbringing or a sad childhood. But they always emerge from something. This has been a commonplace of criticism on eighteenth-century fiction from Hippolyte Taine (the purpose of the new novel is "to depict real life, to describe characters, to suggest plans of conduct, and judge motives of action") to John Bender ("The novel ... articulates reality within a fine network of visible, observationally discoverable causes which are the motor factors of the narrative itself, for example, the internal forces of psychological motivation").[46] The attitude is now so widespread and considered so essential to the genre that beginners' handbooks on novel-writing call motivation the key to realistic characters: "Be sure your characters have motivations for their actions, opinions and decisions," Prudy Taylor Board advises the would-be novelist, "and that the reader understands these motives.... If you don't, ... you have created puppets or caricatures, not believable characters."[47]

Naturally, not all characters are equally "round," to use E. M. Forster's term, and the "flatter" ones often act on no more interesting motivations than the heroes and villains of old. The realistic character's victory was never complete, and simplistic characters persisted, whether the murderous caitiffs of epics and romances or the mustache-twirling dastards of later melodramas. But one of the most important contributions the new realistic novel made to the literary tradition was the character who behaves according to consistent, coherent, and comprehensible motives. By the time we reach Jane Austen, motive has become a far more complex matter than anything found in epic—many of her heroines act on motives that even they do not recognize. But a motive of some sort, however complicated, remains a necessity.

To put it another way, the lack of a motive produces a puzzle that exercises critical ingenuity. As eighteenth-century critics approached literature, whether Shakespeare or the new realistic novel, understanding characters meant understanding their motivations. Unclear motives posed a critical problem, and sometimes required a radical solution. Some of the most controversial readings of Shakespeare arise from passages where a character's motive is unclear. Cordelia's apparent lack of motivation in speaking brusquely to her father was one of the mysteries that demanded solution; it led Nahum Tate to introduce the infamous Cordelia–Edgar love interest:

> 'Twas my good Fortune to light on one Expedient to rectifie what was wanting in the Regularity and Probability of the Tale, which was to run through the whole A *Love* betwixt *Edgar* and *Cordelia*.... This renders *Cordelia*'s Indifference and her Father's Passion in the first Scene probable. It likewise gives Countenance to *Edgar*'s Disguise.[48]

---

46 Taine, *History of English Literature*, 2:192; Bender, *Imagining the Penitentiary*, p. 43. Compare Homer Obed Brown's summary of Walter Scott's attitudes: "the distinction between romance and novel could be measured by shades of degree between motivated action and form and lack of it" (*Institutions of the English Novel*, p. 188).

47 Board, *101 Tips*, p. 35. Compare Sol Stein, who, in a checklist of advice called "Revising Drafts," asks, "Is each character's motivation credible?" (*How to Grow a Novel*, p. 166). Similar advice is common in most such guides.

48 Tate, *King Lear*, sig. A2ᵛ.

A more extreme lack of motivation informs Aaron in *Titus Andronicus*, a villain more nefarious than even Iago. Iago had at least been passed over for a promotion, but Aaron seems to be without even such a simplistic provocation. He gleefully recounts his horrible deeds:

> Ev'n now I curse the day (and yet, I think,
> Few come within the compass of my curse)
> Wherein I did not some notorious Ill,
> As kill a man, or else devise his death;
> Ravish a maid, or plot the way to do it;
> Accuse some innocent, and forswear myself.
>
> . . . .
>
> Tut, I have done a hundred dreadful things,
> As willingly as one would kill a fly;
> And nothing grieves me heartily indeed,
> But that I cannot do ten thousand more.

This was not the kind of characterization the eighteenth century had come to expect from Shakespeare—it was the one-dimensional delight in evil that was found only in old books, not in men. The most common eighteenth-century solution to this problem? Remove the play from the canon. "All the editors and criticks agree with Mr. Theobald in supposing this play spurious," writes Johnson. "I see no reason for differing from them."[49]

Most of these problems, though, could be solved with less drastic measures than revision or rejection; explication was usually enough. It may even be that the need to solve these problems is the most important force behind early character criticism. As a rough guide, the volume of late eighteenth- and nineteenth-century commentary on each of Shakespeare's characters varies proportionately with the difficulty of explaining his or her motives.[50] Understanding motive was behind many of Coleridge's lectures on Shakespeare's characters—Hamlet, Richard III, Falstaff— and prompted his famous remark on "the motive-hunting of motiveless Malignity" in Iago.[51] All malignity had to be motivated malignity, and it seems likely that the difficulty of understanding Hamlet's motivations played a significant part in making it the most studied play of the nineteenth and twentieth centuries.[52]

---

49   Johnson, Yale *Works*, 8:750.

50   Deidre Shauna Lynch makes some perceptive comments on the relationship between Shakespearean character criticism and the early novel, as well as on the development of new conceptions of interiority in the late eighteenth and early nineteenth centuries. See part 2 of *The Economy of Character*, esp. pp. 133–8.

51   Coleridge, *Lectures 1808–1819 on Literature*, 2:315.

52   James Harris, however, was able to dismiss Hamlet's inconsistencies as mere faults. When Hamlet is wronged by Claudius, he says, we expect him to seek revenge; "But should *the same Hamlet* by chance kill an *innocent old Man*, an old Man, from whom he had *never received Offence*; and with whose *Daughter* he *was actually in love*;—what should we expect *then*? Should we not look for *Compassion*, I might add, even for *Compunction*? Should we not be shockt, if, instead of this, he were to prove *quite insensible*—or (what is even worse) were he *to be brutally jocose*?" In this case he says "the MANNERS are *blameable*, because they are

The Bounds of Probability

Literary criticism shows significant advances in the discussion of motivation over the course of the eighteenth century, but in another forum motive is even more essential. It is no coincidence that the increasing attention paid to fictional motive corresponds closely with the increasing attention paid to legal motive.

Once again, there are precedents. Aristotle devotes an entire chapter of his *Rhetoric* (1.10) to considerations of criminal motive. As he explains, "all the actions of men must necessarily be referred to seven causes: chance, nature, compulsion, habit, reason, anger, and desire." In the courtroom, "reason"—the rational desire, or motivation—is the most important. He explains that the prosecution "must examine the number and nature of the motives which are to be found in his opponent; and the defendant, which of them are not to be found in him."[53] But Aristotle's advice was little heeded in England until the late seventeenth century, when motive began to become important in criminal trials. In the new regime, establishing guilt often depended on the prosecutor's ability to convince the jurors that the accused not only had the opportunity to commit a crime, but that he also had a reason to do so. The defense needed only to show that the accused stood to gain nothing from committing the crime; that granted, it would follow that he did not commit it. The task of counsel on either side, therefore, was to construct a narrative that explains the events—the more coherent the narrative, the more convincing the story.

What, though, does "coherent" mean in this context?—what makes for a convincing motive? There is very little explicit discussion of this, but it seems that "coherent" here eventually came to mean satisfying according to the canons of the realistic psychological novel. The literary and the legal understandings of motivation seem mutually influential. To raise the question of motive, whether as a prosecutor or defendant, was to invite auditors to construct a narrative—every juror his own novelist—and the creator of the more compelling narrative usually won the case. Just as we see in eighteenth-century fiction, eighteenth-century legal theory increasingly takes for granted the notion that all actions are prompted by some comprehensible drives or desires: people do not do things without a good reason.

Even when disputes over deception are not actual legal proceedings, they often take a similar form, and the prosecutors of metaphorical criminals often adopt the same techniques as the prosecutors of actual criminals. The detector's ability to create a plausible narrative explaining the existence of a questionable document goes a long way toward exposing it as a fake. One way to discredit an opponent's story, therefore, is to tell a better one of your own, where "better" does not mean more sensational, but rather, more convincing, more plausible, more in line with readers' understanding of human nature. Disputes over authenticity often turn into dueling narratives, with each side offering a story and trying to insist on its plausibility, hoping to convince an increasingly sophisticated audience, schooled in the new literary attention to motive.

---

inconsistent; we should *never conjecture from* HAMLET any thing *so unfeelingly cruel*" (Harris, *Philological Inquiries*, pp. 167–9).

53   Aristotle, *Rhetoric*, 1.10.8 (1369a), 1.10.6 (1368b).

Edmond Malone had real legal training, so we should not be surprised to see him employing this legal approach in his attacks on Ireland. His *Inquiry into the Authenticity of Certain Miscellaneous Papers* (1796) catalogues many inconsistencies, contradictions, and omissions in Ireland's Shakespearean documents, all the while treating them as evidence in a criminal trial. Perhaps in strict logic it would be enough to point to such gaps to reveal the papers as forgeries, but Malone is determined to make his case more convincing than unaided logic will allow. Many of his comments in the *Inquiry* therefore try to make sense of anomalies in the text by constructing a psychological narrative that explains the forger's motivations. A letter supposedly from Shakespeare to Richard Cowley, for instance, "(very prudently) has no date, except *Marche nynthe*"[54]—the parenthesis wickedly suggests that Ireland consciously omitted a more precise date to save himself from the dangers of detection. He thereby explains an omission by telling a story about Ireland's supposed motives: the missing date is not the result of chance, but a "prudent" attempt to make detection difficult. A prosecuting attorney could hardly make a more persuasive case.

Although Malone was the most dedicated teller of stories designed to bring forgeries to light, other detectors constructed similar narratives of how forged documents came to be. Thomas Tyrwhitt noted of the entries in Chatterton's glossary that "Whoever will take pains to examine these interpretations will find, that they are almost all taken from Skinner's *Etymologicon Linguæ Anglicanæ*."[55] Now, it could simply be that both Skinner and Chatterton saw the need to gloss the same obsolete words; for Tyrwhitt, though, the similarity of the word lists is evidence that Chatterton stole his information from the *Etymologicon*. (He is on more solid ground when he notes that Chatterton's errors "may be proved very often to have taken their rise ... from blunders of Skinner himself."[56]) Tyrwhitt invites the reader to participate in the process of making sense of the forgeries: true, it is implausible that a forger would take great trouble to construct a faux-antique document for minimal reward; if, however, the effort can be shown to be small, the forgery becomes more likely in the reader's mind. And it is only logical that an inexperienced forger would try to save time by cribbing from easily available reference books.

Other critics of literary forgers used the same tactic, showing how what appears to be a difficult forgery is in fact the product of little effort. The anonymous author of a satirical jeremiad, *Hell upon Earth* (1729), debunks popular ghost stories by cataloguing the generic conventions. He thereby composes a pseudo-narrative, explaining how fakers might carry out their hoaxes without expending much energy:

> In the Country there are two Sorts of *Ghosts*, a *Plebian Ghost* and a *Ghost of Rank*; and these two bear a different Figure, and have a different Behaviour.
>
> *The Ghost of Dignity* is always known to be the Spirit of a former Landlord of the Parish.... His *Ghost* is the very same Man that he himself was in his Life-time, in every Respect: It wears the self-same Snuff-colour'd Cloaths trimm'd with black, the same Camblet-Cloak, lin'd with red, a little faded, and the same Shoes with Cork-Soals and

---

54   Malone, *An Inquiry*, p. 205.

55   Chatterton, *Poems*, ed. Tyrwhitt, p. 324.

56   Ibid., p. 325.

Square-Toes … and twenty other Signs and Tokens, which are all visible to any Man, Woman, or Child, that can but see clearly in the Dark.[57]

And William Shaw provides a narrative of his own creation of would-be Ossianic forgeries, complete with a DIY kit for the aspiring forger that helpfully provides all the Ossianic clichés:

> I remember, when I travelled that country three years ago, to have sat down on a hill; and, the scene being favourable, in a poetic mood, I jingled together upon paper, with suitable invented Galic names, the epithets of blue-eyed, meek-eyed, mildly-looking, white-bosomed, dark-brown locks, noble, generous, valiant, tears, spears, darts, hearts, harts, quivers, bows, arrows, helmets, steel, streams, torrents, noble deeds, other times, bards, chiefs, storms, songs, &c. and produced a little poem, which reads pretty smoothly; and, if I had a mind to publish it, it would be no difficult matter to persuade some people I had translated it from the Galic: for I might translate a stanza of it into Earse, shew it to the inquisitive, and say I had the rest by me; after which they would never enquire.[58]

The message is clear: spinning out Ossianic verses is easy—in Johnson's formulation, within the grasp of "many men, many women, and many children"[59]—and readers must therefore adjust their expectations about the real challenges and rewards.

Sometimes these arguments about motive take oddly counterintuitive forms. We have already seen Francis Webb's attempt to defend Ireland's impostures by arguing that they looked too much like forgeries to be forgeries: "Imposture, in general, keeps within the bounds of probability." Similar arguments were made by many of the defenders of eighteenth-century fakes. Thus, when Hugh Blair discovers glaring historical inconsistencies in the Ossian poems, they are for him not proof of deception but of authenticity: "Who," after all, "would have been either so hardy or so stupid, as to attempt a forgery which could not have failed of being immediately detected?"[60] And the clumsier the forgers, the more their supporters invoked this argument that turned their incompetence into proof of innocence. Thomas James Mathias uses Chatterton's ineptitude in antiquating his documents as evidence that he could not have intended a forgery: "The very appearance produced by Chatterton's holding the parchment over the candle," he writes, is "not judged to be discriminating marks of antiquity by those who are conversant in those subjects."[61] Thomas Erskine similarly explained to Samuel Ireland: "And as to the Orthography an object so much cavilled at, he said its being unlike that of the period, weigh'd in his opinion more in favor of their authenticity than against it, as No Man would have set about such an imposition, of this amazing magnitude without first weighing well,

---

57 *Hell upon Earth*, p. 47.

58 Shaw, *An Enquiry*, pp. 57–9.

59 Boswell, *Life*, 1:396. Compare Donald Macdonald's satirical parody of the characteristic mode Ossianic poems: "My Vestment of pleasant Linen as white as Milk of the Mountain-Goat, is now, alas! a Mantle of Sorrow, like the green Moss on the Heath that covers the Bogs of Death….Thy Breath is like Mildew from the East; withering the Blossom that promised fair Fruit" (Macdonald, *Three Beautiful and Important Passages*, p. [7]).

60 Blair, *A Critical Dissertation*, p. 402.

61 Mathias, *An Essay on the Evidence*, p. 41 n.

both from Mss & printed books of those times the manner of spelling &c."[62] These arguments make sense only against the background of psychological explanations, in which convictions about motivation are so powerful that they overrule virtually all other criteria. Surely, this style of argument goes, even a minimally competent forger would have recognized that inconsistency is a problem, and would not have committed so obvious a blunder: in avoiding such mistakes, the forger's expenditure of energy is minimal and the gain in credibility is substantial. The inconsistencies become evidence of authenticity.

The converse can also occur: consistency can become evidence of forgery. When Ireland departs from Malone's conception of Shakespeare's style, he is rebuked for it. More surprising is that Ireland could be lambasted for his similarities to Shakespeare as well. When Malone discovers echoes of *The Merchant of Venice* in a supposed letter from Shakespeare to Anne Hathaway, he explains the letter away by suggesting that Ireland borrowed the language from the published play. In doing so, he ignores several other plausible scenarios: Shakespeare may well have recalled his youthful love letter when he came to write his comedy; he may simply have been fond throughout his life of certain phrases and images, which independently found expression in several works. For Malone, none of these explanations will do. By offering his own narrative to account for the presence of familiar lines in an unfamiliar text, he frames the debate and works to set the standard of what is plausible.

The Most Irrational Do Not Act without Some Impulse

The Elizabeth Canning saga of 1753 provides the most complicated case study of the eighteenth-century understanding of motive in an investigation of deception—complicated because motive provides nearly all the evidence we have, and after two-and-a-half centuries we still lack a definitive verdict on what happened. The problem is that the evidence presented by both sides is compelling—and yet at least one of them must be wrong. Canning certainly disappeared and seemed to have been abused; the details she provided are enough to make it at least plausible that she had seen the room in which she claimed to be imprisoned. But Mary Squires produced dozens of witnesses who testified she was not in London at the time of the abduction. This has led some critics to seek for ways to reconcile all the contradictions. In 1897, for example, Courtney Kenny considered the possibility that "Canning might be mistaken as to the identity of the woman who robbed her and the room where she was imprisoned, and yet truly have undergone an imprisonment and a robbery." In her account of 1945, Lillian de la Torre turns to Freud and notes that "The sexual anxiety of hysterical virgins is likely to come out in disturbed physical functions.... The threat of sexual assault ... brought on hysterical fasting, and covered itself with the hysterical blocking of memory called amnesia." Most fancifully of all, in 1940 Barrett R. Wellington immersed himself in H. H. Newman's textbook, *The Biology of Twins*, and arrived at an "inescapable conclusion": that "the old gipsy, grotesque

---

62   BL Add. MS 30346, fol. 157ᵛ.

looking though she was, possibly had a living counterpart; and the chance of it was approximately 1 in 150"—much more plausible, he concludes, than the prospect that dozens of witnesses were either mistaken or perjured themselves.[63] None of these accounts, though, is really convincing, and we are left with the frustrating conclusion that many people must have been either liars or grossly mistaken.

"We have turned it over and over," wrote one Victorian commentator on the case, "looked at it this way and that way, read it backwards and forwards and upside down.... Read the evidence on one side, and it is impossible to refuse our assent to it. Read that on the other, and it is equally conclusive. The *alibi* and the *ibi* are both supported by a train of evidence which appears irresistible." Another late Victorian writer noted that the case was marked by "the collision of the two greatest masses of direct testimony that ever were arrayed in positive contradiction to each other in any English Court."[64] And because the testimony on one side tends to cancel out the testimony on the other, most partisans have tried to settle the case with reference to motive, arguing that their version of the story is plausibly motivated, whereas the other is inconsistent with what we know of human nature. In the Canning case, though, whatever the truth may be, one is left with at least one set of actions that seem entirely without motive.

The difficulty is obvious when one considers the two possibilities in the case: either Canning was held by Mary Squires, as she claimed, or she was not. If her story is true—if she was in fact abducted by ruffians and kept in an attic for four weeks—then it is unclear what could have prompted the men to drag her several miles across London, risking detection all the while, only to lock her in an attic without checking on her for a month. If they actually wanted to recruit her as a prostitute, surely they would have given her the opportunity to "go their way," rather than waiting for her to starve. As John Hill objected early in the affair, "There can be no Cause assigned, why Men should drag her many Miles, or why Women lock her up to perish, without the least Advantage, or the least Prospect of Advantage."[65] An anonymous commentator made the same point a year later:

> is this a Story coherent with Nature, Reason, or even Common-Sense, to believe, that these Fellows, who she says robb'd her by *Moorfields*, should, instead of flying for their Safety from the Vengeance of offended Justice, take upon them the unnecessary and unprofitable Trouble of carrying her ten or twelve Miles in the silent Watches of the Night, in one of the most public Roads in *England*, and thereby run the Risque of being taken and hang'd! Self-preservation is the first and strongest Principle in the Law of Nature.[66]

Ditto another anonymous contributor to the pamphlet war: "Can any Man of common Sense imagine, that two Men should employ themselves seven Hours together, lugging and hauling along for ten Miles, in the Middle of the Night, a poor Creature

---

63 Kenny, "The Mystery of Elizabeth Canning," p. 376; de la Torre, *Elizabeth Is Missing*, pp. 247–8; Wellington, *The Mystery of Elizabeth Canning*, p. 178.

64 Paget, *Paradoxes and Puzzles*, p. 335; Kenny, "The Mystery of Elizabeth Canning," p. 368.

65 John Hill, *The Story of Elizabeth Canning Considered*, p. 20.

66 *Miss Canning and the Gypsey*, p. 9.

that had lost her Senses, and consequently had no Power to give any Motion to her Body, and all this only to divert themselves?"[67] A balladeer was more direct and more scurrilous: Canning was supposed to be seized

> By Men who first plunder'd her under a Wall,
> Then stole her to rob her of—Nothing at all;
> They sought not a Maiden-head, for if they had
> They went to the wrong Shop to find it, Egad.
>   *Derry down,* &c.[68]

If, on the other hand, Canning's story is false—if she never passed any time in Squires's house—then it is difficult to imagine what could have prompted her to accuse a group of innocents of a capital crime, risking her own conviction for perjury. If she simply wanted an excuse for her disappearance, surely she could have invented captors who could not easily be found in London. By providing circumstantial details that could be checked, she simply gave her adversaries opportunities for contradicting her: as Allan Ramsay writes in Canning's defense, "If a lie is made circumstantial, … every one of those circumstances, which at first gave it authority, may administer means of tracing, and discovering its falshood."[69] As we have seen with William Henry Ireland, the very improbabilities of her story therefore become evidence that it could not have been fabricated. "Would a person of common sense," asks another of Canning's defenders, "have clogged a forgery, which she had a month to put together, with a number of difficulties, which might have been left out of the scheme?"[70]

A few commentators were not bothered by the participants' apparent lack of motive. "As to the manner of the robbers carrying her down to Wells's," Daniel Cox explains, "without being discovered on the road, or their motives for doing it, it is no part of my present business, even so much as to guess at."[71] "As to those Objections which arise from the Want of a sufficient Motive in the Transactors of this cruel Scene," writes Henry Fielding, "no great Stress I think can be laid on these." The world is full of unmotivated malice, as he demonstrates by retailing a recent high-profile crime: "I might ask what possible Motive could induce two Ruffians, who were executed last Winter for Murder, after they had robbed a poor Wretch who made no Resistance, to return and batter his Skull with their Clubs, till they fractured it in almost twenty different Places." Such cruelty is beyond the imagination of Fielding's middle-class audience—breaking a defenseless man's skull, especially after all his money has been taken from him, is nigh on inhuman. The case, though, is not unique; London's streets seem to be crawling with such inhuman or subhuman villains:

---

67 *The Truth of the Case*, p. 11.
68 *The Devil Outdone*, p. 4.
69 Ramsay, *A Letter to the Right Honourable the Earl of* ——, pp. 11–12.
70 *A Collection of Several Papers Relating to Elizabeth Canning*, p. 9.
71 Cox, *An Appeal to the Public*, p. 31.

> How many Cruelties indeed do we daily hear of, to which it seems not easy to assign any
> other Motive than Barbarity itself? In serious and sorrowful Truth, doth not History as
> well as our own Experience afford us too great Reason to suspect, that there is in some
> Minds a Sensation directly opposite to that of Benevolence, and which delights and feeds
> itself with Acts of Cruelty and Inhumanity?

He ends by suggesting that "Barbarity itself" is rampant among the scullions, ruffians, and gypsies who figure in Canning's case: "And if such a Passion can be allowed any Existence, where can we imagine it more likely to exist than among such People as these?"[72] Most, though, refused to believe in such unmotivated wickedness. "Acts of Cruelty," admits John Hill, "have been practis'd by Ruffians: I grant you so much, mighty Reasoner! but there has been a Motive, the worst of them have never done it otherwise."[73] Another of Canning's critics expresses shock that Fielding—not only schooled in modern fiction, but a renowned practitioner of the form—should be prepared to accept unmotivated wickedness: "I cannot help being surprized at the conduct of Justice Fielding in this affair, ... who from his witty and humorous writings, appears to be thoroughly versed in all the deceits and weaknesses of the human heart."[74]

In the first trial, when Mary Squires and Susannah Wells were charged with robbery, public sympathy was largely with Canning, and Canning's lack of a clear motive to lie figured prominently in the prosecution's case. "Could any reasonable Motive be assigned," asks one anonymous defender of Canning, "why these two Girls [Canning and Virtue Hall] should agree to take away the Life of a Person, against whom it cannot be supposed they could have any Cause of Malice?"[75] Since few readers could imagine anything that would prompt such behavior, it followed that Canning, with no reason to tell a lie, must be telling the truth. Fielding, though he is prepared to believe that the ruffians acted arbitrarily, will not admit the same of Canning:

> What Motive can be invented for her laying this heavy Charge on those who are innocent?
> ... Will they then imagine, that this Girl hath committed a more deliberate, and, therefore, a
> more atrocious Crime, by endeavouring to take away the Lives of an old Woman, her Son,
> and another Man, as well as to ruin another Woman, without any Motive whatever?[76]

Motive, however, can cut both ways, and serve as a witness for both the prosecution and the defense. For every person who would defend Canning by insisting that she had no reason to accuse Squires, another would defend Squires by insisting she had no reason to abduct Canning. An anonymous pamphlet on the Canning case, *The Arguments on Both Sides the Question* (1753), lays out the problem. Canning's defenders can ask (following Fielding), "What Motive can be invented for her laying this heavy Charge on those who are innocent?"; her accusers can note in return,

---

72 Fielding, *A Clear State of the Case*, pp. 289–90.
73 Hill, *The Story of Elizabeth Canning*, p. 21.
74 *The Imposture Detected*, pp. 42–3.
75 *Genuine and Impartial Memoirs of Elizabeth Canning*, p. 35.
76 Fielding, *A Clear State of the Case*, pp. 292–3.

"It doth not well appear with what Motive these Men carried this poor Girl such a Length of Way, or, indeed, that they had any Motive at all for so doing.... The Gipsy Woman doth not seem to have had any sufficient Motive to her Proceedings."[77] John Hill was quoted above, insisting that all crimes proceed from motives. From this general law he derives a particular application: Squires was accused unjustly. "There could be in Nature no Motive to her doing it," he insists; "and the most irrational do not act without some Impulse."[78] As E. Biddulph explains, "if the Girl is *innocent*, all the Witnesses ... in Number more than Fifty, are to a Man fore-sworn, corruptly, wilfully forsworn: A Thought too horrid to be harboured in the Breast of any, but the Man, whose own abandoned Principles have led him to suppose that the whole human Race are as wicked as himself."[79] "Was it ever known," asks Ramsay, "that any plurality of human creatures were actuated by the same kind of delirium?"[80] This is the first in a long list of Ramsay's rhetorical questions, all beginning "Was it ever known ... ?" stretching to three pages. The implied answer is always no: such a thing is unheard of. Canning, therefore, must be guilty of perjury.

Many thought they had found the answer to what John Treherne has called the "Canning Enigma" when they found a plausible motive. Despite the testimonials in favor of Canning's character, "well supported by several tradesmen of probity and integrity"; despite, too, a physician's testimony "that Elizabeth Canning has never had a child,"[81] some argued that she disappeared in the hopes of concealing a pregnancy. John Hill insists that "Where a Girl, like this, could be; and how employed during the time; is not difficult to imagine. Not with a Lover certainly, say you! ... Eighteen, let me remind you, is a critical Age; and what would not a Woman do, that had made an Escape, to recover her own Credit, and screen her Lover." He admits that this is speculation—"I pretend to no Knowledge of this"—but adds that, "if we are to reason, let us do it freely; and what appears so likely?"[82] Another critic is more confident that he understands exactly what happened: "She was now above five, perhaps six months gone with child; her affairs were coming to a crisis, and what was to be done in this desperate exigence? She would most naturally consult her gallant, or rather her physician, who had so successfully removed her former complaints, to see if possibly he could relieve her from this."[83]

Although there is no clear consensus today, with "Canningites" and "Egyptians" still differing over how to interpret the surviving evidence, my own suspicion is that Canning hid from her relatives to conceal a lying-in, an abortion, or a salivation

---

77   *The Arguments on Both Sides the Question*, pp. 7, 3.

78   John Hill, *The Story of Elizabeth Canning*, pp. 33–4.

79   Biddulph, *Some Account of the Case*, p. 69.

80   Ramsay, *A Letter to the Right Honourable the Earl of* ——, p. 7. Compare Courtney Kenny's review of the case in 1897: he catalogues "Seven great improbabilities ... patent on the face of" Canning's story, beginning with "(1) The absence of motive for the original abduction" and "(2) The absence of motive for the subsequent four weeks' detention" ("The Mystery of Elizabeth Canning," p. 377).

81   Cox, *An Appeal to the Public*, pp. 10, 23.

82   John Hill, *The Story of Elizabeth Canning Considered*, p. 24.

83   *The Imposture Detected*, p. 30.

for a venereal disease.[84] This would account for her four-week disappearance and her return looking much thinner. A pregnancy would have provided her with an embarrassment she would be eager to hide; the embarrassment could have led her to concoct an alibi, which she then allowed to get out of hand. It seems likely that, when she related a vague account of her captivity, ardent investigators inadvertently fed her clues about Squires and her household—might she have lived in such a part of town?—might she have been a gypsy woman?—and Canning, when offered such leads, had only to assent to seem to relate a story rich circumstantial details. And yet, even today, we are entirely without conclusive hard evidence—we have only our own subjective impression of what makes the most psychological sense. There is no positive or even circumstantial evidence about how she passed the mysterious four weeks; there is no record of a lover, a child, an abortion, or a venereal disease. We can do nothing more than her contemporaries, offering narratives in the hope that they will seem plausible, allowing all the major actors in the story to behave in ways we expect real people to behave.

That we still follow this course should be no surprise, because we are the heirs of the eighteenth century's discovery of the importance of motive. It continues to inform our courtroom practice, where prosecution attorneys strive to reveal the defendant's motive. It is likewise all over our popular literature—motive is an absolute necessity in our crime fiction and detective stories. In every novel, film, or television program devoted to crime investigation, the detectives at some point are required to muse aloud, "We have motive and opportunity—all we need now is the weapon." The prospect that someone might commit a crime—whether literal or figurative—for no motive at all was, and is, worrisome. Popular literature's most famous detective, Sherlock Holmes, admitted that worry in a case that did not end to his own satisfaction: "'What is the meaning of it, Watson?' said Holmes, solemnly, as he laid down the paper. 'What object is served by this circle of misery and violence and fear? It must tend to some end, or else our universe is ruled by chance, which is unthinkable. But what end?'"[85] Holmes's question, "But what end?," hangs in the air in Doyle's story; it is never resolved. Holmes and Watson need a comprehensible motive in order to make sense of brutality just as Canning's contemporaries did, and just as we do today. We are all heirs to the eighteenth century's new consideration of the forces that drive the human psyche, and the unthinkability of motiveless malignity continues to haunt us.

84　Something like this has been the conclusion of Voltaire in 1762, Austin Dobson in 1886 (whose *Dictionary of National Biography* entry identifies her as "Canning, Elizabeth, malefactor"), Hugh Childers in 1913, Arthur Machen in 1926 (who calls Canning's story "a lie from beginning to end; a lie as a whole, a lie in all its parts" [*The Canning Wonder*, p. v]), and John Treherne in 1989. I am inclined to agree with them, though with rather less contempt for Canning than some of them display. Judith Moore, however, who offers the most extensive account of the Canning phenomenon to date, writes, "I have come to believe … that Elizabeth Canning's whole story was true." But she notes, too, that "I do not believe that a solution to the Canning case is possible" (Moore, *The Appearance of Truth*, p. 256). Her diffidence is doubtless the best approach to the contradictory evidence.

85　Doyle, "The Adventure of the Cardboard Box," in *The Classic Illustrated Sherlock Holmes*, p. 213.

Chapter 9

Different Kinds of Value

Why, finally, does any of this matter? Who, for instance, is injured by the claim that Mary Toft gave birth to rabbits? Why should we care whether the works published by Macpherson or Chatterton are "genuine poems" (whatever that means)? What, in other words, makes the detection of fraud such a pressing concern?

Ever Willing to Be Deceived

Granted, there are times when deceit is not a concern at all. Some fakes are allowed to pass for true even though no one is really taken in, and counterfeits are allowed the same value as the real article. Henry Fielding provides an example in *Joseph Andrews*: Wilson recalls his London days, when he hoped to be known as a rake. Whether the women with whom he consorted were actually licentious did not matter: they "were all Vestal Virgins for any thing which I knew to the contrary. The Reputation of Intriguing with them was all I sought." He brings about this illusion by forging love letters: "very probably the Persons to whom I shewed their Billets, knew as well as I, that they were Counterfeits"[1]—and yet all were willing to continue playing the game. Early in the nineteenth century, Washington Irving was equally happy with a counterfeit. He traveled to Stratford-upon-Avon in 1815 "on a poetical pilgrimage" to Shakespeare's birthplace. The owner, a Mrs. Hornby, "was peculiarly assiduous in exhibiting the relics with which this, like all other celebrated shrines, abounds." Irving knew that most of these "relics" were bogus, but admitted,

> I am always of easy faith in such matters, and am ever willing to be deceived, where the deceit is pleasant, and costs nothing. I am therefore a ready believer in relics, legends, and local anecdotes of goblins and great men; and would advise all travellers who travel for their gratification to be the same. What is it to us whether these stories be true or false, so long as we can persuade ourselves into the belief of them, and enjoy all the charm of the reality?[2]

The truth was for Irving irrelevant: he and Mrs. Hornby were each playing a role, and with a kind of suspension of disbelief he was happy to be taken in by the story's "charm." A modern analogy may be bouncers in bars in American university towns, who make a pretense of checking identification even though they know that many of those they see are phony: both sides recognize that the game must be played, so

---

1   Fielding, *Joseph Andrews*, p. 203.
2   Irving, *The Sketch Book of Geoffrey Crayon*, pp. 210–11.

underage drinkers continue to present forged driver's licenses and bored bouncers continue to examine them.

Most people would argue that this kind of willingness to be deceived is limited to certain kinds of deceit—with some stories we are "of easy faith," in Irving's words, but that does not mean authenticity is irrelevant. For a few critics, though, it is never really a concern, since authenticity is itself a fiction, a social construction built on a shaky foundation. Some have argued that all forgers and readers are engaged in games such as those Fielding's Wilson and Washington Irving played: writers and readers play their respective parts unconcerned with questions of truth. Oscar Wilde clearly enjoys this paradox, as presented in *The Portrait of Mr W. H.*, when his characters engage in "a long discussion about Macpherson, Ireland, and Chatterton." Speaking of Chatterton, Wilde's protagonist

> insisted that his so-called forgeries were merely the result of an artistic desire for perfect representation; that we had no right to quarrel with an artist for the conditions under which he chooses to present his work; and that all Art being to a certain degree a mode of acting, an attempt to realise one's own personality on some imaginative plane out of the reach of the trammelling accidents and limitations of real life, to censure an artist for a forgery was to confuse an ethical with an æsthetical problem.[3]

Some modern critics echo Wilde's ideas about acting, insisting that all art is a kind of deceit. K. K. Ruthven, for instance, argues that the distinction between authenticity and fakery is entirely factitious: "The relationship between literarity and spuriosity," he argues, "is framed as a binary opposition, in which literature is valorised as the authentic Self and literary forgery disparaged as its bogus Other. The perceived business of literary studies is accordingly to preserve and fortify that distinction by practising a cultural eugenics designed to eliminate the dreck. This is why the outing of a literary forgery is generally admired as a culturally prophylactic event." In likening the detection of forgery to eugenics, he makes the whole business appear unseemly at best and sinister at worst, an unholy exercise in tampering with the natural order. "No writer," he argues, "is permitted to disturb those cultural institutions which accredit and mediate literature by demonstrating inefficiencies in their operations and thus questioning the grounds of their existence."[4] One of the recurring concerns of his book is to argue that these rules of the game are arbitrary, and that we need not have the same obsessions with what is genuine and what fake.

Ruthven has a point. Our culture's valuation of the "authentic" is indeed contingent, for not only is it possible to imagine a society in which our obsession with authenticity does not exist, but we can point to actual societies in which this is the case. Anthropologist Ross Bowden, for example, spent time among the Kwoma of the East Sepik Province of Papua New Guinea, among whom the notion of an "art forgery" is nonsensical. "Kwoma artworks," notes Bowden, "are made from readily perishable materials, principally wood and bark, and when an object decays and becomes too fragile to serve its purpose (e.g., to be displayed ritually) a replica will be made and the original discarded.... Kwoma place no special cultural or aesthetic

3   Wilde, *The Portrait of Mr W. H.*, p. 3.
4   Ruthven, *Faking Literature*, pp. 2–3.

value on what in the West would be called 'original' works of art." He observes, further, that "in radical contrast to modern European societies Kwoma attribute no culturally significant creativity to artists. No artist, however skilled, is considered to contribute anything essentially *new* to a work he produces."[5] Ruthven is therefore justified in considering forgery as the violation of a culturally contingent set of norms, not a God-given law.

It is easy, though, for critics to go too far in this direction, and to argue that the distinction between truth and falsehood is not merely contingent but meaningless. Sometimes Ruthven, it seems to me, indulges too much in Wildean paradox. "There is no 'line dividing quotation from plagiarism,'" he writes, "since the identical practice can be classified as either a literary felony or the ultimate in literary sophistication."[6] Ruthven, in fact, works throughout his book to worry the line between the genuine and the fake, always suggesting that fiction is nothing but lies, with no essential distinction from other kinds of deception.

The Abiding Perversion

Nick Groom shares Ruthven's interest in the ways one variety of mendacious imitation (literature) became celebrated while another (forgery) became transgressive, and he argues that the two are mutually defining: "authenticity and forgery," he writes, "seem less to be absolute terms than mutually supporting concepts. The definition of each element is determined by the other."[7] He stops shy, however, of conflating the two, and expresses his reservations about "the postmodern iconoclasts" who "are perpetually juggling signs and mixing codes, questioning all faith in representation." Why, he asks, "are the creative powers of the forger not straightforwardly ranked with those of the genius?" His answer is less pat and more historically informed than Ruthven's, and it has to do with shifting notions of originality and authenticity: "Forged work has not been treated with the respect bestowed upon a Leonardo because in the early nineteenth century authenticity became so crucial to Romantic aesthetics that it profoundly redrew the map of literary culture and we are still living with its assumptions today." Changing conceptions of authorial genius in the late eighteenth and early nineteenth centuries worked to exclude certain imaginative uses of the past, and in this revolution forgers like Macpherson and Chatterton were the losers. It did not have to be that way, but we now live in a world dominated by conceptions of authenticity that exclude those writers who made the "wrong" choice in their relation to their material and the past. "Authenticity," Groom declares, "is the abiding perversion of our times. It is indulged as a vice, worshipped as a fetish, embraced as a virtue."[8]

Whatever the reasons, the fact remains that in eighteenth-century Britain, authenticity was for virtually all readers a real concern—Johnson, Douglas, Walpole,

---

5   Bowden, "What Is Wrong with an Art Forgery?," pp. 333, 335.

6   Ruthven, *Faking Literature*, p. 125, quoting E. E. Kellett, *Literary Quotation and Allusion*, pp. 11, 12.

7   Groom, *The Making of Percy's "Reliques,"* p. 242.

8   Groom, *The Forger's Shadow*, pp. 299, 58, 293.

and Malone were not Kwoma. They cared about deception. Philip Dormer Stanhope, the fifth earl of Chesterfield, cared very much when William Dodd forged his name on a bill of exchange for £4,200—cared enough, in fact, to send his former tutor to the gallows.[9] More complicated, though, and therefore more interesting than forged currency or counterfeit banknotes, are phony works of art, since questions of their value are more complex. It is true that the monetary value of many works of art is bound up with notions of authenticity—works recognized as genuine usually fetch higher prices than comparable works believed to be forged—but this does not on its own explain why people care about excluding fakes from an artistic canon. To say that people want to identify "genuine" works because they are worth more is to beg the question: "authentic" works are valuable because they are desirable, not desirable because they are valuable.

Fakery matters because, at least in eighteenth-century British culture, not only the monetary worth but also the aesthetic worth of a work of art depends to a large degree on its perceived authenticity. Some aestheticians have argued that this is an unthinking prejudice, and that there is no reason to fetishize the "authentic"; they find it absurd that for 40 years museums have been paying good money to the Rembrandt Research Project to reduce their supposed Rembrandt masterpieces into second-rate imitations, moving them from the most conspicuous galleries to the basement—even though they are exactly the same physical objects that once drew reverent crowds. Some view this as, in Wilde's words, "confus[ing] an ethical with an æsthetical problem."[10] The fact is, though, that most people *do* care about such matters, and have for a long time. Most eighteenth-century commentators found fakes inferior to the genuine articles—even when the fakes were beautiful in their own right. The authentic always shone more brightly. François de Chassepol put it well in 1741, when he discussed "Medals struck in modern Dies": "We have a prodigious quantity of those modern pieces, not to be surpassed in their beauty and nobleness by any thing but the Antique itself."[11]

Worth and authenticity, however, are not always inseparable, and the qualifications above—"most," "usually"—must be taken seriously. The most interesting case study of an attempt to treat the two separately is the reception of the Rowleian poems. Rowley was almost unanimously recognized as a fiction by the late 1780s, but Chatterton's reputation for genius continued to rise through the late eighteenth and early nineteenth centuries. The major Romantics praised his poetic ability extravagantly: Wordsworth declared him "the marvellous boy"; Coleridge lamented, "O, CHATTERTON! that thou wert yet alive!"; and Keats dedicated *Endymion* "TO THE MEMORY OF THOMAS CHATTERTON," the "child of sorrow." The passion stayed alive well into the Victorian era: Dante Gabriel Rossetti considered him "as great as any

---

9   The standard account is Howson, *The Macaroni Parson*; see also Radzinowicz, *A History of English Criminal Law*, 1:450–472.

10   For a pair of philosophical discussions of the question, see four essays gathered in the collection *The Forger's Art: Forgery and the Philosophy of Art*: Meiland, "Originals, Copies, and Aesthetic Value"; Goodman, "Art and Authenticity"; Meyer, "Forgery and the Anthropology of Art"; and Wreen, "Is, Madam? Nay, It Seems!"

11   Chassepol, *A Treatise of the Revenue*, p. 191.

English poet whatever," noting that he "might absolutely, had he lived, have proved the only man in England's theatre of imagination who could have bandied parts with Shakspeare."[12]

Considered Merely as a Poem

It is useful to juxtapose two conflicting views of Chatterton's worth to see how and when they associate authenticity with worth. Anna Seward records a conversation about Chatterton with Samuel Johnson, in which Johnson expresses a low estimate of the worth of the Rowleian poems:

> I spoke of its author to Johnson, with the warmest tribute of my admiration; but he would not hear me on the subject, exclaiming,—"Pho, child! don't talk to me of the powers of a vulgar uneducated stripling. He may be another Stephen Duck. It may be extraordinary to do such things as he did, with means so slender;—but what did Stephen Duck do, what could Chatterton do, which, abstracted from the recollection of his situation, can be worth the attention of learning and taste? Neither of them had opportunities of enlarging their stock of ideas. No man can coin guineas, but in proportion has he has gold."[13]

In Johnson's comments we see the usual association of authenticity with worth: Chatterton may have done remarkable things for a charity-school boy, but the only guineas his meager stock of ideas allowed him to coin were counterfeits. Seward, though, will have none of it, and instead declares that Chatterton is

> the most extraordinary genius which perhaps ever existed. This ill-starred youth certainly found ancient and curious manuscripts, which furnished the hint of his design, and upon which he poured the splendours of his rich imagination, kindling and flowering as he proceeded. Very superficially, indeed, is the perfection of modern harmony, and the grace of modern imagery, veiled by obsolete verbalism.[14]

Many poetic enthusiasts sided with Seward, dismissing objections like Johnson's as pedantic nitpicking. As Thomas Twining wrote to Charles Burney about Chatterton's poems, "Whatever [Mason] may think of their authenticity, if he did not allow them

---

12 Wordsworth, "Resolution and Independence," line 43, in *Poems in Two Volumes*; Coleridge, "Monody on the Death of Chatterton," line 126, in *Poetical Works*; Keats, *Endymion* and "Oh Chatterton! How Very Sad Thy Fate," line 2, in *Poems*; Caine, *Recollections of Dante Gabriel Rossetti*, pp. 184–5. Blake's praise intentionally conflates worth and authenticity: "I Believe both Macpherson & Chatterton," he wrote in his copy of Wordsworth's *Poems*, "that what they say is Ancient, Is so" (*Poetry and Prose*, p. 655). For an extensive survey of Chatterton's influence on Romantic literature, see Fairer, "Chatterton's Poetic Afterlife," and Stafford, "'Dangerous Success.'"

13 Seward to Thomas Park, 30 Jan. 1800, in Seward, *Letters*, 5:272. But compare Johnson's impression of Chatterton as published by Boswell nine years earlier: "This is the most extraordinary young man that has encountered my knowledge. It is wonderful how the whelp has written such things" (Boswell, *Life*, 3:51). Here I am less concerned with Johnson's own position than with how Seward depicts it.

14 Seward to Dr. Gregory, 25 March 1792, in Seward, *Letters*, 3:125.

to be full of genius I should scarce be able to think him sincere. What a fuss people make whether Rowley or Chatterton wrote them, as if the whole merit of the poetry depended on that point!"[15] Vicesimus Knox too dismissed the fussy antiquaries: "the genuine beauties of poetry are capable of being relished by those who are perfectly regardless whether or not it was printed in the black letter, and written by Rowley or by Chatterton."[16] Lord Dacre wrote in 1777 of "the Mss. which ... if devoid of the Merit of Antiquity, are ... still Extremely valuable, and worth publication; the beauty of the Poetry being the same whether Ancient or Modern."[17] And a contributor to the *Gentleman's Magazine*, signing himself "A Detester of Literary Imposition, but a Lover of good Poetry," tried explicitly to distinguish aesthetic worth from antiquarian authenticity: "whatever may be thought of the *author*, I cannot see any reason to depreciate the work. 'If the pieces are modern,' it has been hinted, 'they are of little value.' I must own, I am of a contrary opinion. Whether a poem was written three centuries ago, by a Romish priest, in real old English, or seven years ago, in fictitious old English, by a lawyer's clerk, surely, cannot either enhance or diminish its merit, considered merely as a poem."[18]

This opinion, though, was far from unanimous, and for Johnson and others like him a Rowleian poem should not, could not, be "considered merely as a poem"—it was also material for a history of English literature, among other things. Thomas Warton, like Johnson, was perfectly willing to grant a measure of genius to Chatterton, irrespective of whether the poems were written in the fifteenth century: "This youth," he writes, "who died at eighteen, was a prodigy of genius: and would have proved the first of English poets, had he reached a maturer age."[19] Individual genius, however, was not his sole concern in *The History of English Poetry*, and in his attempt to tell the story of English verse, questions of authenticity matter very much. "Insignificant as it may seem," he writes, "the determination of these questions affects the great lines of the history of poetry, and even of general literature." For Warton, in fact, the genuine may be *less* impressive than a modern imitation; still, it is the literary historian's job to determine what is true and what is false. He offers a painterly analogy: "If a portrait by Hans Holbein was to be retouched, or rather repainted, by Reynolds, it would undoubtedly be made a much finer picture. But it would not be a picture by Hans Holbein."[20]

The real reason it matters for the literary historian is that the presence of a modern variety of genius in fifteenth-century Bristol would require a significant rewriting of English literary history. Warton resorts to the conditional mood in considering Rowley's merits: "a want of genius will be no longer imputed to this period of our poetical history, if the poems lately discovered at Bristol ... are genuine."[21] A

---

15   Thomas Twining to Charles Burney, 16 June 1777, in Twining, *Recreations and Studies*, p. 53.

16   Knox, "On the Prevailing Taste for the Old English Poets," in *Essays*, 1:215.

17   Lord Dacre to Barrett, 14 Sept. 1777, BL Add. MS 47865, fol. 30ʳ.

18   *Gentleman's Magazine* 47 (Aug. 1777): 364.

19   Warton, *The History of English Poetry*, 2:157.

20   Warton, *An Enquiry*, pp. 7, 32.

21   Warton, *The History of English Poetry*, 2:139.

writer in the *Monthly Review* agreed. When the regularity of the versification tipped him off that the Rowleian poems may be merely "Mock Ruins," he laid out the implications:

> If such they are, their merit is of no high estimation, it being as easy for a person accustomed to versification, and acquainted with obsolete terms, to fabricate an old poem as to write a new one: but if, on the contrary, they are really productions of the fifteenth century, they are the most extraordinary literary curiosities that this or any recent period has produced: for they would shew us that the graces of numbers, and the refinements of poetical melody, are of no modern date, but belonged to one of the first adventurers in English poetry.[22]

The result was a pair of incommensurable evaluations: one for the Rowleian poems written by Rowley, the other for the Rowleian poems written by Chatterton. It mattered not at all that the sole difference between the two collections was the byline. As the *Gentleman's Magazine* put it, "curiosities in literature, like those of Nature, are of very different kinds of value and importance, according to the certainty of their genuineness, and the consequences that may be established from them."[23] Notice the difference is one of *kind*, rather than of *degree*: both works may have value and importance; both may be of great value an importance—but the value of "authentic" works is of a different sort from the value of a fake. The *Critical* was even more direct: it is important to separate the true from the false "not only because genuine productions are more valuable than forgeries; but because there is something scandalous and detestable in such literary frauds. Cheats and knaves have disgraced the republic of letters by their spurious publications. He therefore deserves to be branded as the worst of impostors, WHO OBTRUDES ANY THING UPON THE WORLD, UNDER THE VENERABLE NAME OF ANTIQUITY, WHICH HAS NOT AN HONEST TITLE TO THAT CHARACTER."[24]

A Literary Imposture upon Which Facts Could Be Founded

Chatterton's legacy is therefore divided: he was attacked as "the worst of impostors" but celebrated as "the most extraordinary genius which perhaps ever existed," condemned as a forger but praised as a genius, suggesting that at least some commentators were willing to distinguish his historical importance from his aesthetic worth. James Macpherson was not so lucky. Many of Chatterton's adherents were prepared to admit that the historical authenticity of the Rowleian poems was

---

22 *Monthly Review* 56 (April 1777): 256. One commentator writing a few months later was less concerned with the history of literature than the history of Bristol: "It is of the highest importance to have this literary imposture detected; not for the sake of adding to the list of our poets or antiquaries, but for the honour of the city of Bristol, which either has or has not preserved the memorial of her benefactor, and done justice to his liberality" (*Gentleman's Magazine* 47 [Oct. 1777]: 481).

23 *Gentleman's Magazine* 47 (May 1777): 205.

24 *Critical Review* 46 (Aug. 1778): 115.

unimportant, but few readers of the Ossianic poems were willing to extend the same courtesy to Macpherson.

The problem was evident from the beginning. Just one month after the first *Fragments* appeared in the *Gentleman's Magazine*, a correspondent wrote to Mr. Urban, "The two Pieces in your last, called Fragments of *Scots* Poetry, translated from the Erse, pleased me so well, though I believe them to be modern Compositions."[25] A few months later, the *Monthly Review* expressed the same reservations: "We are told in a Preface to this little work, that the public may depend on these Fragments as genuine remains of ancient Scottish poetry.... and yet, did we put no confidence in the assertion of the anonymous Editor, we should think, notwithstanding such evident marks of authenticity, that they *might be* the production of a later age."[26] History and aesthetics were intertwined from the very beginning of the Ossianic episode.

Macpherson's reputation, as we have seen in Chapter 6, has suffered largely because he made specific historical claims about third-century Scotland and, more important, he and his supporters closely associated the worth of those poems with their historical origins. The important fact here is that, for many readers, the historical information contained in the poems—which even Macpherson's modern defenders have to admit is often wholly chimerical—trumped the poetic value of Ossian's works. Consider William Duff, who wrote that "It will at first view appear to the attentive reader, that the poems of Ossian are in the main historical, not fictitious.... We are necessarily led to consider the whole collection of these poems as forming a kind of poetical history of the times." Duff even insists that Ossian's generous and sensible characters are "not fictitious, ... but real; for as the manners and spirit of the times had a natural tendency to propagate generosity of sentiment, and martial virtue, the person most eminent in these, became by undoubted right the hero of his poems, and he had no occasion for inventing one altogether imaginary."[27] For many Edinburghers of the later eighteenth century, Ossian's works were more than belles lettres: they were repositories of data about ancient British history.

Several commentators did try to separate the questions of authenticity and poetic merit. Hugh Blair insisted, "Of the poetical merit of these fragments, nothing shall here be said. Let the public judge, and pronounce."[28] Anna Seward also averred that the historical questions held no interest for her: "Excepting Dr Johnson's contumelious and angry assertions," she wrote to Walter Scott, "I have not examined any of the arguments that seek to prove [the Ossianic poems] forgery. I liked not to have my mind disturbed. It was sufficient for me that my imagination was raised, my passions interested, and my ear gratified even to luxury, whenever I opened those pages of dubious origin."[29] Even William Shaw was willing to admit, albeit probably

---

25   *Gentleman's Magazine* 30 (July 1760): 335.
26   *Monthly Review* 23 (Sept. 1760): 204–5.
27   Duff, *Critical Observations*, pp. 67, 71.
28   Blair, Preface to *Fragments*, p. 6.
29   Seward to Walter Scott, 20 June 1806, in Seward, *Letters*, 6:279.

disingenuously, "I have nothing to say of the merit or demerit of the criticism, because that will be the same, whether genuine or false."[30]

Yet those who treated the Ossianic poems as historical documents as well as poems had reasons to care about their origin. The danger of mining imaginative works for historical facts is evident in the works of the historians who began picking up on Macpherson's assertions about the British peoples. Robert Henry routinely cites Ossian's poems and Macpherson's supporting materials in his *History of Great Britain* (1771): his information on ancient Scottish obstetrics bears the citation "Ossian's Poems, v. 1. p. 115," and his account of feasts comes from "Ossian's Poems, v. 2. p. 8, &c."[31] Macpherson and Ossian are cited dozens of times in the first volume and in many other works of the era, without any indication that the historical information may be imaginary. Edmund Burke asserts that this is his biggest objection to Macpherson: "it was culpable to carry on a literary imposture upon which facts could be founded," he told Boswell in 1787, "so as that the world should be deceived as to manners and ancient history."[32]

For readers like Burke, history trumped aesthetics and Macpherson the poet became Macpherson the forger. Largely because of the association between the Ossianic literature and ancient British history, "Disbelievers," writes Paul J. deGategno, "refused to grant any distinction between the historical authenticity and the literary worth of the poems. If they were not ancient, they had no value as literature."[33] We see this strong association of authenticity and worth both among experts—"the Laird of Macfarlane," writes David Hume, "the greatest Antiquarian whom we have in this country, ... insists as strongly on the historical truth, as well as the poetical beauty of these productions"[34]—and among the literary public—"There is a second Edition of the Scotch Fragments," writes Gray to Walpole, "yet very few admire them, & almost all take them for fictions."[35] The proximity of admiration and historical evaluation suggests their interdependence. Walpole too is unable to dissociate historicity from poetic worth, for his ostensibly purely aesthetic complaint that "It tires me to death to read how many ways a warrior is like the moon, or the sun, or a rock, or a lion, or the ocean" is followed immediately by the more historical justification that "I cannot believe it genuine," and in 1781 he finally dismissed the poems as "dull forgeries."[36]

What is significant about these examples is that authenticity and worth, author and authority, are inseparable: historical truth with poetical beauty on the one hand, or dull forgeries on the other, yes; but the category of poetical forgery is for many

---

30 Shaw, *An Enquiry*, p. 39.

31 Henry, *The History of Great Britain*, 1:460, 486. Other uncritical citations of Macpherson include Arnot, *The History of Edinburgh* (1779), pp. 52, 74, 184; and Troil, *Letters on Iceland* (1780), pp. 21–3. See also Baines, *The House of Forgery*, pp. 114–15.

32 *Boswell: The English Experiment, 1785–1789*, p. 150.

33 DeGategno, *James Macpherson*, p. 5.

34 Hume to Gray, in Gray, *Correspondence*, 3:1227; quoted with slight changes in Gray to Mason, *c.* 31 Aug. 1760, in Gray, *Correspondence*, 2:695 (letter 319*).

35 Gray to Wharton, Oct. 1760, in Gray, *Correspondence*, 2:704 (letter 321).

36 Walpole to George Montagu, 8 Dec. 1761, in Walpole, *Correspondence*, 9:407; Walpole to Mason, 5 Feb. 1781, in Walpole, *Correspondence*, 29:105.

of these readers inconceivable. Beauty may not be Keats's truth, nor truth Keats's beauty, but beauty certainly cannot be expected to lodge with falsehood. Recall that Sir Philip Sidney was largely successful in defending writers of fiction from charges of deceit by arguing that the poet "nothing affirms, and therefore never lieth."[37] Poets like Macpherson, though, began to affirm, and therefore left themselves open to accusations that they lied. Insofar as the study of literature is a matter of acquiring objective knowledge about the extra-literary world, it is subject to the kinds of judgments about truth and falsehood that apply outside the literary arena, and forgers' reputations have largely depended on the degree to which they claimed to make objective claims about the real world.

A Much Greater Share of Gross Credulity

All of these objections to the inaccurate factual claims in literature make sense against a background of Lockean epistemology, the foundation of most eighteenth-century British thinkers' conception of the mind, and they give us some idea of the real reason for the age's tremendous obsession with and vigilance against fakery. Deception and detection are among the central preoccupations of such eighteenth-century philosophers as Locke, Berkeley, and Hume. Empirical philosophy begins by jettisoning innate ideas, leaving a blank slate awaiting the impressions of the senses. If all knowledge is *a posteriori*, our ability to know anything at all depends on the truth of our experience. The question is, what happens when someone maliciously scribbles graffiti on our *tabulae rasae*?

Locke's famous metaphor of a blank slate, however appropriate for perception, is less fitting for the other Lockean faculty, reflection. Reflection allows us to reorganize our perceptions, to connect them to one another, and to build them into structures. Better than a slate, then, might be a more three-dimensional metaphor, perhaps something architectural, or at least children's building blocks, which can be rearranged and piled on one another. A useful implication of this metaphor is its recognition that ideas depend on one another for their positions. If, after one of these stacks of mental building blocks has been created, we discover that the bottom block is bogus, the whole tower comes crashing down—or at least has to be painstakingly disassembled and reassembled. Lies and hoaxes threaten to upset the entire system of knowledge and belief.

It is therefore only natural that the fear of being duped haunted the eighteenth century, and that many writers recognized the need for vigilance. But this need was worrisome, because vigilance can never be perfect—one can never prove convincingly that something is *not* a fake. Our stories of perfidious fakers brought to justice have something unsettling in common. If we consider the fake as a literary kind, we know only the inferior exemplars of the genre: the best are by definition unknown to us. Some may even be undetectable. Even if the story has no internal or external inconsistencies; even if the poem is free of anachronisms; even if the orthography and watermarks of a document are all consistent with its supposed

---

37   Sidney, *Apology for Poetry*, p. 52.

origin—still, it may simply have been the work of an exceptionally skillful faker. William Shaw expressed optimism when he argued that, "In an imposture, a man cannot shut every avenue to detection."[38] But neither can the detector hope to go down every open avenue.

What is worse, even *detectable* forgeries are not always *detected*, because we do not always think to put the question or examine the evidence critically. Some fakes are so outrageous that they force themselves on our attention: an orange dollar bill, for instance, would never make it into our wallets. But who can say for certain that he or she is not carrying a dollar bill on which George Washington sports Groucho glasses or a novelty-store arrow-through-the-head? We could spot such a counterfeit in an instant if we thought to look for it, but who among us is so conscientious as to check every dollar bill we receive with an eye for forgeries? Why, then, should we have any confidence that our canon is not filled with literary Groucho glasses and arrows-through-the-head we never thought to look for?

Thoughts like these nagged many eighteenth-century thinkers, who were almost obsessed with questions of authenticity, and with good reason, because several outrageous hoaxes still managed to fool at least some of the people some of the time. The most brazen example of a fake hiding in plain sight was William Lauder's *Essay on Milton*. The book (first published as a series of articles) begins modestly enough by alluding to the "four or five modern authors in *Latin* verse, whom I have reason to believe *Milton* has consulted in composing his poem." "I no way intend," he avows, "unjustly to derogate from the real merit of that noble poet, who certainly is entitled to a high degree of praise." But soon come a series of escalating attacks: Lauder blames Milton not "for this unlimited freedom" in copying authors, "but for his industriously concealing it," and eventually concludes that Milton "is not the original author of any one single thought in *Paradise Lost*; but has only digested into order the thoughts of others, and cloathed them in an elegant *English* dress." He then lays out a long list of passages from neo-Latin authors, with Grotius's *Adamus Exsul* "in the front of this catalogue," and shows convincingly that Milton's English is nothing more than a literal translation of his Latin predecessors. By the book's end, the poet whose reputation Lauder was loath to derogate "is reduced to his true standard, appears mortal and uninspired, and in ability little superior to the poets abovementioned; but in honesty and open dealing, the best quality of the human mind, not inferior, perhaps, to the most unlicensed plagiary that ever wrote."[39] The case seemed clinched.

Only when John Douglas bothered to track down the obscure citations to the neo-Latin poets Lauder had listed did it occur to him that the citations were bogus—they were simply fabricated. "It did not enter into my Head," Douglas confesses, "that our Critic cou'd have the Assurance to urge false Quotations in support of his Charge; and therefore I, as, I imagine, did every other Person, into whose Hands his Book has fallen, implicitly took it for granted that the Authors he quotes really contain those Lines which he attributes to them." Neither would it enter into our heads today: although we appreciate the chance to verify the authenticity of quotations with

---

38 Shaw, *An Enquiry*, pp. 54–5.
39 Lauder, *An Essay on Milton*, pp. 1, 2, 77, 155, 49, 163.

accurate citations, in practice few of us are so meticulous as to question the truth of such claims. When critics tell us these sentences appear in this book, we rarely think to challenge them. "It seems so extremely improbable," Douglas admits, "that any one shou'd ever venture to put so gross an Imposition on the World, that ... I almost despair of being believed."[40] His record of success, however, earned him the reputation as "The scourge of impostors, the terror of quacks."[41]

How many, though, could maintain Douglas's degree of scrutiny around the clock and around the calendar? Our natural inclination is to accept an account as true unless we have specific reason to doubt it, but that habit of trust makes us easy marks for con artists of every kind. Many eighteenth-century Britons were therefore afraid of being labeled over credulous. The anonymous author of *The Imposture Detected*, a tract on the Canning affair, admits he "cannot help imputing to the modern English, particularly the Londoners, a much greater share of gross credulity, than can be said to have possessed the ancient Greeks and Romans." Greek and Roman superstition, he suggests, is at least understandable, but "the credulity of the English is inexcusable, for they believe the most absurd things imaginable, without having recourse to any supernatural interposition at all." He adduces as evidence a number of high-profile deceptions from the first half of the eighteenth century: "The rabbit-woman, the adventure of the quart-bottle, and the migration of the Londoners to the fields, occasioned by the soldiers prophesying a third earthquake, are recent and notorious instances of this truth."[42] This willingness to believe even absurd fictions was often pointed out. The Canning case became proverbial—nearly 30 years after Canning's supposed abduction, the affair was being adduced as evidence of English credulity. Charlotte Cowley, writing in 1780, complained that "the influence which [the Canning affair] had on the minds of the people, will serve, in some measure, to mark our national characteristic; at least it will tend to prove, that credulity is a part of the English character."[43] Similar attacks on this "national characteristic" abound in eighteenth-century British writings, and betray a real fear of being taken in.

I Doubt, I Have Very Bad Judgment

There is one sure way not to be duped by fakes: simply disbelieve everything. This was the approach of the Jesuit historian Jean Hardouin, who in 1697 suggested that virtually every surviving classical text was a medieval forgery. Out of the entire classical corpus, he admitted only Pliny's *Natural History*, Virgil's *Georgics*, Horace's *Satires* and *Epistles*, and a few of the writings of Homer, Herodotus, Plautus, and Cicero. The rest, he declared, were composed by thirteenth-century monks under the

---

40   John Douglas, *Milton Vindicated*, pp. 26, 40.

41   Goldsmith,"Retaliation," line 79, in *Collected Works*, 4:356–7.

42   *The Imposture Detected*, pp. 2–3. See also Benedict, *Curiosity*, pp. 28–9, 160.

43   Cowley, *The Ladies History of England*, p. 508. Even in 1789, Gilbert Francklyn could note that "The story of Elizabeth Canning and Squires the Gipsey is yet fresh in our memories" (Francklyn, *An Answer to the Rev. Mr. Clarkson's Essay*, p. vii).

direction of one Severus Archontius.[44] The same attitude can be found on the fringes of the scholarly world even today: the Russian mathematician Anatoly Fomenko argues that virtually all of our knowledge of the chronology of Western civilization is mistaken, and that "The dominating historical discourse in its current state was essentially crafted in the XVI century.... Nearly all of its components are blatantly untrue!"[45] This creeping fear of forgers under every rock and around every corner is a paranoia worthy of John Birch or Joseph McCarthy. But one need not be unbalanced to see fakes everywhere: when Varro looked at the 130 plays attributed to Plautus, he deemed only 21 genuine. Even the ever-reasonable Anthony Grafton admits that "perhaps half the legal documents we possess from Merovingian times, and perhaps two-thirds of all documents issued to ecclesiastics before A.D. 1100, are fakes."[46]

For people like Hardouin, then, it is but a short step from Grafton's estimates to disbelieving everything. But mindless skepticism is no healthier than mindless credulity. The French historian Marc Bloch, recalling "a worthy veterinarian" who "refused categorically to believe anything in the newspapers," concludes that "skepticism on principle is neither a more estimable nor a more productive attitude than ... credulity."[47] Among those bitten by the seemingly ubiquitous forgers, suspicion was an almost automatic reaction to anything new. Hume notes of Macpherson's fragments: "The first time I was shown the copies ... I was inclined to be a little incredulous."[48] "There is said to be a poem of Homer's of above 500 lines found lately in the Royal Library at Moscow," wrote Michael Lort in 1778. "Possibly this also may be a forgery ... in this age of forgeries."[49] Horace Walpole too worried about getting it wrong: in 1781, as Chatterton's star was rising, he lamented, "I believed in Ossian, who is now tumbled into the Apocrypha; and I doubted of Rowley, who is now to rank with Moses and the prophets!—I doubt, I have very bad judgment."[50] This sort of thinking is dangerous: it can lead us to a more-than-Humean skepticism bordering on Pyrrhonism, a radical doubt that we can know anything, with no Cartesian *cogito* to break the stalemate. Creeping doubt is bad medicine, and many eighteenth-century thinkers were afflicted with it.

The topic was widely discussed among early eighteenth-century French historians and philosophers. For the authors of the Port Royal *Logic*, "the harm is that ... people who take pleasure in doubting everything either prevent the mind from focusing on what could persuade them, or they apply themselves to it only

---

44   The most thorough and reliable account of Hardouin is Grafton, "Jean Hardouin: The Antiquary as Pariah."

45   Fomenko, *History, Fiction or Science?: Chronology*, p. xx. On the same page he asserts that "Jesus Christ was born in 1152 A.D. and crucified in 1185 A.D."

46   Hardouin makes his case in *Prolegomena ad censuram veterum scriptorum* (1696) and *Chronologia veteris testamenti* (1697). Among his other curious theories was that the New Testament was originally written in Latin. Anthony Grafton discusses Hardouin in *Forgers and Critics*, pp. 72–3; Varro's Plautine canon, p. 13; and Merovingian legal documents, p. 24.

47   Bloch, *The Historian's Craft*, pp. 79–80.

48   Hume to Sir David Dalrymple, 16 Aug. 1760, in Hume, *Letters*, 1:328 (letter 176).

49   Lort to Walpole, 14 Sept. 1778, in Walpole, *Correspondence*, 16:179.

50   Walpole to Lady Ossory, 22 Dec. 1781, in Walpole, *Correspondence*, 33:317.

imperfect."[51] Similar French comments on Pyrrhonism made their way into English works late in the seventeenth century and continued to influence British thought throughout the eighteenth. The Pyrrhonists were the eighteenth century's favorite philosophical straw men. In 1704, Robert Burscough summed up the danger they posed to secular and divine order: "our Compliance [to Church principles] is a Duty; and what is so, cannot be Cancel'd by our Doubts and Scruples. Otherwise the more of these a Person entertains, the less Regard need he pay to the Laws of God or Man: and he that can be a *Pyrrhonian*, may be freed from all Obligations to Vertue and Obedience."[52] Richard Blackmore, who wrote an essay called "Of the Pyrrhonian Scepticks," singled them out in his attack on atheism, *Creation* (1712):

> *Pyrrhonians* next of like Ambitious Aim,
> Wanton of Wit, and panting after Fame,
> Who strove to sink the Sects of Chief Renown,
> And on their ruin'd Schools to raise their own,
> Boldly presum'd, with Rhetorician Pride,
> To hold of any Question either side.
> They thought in ev'ry Subject of Debate,
> In either Scale the proof of equal Weight.[53]

And Lord Bolingbroke may have the definitive summing-up of the Pyrrhonists' eighteenth-century reputation: "The Pyrrhonian is against all sides: and all sides are against him. He is the common enemy, 'hostis philosophici generis.' The academician would pass, if he could, for a neuter, who is for no side, nor against any; or else for a trimmer, who changes sides often, and finds the probable sometimes on one, sometimes on the other."[54] Even the most famous British skeptic, David Hume, acknowledged that true Pyrrhonism, however appealing it may be when a philosopher is in his study, is untenable for the man who lives in the world:

> Shou'd it here be ask'd me, whether I sincerely assent to this argument, which I seem to take such pains to inculcate, and whether I be really one of those sceptics, who hold that all is uncertain, and that our judgment is not in *any* thing possest of *any* measures of truth and falshood; I shou'd reply, that this question is entirely superfluous, and that neither I, nor any other person was ever sincerely and constantly of that opinion. Nature, by an absolute and uncontroulable necessity has determin'd us to judge as well as to breathe and feel.[55]

---

51   Arnauld and Nicole, *Logic*, p. 8/20. It is noteworthy that some defenders of the authenticity of questioned documents accused their skeptical opponents of Pyrrhonism, as when the *Gazette littéraire* tried to suggest that disbelievers in the Ossianic poems were just as incredulous as the notorious Hardouin: "s'il est extraordinaire qu'un Barde Celte du IIIᵉ ou du IVᵉ siecle ait composé ses Poëmes, il seroit bien plus merveilleux encore qu'ils fussent l'ouvrage d'un Moderne; nous aimerions autant croire, avec le P. Hardouin, que les Odes d'Horace & l'Énéïde de Virgile ont été fabriquées par des Moines du XIIIᵉ siecle" (*Gazette littéraire* 6 [Aug. 1765]: 251).

52   Burscough, *A Discourse*, p. 143.

53   Blackmore, *Creation*, p. 140 (3.509–16).

54   Bolingbroke, *Philosophical Works*, 4:220.

55   Hume, *A Treatise of Human Nature*, p. 183 (4.1).

For all his doubts, Hume knew that living in the world demands a belief in reality: the most radical Pyrrhonist in his study has no choice but to accept many things on faith when he leaves his house, even if many of those things will prove false. Jeremy Bentham made the same point in the early nineteenth century: "as the true assertions greatly surpass the false in number, the disposition to believe is our habitual state; disbelief is the exception…. Were it otherwise, social business could not go on; every movement of society would be paralyzed; we would not dare to act."[56] And at the end of the twentieth century, Steven Shapin returned to the same theme: "Persistent distrust," he writes, "has a moral terminus: expulsion from the community. If you will not know, and accept the adequate grounds for, what the community knows, you will not belong to it."[57]

Imposture Weakens Confidence and Chills Benevolence

This is why deception was such an important topic in the eighteenth century: everything seemed to depend on it. Washington Irving may have been "willing to be deceived, where the deceit is pleasant, and costs nothing," but too often it was not pleasant and the cost was high. The stakes were knowledge itself, which is why Samuel Johnson was always unwilling to be deceived. In an age crowded with remarkable literary hoaxes, few people had contact with more of them than Johnson. He was involved in nearly all the noteworthy fakes of his day, and in a multitude of roles: to the bullying antiquarian Macpherson, he played debunker; to the suicidal prodigy Chatterton, a skeptical inquirer; to the convicted forger Dodd, a consoler; to the penitent faux-Formosan Psalmanazar, a friend. And though he is best known for being on the side of righteousness, he several times strayed to the dark side—both unwillingly, when Lauder convinced him publicly to defend his lies about Milton's plagiarism, and willingly, when as a young hack he passed off his own debates in Parliament as the actual words of Walpole and Pitt.

Perhaps because of this experience, few things were more important for him than distinguishing the real from the spurious. Deception colored the way Johnson looked at the world, and it provides one of the keys to his intellectual character. Hester Thrale Piozzi, in recounting his unwitting involvement in the Lauder controversy, notes that his "ruling passion may be said to be the love of truth," an assessment echoed by many of his acquaintances. Sir John Hawkins observed that "His notions of morality were so strict, that he would scarcely allow the violations of truth in the most trivial instances." Boswell elaborates: "The importance of strict and scrupulous

---

56 Bentham, *A Treatise on Judicial Evidence*, p. 16.

57 Shapin, *A Social History of Truth*, p. 20. Later in the same work he argues that, "Although much seventeenth-century rhetoric pointed to a golden mean between radical skepticism and naive credulity, the local politics of the 'modern' English scientific community pitched it forcefully against Scholastic ontological restrictions, while … the critique of skepticism flowed from predicaments and interests shared between scientific practitioners, theologians, and everyday actors. I hazard an impressionistic guess that, for these reasons, early Royal Society members were marginally *more* worried by illegitimate skepticism than by illegitimate credulity" (p. 244).

veracity cannot be too often inculcated. Johnson was known to be so rigidly attentive to it, that even in his conversation the slightest circumstance was mentioned with exact precision." Arthur Murphy concurs: "Johnson always talked as if he was talking upon oath."[58]

These early commentators were right: indignation at misrepresentation of any sort fills Johnson's writings and conversation, informing his comments on the status of fiction, fantastic narratives (including travel writing), and literary attribution—including not only forgery and plagiarism, but even anonymous and pseudonymous publishing (he berated Joseph Warton for his anonymous *Essay on Pope*, "That way of publishing … is a wicked trick"[59]). Johnson's career amounts to a prolonged assault on falsehood. His attitudes toward fakery therefore take us to the heart of his attitudes toward the nature of belief, and even of truth itself.

Johnson famously worked to save William Dodd from execution, and he considered George Psalmanazar "the *best* man he had ever known."[60] But whatever palliation of the crimes he saw in these individual penitents, he never stopped denouncing their sins. When Anna Seward put the question to him—"But, Dr. Johnson, would *you* have pardoned Dr. Dodd?"—he replied, "Madam, had I been placed at the head of the legislature, I should certainly have signed his death-warrant." He could only add that "no law, either human or divine, forbids our deprecating punishment, either from ourselves or others."[61] General severity tempered by occasional leniency was his policy. In this spirit he invokes Matthew 7:12: "The great rule, by which religion regulates all transactions between one man and another," he declared in a sermon, "is, that every man 'should do to others what he would expect that others,' in the same case, 'should do to him.' This rule is violated in every act of fraud."[62] Even more pointed is *Adventurer* 50:

> The liar, and only the liar, is invariably and universally despised, abandoned, and disowned; he has no domestic consolations, which he can oppose to the censure of mankind; he can retire to no fraternity where his crimes may stand in the place of virtues; but is given up to the hisses of the multitude, without friend and without apologist.[63]

The vehemence of this spirited blast is almost unmatched in Johnson's works. What provoked such ire in a man so rarely given to hyperbole? One might explain it simply with reference to Johnson's Christian morality: "Lying lips are abomination to the Lord," says Proverbs 12:22, "but they that deal truly are His delight." That, however, does not go far enough. No Christian moralist has gone on record as an advocate of mendacity, but few have been such tireless crusaders for truth as Johnson.

---

58 Piozzi, *Anecdotes*, p. 398; Hawkins, *Life*, p. 123; Boswell, *Life*, 2:434 and n. 2.

59 Johnson to Joseph Warton, 15 April 1756, in Johnson, *Letters*, 1:133–4.

60 Piozzi, *Anecdotes*, in Hill, ed., *Johnsonian Miscellanies*, 1:266. For Johnson's relationship with Dodd, see Barker, "Samuel Johnson and the Campaign to Save William Dodd."

61 Hastings Robinson, in Hill, ed., *Johnsonian Miscellanies*, 2:418.

62 Johnson, Sermon 18, in Yale *Works*, 14:198.

63 Johnson, Yale *Works*, 2:361.

His resentment at fraud comes from his grounding in Lockean epistemology, and his realization that having our mental towers tumble will eventually discourage our attempts to rebuild, or even to build them in the first place. Charlatans take advantage of a necessary faculty: "The nature of fraud, as distinct from other violations of right or property," Johnson speculates, "seems to consist in this, that the man injured is induced to concur in the act by which the injury is done."[64] This helps us appreciate a passage in *Rasselas*. When Nekayah and Pekuah consider assuming false identities to insinuate their way into the astronomer's company, Rasselas chastises them:

> I have always considered it as treason against the great republick of human nature, to make any man's virtues the means of deceiving him, whether on great or little occasions. All imposture weakens confidence and chills benevolence.... The distrust, which he can never afterwards wholly lay aside, may stop the voice of counsel, and close the hand of charity.[65]

Fakery dampens faith, and without faith there can be no benevolence—Johnson thereby avoids a theological quagmire by suggesting faith and works are inseparable. As he explains in *Rambler* 79, "Whoever commits a fraud is guilty not only of the particular injury to him whom he deceives, but of the diminution of that confidence which constitutes not only the ease but the existence of society."[66] He gets to the heart of the problem in *Adventurer* 50: "When Aristotle was once asked, what a man could gain by uttering falsehoods; he replied, 'not to be credited when he shall tell the truth.'"[67] Fraud, in other words, deters us from trusting our perception and exercising our reflection; it forces us to be unwilling skeptics. Watching our building blocks tumble one too many times discourages us from playing with our blocks at all, and intellectual indolence terrified Johnson.

That is the real source of Johnson's indignation: fakery reduces us to a state of perpetual doubt, and teaches us not to trust. Johnson was never naively credulous about anything, and even recognized that "Credulity on one part is a strong temptation to deceit on the other."[68] Unwarranted skepticism about important matters, however, was a recurring fear, as his prayers make clear: "Let me not linger in ignorance and doubt," he asked God; and later, "Deliver me, gracious Lord from the bondage of doubt."[69] The "doubt" here is specifically Christian unbelief, but Johnson regarded religious skepticism as not fundamentally different from other kinds. (In fact, religious doubts might be assuaged more easily than mundane doubts. Though heresies of every stripe abounded, true atheists were rare in eighteenth-century Britain; the existence of a Creator, whatever His nature, was considered proven beyond question through many arguments, whereas the truth of quotidian details lacked obvious evidence.) Thus, Johnson turns to Thomas Browne to find a "method

---

64   Ibid., 14:196–7.

65   Ibid., 16:158–59.

66   Johnson, *Rambler* 79, in Yale *Works*, 4:55.

67   Johnson, Yale *Works*, 2:360.

68   Johnson, *A Journey to the Western Islands of Scotland*, p. 89.

69   Johnson, "Prayer on Study of Religion" and birthday prayer for 1766, in Yale *Works*, 1:62, 110. I discuss these passages and Johnson's concerns about skepticism in "Samuel Johnson, Unbeliever."

of encountering these troublesome irruptions of skepticism, with which inquisitive minds are frequently harassed."[70] Preventing such skepticism is for him a moral obligation: "It is our duty not to suppress tenderness by suspicion; it is better to suffer wrong than to do it, and happier to be sometimes cheated than not to trust."[71]

Fakers were the biggest problem, but even those without criminal intentions could threaten the foundations of belief. Most commentators on duplicity have been careful to distinguish outright lies from honest misrepresentations, or at least to highlight the difficulty of placing a specific falsehood on the virtuous-to-vicious continuum. Johnson, on the other hand, was impatient with what he regarded as casuistry, probably because to him the effect on belief was the same. As Boswell noticed, "Johnson had accustomed himself to use the word *lie*, to express a mistake or an errour in relation; in short, when the *thing was not so as told*, though the relator did not *mean* to deceive. When he thought there was intentional falsehood in the relator, his expression was, 'He *lies*, and he *knows* he *lies*.'"[72] Any error, even one expressed ingenuously by someone who does not know he lies, might be harmful, and vigilance is therefore an ethical duty: Johnsonian epistemology slides into moral philosophy. Locke defines *falshood* as "the marking down in Words, the agreement or disagreement of *Ideas* otherwise than it is," a value-neutral definition without regard for blame. Johnson's first definition of *false*, on the other hand, is "Not morally true."[73] Truth is a kind of discipline, a perpetual vigilance against falsehood. The true sin of Macpherson, Chatterton, and other members of their nefarious fraternity is the same as that of anyone simply careless with the truth: they weaken confidence in belief, and therefore in thought itself.

Skepticism touched a Johnsonian nerve, and this knowledge helps us understand many of Johnson's critical and moral pronouncements. It makes sense, for example, of his impassioned attacks on those who do not share his love of truth, whether Scots who "love Scotland better than truth," politicians who "prefer safety to truth," senators who "prefer civility to truth," or even Clarissa Harlowe—who, though a paragon of virtue in many respects, always found "something which she prefers to truth."[74] On the other side, it makes sense of his extravagant praise for literature's greatest dupe: "Was there ever yet any thing written by mere man that was wished longer by its readers, excepting Don Quixote, Robinson Crusoe, and the Pilgrim's Progress?" Johnson found Cervantes's extended fable on the dangers of delusion "the greatest [work] in the world," excepting only the *Iliad*.[75] He saw himself and everyman in Cervantes's hero, and had him in mind as he worked to stave off doubt on the one hand and credulity on the other.

Boswell provides perhaps the best summary of the disturbing implications of fraud:

---

70 Johnson, *Life of Browne*, in 1825 *Works*, 6:498.

71 Johnson, *Rambler* 79, in Yale *Works*, 4:55.

72 Boswell, *Life*, 4:49.

73 Locke, *Essay concerning Human Understanding*, p. 578; Johnson, *Dictionary*, s.v. *false*.

74 Johnson, Yale *Works*, 9:119, 10:94; Johnson, 1825 *Works*, 11:3 (parliamentary debate of 8 Dec. 1741); Piozzi, in Hill, ed., *Johnsonian Miscellanies*, 1:297.

75 Hill, ed., *Johnsonian Miscellanies*, 1:332–3.

That *Fingal* is not from beginning to end a translation from the Gallick, but that *some* passages have been supplied by the editor to connect the whole, I have heard admitted by very warm advocates for its authenticity. If this be the case, why are not these distinctly ascertained? Antiquaries, and admirers of the work, may complain, that they are in a situation similar to that of the unhappy gentleman, whose wife informed him, on her death-bed, that one of their reputed children was not his; and, when he eagerly begged her to declare which of them it was, she answered, "*That* you shall never know"; and expired, leaving him in irremediable doubt as to them all.[76]

Irremediable doubt: few things bothered Johnson more, and in this respect he embodied all the anxieties of his age. Our own era can often enjoy the kinds of paradoxes that fascinated Oscar Wilde, in which truth and falsehood are wholly factitious and the world has "no right to quarrel with an artist for the conditions under which he chooses to present his work."[77] Eighteenth-century Britons thought they could not afford to be so casual. They were convinced their world depended on it.

---

76 Boswell, *Life*, 5:389–90.
77 Wilde, *The Portrait of Mr W. H.*, p. 3.

Bibliography

Named Manuscripts

Catcott, George Symes. *Chattertoniana*. Bristol Central Library.
Ireland, William Henry. *Frogmore Fete*. Hyde Collection Case 9 (2).
——. *A Full and Explanatory Account of the Shaksperian Forgery by Myself the Writer William Henry Ireland: Illustrated with Picturesque Family Documents, &c.* Hyde Collection Case 9 Folio (3).
Seyer, Samuel. *Mr. Seyer's MSS. Relating to the History of Bristol*. Bristol Central Library, MS B4533.
Stukeley, William. *Notes on Ossian*. Bodleian MS Eng.misc.e.383.
Whiston, William. *Predictions of William Whistons*. Morgan E2 77 C.

Printed Books with Manuscript Annotations

Chatterton, Thomas. *Poems Supposed to Have Been Written at Bristol*. Ed. Jeremiah Milles. London, 1782 [i.e., 1781]. With Horace Walpole's autograph annotations. British Library, shelfmark C.39.i.19.
Macpherson, James. *The Poems of Ossian*. 2 vols. London, 1773. With Joseph Ritson's autograph annotations. Yale Osborn pc124.

Early Periodicals

The Annual Register; or, A View of the History, Politics, and Literature for the Year .... London, 1758–1837.
The Critical Review; or, Annals of Literature. London, 1756–1817.
Gazette littéraire de l'Europe. Paris, 1764–66.
The Gentleman's Magazine, and Historical Chronicle. London, 1731–1833.
The Lady's Magazine; or, Entertaining Companion for the Fair Sex. London, 1770–1818.
The Monthly Review. London, 1749–1845.
The Telegraph. London, 1794–97.

Printed Books

Adams, Percy G. *Travelers and Travel Liars, 1660–1800*. Berkeley and Los Angeles: Univ. of California Press, 1962.
Adams, William. *A Test of True and False Doctrines: A Sermon Preached in the Parish Church of St. Chad, Salop, on September 24, 1769*. London, 1770.

Ahlers, Cyriacus. *Some Observations Concerning the Woman of Godlyman in Surrey: Made at Guilford on Sunday, Nov. 20. 1726: Tending to Prove Her Extraordinary Deliveries to Be a Cheat and Imposture.* London, 1726.

Allen, Paul Marshall, and Joan deRis Allen. *Fingal's Cave, the Poems of Ossian, and Celtic Christianity.* New York: Continuum, 1999.

Allen, Woody. "The Scrolls." In *Without Feathers*, pp. 21–5. New York: Random House, 1975.

Ancient Scottish Poems, Never Before in Print, but Now Published from the MS. Collections of Sir Richard Maitland. 2 vols. London, 1786.

Appleton, William W. *A Cycle of Cathay: The Chinese Vogue in England during the Seventeenth and Eighteenth Centuries.* New York: Columbia Univ. Press, 1951.

À Propos Mr. St. André's Case and Depositions as Publish'd in the London Gazette of February 23, 1724. and the Daily Post of March 4, 1725. London, [1727?].

Archenholz, Johann Wilhelm von. *A Picture of England: Containing a Description of the Laws, Customs, and Manners of England.* 2 vols. London, 1789.

The Arguments on Both Sides the Question in the Intricate Affair of Elizabeth Canning. [London?], 1753.

Aristotle. *The "Art" of Rhetoric.* Trans. John Henry Freese. London: William Heinemann, 1926.

——. *Hobbes's Translation of Aristotle's Art of Rhetorick: A New Edition, with Alterations, and a New Preface by a Gentleman.* London, 1759.

Arnauld, Antoine, and Pierre Nicole. *Logic or the Art of Thinking: Containing, besides Common Rules, Several New Observations Appropriate for Forming Judgment.* Ed. and trans. Jill Vance Buroker. Cambridge: Cambridge Univ. Press, 1996.

Arnot, Hugo. *The History of Edinburgh.* Edinburgh, 1779.

Astle, Thomas. *The Origin and Progress of Writing.* 2nd ed. London, 1803.

Atherton, Margaret. "Locke's Theory of Personal Identity." *Midwest Studies in Philosophy* 14 (1984): 273–93.

Augustine. *Saint Augustine: Treatises on Various Subjects.* Ed. Roy J. Deferrari. Vol. 16 of The Fathers of the Church. New York: Fathers of the Church, 1952.

Authentic Memoirs of William Wynne Ryland, Containing a Succinct Account of the Life and Transactions of That Great but Unfortunate Artist. London, 1784.

Bacon, Francis. *The Essayes or Counsels, Civill and Morall.* Ed. Michael Kiernan. Cambridge, Mass.: Harvard Univ. Press, 1985.

Baines, Paul. *The House of Forgery in Eighteenth-Century Britain.* Aldershot: Ashgate, 1999.

Balston, Thomas. *James Whatman Father & Son.* London: Methuen & Co., 1957.

Baretti, Giuseppe. *Easy Phraseology, for the Use of Young Ladies, Who Intend to Learn the Colloquial Part of the Italian Language.* London, 1775.

Barker, A. D. "Samuel Johnson and the Campaign to Save William Dodd." *Harvard Library Bulletin* 31 (1983): 147–80.

Bate, Jonathan. "Shakespearean Allusion in English Caricature in the Age of Gillray." *Journal of the Warburg and Courtauld Institutes* 49 (1986): 196–210.

Beattie, James. *Evidences of the Christian Religion, Briefly and Plainly Stated.* 2 vols. Edinburgh, 1786.

Bender, John. *Imagining the Penitentiary: Fiction and the Architecture of Mind in Eighteenth-Century England.* Chicago: Univ. of Chicago Press, 1987.

Benedict, Barbara. *Curiosity: A Cultural History of Early Modern Inquiry.* Chicago: Univ. of Chicago Press, 2001.

Bennet, Benjamin. *The Truth, Inspiration, and Usefulness of the Scripture Asserted and Proved.* London, 1730.

Bentham, Jeremy. *Rationale of Judicial Evidence, Specially Applied to English Practice.* 5 vols. London, 1827.

——. *A Treatise on Judicial Evidence, Extracted from the Manuscripts of Jeremy Bentham, Esq. by M. Dumont.* London, 1825.

Bentley, Richard. *A Dissertation upon the Epistles of Phalaris, with an Answer to the Objections of the Honourable Charles Boyle, Esquire.* London, 1699.

Biddulph, E. *Some Account of the Case between Elizabeth Canning and Mary Squires; As It Now Stands upon the Foot of the Evidence Given on Both Sides, upon the Late Trial at the Old-Bailey.* London, 1754.

Bielfield, Jacob Friedrich, Freiherr von. *The Elements of Universal Erudition: Containing an Analytical Abridgment of the Sciences, Polite Arts, and Belles Lettres.* Trans. W. Hooper. Dublin, 1771.

Blackburne, Francis. *Remarks on Johnson's Life of Milton.* London, 1780.

Blackmore, Sir Richard. *Creation: A Philosophical Poem in Seven Books.* London, 1712.

Blackstone, Sir William. *Commentaries on the Laws of England.* 4 vols. Oxford, 1765–69.

Blair, Hugh. *A Critical Dissertation on the Poems of Ossian.* In Macpherson, *The Poems of Ossian,* ed. Howard Gaskill, pp. 345–408.

——. "A Dissertation." In Macpherson, *The Poems of Ossian,* ed. Howard Gaskill, pp. 205–24.

——. Preface to *Fragments of Ancient Poetry.* In Macpherson, *The Poems of Ossian,* ed. Howard Gaskill, pp. 5–6.

Blake, William. *The Poetry and Prose of William Blake.* Ed. David V. Erdman. Garden City: Doubleday, 1965.

Bloch, Marc. *The Historian's Craft.* Trans. Peter Putnam. New York: Knopf, 1953.

Board, Prudy Taylor. *101 Tips on Writing and Selling Your First Novel.* New York: Mystery and Suspense Press, 2003.

Bolingbroke, Henry St. John, Viscount. *The Philosophical Works of the Late Right Honourable Henry St. John, Lord Viscount Bolingbroke.* 5 vols. London, 1754.

Boswell, James. *Boswell: The English Experiment, 1785–1789.* Ed. Irma S. Lustig and F. A. Pottle. New York: McGraw-Hill, 1986.

——. *Boswell: The Ominous Years, 1774–1776.* Ed. Charles Ryskamp and Frederick A. Pottle. New York: McGraw-Hill, 1963.

——. *Boswell's London Journal, 1762–1763.* Ed. Frederick A. Pottle. New York: McGraw-Hill, 1950.

——. *Letters of James Boswell.* Ed. Chauncey Brewster Tinker. 2 vols. Oxford: Clarendon Press, 1924.

——. *The Life of Samuel Johnson.* Ed. G. B. Hill, rev. L. F. Powell. 6 vols. Oxford: Clarendon Press, 1934–64.

Bowden, Ross. "What Is Wrong with an Art Forgery?: An Anthropological Perspective." *The Journal of Aesthetics and Art Criticism* 37, no. 3 (Summer 1999): 333–43.

Boyle, Charles, Earl of Orrery [i.e., Francis Atterbury]. *Dr. Bentley's Dissertations on the Epistles of Phalaris, and the Fables of Æsop, Examin'd*. London, 1699.

Brainerd, C. J., and V. F. Reyna. *The Science of False Memory*. Oxford: Oxford Univ. Press, 2005.

Brathwaite, Thomas. *Remarks on a Short Narrative of an Extraordinary Delivery of Rabbets*. London, 1726.

Bristol, Michael D. "How Many Children Did She Have?" In *Philosophical Shakespeares*, pp. 18–33. Ed. John J. Joughin. London: Routledge, 2000.

Brooke, Christopher N. L. "Approaches to Medieval Forgery." *Journal of the Society of Archivists* 3 (1965–1969): 377–86

Brosses, Charles de. *Terra Australis Cognita; or, Voyages to the Terra Australis, or Southern Hemisphere, during the Sixteenth, Seventeenth, and Eighteenth Centuries*. 3 vols. Edinburgh, 1766–68.

Bryant, Jacob. *Observations upon the Poems of Thomas Rowley, in Which the Authenticity of Those Poems Is Ascertained*. London, 1781.

Burn, Richard. *The Justice of the Peace, and Parish Officer*. 3rd ed. London, 1756.

Burscough, Robert. *A Discourse, I. of the Unity of the Church. II. Of the Separation of the Dissenters from the Church of England. III. Of Their Setting up Churches against the Conforming Churches; and of the Ordination of Their Teachers: Being an Answer to a Book, Entituled, Dissenters No Schismaticks, &c*. Exeter, 1704.

Butler, Joseph. *The Analogy of Religion, Natural and Revealed, to the Constitution and Course of Nature*. London, 1736.

Caine, Hall. *Recollections of Dante Gabriel Rossetti*. London, 1882.

Cameron, Ewen. *The Fingal of Ossian, an Ancient Epic Poem in Six Books: Translated from the Original Galic Language, by Mr. James Macpherson; and Now Rendered into Heroic Verse*. Warrington, 1776.

Campbell, Thomas. *A Philosophical Survey of the South of Ireland: In a Series of Letters to John Watkinson, M.D.* London, 1777.

Canning's Magazine; or, A Review of the Whole Evidence That Has Been Hitherto Offered for or against Elizabeth Canning, and Mary Squires: Including Some Memorable Occurrences, Never Before Imparted to the Publick. London, 1754.

Carleton, John. *The Ultimum Vale of John Carleton, of the Middle Temple London, Gent.: Being a True Description of the Passages of That Grand Impostor, Late a Pretended Germane-Lady*. London, 1663.

Carruthers, R. *The Highland Note-Book; or, Sketches and Anecdotes*. Edinburgh, 1843.

A Certaine Relation of the Hog-Faced Gentlewoman Called Mistriss Tannakin Skinker. London, 1640.

Chassepol, François de. *A Treatise of the Revenue and False Money of the Romans, to Which Is Annexed a Dissertation upon the Manner of Distinguishing Antique Medals from Counterfeit Ones*. London, 1741.

Chatterton, Thomas. *The Complete Works of Thomas Chatterton: A Bicentenary Edition*. Ed. Donald S. Taylor. 2 vols. Oxford: Oxford Univ. Press, 1971.

——. *Poems, Supposed to Have Been Written at Bristol, by Thomas Rowley, and Others, in the Fifteenth Century.* Ed. Thomas Tyrwhitt. 3rd ed. London, 1778.

——. *Poems, Supposed to Have Been Written at Bristol, in the Fifteenth Century, by Thomas Rowley, Priest, &c.: With a Commentary, in Which the Antiquity of Them is Considered, and Defended by Jeremiah Milles, D.D., Dean of Exeter.* London, 1782 [i.e., 1781].

Childers, Hugh Robert Eardley. *Romantic Trials of Three Centuries.* London: J. Lane, 1913.

Churchill, Charles. *Poetical Works of Charles Churchill.* Ed. Douglas Grant. Oxford: Clarendon Press, 1956.

Clark, John. *An Answer to Mr Shaw's Inquiry into the Authenticity of the Poems Ascribed to Ossian.* Edinburgh, 1781.

Clarke, Samuel. *Sermons on the Following Subjects, viz., Of Faith in God ...* 10 vols. London, 1730–31.

Cody, Lisa Forman. *Birthing the Nation: Sex, Science, and the Conception of Eighteenth-Century Britons.* Oxford: Oxford Univ. Press, 2005.

Coke, Sir Edward. *The First Part of the Institutes of the Lawes of England; or, A Commentarie upon Littleton, Not the Name of a Lawyer Onely, but of the Law It Selfe.* London, 1628.

Coleridge, Samuel Taylor. *Lectures 1808–1819 on Literature.* Ed. R. A. Foakes. 2 vols. Princeton: Princeton Univ. Press, 1987.

——. *Poetical Works.* 6 vols. Ed. J. C. C. Mays. Princeton: Princeton Univ. Press, 2001.

A Collection of Several Papers Relating to Elizabeth Canning. London, 1754.

Collins, Anthony. *An Essay concerning the Use of Reason in Propositions, the Evidence Whereof Depends upon Human Testimony.* 2nd ed. London, 1709.

Colman, George. *Prose on Several Occasions: Accompanied with Some Pieces in Verse.* 3 vols. London, 1787.

Congreve, Sir William. *An Analysis of the True Principles of Security against Forgery; Exmplified by an Enquiry into the Sufficiency of the American Plan for a New Bank Note.* London, 1820.

Cowley, Charlotte. *The Ladies History of England; from the Descent of Julius Cæsar, to the Summer of 1780.* London, 1780.

Cox, Daniel. *An Appeal to the Public, in Behalf of Elizabeth Canning, in Which the Material Facts in Her Story Are Fairly Stated, and Shewn to Be True, on the Foundation of Evidence.* 2nd ed. London, 1753.

Croft, Herbert. *Love and Madness: A Story Too True.* London, 1780.

Curley, Thomas M. "Johnson's Last Word on Ossian: Ghostwriting for William Shaw." In *Aberdeen and the Enlightenment,* ed. Jennifer J. Carter, pp. 375–431. Aberdeen: Aberdeen Univ. Press, 1987.

——. "Samuel Johnson and Truth: The First Systematic Detection of Literary Deception in James Macpherson's *Ossian.*" *The Age of Johnson: A Scholarly Annual* 17 (2006): 119–96.

Dalrymple, David. *Remarks on the History of Scotland.* Edinburgh, 1773.

Davies, Edward. *The Claims of Ossian, Examined and Appreciated.* Swansea, 1825.

Defoe, Daniel. *The Life and Strange Surprizing Adventures of Robinson Crusoe, of York, Mariner.* Ed. J. Donald Crowley. Oxford: Oxford Univ. Press, 1972.

DeGategno, Paul J. *James Macpherson.* Boston: Twayne, 1989.

de Grazia, Margreta. *Shakespeare Verbatim: The Reproduction of Authority and the 1790 Apparatus.* Oxford: Clarendon Press, 1991.

de la Torre, Lillian. *"Elizabeth Is Missing"; or, Truth Triumphant: An Eighteenth Century Mystery.* New York: Alfred A. Knopf, 1945.

De Quincey, Thomas. *De Quincey's Collected Writings: New and Enlarged Edition.* Ed. David Masson. 14 vols. Edinburgh, 1889–90.

The Devil Outdone, in a Contest between Elizabeth Canning, Mary Squires, and Dr. C——: A Ballad. London, [1753?].

"The Doctors in Labour; or, A New Whim Wham from Guildford." London, [1726?].

Dix, John Ross. *The Life of Thomas Chatterton, Including His Unpublished Poems and Correspondence.* London, 1837.

Dodd, James Solas. *A Physical Account of the Case of Elizabeth Canning: With an Enquiry into the Probability of Her Subsisting in the Manner Therein Asserted, and Her Ability for Escape after Her Suppos'd Ill Usage.* London, 1753.

Donne, John. *Fifty Sermons Preached by That Learned and Reverend Divine, John Donne.* London, 1649.

Douglas, James. *An Advertisement Occasion'd by Some Passages in Sir R. Manningham's Diary, Lately Publish'd.* London, 1727.

Douglas, John. *Milton Vindicated from the Charge of Plagiarism, Brought against Him by Mr. Lauder, and Lauder Himself Convicted of Several Forgeries and Gross Impositions on the Public.* London, 1751.

——. *Six Letters from A——d B——r to Father Sheldon, Provincial of the Jesuits in England; Illustrated with Several Remarkable Facts, Tending to Ascertain the Authenticity of the Said Letters, and the True Character of the Writer.* London, 1756.

Doyle, Arthur Conan. *The Classic Illustrated Sherlock Holmes.* Stamford, Conn.: Longmeadow Press, 1987.

Duff, William. *Critical Observations on the Writings of the Most Celebrated Original Geniuses in Poetry.* London, 1770.

Duranti, Luciana. *Diplomatics: New Uses for an Old Science.* Lanham, Md.: The Scarecrow Press, 1998.

Eco, Umberto. *The Limits of Interpretation.* Bloomington and Indianapolis: Indiana Univ. Press, 1990.

Edwards, Jonathan. *A Careful and Strict Enquiry into the Modern Prevailing Notions of That Freedom of Will, Which Is Supposed to Be Essential to Moral Agency.* London, 1762.

Einstein, Albert. "On the Electrodynamics of Moving Bodies." Trans. W. Perrettt and G. B. Jeffery. In *Selections from the Principle of Relativity*, ed. Stephen Hawking, pp. 1–23. Philadelphia: Running Press, 2004.

Elliot, Adam. *A Modest Vindication of Titus Oates the Salamanca-Doctor from Perjury; or, An Essay to Demonstrate Him Only Forsworn in Several Instances.* London, 1682.

Ellis, John M. *One Fairy Story Too Many: The Brothers Grimm and Their Tales.* Chicago: Univ. of Chicago Press, 1983.

Encyclopædia Britannica; or, A Dictionary of Arts, Sciences, &c. on a Plan Entirely New. 2nd ed. 10 vols. Edinburgh, 1778–83.

Erskine-Baker, David. *The Muse of Ossian: A Dramatic Poem, of Three Acts.* Edinburgh, 1763.

Fairer, David. "Chatterton's Poetic Afterlife, 1770–1794: A Context for Coleridge's *Monody*." In *Thomas Chatterton and Romantic Culture*, ed. Nick Groom, pp. 228–52.

Ferguson, Adam. *An Essay on the History of Civil Society, 1767.* Ed. Duncan Forbes. Edinburgh: Edinburgh Univ. Press, 1966.

Fielding, Henry. *A Clear State of the Case of Elizabeth Canning.* In *An Enquiry into the Causes of the Late Increase of Robbers and Related Writings.* Ed. Malvin R. Zirker. Middletown, Conn.: Wesleyan Univ. Press, 1988.

——. *Joseph Andrews.* Ed. Martin Battestin. Middletown, Conn.: Wesleyan Univ. Press, 1967.

Fissell, Mary, and Roger Cooter. "Exploring Natural Knowledge: Science and the Popular." In *The Cambridge History of Science: Volume 4, Eighteenth-Century Science*, pp. 129–58. Ed. Roy Porter, David C. Lindberg, and Ronald L. Numbers. Cambridge: Cambridge Univ. Press, 2003.

Fomenko, Anatoly T. *History, Fiction or Science?: Chronology.* Douglas, Isle of Man: Delamere, 2003.

Formey, Jean-Henri-Samuel. *Elementary Principles of the Belles Lettres.* Trans. Sloper Foreman. London, 1766.

Foucault, Michel. "What Is an Author?" In *The Foucault Reader*, ed. Paul Rabinow, pp. 101–20. New York: Pantheon Books, 1984.

Francklyn, Gilbert. *An Answer to the Rev. Mr. Clarkson's Essay on the Slavery and Commerce of the Human Species, Particularly the African.* London, 1789.

Franklin, Benjamin. *The Papers of Benjamin Franklin.* Ed. Leonard W. Labaree. 38 vols. to date. New Haven: Yale Univ. Press, 1959–.

Franklin, James. *The Science of Conjecture: Evidence and Probability before Pascal.* Baltimore: Johns Hopkins Univ. Press, 2001.

Freeman, Arthur, and Janet Ing Freeman. *John Payne Collier: Scholarship and Forgery in the Nineteenth Century.* 2 vols. New Haven: Yale Univ. Press, 2004.

Gaskill, Howard. "The Manuscript Myth." In *Ossian Revisited*, ed. Howard Gaskill, pp. 6–16.

——. "Ossian in Europe." *Canadian Review of Comparative Literature* 21 (Dec. 1994): 643–75.

——. "'Ossian' Macpherson: Towards a Rehabilitation." *Comparative Criticism* 8 (1986): 113–46.

Gaskill, Howard, ed. *Ossian Revisited.* Edinburgh: Edinburgh Univ. Press, 1991.

Genuine and Impartial Memoirs of Elizabeth Canning. London, 1754.

The Genuine Copy of a Letter Found Nov. 5, 1762, Near Strawberry Hill, Twickenham, Addressed to the Hon. Mr. H——ce W——le. London, 1783.

Gibbon, Edward. *The History of the Decline and Fall of the Roman Empire.* Ed. David Womersley. 3 vols. London: Allen Lane, The Penguin Press, 1994.

Gifford, George. *A Discourse of the Subtill Practises of Deuilles by Witches and Sorcerers.* London, 1587.

Gilbert, Geoffrey. *The Law of Evidence.* London, 1756.

Gilbert, William. *De Magnete.* Trans. P. Fleury Mottelay. New York: John Wiley & Sons, 1893.

Gillies, Alexander. *A Hebridean in Goethe's Weimar: The Reverend James Macdonald and the Cultural Relations between Scotland and Germany.* Oxford: Basil Blackwell, 1969.

Giry, A. *Manuel de diplomatique.* Paris, 1894.

Gisbal, an Hyperborean Tale: Translated from the Fragments of Ossian the Son of Fingal. London, 1762.

Goethe, Johann Wolfgang von. *Die Leiden des jungen Werthers; Die Wahlverwandtschaften; Kleine Prosa; Epen.* Ed. Waltraud Wiethölter. Frankfurt am Main: Deutscher Klassiker Verlag, 1994.

———. *The Sorrows of Werter: A German Story.* 2 vols. London, 1779.

Goldsmith, Oliver. *Collected Works of Oliver Goldsmith.* Ed. Arthur Friedman. 5 vols. Oxford: Clarendon Press, 1966.

Goodman, Nelson. "Art and Authenticity." In *The Forger's Art: Forgery and the Philosophy of Art,* ed. Denis Dutton, pp. 97–114. Berkeley and Los Angeles: Univ. of California Press, 1983.

Gordon, John. *Occasional Thoughts on the Study and Character of Classical Authors, on the Course of Litterature, and the Present Plan of a Learned Education: With Some Incidental Comparisons between Homer and Ossian.* London, 1762.

Gosson, Stephen. *The Schoole of Abuse: Contayning a Pleasaunt Inuective against Poets, Pipers, Players, Iesters, and Such Like Caterpillers of a Common Wealth.* London, 1587.

Gould, Stephen Jay. *Triumph and Tragedy in Mudville: A Lifelong Passion for Baseball.* New York: W. W. Norton, 2003.

Grafton, Anthony. "Jean Hardouin: The Antiquary as Pariah." In *Bring Out Your Dead: The Past as Revelation,* pp. 181–207. Cambridge, Mass.: Harvard Univ. Press, 2001.

———. *Forgers and Critics: Creativity and Duplicity in Western Scholarship.* Princeton: Princeton Univ. Press, 1990.

Graham, Patrick. *Essay on the Authenticity of the Poems of Ossian; in Which the Objections of Malcolm Laing, Esq. Are Particularly Considered and Refuted.* Edinburgh, 1807.

Gray, Thomas. *Correspondence of Thomas Gray.* Ed. Paget Toynbee and Leonard Whibley. 3 vols. Oxford: Clarendon Press, 1935.

Greene, Edward Burnaby. *Strictures upon a Pamphlet Intitled, Cursory Observations on the Poems Attributed to Rowley, a Priest of the Fifteenth Century,* 1982.

Groom, Nick. "The Case against Chatterton's 'Lines to Walpole' and 'Last Verses.'" *Notes & Queries* 50, no. 3 (Sept. 2003): 278–80.

———. *The Forger's Shadow: How Forgery Changed the Course of Literature.* London: Picador, 2002.

———. *The Making of Percy's "Reliques."* Oxford: Clarendon Press, 1999.

———. "Original Copies; Counterfeit Forgeries." *Critical Quarterly* 42, no. 2 (Summer 2001): 6–18.

Groom, Nick, ed. *Thomas Chatterton and Romantic Culture*. Houndmills: Macmillan; New York: St. Martin's, 1999.

Gulliver, Lemuel [pseud.]. *The Anatomist Dissected; or, The Man-Midwife Finely Brought to Bed: Being an Examination of the Conduct of Mr. St. Andre: Touching the Late Pretended Rabbit-Bearer; as It Appears from His Own Narrative.* Westminster, 1727.

Hacking, Ian. *The Emergence of Probability: A Philosophical Study of Early Ideas about Probability, Induction and Statistical Inference*. London: Cambridge Univ. Press, 1975.

Hald, Anders. *A History of Probability and Statistics and Their Applications before 1750*. New York: John Wiley & Sons, 1990.

Hardinge, George. *Rowley and Chatterton in the Shades; or, Nugæ Antiquæ et Novæ*. Ed. Joan Pittock. Los Angeles: William Andrews Clark Memorial Library, 1979.

Hardouin, Jean. *Chronologia veteris testamenti*. Paris, 1697.

———. *Prolegomena ad censuram veterum scriptorum*. Paris, 1696.

Harris, James. *Philological Inquiries in Three Parts*. London, 1781.

Hawes, Clement. *The British Eighteenth Century and Global Critique*. Houndmills: Palgrave Macmillan, 2005.

Hawkins, Sir John. *The Life of Samuel Johnson*. Volume 1 of *The Works of Samuel Johnson*. 11 vols. London, 1787.

Haywood, Ian. *Faking It: Art and the Politics of Forgery*. New York: St. Martin's, 1987.

———. *The Making of History: A Study of the Literary Forgeries of James Macpherson and Thomas Chatterton in Relation to Eighteenth-Century Ideas of History and Fiction*. Rutherford, N.J.: Fairleigh Dickinson Univ. Press, 1986.

Hell upon Earth; or, The Town in an Uproar. London, 1729.

Helvétius, Claude Adrien. *De l'Esprit; or, Essays on the Mind, and Its Several Faculties: Written by Helvetius, Translated from the Edition Printed under the Author's Inspection*. London, 1759.

Henry, Robert. *The History of Great Britain, from the First Invasion of It by the Romans under Julius Cæsar: Written on a New Plan*. 6 vols. London, 1771–93.

Heron, Robert. *Observations Made in a Journey through the Western Counties of Scotland in the Autumn of M,DCC,XCII*. 2 vols. Perth, 1793.

Hickford, Raynor. *Observations on the Poems Attributed to Rowley, Tending to Prove that They Were Really Written by Him and Other Ancient Authors: To Which Are Added Remarks on the Appendix of the Editor of Rowley's Poems*. London, 1783.

Hill, G. B., ed. *Johnsonian Miscellanies*. 2 vols. Oxford: Clarendon Press, 1897.

Hill, John. *The Story of Elizabeth Canning Considered*. London, 1753.

Hirschman, Albert O. *The Passions and the Interests: Political Arguments for Capitalism Before Its Triumph*. Princeton: Princeton Univ. Press, 1977.

Hoffman, Calvin. *The Murder of the Man Who Was "Shakespeare."* New York: J. Messner, 1955.

Howson, G. *The Macaroni Parson: The Life of the Unfortunate Dr Dodd*. London: Hutchinson, 1973.

Hudson, Nicholas. "Constructing Oral Tradition: The Origins of the Concept in Enlightenment Intellectual Culture." In *The Spoken Word: Oral Culture in Britain, 1500–1850*, ed. Adam Fox and Daniel Woolf, pp. 240–55. Manchester: Manchester Univ. Press, 2003.

——. "'Oral Tradition': The Evolution of an Eighteenth-Century Concept." In *Tradition in Transition: Women Writers, Marginal Texts, and the Eighteenth-Century Canon*, pp. 161–76. Oxford: Clarendon Press, 1996.

——. *Writing and European Thought, 1600–1830*. Cambridge: Cambridge Univ. Press, 1994.

Hull, Thomas, ed. *Select Letters between the Late Duchess of Somerset, Lady Luxborough, Miss Dolman, Mr. Whistles, Mr. R. Dodsley, William Shenstone, Esq., and Others*. 2 vols. London, 1788.

Hume, David. *Enquiries concerning Human Understanding and concerning the Principles of Morals*. Ed. L. A. Selby-Bigge, rev. P. H. Nidditch. 3rd ed. Oxford: Clarendon Press, 1975.

——. *The Letters of David Hume*. Ed. J. Y. T. Greig. 2 vols. Oxford: Clarendon Press, 1932.

——. "Of the Authenticity of Ossian's Poems." In *The Philosophical Works of David Hume*, 4:415–24. Ed. T. H. Green and T. H. Grose. 4 vols. London, 1875.

——. *A Treatise of Human Nature*. Ed. L. A. Selby-Bigge, rev. P. H. Nidditch. 2nd ed. Oxford: Clarendon Press, 1978.

Hurd, Richard. *The Early Letters of Richard Hurd, 1739–1762*. Ed. Sarah Brewer. Woodbridge: Boydell Press and the Church of England Record Society, 1995.

The Imposture Detected; or, The Mystery and Iniquity of Elizabeth Canning's Story Displayed. London, 1753.

Ireland, William Henry. *An Authentic Account of the Shaksperian Manuscripts, &c.* London, 1796.

——. *Chalcographimania; or, The Portrait-Collector and Printseller's Chronicle, with Infatuations of Every Description*. London, 1814.

——. *The Confessions of William-Henry Ireland: Containing the Particulars of His Fabrication of the Shakspeare Manuscripts*. London, 1805.

——. *Miscellaneous Papers and Legal Instruments under the Hand and Seal of William Shakespeare*. London, 1796.

Irving, Washington. *The Sketch Book of Geoffrey Crayon, Gent.* Ed. Haskell Springer. Boston: Twayne Publishers, 1978.

Jacob, Giles. A *Treatise of Laws; or, A General Introduction to the Common, Civil, and Canon Law: In Three Parts*. London, 1721.

Jameson, Fredric. *The Political Unconscious: Narrative as a Socially Symbolic Act*. Ithaca: Cornell Univ. Press, 1981.

John, of Salisbury, Bishop of Chartres. *Entheticus Maior and Minor*. Ed. Jan van Laarhoven. 3 vols. Leiden: E. J. Brill, 1987.

——. *Ioannis Saresberiensis Policraticus I–IV*. Ed. K. S. B. Keats-Rohan. Turnholt: Brepols Editores Pontificii, 1993.

Johnson, David. *Hume, Holism, and Miracles*. Ithaca: Cornell Univ. Press, 1999.

Johnson, Samuel. *A Dictionary of the English Language*. 2 vols. London, 1755.

——. *The Letters of Samuel Johnson.* Ed. Bruce Redford. 5 vols. Princeton: Princeton Univ. Press, 1992–94.

——. *The Lives of the Most Eminent English Poets: With Critical Observations on Their Works.* Ed. Roger Lonsdale. 4 vols. Oxford: Oxford Univ. Press, 2006.

——. *A Journey to the Western Islands of Scotland.* Ed. J. D. Fleeman. Oxford: Clarendon Press, 1985.

——. *The Works of Samuel Johnson.* 11 vols. Oxford, 1825.

——. *The Yale Edition of the Works of Samuel Johnson.* 16 vols. to date. New Haven: Yale Univ. Press, 1958–.

Johnson, Samuel, and Thomas Osborne. *Catalogus Bibliothecæ Harleianæ.* 5 vols. London, 1743–45.

Kames, Henry Home, Lord. *Essays on the Principles of Morality and Natural Religion: In Two Parts.* Edinburgh, 1751.

——. *Sketches of the History of Man.* 2nd ed. 4 vols. Edinburgh, 1778.

Kaminski, Thomas. *The Early Career of Samuel Johnson.* Oxford: Oxford Univ. Press, 1987.

Keats, John. *The Poems of John Keats.* Ed. Jack Stillinger. London: Heinemann, 1978.

Keevak, Michael. *The Pretended Asian: George Psalmanazar's Eighteenth-Century Formosan Hoax.* Detroit: Wayne State Univ. Press, 2004.

Kellett, E. E. *Literary Quotation and Allusion.* Port Washington, N.Y.: Kennikat Press, 1969.

Kenny, Courtney. "The Mystery of Elizabeth Canning." *Law Quarterly Review* 13 (1897): 368–82.

Kitson Clark, G. *The Critical Historian.* London: Heinemann, 1967.

Knights, L. C. *How Many Children Had Lady Macbeth?: An Essay in the Theory and Practice of Shakespeare Criticism.* Cambridge: Gordon Fraser, 1933.

Knowles, David. *The Historian and Character, and Other Essays.* Cambridge: Cambridge Univ. Press, 1963.

Knox, Vicesimus. *Essays Moral and Literary.* New ed. 2 vols. London, 1782.

Koppenhaver, Katherine M. *Attorney's Guide to Document Examination.* Westport, Conn.: Quorum Books, 2002.

Körner, Stephan. *Fundamental Questions of Philosophy: One Philosopher's Answers.* 4th ed. Brighton: Harvester Press, 1979.

Korshin, Paul J. "Evidence: Toward a History and Theory." In *Alteratives*, ed. Warren Motte and Gerald Prince, pp. 133–47. Lexington: French Forum, 1993.

——. "Reconfiguring the Past: The Eighteenth Century Confronts Oral Culture." *The Yearbook of English Studies* 28 (1998): 235–49.

Kurz, Otto. *Fakes: A Handbook for Collectors and Students.* London: Faber, 1948.

Laing, Malcolm. *The History of Scotland, from the Union of the Crowns on the Accession of James VI. to the Throne of England, to the Union of the Kingdoms in the Reign of Queen Anne.* 2 vols. London, 1800.

Laing, Malcolm, ed. *The Poems of Ossian.* 2 vols. Edinburgh, 1805.

Langbein, John H. "The Criminal Trial before the Lawyers." *University of Chicago Law Review* 45 (1977–78): 263–316.

Lauder, William. *An Essay on Milton's Use and Imitation of the Moderns, in His Paradise Lost.* London, 1750.

——. *King Charles I. Vindicated from the Charge of Plagiarism, Brought against Him by Milton, and Milton Himself Convicted of Forgery.* London, 1754.

Lay-Craft Exemplified in a Discovery of the Weakness of the Late Attempts of the Author of "Priest-Craft in Perfection" and Mr. Benjamin Robinson Minister of the Gospel, to Prove the English Clergy Guilty of Forgery. London, 1710.

L'Estrange, Roger. *A Further Discovery of the Plot: Dedicated to Dr. Titus Oates.* 3rd ed. London, 1680.

A Letter from a Male Physician in the Country, to the Author of the Female Physician [John Maubray] in London; Plainly Shewing, that for Ingenuity, Probity, and Extraordinary Productions, He Far Surpasses the Author of the Narrative: To Which Is Added, a Short Dissertation upon Generation, Whereby Every Child-Bearing Woman May Be Satisfied, that 'Tis as Impossible for Women to Generate and Bring Forth Rabbets, as 'Tis Impossible for Rabbits to Bring Forth Women. London, 1726.

The Life of Titus Oats from His Cradle to His First Pilloring for Infamous Perjury; with a True Account of His Birth and Parentage: Impartially Set Forth for the Satisfaction of All Persons. London, 1685.

Locke, John. *An Essay concerning Human Understanding.* Ed. Peter H. Nidditch. Oxford: Clarendon Press, 1975.

Lynch, Deidre Shauna. *The Economy of Character: Novels, Market Culture and the Business of Inner Meaning.* Chicago: Univ. of Chicago Press, 1998.

Lynch, Jack. *The Age of Elizabeth in the Age of Johnson.* Cambridge: Cambridge Univ. Press, 2003.

——. "Samuel Johnson, Unbeliever." *Eighteenth-Century Life* 29, no. 3 (Fall 2005): 1–19.

Maas, Paul. *Textual Criticism.* Translated by Barbara Flower. Oxford: Clarendon Press, 1958.

Mabillon, Jean. *De re diplomatica libri VI.* Paris, 1681.

McCann, Edwin. "Locke on Identity: Matter, Life, Consciousness." *Archiv für Geschichte der Philosophie* 69 (1987): 55–77.

Macdonald, Donald [pseud.]. *Three Beautiful and Important Passages Omitted by the Translator of Fingal.* London, 1762.

Machen, Arthur. *The Canning Wonder.* New York: Alfred A. Knopf, 1926.

Mackenzie, Henry, ed. *Report of the Committee of the Highland Society of Scotland, Appointed to Inquire into the Nature and Authenticity of the Poems of Ossian.* Edinburgh, 1805.

McKeon, Michael. *The Origins of the English Novel, 1600–1740.* Baltimore: Johns Hopkins Univ. Press, 1987.

M'Kinnon, Charles. *Essays on the Following Subjects: Wealth and Force of Nations, Authenticity of Ossian, Accompanyment, Existence of Body, Fortification, Battle.* Edinburgh, 1785.

Mackintosh, Donald T. "James Macpherson and the Book of the Dean of Lismore." *Scottish Gaelic Studies* 6, part 1 (Sept. 1947): 11–20.

M'Nicol, Donald. *Remarks on Dr. Samuel Johnson's Journey to the Hebrides; in Which Are Contained, Observations on the Antiquities, Language, Genius, and Manners of the Highlanders of Scotland.* London, 1779.

Macpherson, James. *The Poems of Ossian and Related Works.* Ed. Howard Gaskill. Edinburgh: Edinburgh Univ. Press, 1996.

Maechler, Stefan. *The Wilkomirski Affair: A Study in Biographical Truth.* Trans. John E. Woods. London: Picador, 2001.

Mahoney, Michael S. "Die Anfänge der algebraischen Denkweise im 17. Jahrhundert," *Rete* 1 (1971): 15–31.

Malone, Edmond. *Cursory Observations on the Poems Attributed to Thomas Rowley.* 2nd ed. (i.e., first collected edition). London, 1782.

——. *An Inquiry into the Authenticity of Certain Miscellaneous Papers and Legal Instruments, Published Dec. 24, M DCC XCV. and Attributed to Shakspeare, Queen Elizabeth, and Henry, Earl of Southampton.* London, 1796.

Manningham, Richard. *An Exact Diary of What Was Observ'd during a Close Attendance upon Mary Toft, the Pretended Rabbet-Breeder of Godalming in Surrey.* London, 1726.

Marcuse, Michael J. "*The Gentleman's Magazine* and the Lauder/Milton Controversy." *Bulletin of Research in the Humanities* 81 (1978): 179–209.

——. "Miltonoklastes: The Lauder Affair Reconsidered." *Eighteenth-Century Life* 4 (1978): 86–91.

——. "The Pre-Publication History of William Lauder's *Essay on Milton's Use and Imitation of the Moderns in His Paradise Lost.*" *Papers of the Bibliographical Society of America* 72 (1978): 37–57.

——. "'The Scourge of Impostors, the Terror of Quacks': John Douglas and the Exposé of William Lauder." *The Huntington Library Quarterly* 42 (1978–79): 231–61.

Martin, Peter. *Edmond Malone, Shakespearean Scholar: A Literary Biography.* Cambridge: Cambridge Univ. Press, 1995.

Mason, William. *An Archaeological Epistle to the Reverend and Worshipful Jeremiah Milles, D.D., Dean of Exeter, President of the Society of Antiquaries, and Editor of a Superb Edition of the Poems of Thomas Rowley, Priest.* London, 1782.

Mathias, Thomas James. *An Essay on the Evidence, External and Internal, Relating to the Poems Attributed to Thomas Rowley: Containing a General View of the Whole Controversy.* London, 1783.

Meek, Thomas. *A Small Tribute to the Memory of Ossian; Containing an Original Method of Vindicating the Authenticity of His Poems.* Edinburgh, 1809.

Meiland, Jack W. "Originals, Copies, and Aesthetic Value." In *The Forger's Art: Forgery and the Philosophy of Art,* ed. Denis Dutton, pp. 115–30. Berkeley and Los Angeles: Univ. of California Press, 1983.

Memoirs of the Life of John Matthieson, Executed for Forgery on the Bank of England, on Wednesday the 28th of July, 1779. London, 1779.

Meyer, Leonard B. "Forgery and the Anthropology of Art." In *The Forger's Art: Forgery and the Philosophy of Art,* ed. Denis Dutton, pp. 77–92. Berkeley and Los Angeles: Univ. of California Press, 1983.

Meyerstein, E. H. W. *A Life of Thomas Chatterton.* London: Ingpen and Grant, 1930.

Miss Canning and the Gypsey; or, A More Particular Inlet into the Knowledge of That Paradoxical Affair, than Any Attempts Hitherto Made to Bring It to Light. 2nd ed. London, 1754.

Moivre, Abraham de. *The Doctrine of Chances; or, A Method of Calculating the Probability of Events in Play.* London, 1718.

Montagu, Elizabeth. *The Letters of Mrs. Elizabeth Montagu, with Some of the Letters of Her Correspondents.* 4 vols. London, 1809–13.

Montaigne, Michel de. *Essays of Michael Seigneur De Montaigne: In Three Books, with Marginal Notes and Quotations: And an Account of the Author's Life.* Trans. Charles Cotton. 4th ed. 3 vols. London, 1711.

Moore, Dafydd. *Enlightenment and Romance in James Macpherson's "The Poems of Ossian": Myth, Genre and Cultural Change.* Aldershot: Ashgate, 2004.

Moore, Judith. *The Appearance of Truth: The Story of Elizabeth Canning and Eighteenth-Century Narrative.* Newark: Univ. of Delaware Press, 1994.

Morgan, Thomas. *Philosophical Principles of Medicine, in Three Parts.* London, 1725.

Mossner, Ernest Campbell. *The Forgotten Hume: Le Bon David.* New York: Columbia Univ. Press, 1943.

Much Ado about Nothing; or, A Plain Refutation of All That Has Been Written or Said Concerning the Rabbit-Woman of Godalming: Being a Full and Impartial Confession from Her Own Mouth, and under Her Own Hand, of the Whole Affair, from the Beginning to the End: Now Made Publick for the General Satisfaction. London, 1727.

Mumford, Jeremy. "Clara Miccinelli's Cabinet of Wonders: Jesuits, Incas, and the Mysteries of Colonial Peru." *Lingua Franca* 10, no. 1 (Feb. 2000): 36–45.

Nelson, William. *The Law of Evidence: Wherein All the Cases That Have Yet Been Printed ... Are Collected and Methodically Digested under Their Proper Heads.* London, 1717.

Newman, Eric P. "Franklin Making Money More Plentiful." *Proceedings of the American Philosophical Society* 115, no. 5 (15 Oct. 1971): 341–9.

——. "Nature Printing on Colonial and Continental Currency." *The Numismatist* 77 (1964): 147–54, 299–305, 457–65, 613–23.

Nichols, John. *Illustrations of the History of the Eighteenth Century.* 8 vols. London, 1817–58.

——. *Literary Anecdotes of the Eighteenth Century.* 9 vols. London, 1812–16.

Nixon, John. *The Oaken Chest or the Gold Mines of Ireland a Farce.* London, [1797?].

Oates, Titus. *An Exact and Faithful Narrative of the Horrid Conspiracy of Thomas Knox, William Osborne, and John Lane, to Invalidate the Testimonies of Dr. Titus Oates, and Mr. William Bedlow; by Charging Them with a Malicious Contrivance against the E. of Danby, and the Said Dr. Oates with an Attempt of Sodomy.* London, 1680.

O'Conor, Charles. *Dissertations on the History of Ireland: To Which Is Subjoined, a Dissertation on the Irish Colonies Established in Britain: With Some Remarks on Mr. Mac Pherson's Translation of Fingal and Temora.* 2 vols. in 1. Dublin, 1766.

O'Halloran, Sylvester. *An Introduction to the Study of the History and Antiquities of Ireland.* Dublin, 1772.

Osborn, Albert S. *Questioned Documents: A Study of Questioned Documents with an Outline of Methods by Which the Facts May Be Discovered and Shown.* Rochester, N.Y.: Lawyers' Co-operative, 1910.

Oulton, Whalley Chamberlain. *Vortigern under Consideration; with General Remarks on Mr. James Boaden's Letter to George Steevens, Esq.* London, 1796.

Paget, John. *Paradoxes and Puzzles, Historical, Judicial, and Literary.* Edinburgh: Blackwood & Sons, 1874.

Paley, William. *The Principles of Moral and Political Philosophy.* London, 1785.

Parr, Samuel. *The Works of Samuel Parr, LL.D., Prebendary of St. Paul's, Curate of Hatton, &c., with Memoirs of His Life and Writings, and a Selection from His Correspondence.* Ed. John Johnstone. 8 vols. London, 1828.

Patey, Douglas Lane. *Probability and Literary Form: Philosophic Theory and Literary Practice in the Augustan Age.* Cambridge: Cambridge Univ. Press, 1984.

Paull, H. M. *Literary Ethics: A Study in the Growth of the Literary Conscience.* London: Thornton Butterworth, 1928.

Peake, Thomas. *A Compendium of the Law of Evidence.* London, 1801.

Pennant, Thomas. *A Tour in Scotland: MDCCLXIX.* Chester, 1771.

Percy, Thomas. *The Percy Letters.* Ed. David Nichol Smith, Cleanth Brooks, and A. F. Falconer. 9 vols. Baton Rouge: Louisiana State Univ. Press; New Haven: Yale Univ. Press, 1944–88.

——. *Reliques of Ancient English Poetry: Consisting of Old Heroic Ballads, Songs, and Other Pieces of Our Earlier Poets, Chiefly of the Lyric Kind.* 2nd ed. 3 vols. London, 1767.

Philologus [pseud.]. *The Inspector Inspected; or, Dr. Hill's Story of Elizabeth Canning Examined and Impartially Considered: In a Letter to That Gentleman, in Which All His Vain Subterfuges Are Detected and Confuted.* London, 1753.

A Philosophical Enquiry into the Wonderful Coney-Warren, Lately Discovered at Godalmin Near Guilford in Surrey. London, 1726.

Pinkerton, John. *An Enquiry into the History of Scotland Preceding the Reign of Malcolm III.* 2 vols. London, 1789.

——. *Select Scotish Ballads.* 2nd ed. 2 vols. London, 1783.

Piozzi, Hester Thrale. *Anecdotes of the Late Samuel Johnson.* London, 1786.

Pittock, Murray G. H. *Inventing and Resisting Britain: Cultural Identities in Britain and Ireland, 1685–1789.* New York: St. Martin's Press, 1997.

Plato. *Republic.* In *The Collected Dialogues of Plato, Including the Letters.* Ed. Edith Hamilton and Huntington Cairns. Princeton: Princeton Univ. Press, 1961.

Pope, Alexander. *The Twickenham Edition of the Poems of Alexander Pope.* Ed. John Butt *et al.* 11 vols. in 12. New Haven: Yale Univ. Press, 1939–69.

Porter, James. "'Bring Me the Head of James Macpherson': The Execution of Ossian and the Wellsprings of Folkloristic Discourse." *Journal of American Folklore* 114, no. 454 (Fall 2001): 396–435.

Prance, Miles. *A True Narrative and Discovery of Several Very Remarkable Passages Relating to the Horrid Popish Plot: As They Fell within the Knowledge of Mr Miles Prance of Covent-Garden, Goldsmith.* London, 1679.

Priest, Graham, J. C. Beall, and Bradley Armour-Garb, eds. *The Law of Non-Contradiction: New Philosophical Essays.* Oxford: Clarendon Press, 2004.

Priestley, Joseph. *The Doctrine of Philosophical Necessity Illustrated: Being an Appendix to the Disquisitions Relating to Matter and Spirit*. London, 1777.

Prior, Sir James. *Life of Edmond Malone, Editor of Shakspeare: With Selections from His Manuscript Anecdotes*. London, 1860.

Psalmanazar, George. *An Enquiry into the Objections against George Psalmanaazaar of Formosa: In Which the Accounts of the People, and Language of Formosa by Candidius, and the Other European Authors, and the Letters from Geneva, and from Suffolk, about Psalmanaazaar, Are Proved Not to Contradict His Account*. London, *c*. 1710.

——. *An Historical and Geographical Description of Formosa*. London, 1704.

——. *An Historical and Geographical Description of Formosa*. 2nd ed. London, 1705.

——. *Memoirs of ****, Commonly Known by the Name George Psalmanazar; a Reputed Native of Formosa*. London, 1764.

Radzinowicz, Leon. *A History of English Criminal Law and Its Administration from 1750*. 5 vols. New York: Macmillan, 1948.

Ramsay, Allan. *A Letter to the Right Honourable the Earl of —— concerning the Affair of Elizabeth Canning*. London, 1753.

Raveneau, Jacques. *Traité des inscriptions en faux et reconnoissances d'escritures et signatures par comparaison et autrement*. Paris, 1666.

Reisner, Thomas A. "Graphic Affinities: Statistical Approaches to Psalmanazar's Pseudo-Formosan." *Langues et linguistique* 20 (1994): 81–107.

——. "'Tongue with a Tang': Survey of an 18th Century Pseudo-Language." *Langues et linguistique* 19 (1993): 187–203.

Rhodes, Henry T. F. *The Craft of Forgery*. London: John Murray, 1934.

Richardson, William. *A Philosophical Analysis and Illustration of Some of Shakespeare's Remarkable Characters*. New ed. London, 1780.

Ricoeur, Paul. *History, Memory, Forgetting*. Trans. Kathleen Blamey and David Pellauer. Chicago: Univ. of Chicago Press, 2004.

Riffaterre, Michael. *Fictional Truth*. Baltimore: Johns Hopkins Univ. Press, 1990.

Ritson, Joseph. *The Letters of Joseph Ritson, Esq., Edited Chiefly from Originals in the Possession of His Nephew*. 2 vols. London, 1833.

Ruthven, K. K. *Faking Literature*. Cambridge: Cambridge Univ. Press, 2001.

St. André, Nathanael. *A Short Narrative of an Extraordinary Delivery of Rabbets, Perform'd by Mr. John Howard, Surgeon at Guilford*. 2nd ed. London, 1727.

Sandys, John Edwin. *History of Classical Scholarship*. 3 vols. Cambridge: Cambridge Univ. Press, 1903–8.

Saunders, Bailey. *The Life and Letters of James Macpherson: Containing a Particular Account of His Famous Quarrel with Dr. Johnson, and a Sketch of the Origin and Influence of the Ossianic Poems*. London, 1894.

Scott, Sir Walter. *Letters of Sir Walter Scott*. Ed. H. J. C. Grierson. 12 vols. London: Constable & Co., 1932–37.

Seward, Anna. *The Letters of Anna Seward*. 6 vols. Edinburgh, 1811.

Shaftesbury, Anthony Ashley Cooper, third Earl of. *Characteristics of Men, Manners, Opinions, Times*. Ed. Lawrence E. Klein. Cambridge: Cambridge Univ. Press, 1999.

Shakespeare: Concerning the Traits of His Characters. London, [1774?].

Shapin, Steven. *A Social History of Truth: Civility and Science in Seventeenth-Century England*. Chicago: Univ. of Chicago Press, 1994.

Shapiro, Barbara J. *"Beyond Reasonable Doubt" and "Probable Cause": Historical Perspectives on the Anglo-American Law of Evidence*. Berkeley and Los Angeles: Univ. of California Press, 1992.

Shaw, William. "Appendix, Containing a Reply to Mr. Clark." In *Enquiry into the Authenticity of the Poems Ascribed to Ossian*. 2nd ed. London, 1782.

———. *An Enquiry into the Authenticity of the Poems Ascribed to Ossian*. Dublin, 1782.

———. *Memoirs of the Life and Writings of the Late Dr. Samuel Johnson*. London, 1785.

———. *Reply to Mr. Clark*. London, 1782.

Sher, Richard B. "Percy, Shaw and the Ferguson 'Cheat': National Prejudice in the Ossian Wars." In *Ossian Revisited*, ed. Howard Gaskill, pp. 207–45.

Sheridan, Richard Brinsley. *The Dramatic Works of Richard Brinsley Sheridan*. Ed. Cecil Price. 2 vols. Oxford: Clarendon Press, 1973.

Sidney, Sir Philip. *An Apology for Poetry or the Defense of Poetry*. Ed. Geoffrey Shepherd. London: Nelson, 1965.

Sinclair, Sir John. "A Dissertation on the Authenticity of the Poems of Ossian." In *The Poems of Ossian, in the Original Gaelic, with a Literal Translation into Latin*, ed. John Sinclair, 3 vols., 1:i–ccxxxii. London, 1807.

Smith, Adam. *An Inquiry into the Nature and Causes of the Wealth of Nations*. Ed. Edwin Cannan. 2 vols. in 1. Chicago: Univ. of Chicago Press, 1976.

Smith, John. *Galic Antiquities: Consisting of a History of the Druids, Particularly of Those of Caledonia; a Dissertation on the Authenticity of the Poems of Ossian; and a Collection of Ancient Poems, Translated from the Galic of Ullin, Ossian, Orran, &c*. Edinburgh, 1780.

Smyth, John Vignaux. *The Habit of Lying: Sacrificial Studies in Literature, Philosophy, and Fashion Theory*. Durham: Duke Univ. Press, 2002.

Stafford, Fiona. "'Dangerous Success': Ossian, Wordsworth, and English Romantic Literature." In *Ossian Revisited*, ed. Howard Gaskill, pp. 49–72.

———. "Dr Johnson and the Ruffian: New Evidence in the Dispute between Samuel Johnson and James Macpherson." *N&Q* 36, no. 1 (March 1989): 70–77.

———. *The Sublime Savage: A Study of James Macpherson and the Poems of Ossian*. Edinburgh: Edinburgh Univ. Press, 1988.

Stein, Sol. *How to Grow a Novel: The Most Common Mistakes Writers Make and How to Overcome Them*. New York: St. Martin's Griffin, 1999.

Stephen, Leslie. *Hours in a Library*. New ed. 3 vols. London, 1892.

Stewart, Susan. *Crimes of Writing*. Oxford: Oxford Univ. Press, 1991; Durham: Duke Univ. Press, 1994.

Stukeley, William. *A Letter from Dr. Stukeley to Mr. Macpherson, on His Publication of Fingal and Temora*. London, 1763.

Swift, Jonathan. *The Correspondence of Jonathan Swift*. Ed. Harold Williams. 5 vols. Oxford: Clarendon Press, 1963–65.

———. *The Correspondence of Jonathan Swift, D.D.* Ed. David Woolley. 4 vols. Frankfurt am Main: Peter Lang, 1999–.

——. *A Tale of a Tub: To Which Is Added the Battle of the Books and the Mechanical Operation of the Spirit.* Ed. A. C. Guthkelch and D. Nichol Smith. 2nd ed. Oxford: Clarendon Press, 1958.

Symons, William. *An Essay on the Weighing of Gold, &c.: Wherein Is Shewn an Effectual Method for Discovering and Detecting of Counterfeit Pieces of Money, on the Principles of Hydrostatics.* 2nd ed. London, 1770.

Taine, H. A. *History of English Literature.* Trans. Henri Van Laun. 2 vols. in 1. New York: A. L. Burt, n.d.

Tassin, René Prosper, and Charles Toustain. *Nouveau traité de diplomatique.* 6 vols. Paris, 1750–65.

Tate, Nahum. *The History of King Lear: Acted at the Duke's Theatre: Reviv'd with Alterations.* London, 1681.

Temple, William. *The Epistles of Phalaris, Translated into English from the Original Greek by S. Whately ... to Which Is Added Sir W. Temple's Character of the Epistles of Phalaris.* London, 1699.

——. *Miscellanea: The Third Part.* London, 1701.

Thomson, Derick S. *The Gaelic Sources of Macpherson's "Ossian."* London: Oliver and Boyd, 1951.

——. "'Ossian' Macpherson and the Gaelic World of the Eighteenth Century." *Aberdeen University Review* 40 (1963): 7–20.

Todd, Dennis. *Imagining Monsters: Miscreations of the Self in Eighteenth-Century England.* Chicago: Univ. of Chicago Press, 1995.

Treherne, John. *The Canning Enigma.* London: Jonathan Cape, 1989.

The Trial of Elizabeth Canning, Spinster, for Wilful and Corrupt Perjury; At Justice Hall in the Old-Bailey. London, 1754.

Troil, Uno von. *Letters on Iceland: Containing Observations on the Civil, Literary, Ecclesiastical, and Natural History; Antiquities, Volcanos, Basaltes, Hot Springs; Customs, Dress, Manners of the Inhabitants, &c. &c.* 2nd ed. London, 1780.

The Truth of the Case; or, Canning and Squires Fairly Opposed: Being, an Impartial Examination of the Merits of This Surprising Cause: Wherein the Gipsey is Vindicated, as Far as Probability and the Circumstances of the Case Will Allow. London, 1753.

Truth Triumphant; or, The Genuine Account of the Whole Proceedings against Elizabeth Canning, Tried and Convicted of Perjury, at the Sessions-House in the Old-Bailey, Tuesday, May 7. for Falsely Swearing a Robbery against Mary Squires, the Gypsey, for Which Robbery She Was Capitally Convicted, and Afterwards Received His Majesty's Most Gracious Pardon. London, 1754.

The Tryals of William Ireland, Thomas Pickering, and John Grove; for Conspiring to Murder the King: Who upon Full Evidence Were Found Guilty of High Treason, at the Sessions-House in the Old Baily, December the 17th 1678, and Received Sentence Accordingly. London, 1678.

Twining, Thomas. *Recreations and Studies of a Country Clergyman of the Eighteenth Century: Being Selections from the Correspondence of the Rev. Thomas Twining, M.A.* London, 1882.

Twining, William. *Rethinking Evidence: Exploratory Essays.* Oxford: Basil Blackwell, 1990.

Valla, Lorenzo. *The Treatise of Lorenzo Valla on the Donation of Constantine: Text and Translation into English*. Ed. and trans. Christopher B. Coleman. New Haven: Yale Univ. Press, 1922.

Virgil. *P. Vergili Maronis opera*. Ed. R. A. B. Mynors. Oxford: Clarendon Press, 1969.

Waldron, F. G. *Free Reflections on Miscellaneous Papers and Legal Instruments, under the Hand and Seal of William Shakspeare, in the Possession of Samuel Ireland, of Norfolk-Street; to Which Are Added, Extracts from an Unpublished MS. Play, Called The Virgin Queen, Written by, or in Imitation of, Shakspeare*. London, 1796.

Walpole, Horace. *The Castle of Otranto*. Ed. W. S. Lewis. Oxford: Oxford Univ. Press, 1964.

——. *The Works of Horatio Walpole, Earl of Orford*. 5 vols. London, 1797–98.

——. *The Yale Edition of Horace Walpole's Correspondence*. Ed. W. S. Lewis. 48 vols. New Haven: Yale Univ. Press, 1937–83.

Warton, Thomas. *The Correspondence of Thomas Warton*. Ed. David Fairer. Athens: Univ. of Georgia Press, 1995.

——. *An Enquiry into the Authenticity of the Poems Attributed to Thomas Rowley*. London, 1782.

——. *The History of English Poetry*. 4 vols. London, 1775–81.

Watt, Ian. *The Rise of the Novel*. Berkeley and Los Angeles: Univ. of California Press, 1957.

Watts, Isaac. *Philosophical Essays on Various Subjects, Viz. Space, Substance, Body, Spirit, ... with Some Remarks on Mr. Locke's Essay on the Human Understanding*. London, 1733.

Webb, Francis. *Shakspeare's Manuscripts, in the Possession of Mr. Ireland, Examined, respecting the Internal and External Evidence of Their Authenticity*. London, 1796.

Wellington, Barrett R. *The Mystery of Elizabeth Canning, as Found in the Testimony of the Old Bailey Trials and Other Records*. New York: J. Ray Peck, 1940.

Welsh, Alexander. *Strong Representations: Narrative and Circumstantial Evidence in England*. Baltimore: Johns Hopkins Univ. Press, 1992.

White, John. *The Protestant Englishman Guarded against the Arts and Arguments of Romish Priests and Emissaries*. London, 1753.

Whitman, Walt. *Leaves of Grass: Comprehensive Reader's Edition*. Ed. Harold W. Blodgett and Sculley Bradley. New York: New York Univ. Press, 1965.

Wickman, Matthew. "The Allure of the Improbable: Fingal, Evidence, and the Testimony of the 'Echoing Heath.'" *PMLA* 115, no. 2 (March 2000): 181–94.

Wilde, Oscar. *The Portrait of Mr W. H.: The Greatly Enlarged Version Prepared by the Author after the Appearance of the Story in 1889 but Not Published*. Ed. Vyvyan Holland. London: Methuen, 1958.

Wilkins, John. *Of the Principles and Duties of Natural Religion*. London, 1675.

Wilson, James. *The Works of James Wilson, Associate Justice of the Supreme Court of the United States, and Professor of Law in the College of Philadelphia*. Ed. James DeWitt Andrews. 2 vols. Chicago, 1896.

Wolf, F. A. *Prolegomena to Homer*. Trans. Anthony Grafton, Glenn W. Most, and James E. G. Zetzel. Princeton: Princeton Univ. Press, 1985.

Wolf, Matt. "Marlowe Was Shakespeare." *The Sunday Mail (Queensland)*, 7 July 1985.

The Wonder of Wonders; or, A True and Perfect Narrative of a Woman Near Guildford in Surrey, Who Was Delivered Lately of Seventeen Rabbets, and Three Legs of a Tabby Cat, &c.: In a Letter from a Gentleman at Guildford, to His Friend a Physician in Ipswich, Suffolk: With Remarks upon the Same by Way of Answer: To Which Is Added, an Abstract of a Letter from Mr. Howard, Who Was the Man-Midwife That Deliver'd Her. Ipswich, 1726.

Wordsworth, William. *Poems in Two Volumes, and Other Poems, 1800–1807*. Ed. Jared Curtis. Ithaca: Cornell Univ. Press, 1983.

Wreen, Michael, "Is, Madam? Nay, It Seems!" In *The Forger's Art: Forgery and the Philosophy of Art*, ed. Denis Dutton, pp. 188–224. Berkeley and Los Angeles: Univ. of California Press, 1983.

Zunshine, Lisa. "Eighteenth-Century Print Culture and the 'Truth' of Fictional Narrative." *Philosophy and Literature* 25, no. 2 (2001): 215–32.

Index